NYC: B&W

Photographs, 1965-2018

PHOTOGRAPHS

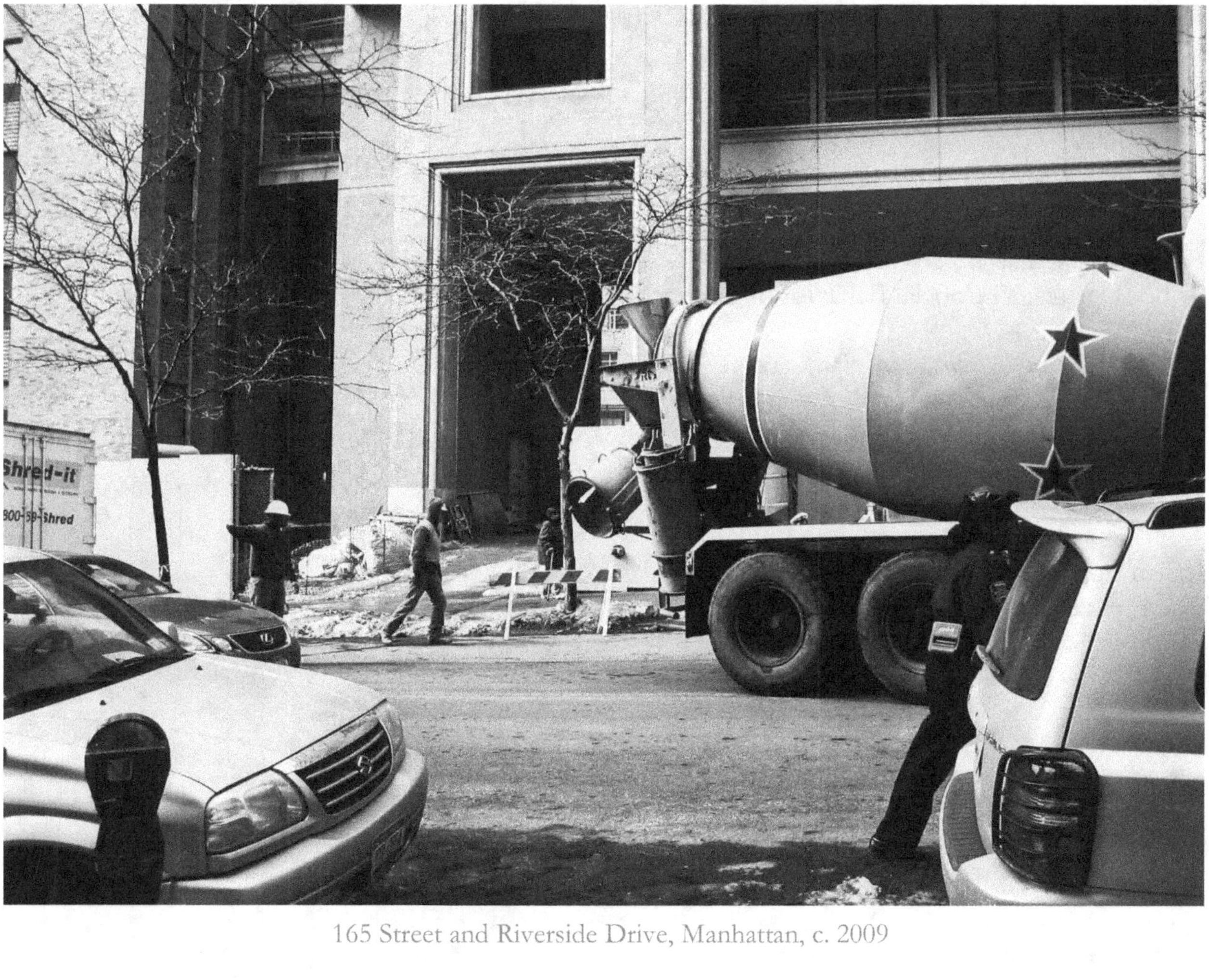

165 Street and Riverside Drive, Manhattan, c. 2009

NYC: B&W
Photographs, 1965-2018
© 2019 Alan Pakaln
First published with color chapters as
New York Shadow: Behind The Scenes
All rights reserved.
www.alanpakaln.com

Books by Alan Pakaln:

New York Shadow: Behind The Scenes
Color & black and white photographs
Same photos as NYC: B&W, coated paper, color printing, more expensive
© 2018

Robot Desires: The Social Behavior of Technology
© 2018

We Are The Machine: Only Following Orders
© 2019
First published as
Robot Desires: The Social Behavior of Technology

The Feast of San Gennaro, Little Italy, New York, 1971:
A Photographic Essay, The People, Food, Activities
© 2017

La Festa di San Gennaro
© 2017
Italian translation of
The Feast of San Gennaro, Little Italy, New York, 1971

Acknowledgement

To my wonderful editor, Valerie Lyle.

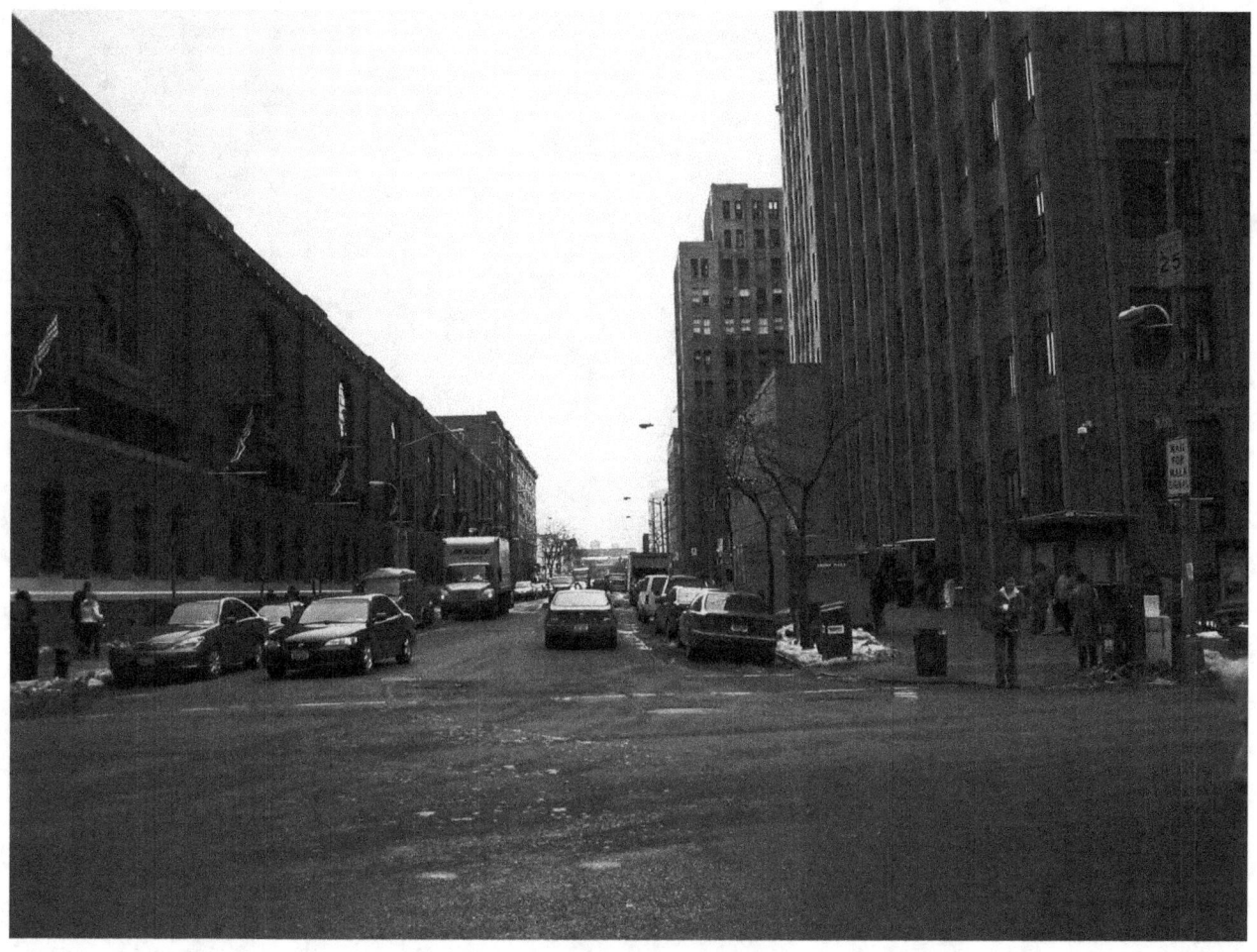

168 Street and Ft. Washington, Manhattan, c. 2009

Foreword

About the photographer

By profession, I am a biomedical engineer with many years of experience overseeing the application of medical technology in New York City hospitals. By desire, I am a photographer with many more years experience than working in my profession. I am an amateur in the classic sense; I photograph what I care about.

I was born in New York City (Doctor's Hospital, now a luxury condominium), and have lived and worked in and around NYC all my life. My education in photography began about age 17, and took place in a small darkroom, a closet under the stairs leading to the basement of the house I grew up in. Eventually, my darkroom had two enlargers, one for medium format, and I could produce both color and black-and-white images. Now, like most, I use a digital camera, scanner, and printer. Not better, just different.

I've never been a high-tech enthusiast, although I have studied aspects of Weston's and Adams' zone system. My favorite cameras were the Nikkormat 35mm and the inexpensive, early point-and-shoot cameras, like a Brownie with 127 film. And now - simple, inexpensive, point-and-shoot cameras.

Different technologies offer different ways of feeling about the process of photographing: SLR with film – careful, exacting; Brownie with film and viewfinder – playful; digital point and shoot – casual, careless.

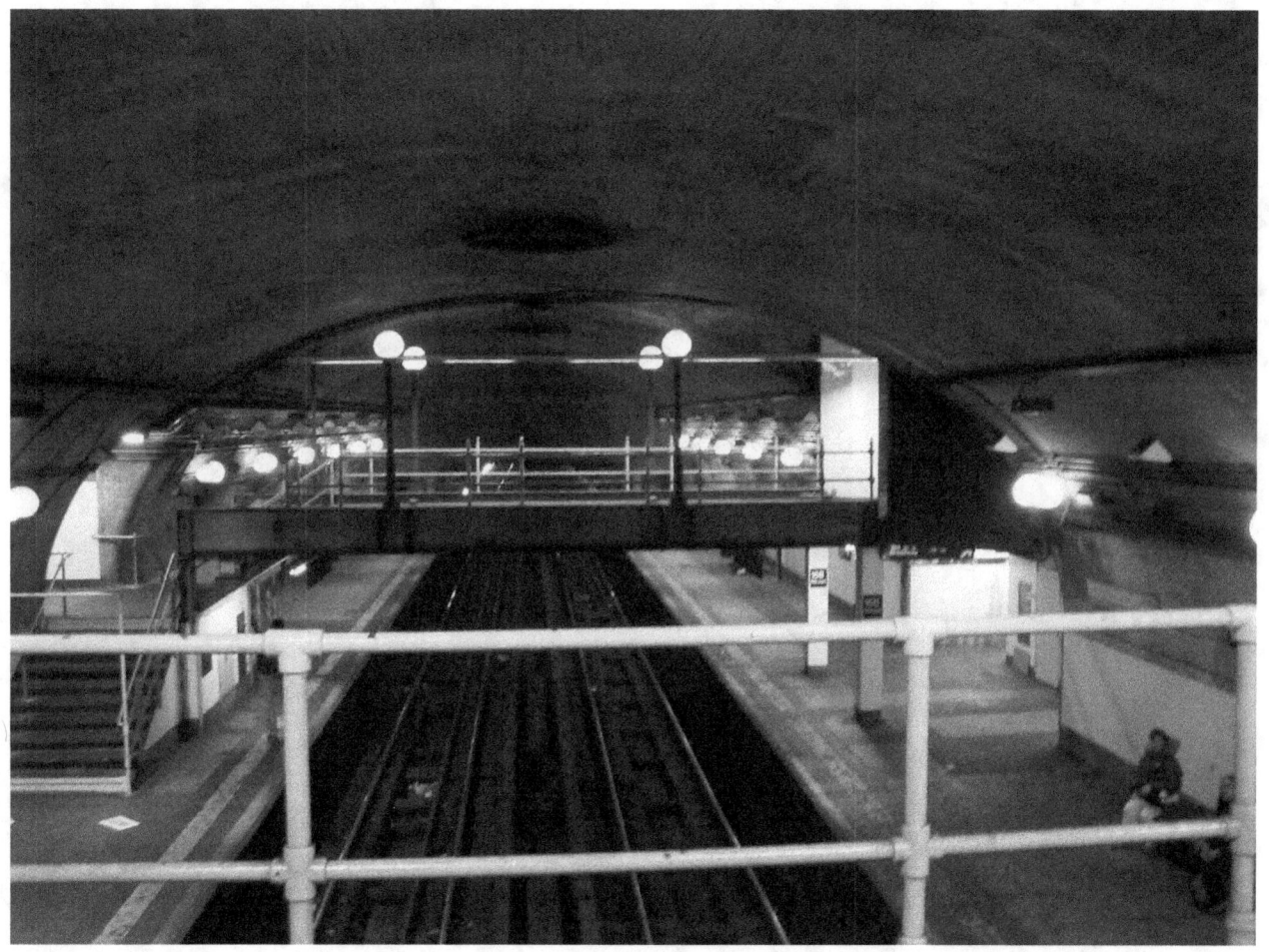

168 Street stop, Broadway 1, subway line, Manhattan, c. 2009

Contents

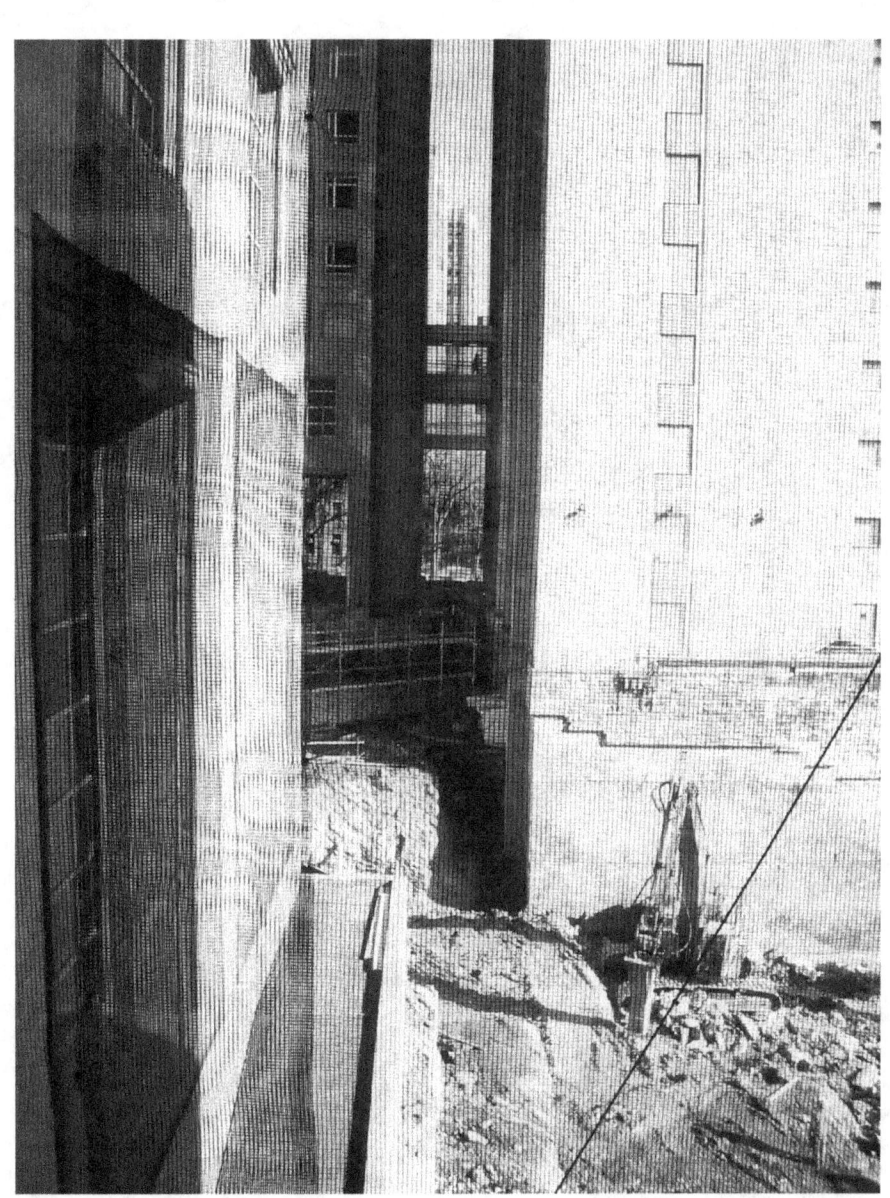

Heart Center construction site, NY Presbyterian Hospital, c. 2009

Introduction

Accidental Photographer

Each of these chapters is a story about New York City, and of course, the experience of the person taking the pictures. I suppose I could be referred to as "an accidental photographer" because I never thought about becoming one, even though I have mountains of prints and boxes of negatives. Sometimes we are also what we least expect.

It's always "the new era." It goes without saying - except to notice the difference - that this twenty-first century era is markedly different from previous ones. Today's New York City appears to me denser in terms of people and vehicles (bicycles included), and faster everywhere all the time. I wonder if the staff at Bellevue Hospital today would, or could, stand still long enough to be photographed. Would they appear to be as relaxed as in the scenes shown here?

It's a funny thing, taking photographs. When the process really works, there is no "visualizing" or reflecting on what is seen. When it works, I am not really feeling present; I just am present. This is not some romantic notion, and certainly it is subjective to say, but for me, I am the picture when I "take" it. And certainly, I am *not* thinking about the device I am taking the picture with.

All photographs are presented full-frame, that is, without cropping, and without alterations other than brightness and contrast adjustments for printing.

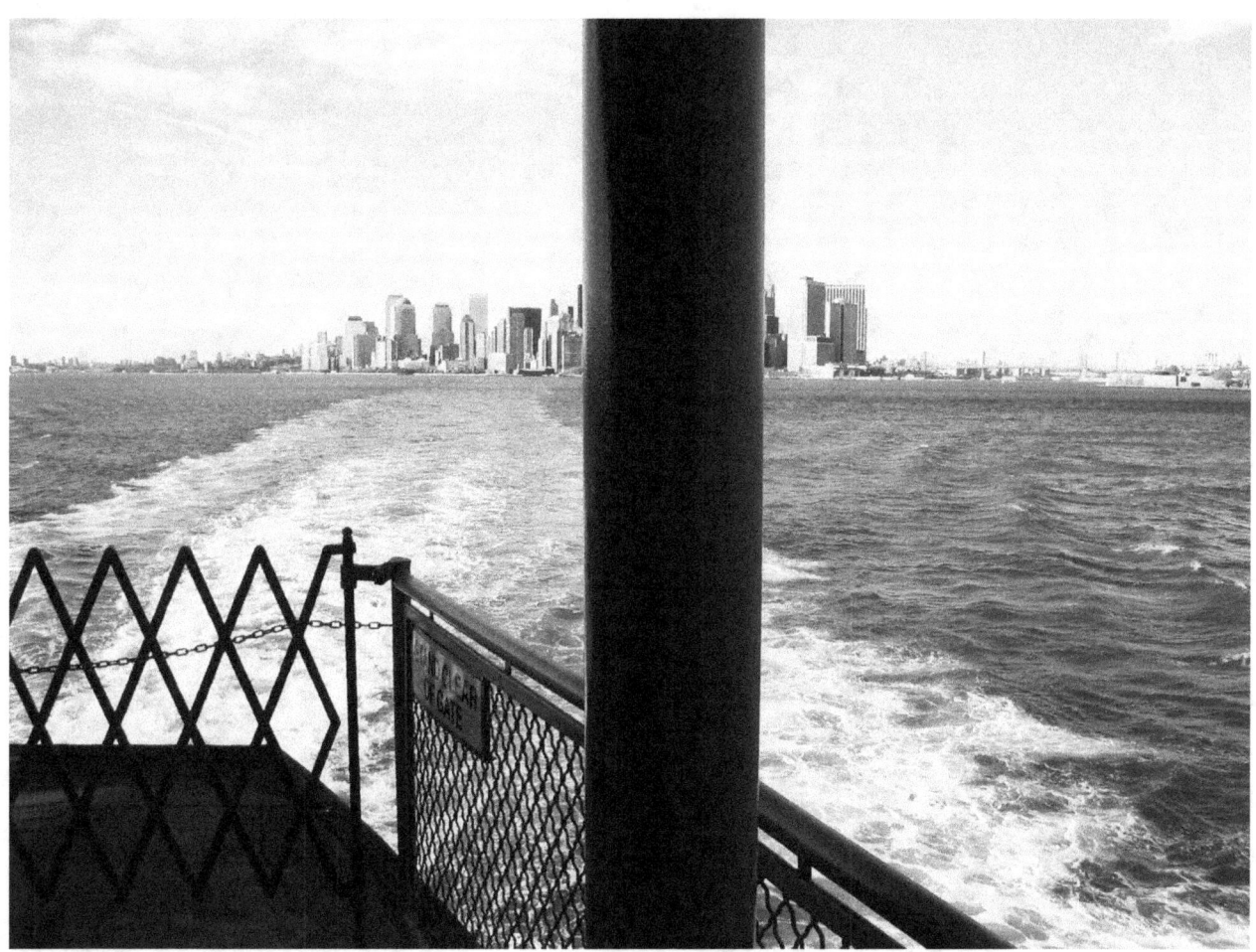

Staten Island Ferry, Manhattan skyline

Coney Island, 1965

It's 1965. I am 18 years old, just graduated from high school. A few of my friends pile into my "brand new" 1955 Pontiac Star Chief (cost, $125) and head out on a Saturday for some exploration. We decide on Coney Island.

Almost "raised New York City," but not quite: I probably hadn't been to Coney Island before. The first half of my childhood was spent in the extreme southeast corner of Yonkers. We lived one block from the Bronx in a house my grandfather built. The second half, my family moved a few miles north and west, to a suburban Westchester County village. Of course we knew about Coney Island, but we didn't know much. We wanted to see something strange and different.

It's funny what a camera can do for - or to - one's memory. I often don't remember what I did as well as I remember taking the picture. In retrospect, I'm disappointed I didn't take more pictures. I was too young and naïve, and distracted, to act on what was in front of me. Plus I did not yet have a real sense of what time can do to history.

What is shown here is basically every shot I took that night. I didn't waste film. I composed carefully and clicked the shutter only when I saw something I really liked. Spontaneity, but nothing silly.

The camera has always been more of a friend to me than a toy. It was an important part of my growing up, introducing me to the idea that there was a world around me worth knowing, worth exploring. Back then, it was a revelation.

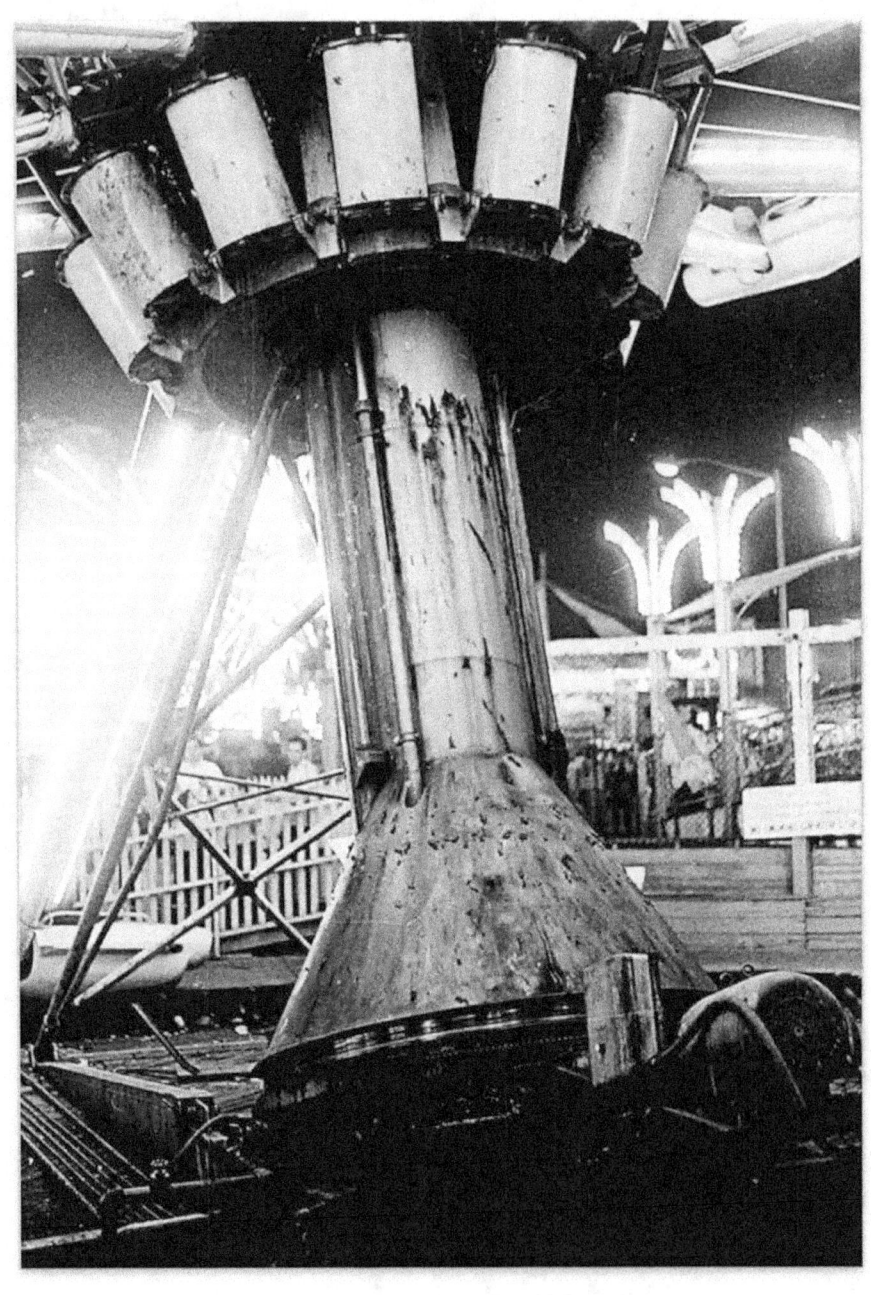

Coney Island, 1965

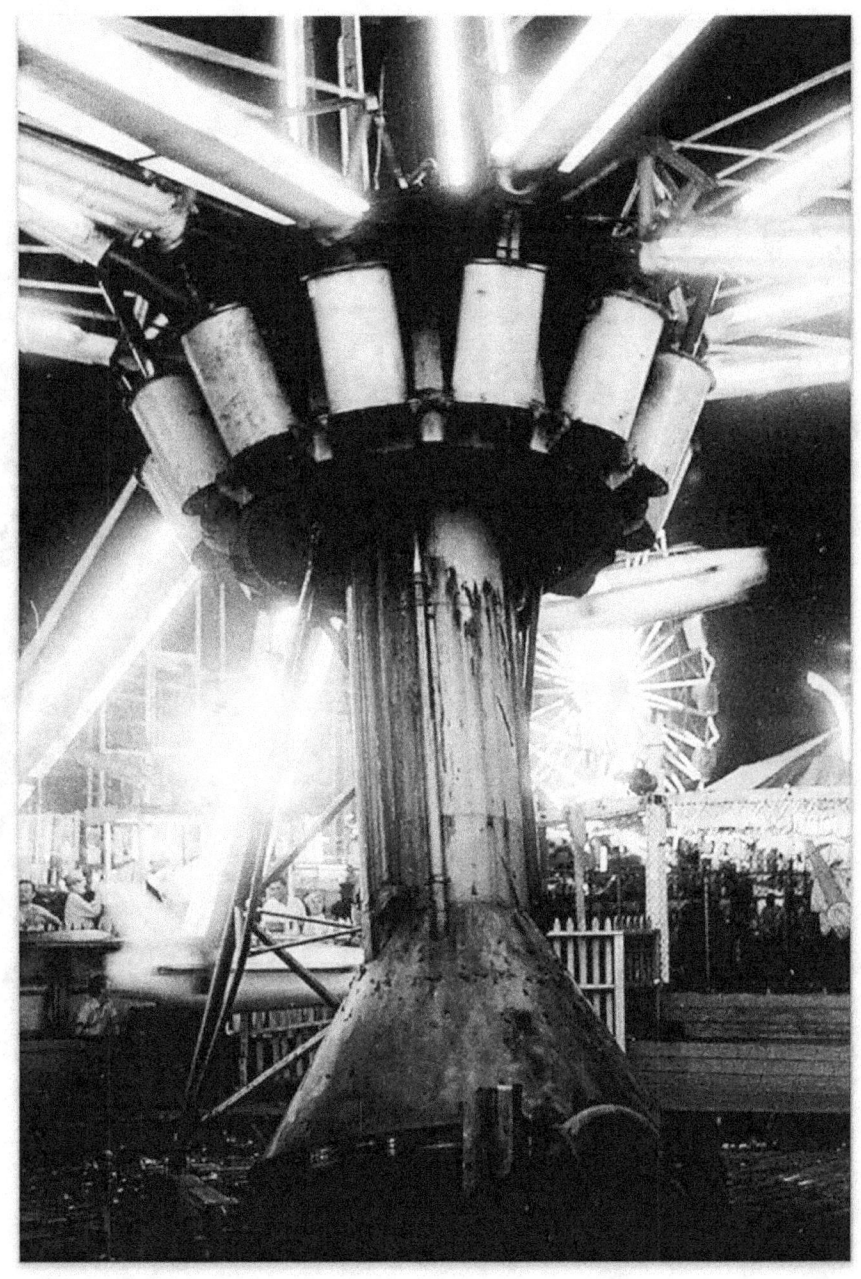

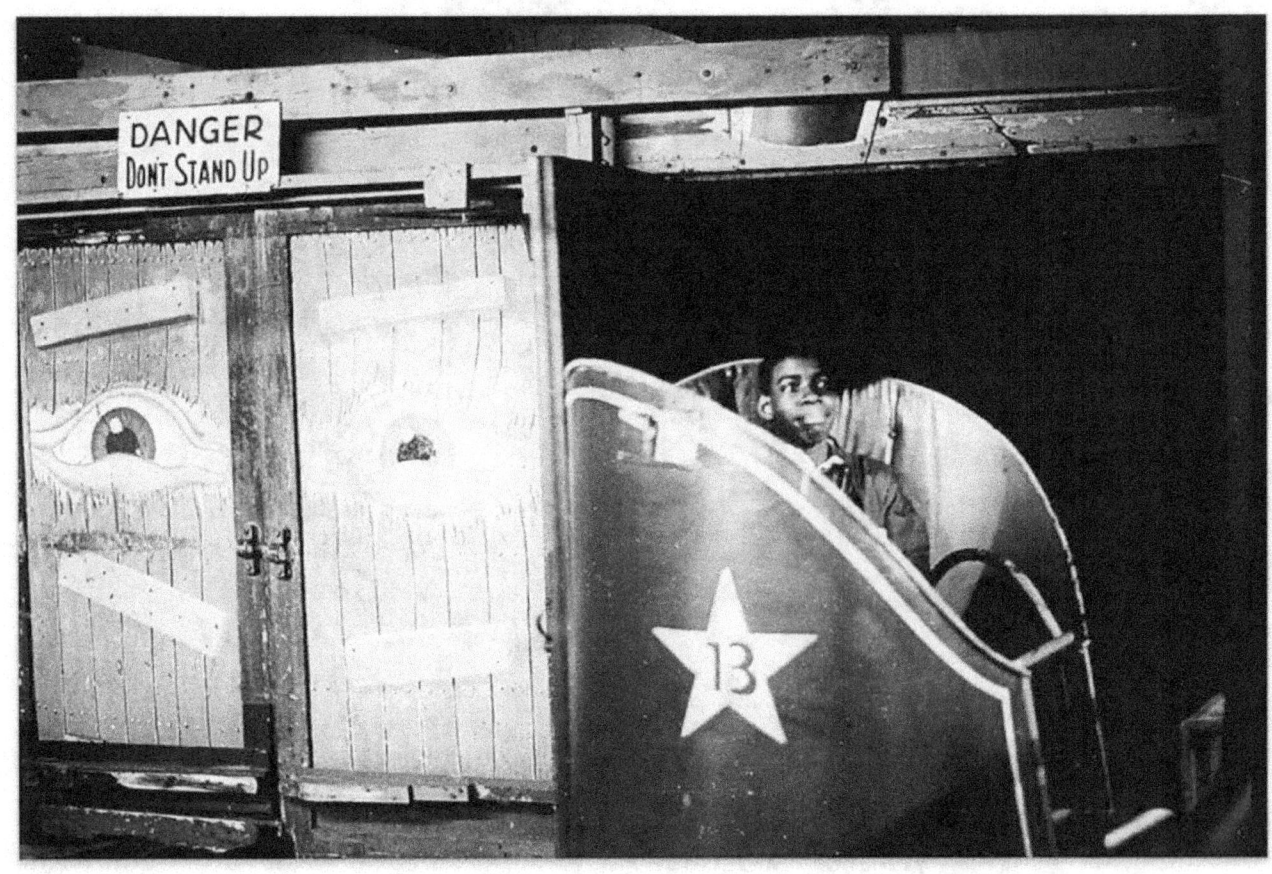

Coney Island, 1965

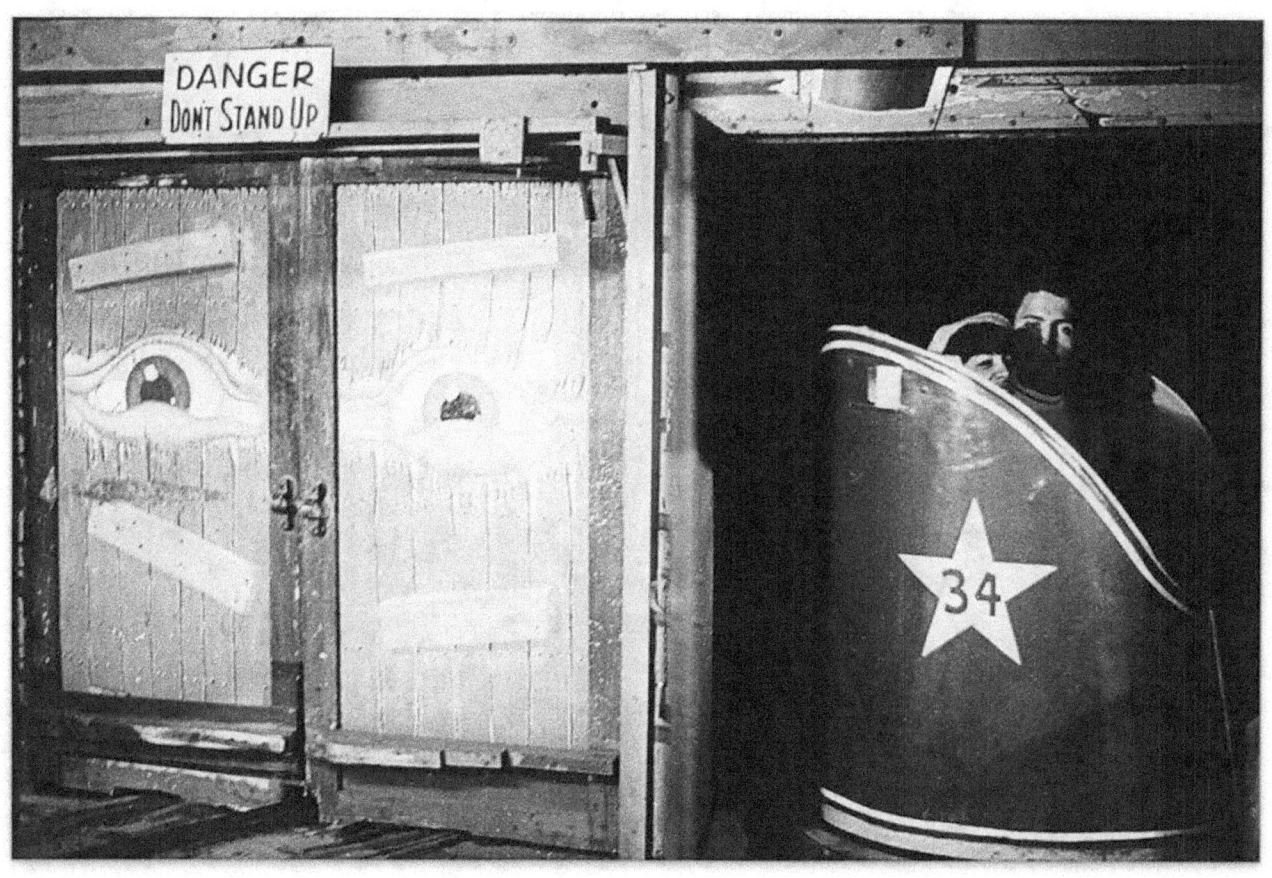

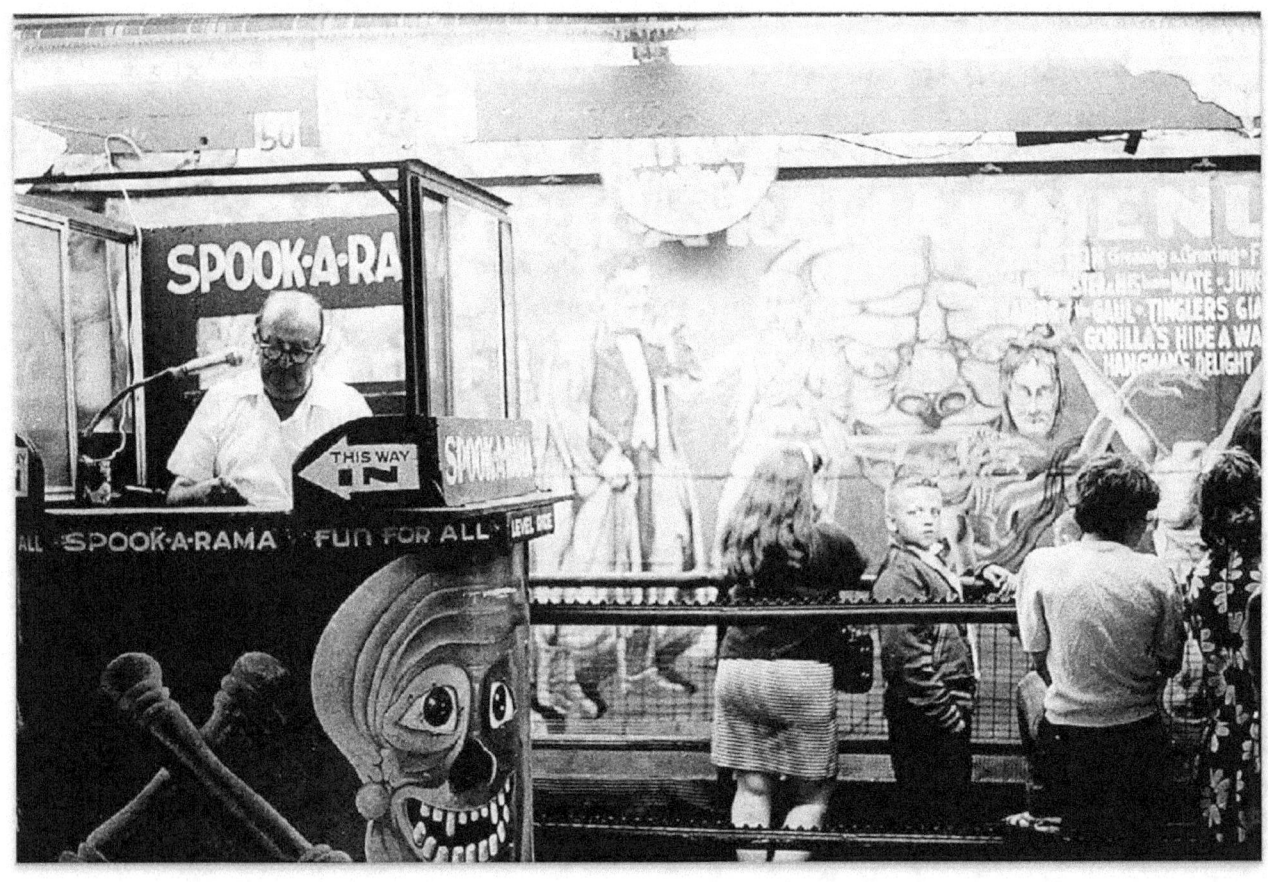

Coney Island, 1965

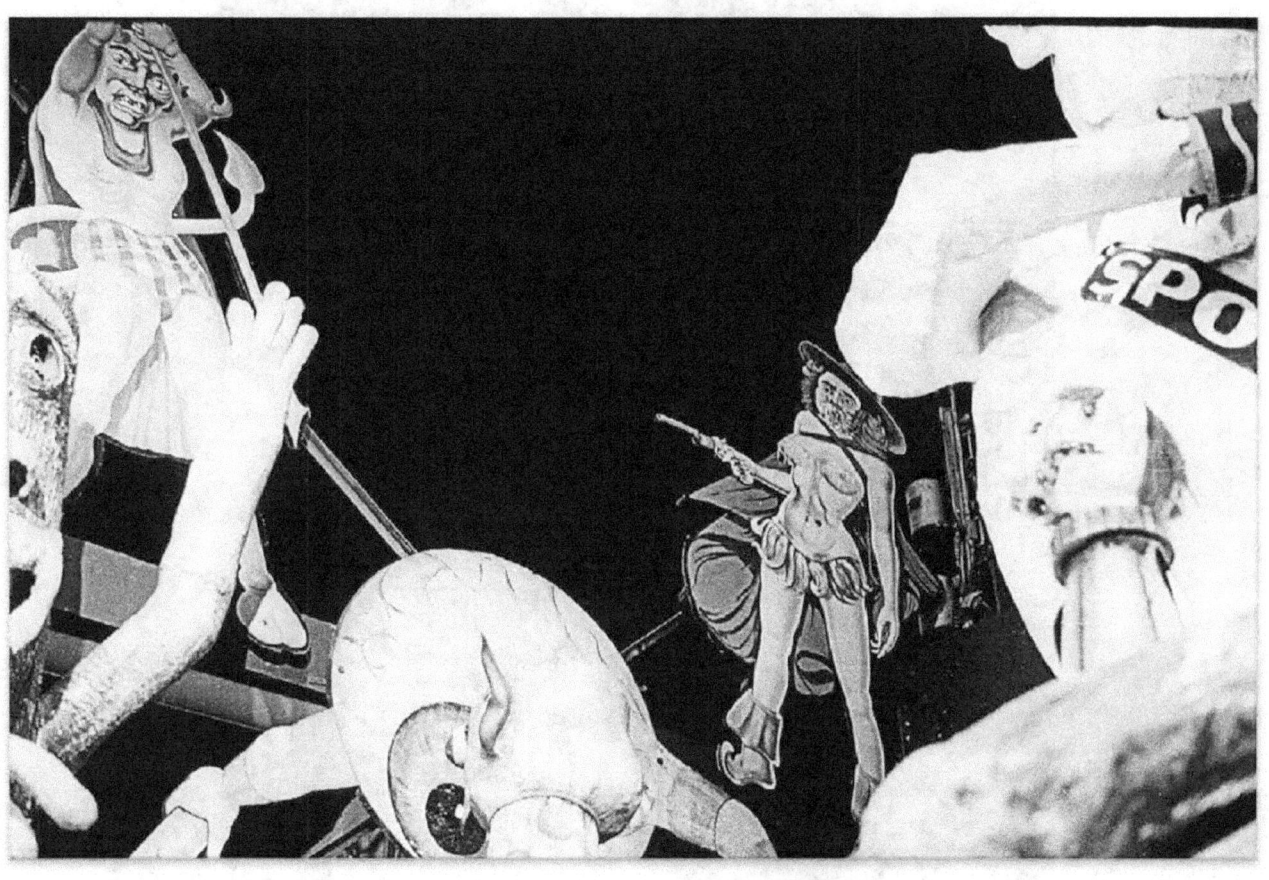

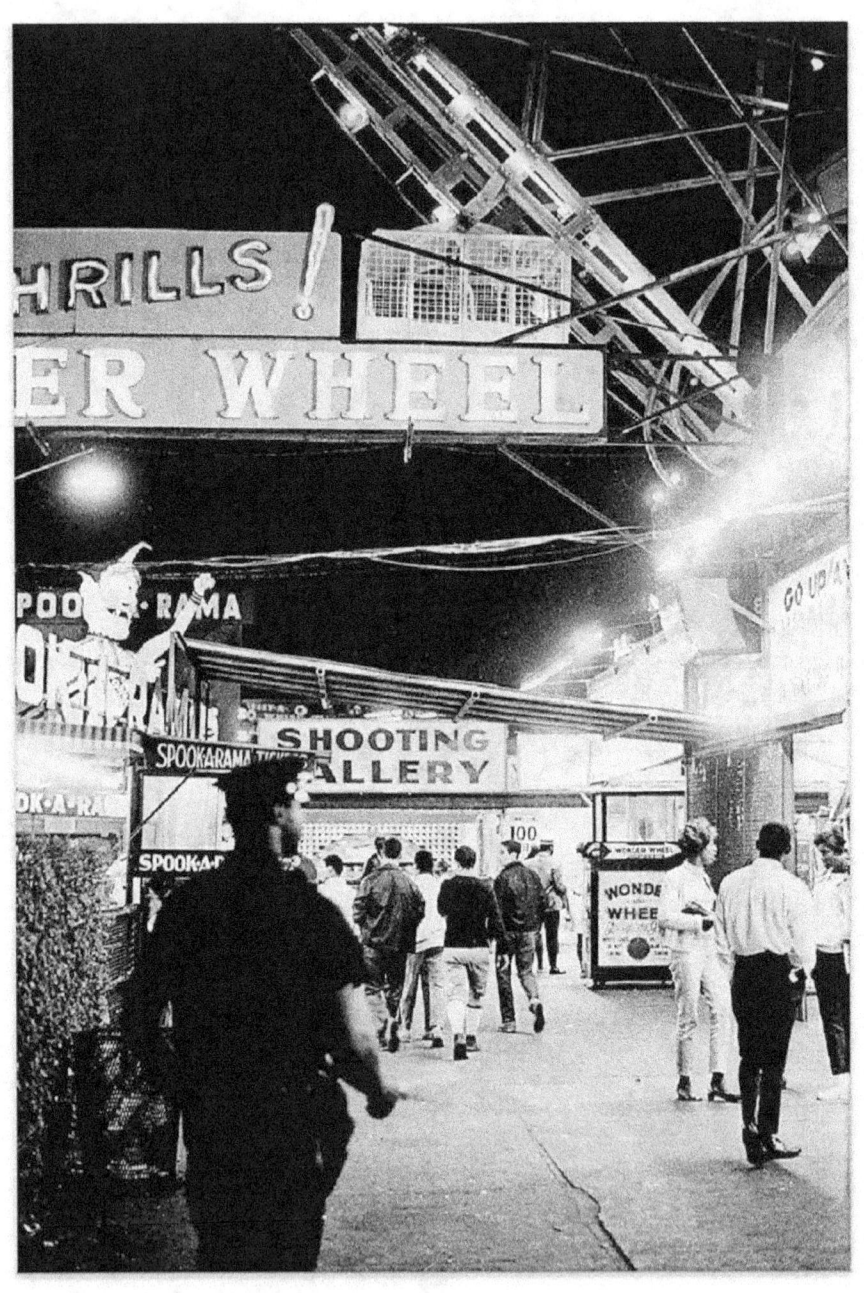

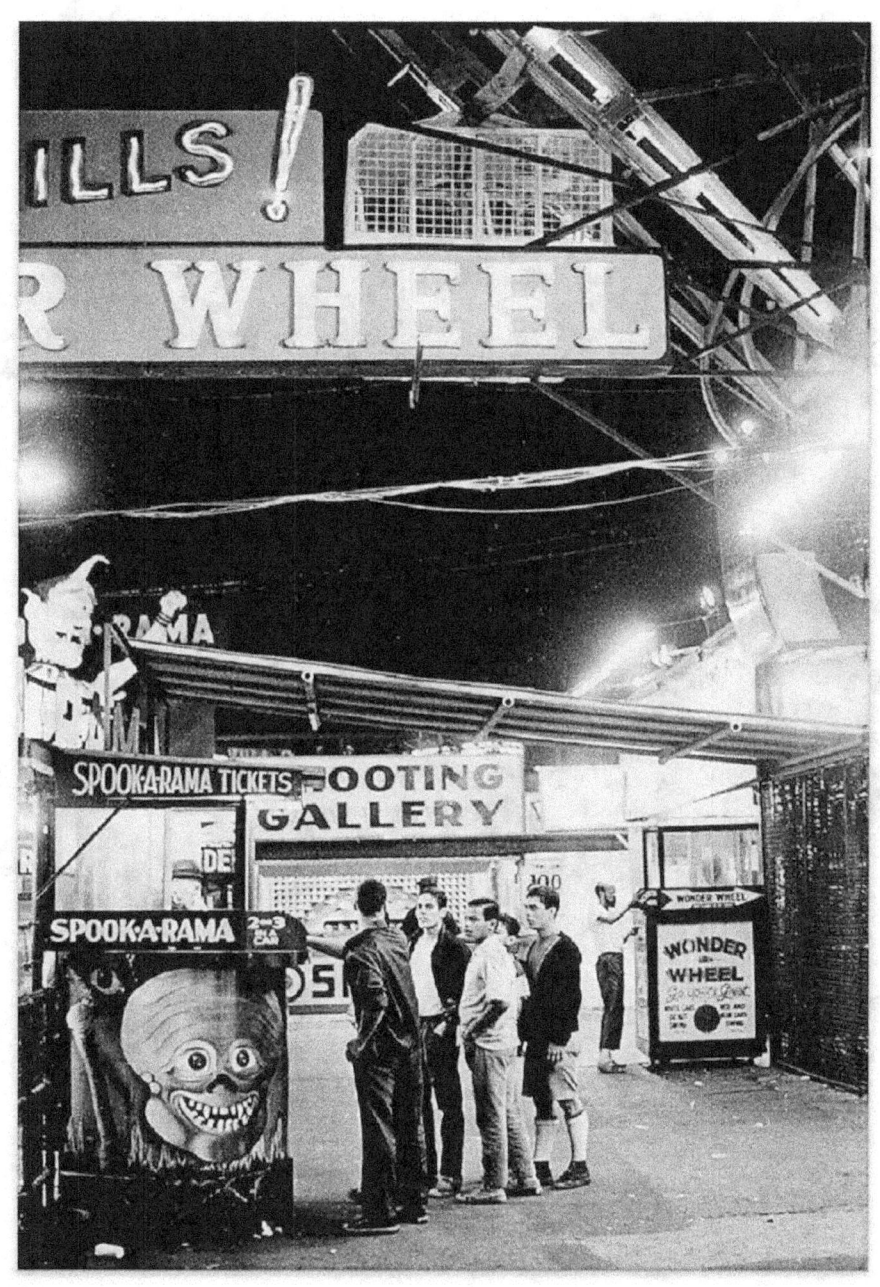

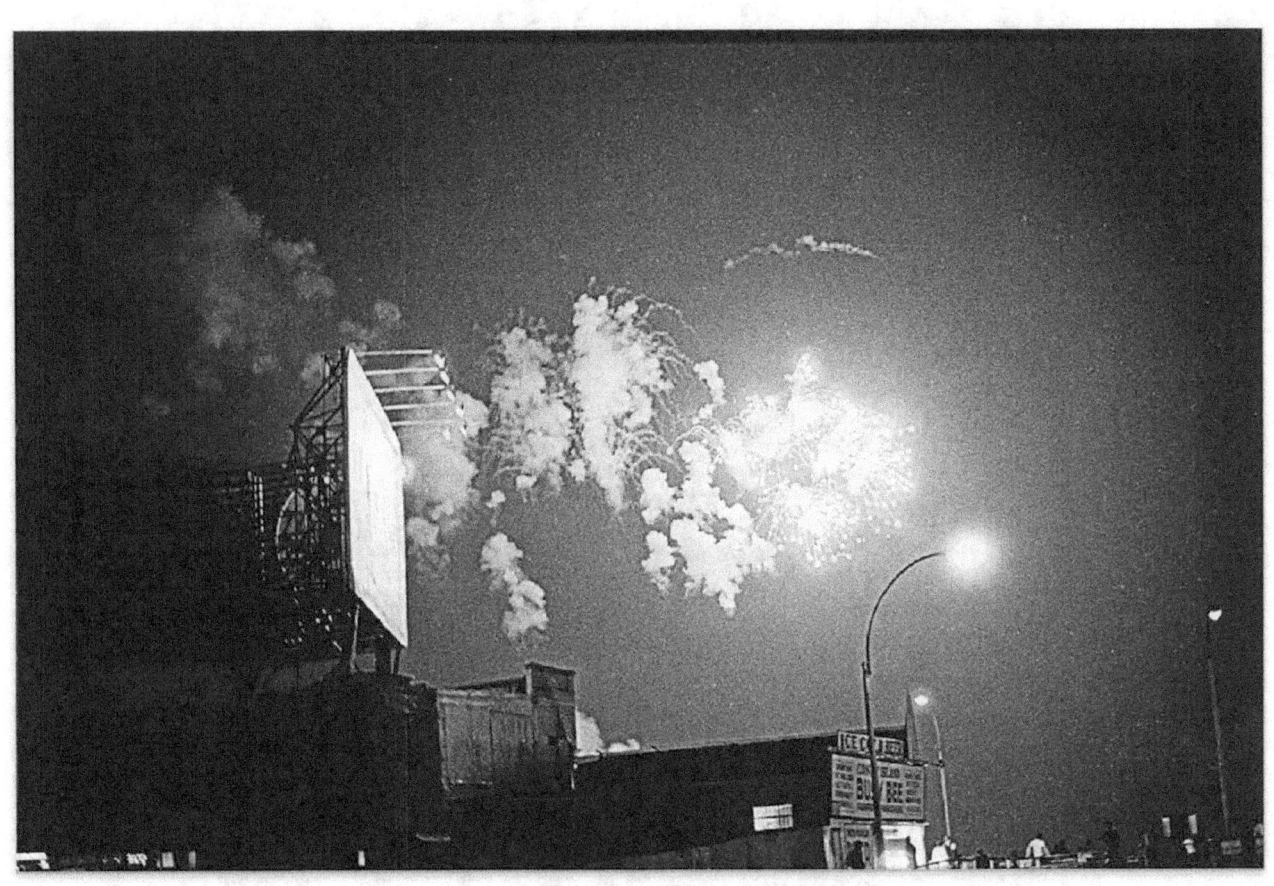

Coney Island, 1965

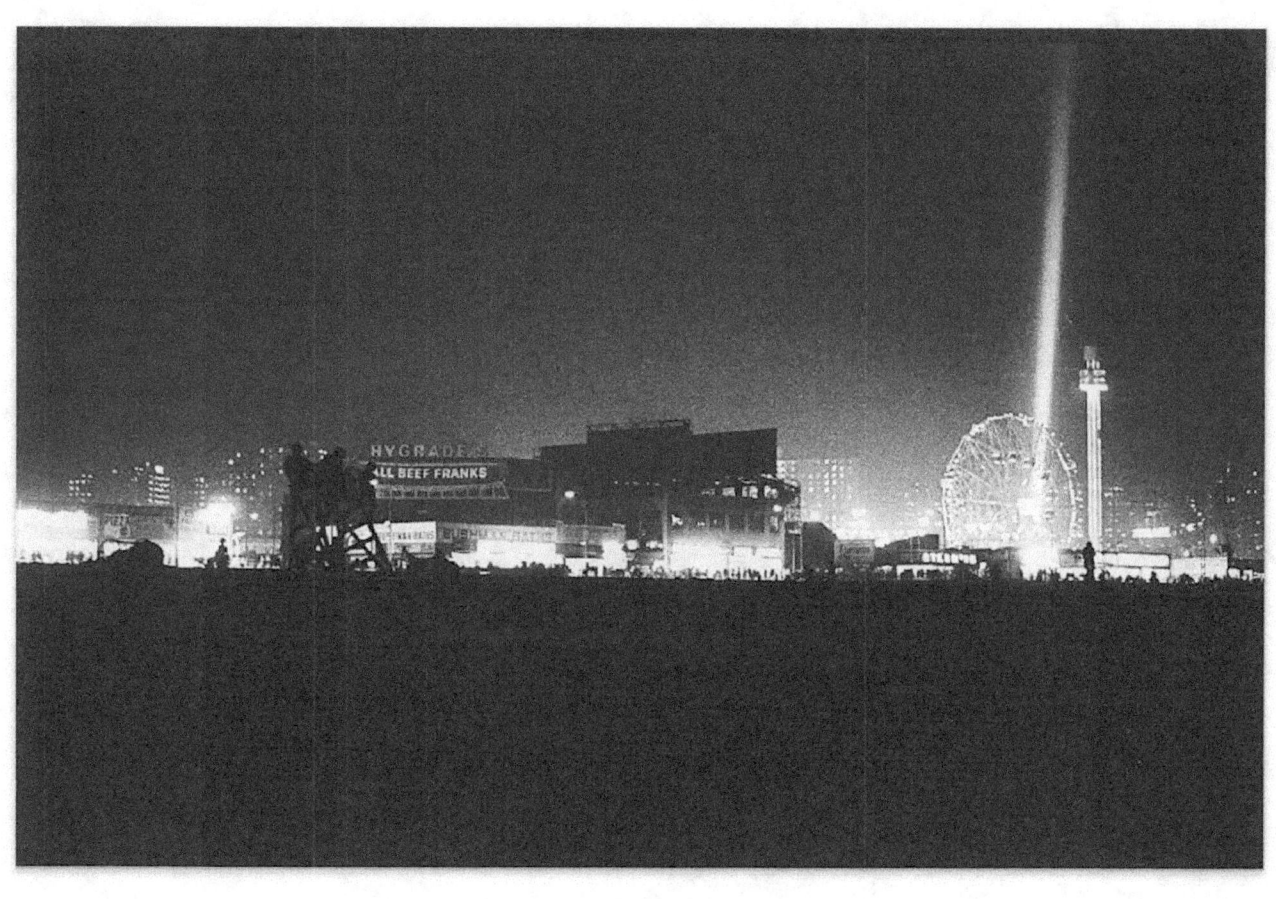

Night from a Car Window, 1965

It's a warm summer night. I'm out with a friend, heading home, and driving down Broadway. It's the same Broadway that runs through New York City, only I'm about 12 miles north of the city line in Westchester County. I'm in the passenger seat, traveling through the Hudson River town of Ossining - the Ossining that has Sing Sing Prison (New York's infamous electric chair executions). I'm hanging out the car window with my camera. We aren't going very fast.

Broadway, or NY Route 9, was originally called Albany Post Road, and in its earliest forms was a trail used by Native Americans. In 1965, it was (and still is) a way to travel from one Hudson River town to another, from work to a favorite hangout, or just to ride around. If you wanted, you could travel toll free from north of the city to Manhattan via the Broadway Bridge in Marble Hill (which is still in Manhattan even though it's on the mainland).

I was young and open to exploring. It was a different era. Going for rides to somewhere or nowhere and photographing was a combination that fit me and the times. "The sixties" produced its own subject matter, but for me, I could escape from that era and visit wherever I wanted and however I wanted.

Tonight it was soft summer air, moving past what I knew at that point in time.

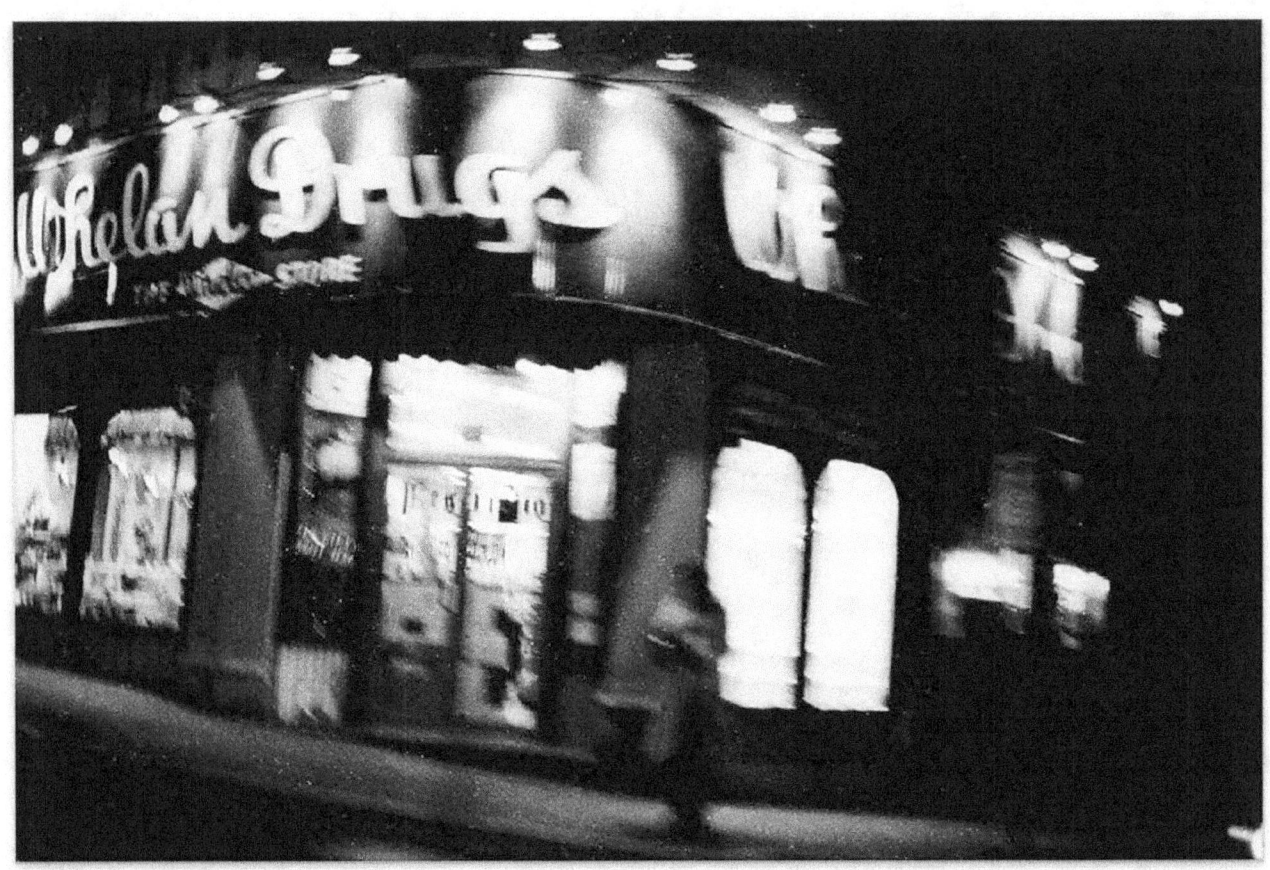

Night From a Car Window, 1965

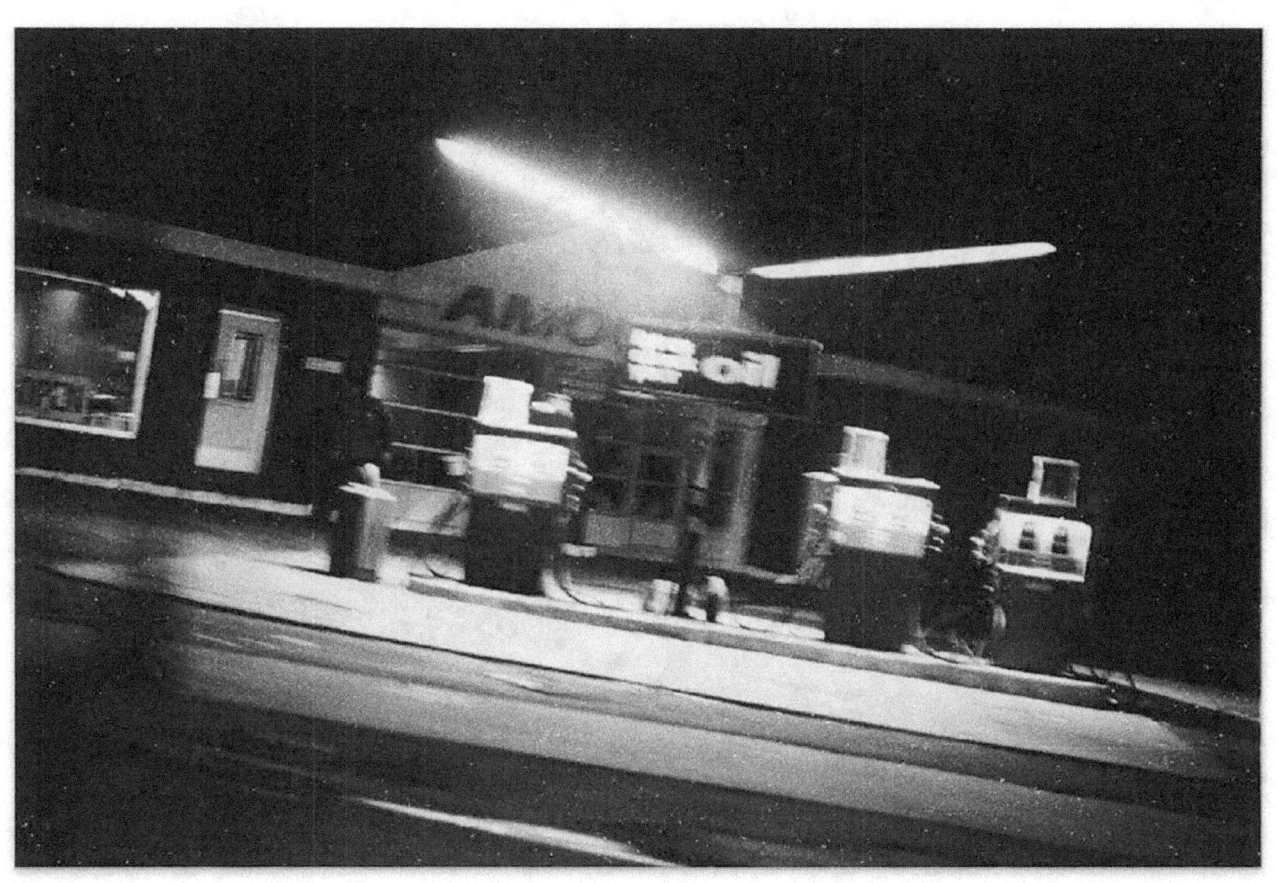

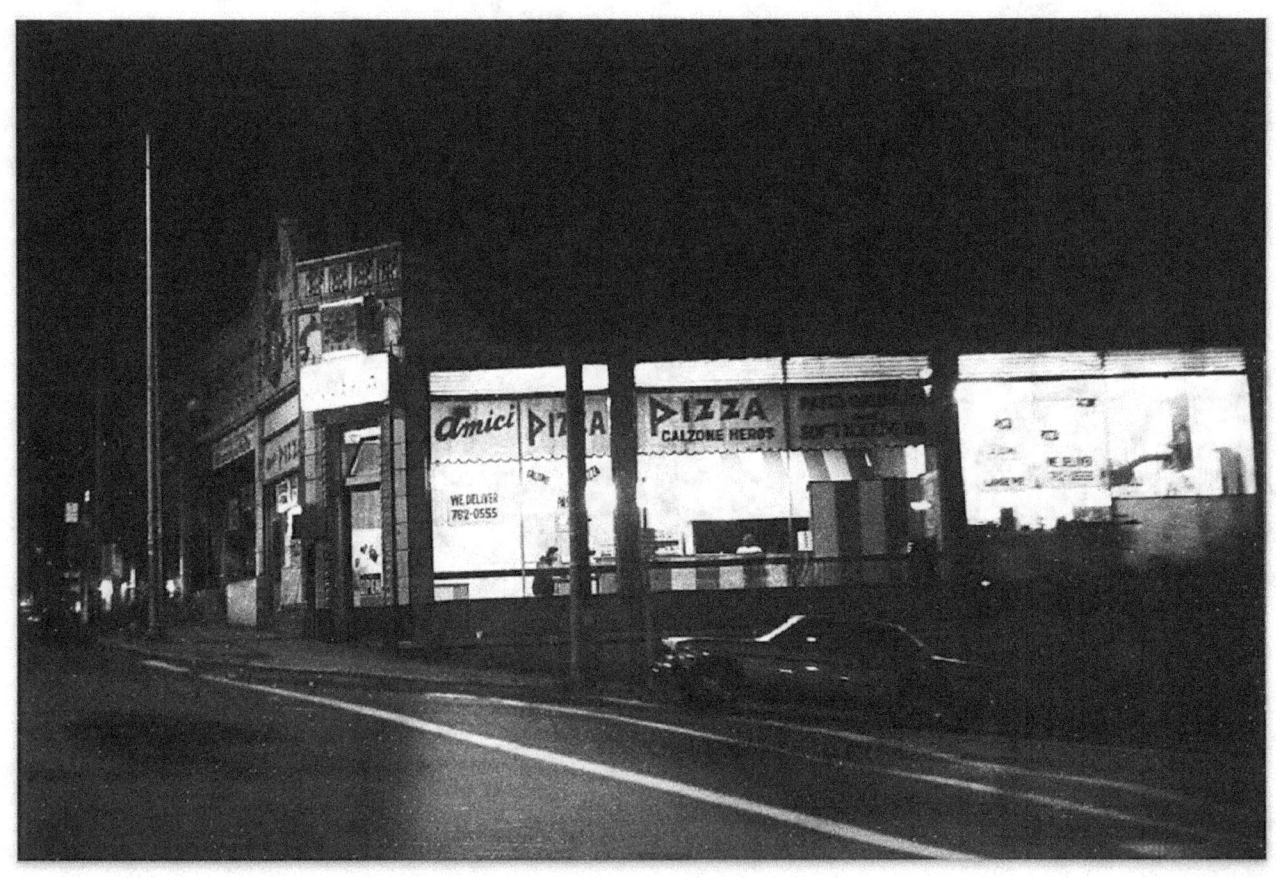

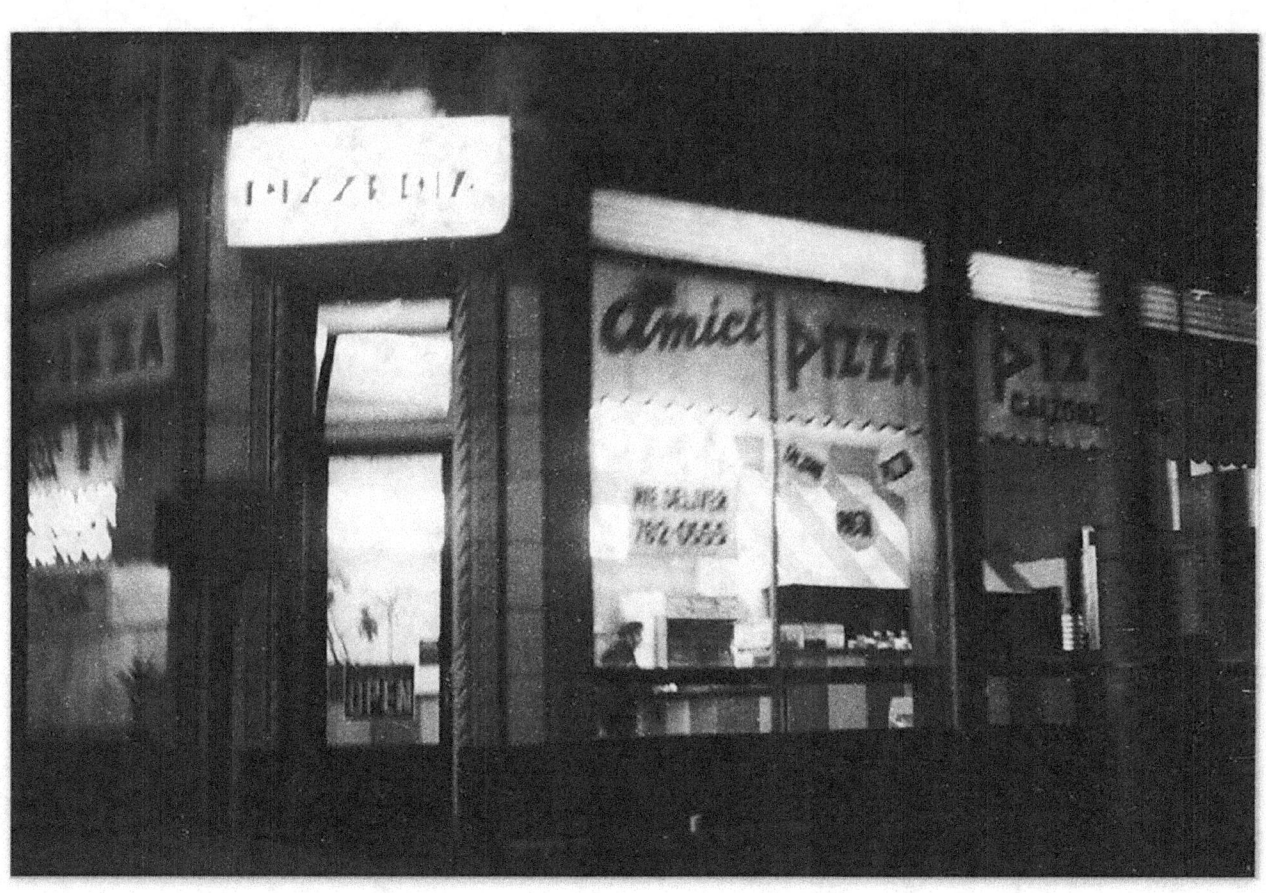

Night From a Car Window, 1965

Night From a Car Window, 1965

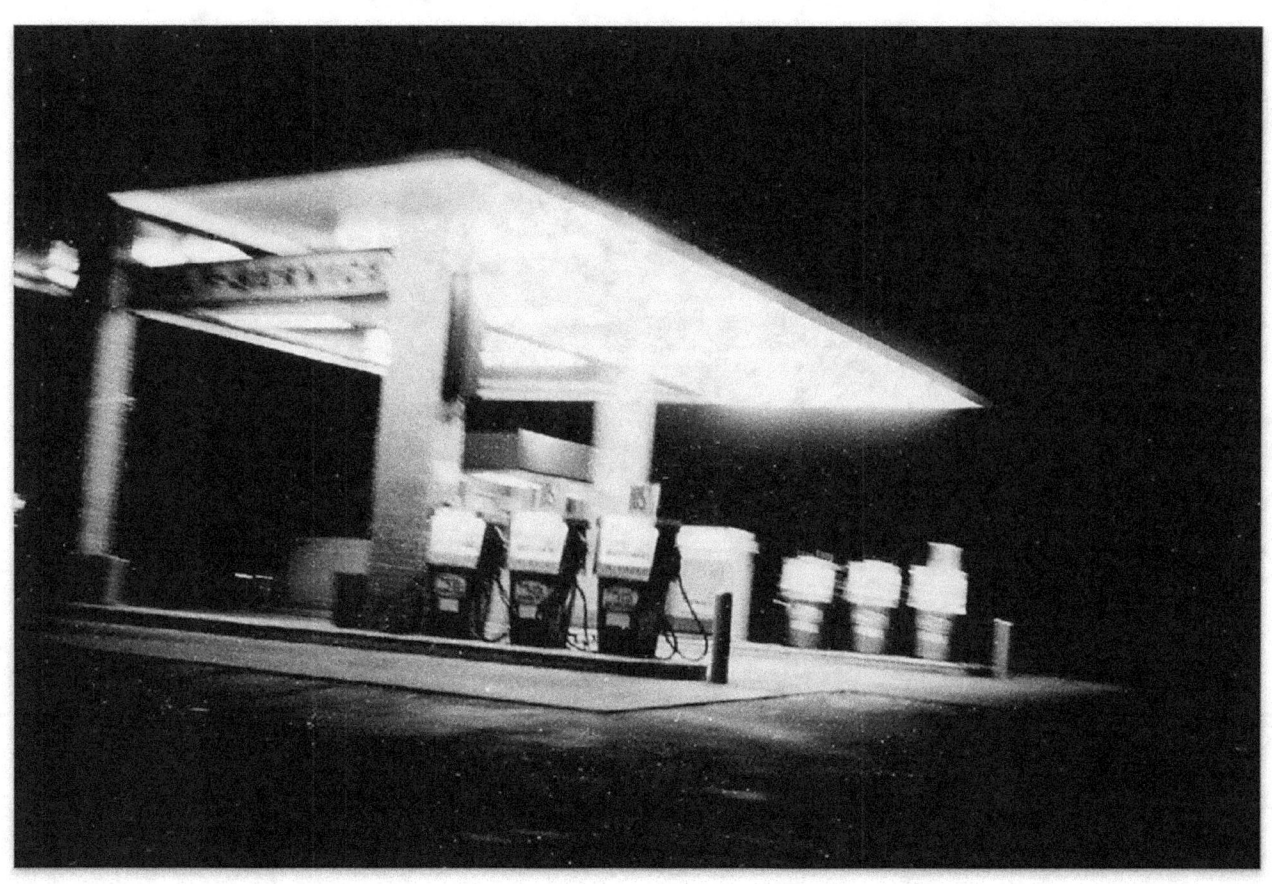

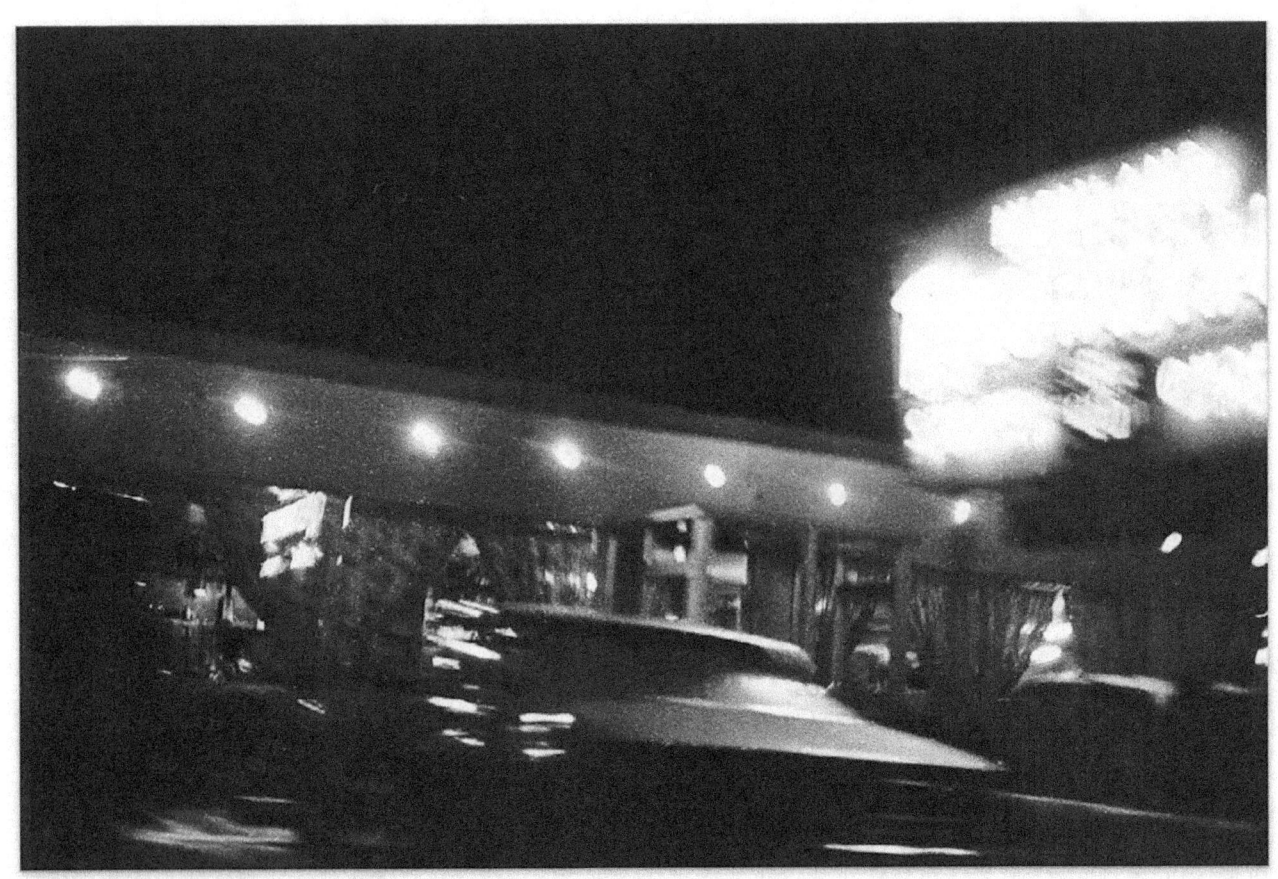

Night From a Car Window, 1965

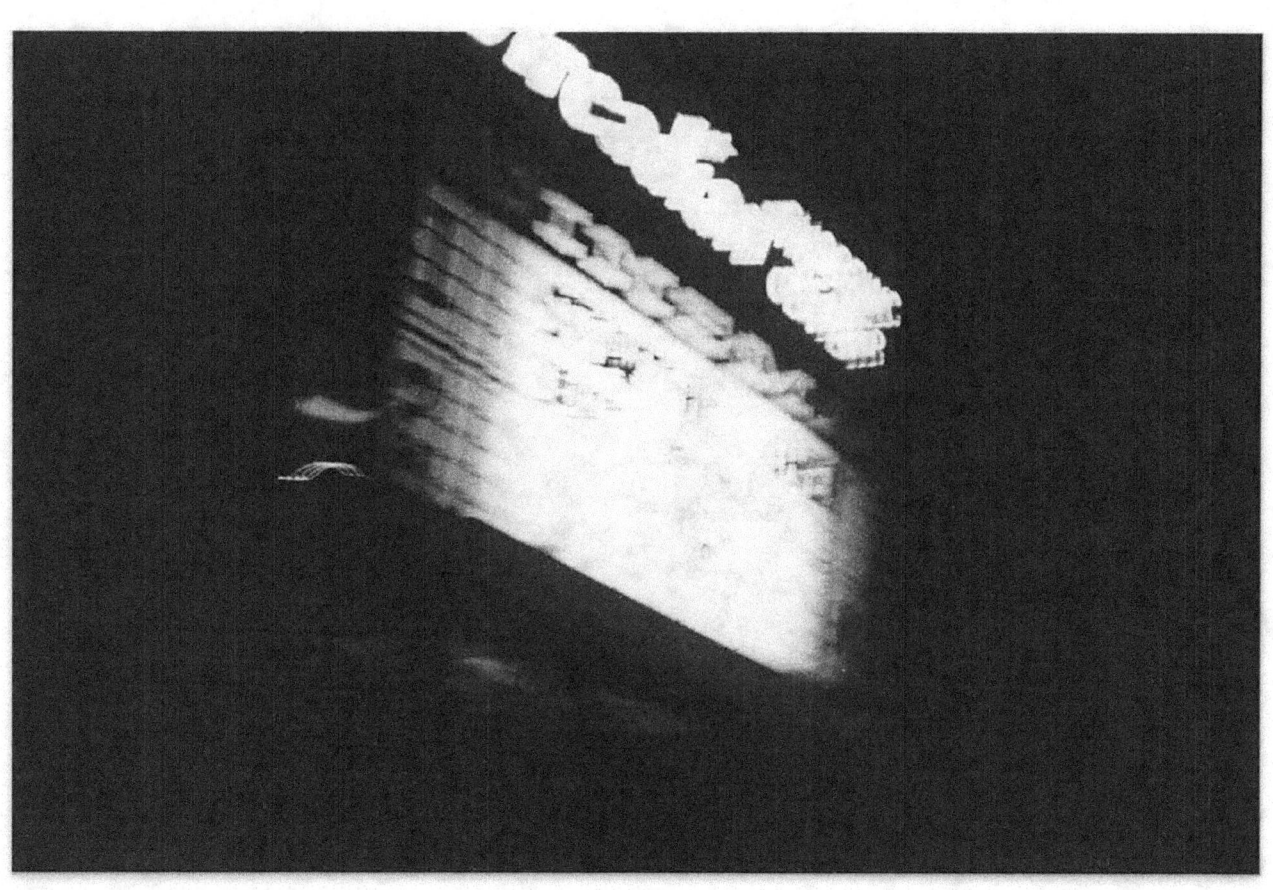

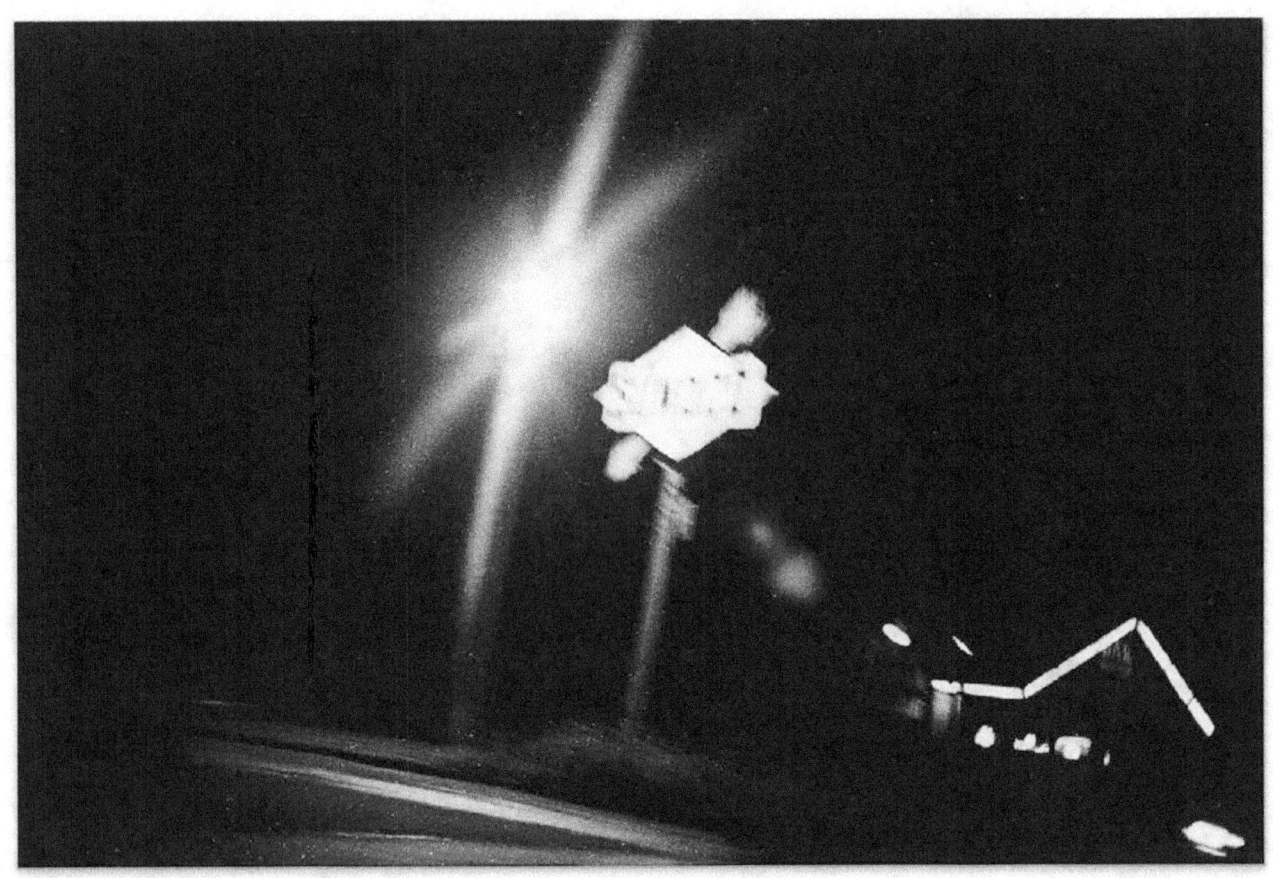

Night From a Car Window, 1965

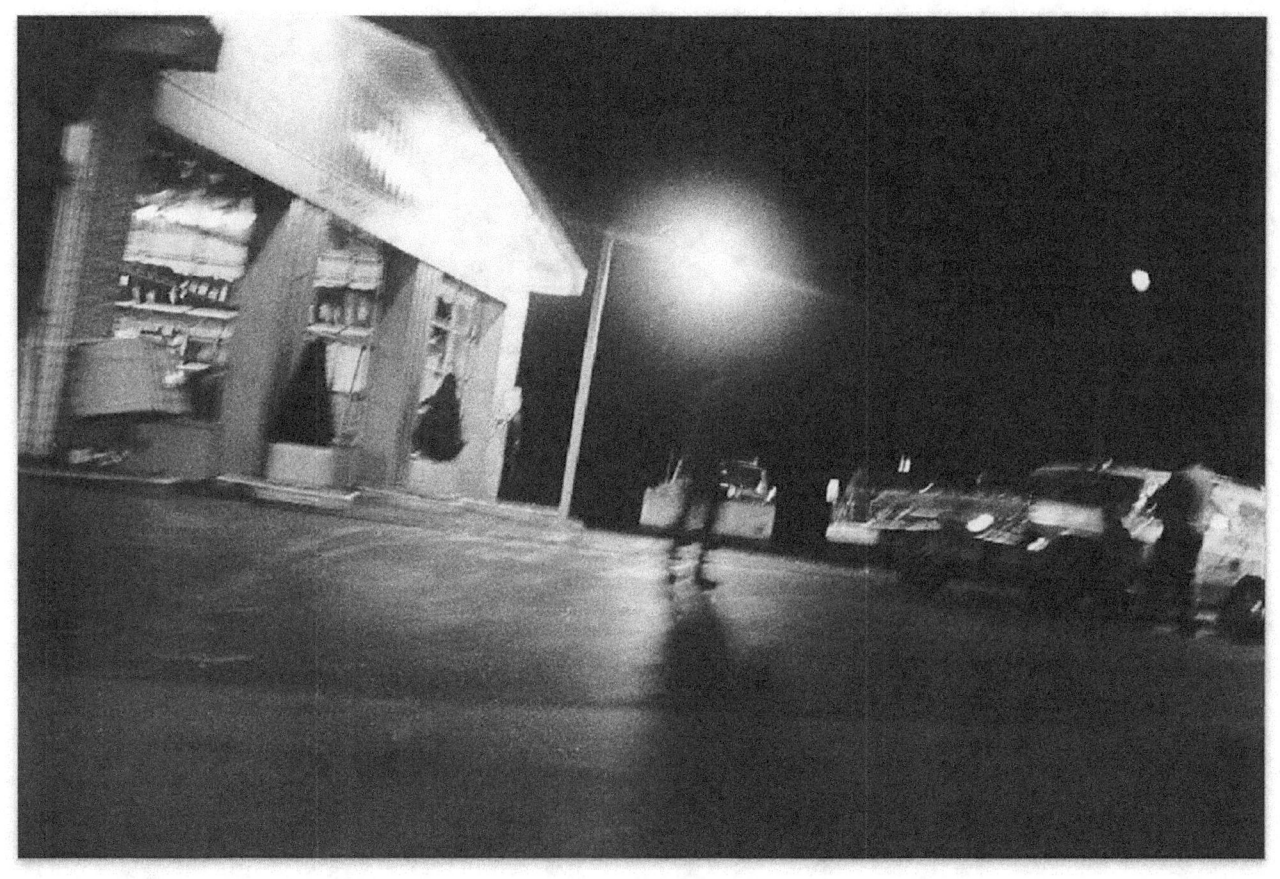

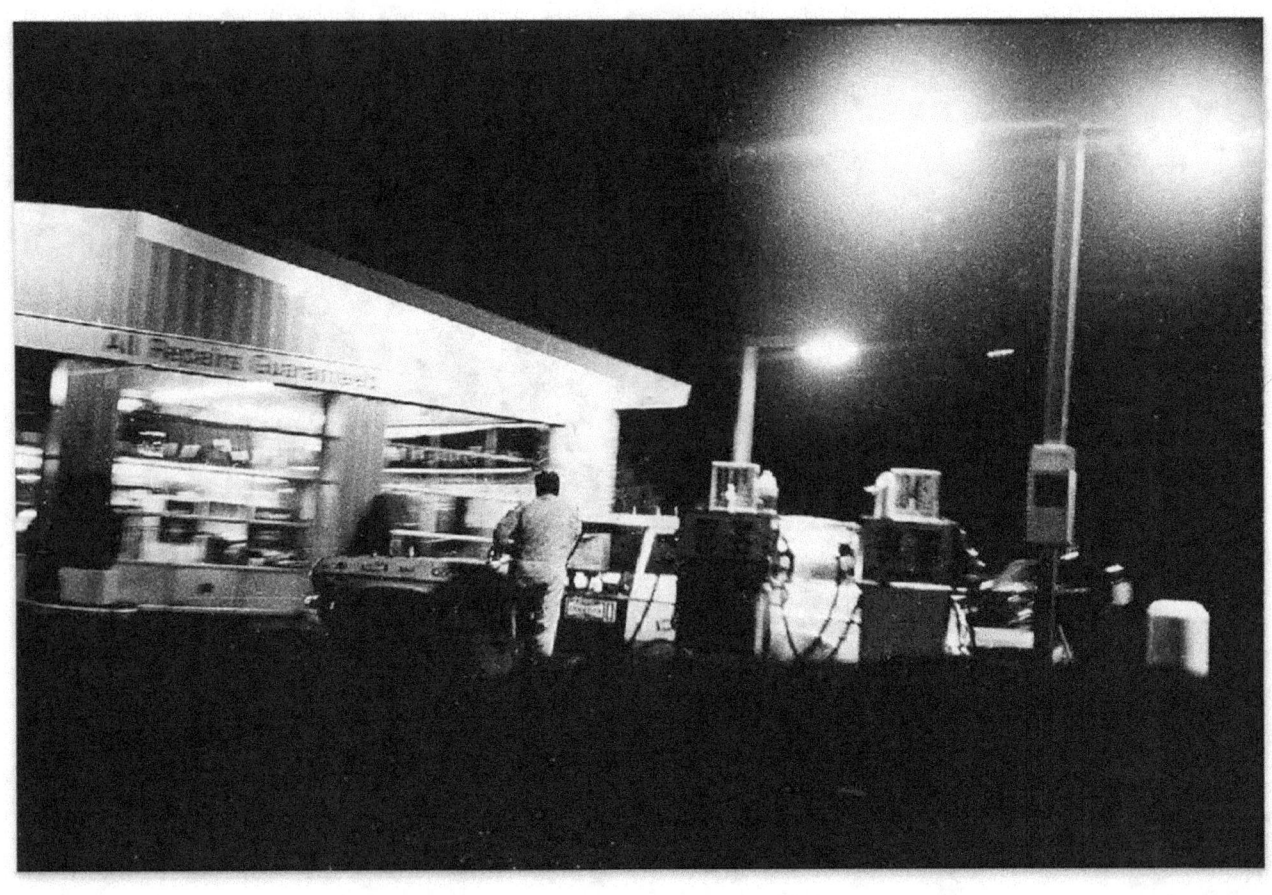

Night From a Car Window, 1965

The Feast of San Gennaro, 1971

Background

In the early 1970s New York City was beginning a slide into a state of disrepair that would peak in the late 1970s. Even as tenants had begun moving into the new World Trade Center complex, several of the boroughs were losing population, arsonists torched buildings for the insurance, graffiti was everywhere, crime was up, and the city was broke.

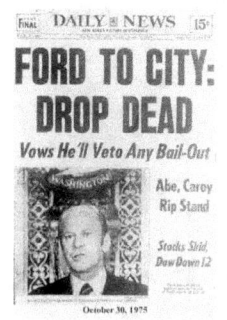

How this all happened is a story in itself, but one thing was clear: the city was not pretty to look at. In New York City, you could say that 1971 represented a lull between storms: the social revolutions of the 1960s, and the deterioration of the late 1970s.

Recorded histories about The Feast of San Gennaro do not offer much detail regarding the 1960s and early 1970s other than basic facts of its existence. The Feast had not yet been fully media-exposed; it was not very well known beyond locals, visiting relatives, and some adventurous tourists looking for exotic corners of the city.

Prior to the 1960s some photographs and descriptions exist - crime scenes, and other historical accounts - but one could guess that attention to this festival might have been limited due to a society distracted by the war in Vietnam, and politics and people in rebellion. As an attention grabber, The Feast did not scream loudly. That would begin to change by 1974 when, commenting on its size, New York Magazine called the festival "no place for the fainthearted."

The Feast takes place in little Italy, Manhattan. Roughly speaking, the area is bordered north and south by East Houston and Canal streets, and west and east by Lafayette and Bowery. By most accounts, the Italian population of Little Italy in the twenty-first century is a fraction of what it was in the twentieth century. Today, that culture is represented mainly by a few restaurants and shops, and also by the festival.

The genesis of the festival is Gennaro, the Bishop of Benevento and the patron saint of Naples. He was born around 272 AD. The centerpiece of the festival is really the procession, which expresses the passion and belief in what the Bishop has come to represent: his faith, dedication, and determination in the face of many challenges. Gennaro's history is a mix of fact and myth stemming from his arrest for visiting a prisoner, his avoidance of punishment, and the representation of blood saved after his execution. It is this vial of blood that forms the centerpiece of the procession on the first day of the festival.

The first festival was in 1926 and has run continuously every September since then. It is now presented by Figli di San Gennaro (Children of San Gennaro), a not-for-profit community organization.

The photographs, September, 1971

What I mostly see when I look at these photographs are the faces of those who made the festival work, faces of a different time, a different era. An era just prior to the Genovese Family, and before Rudy Giuliani interfered, before Mean Streets, and The French Connection. When I look at these faces I see acceptance of a person's place, and of the festival's place in the community. It was an era of its own making, one based on hard work and exhibiting what we might now call innocence (In fact, the only indication I could find as to who actually ran the festival is in one of my photographs, Luigi's Pizzeria & Heros, a sign in the window is signed, "THE COMMITTEE.").

It was perhaps 5:30 in the afternoon when I came upon the Feast of San Gennaro in lower Manhattan. I was living nearby at the time and would often wander the streets with my camera, a Nikkormat with Plus-x, black and white film, set at ASA 200. I realized I had little light remaining in the day with which to shoot. I saw many wonderful scenes and began taking pictures, starting at one end of the festival and finishing at the other. Some people thought I was from the press; one person asked if I was from the *Village Voice* - remember, this was before the festival's extreme popularity and long before everyone carried a camera in their phone!

All photographs were taken in about 45 minutes, which for me was an extraordinary experience. All photographs are shown exactly as they were taken: full-frame, no manipulation.

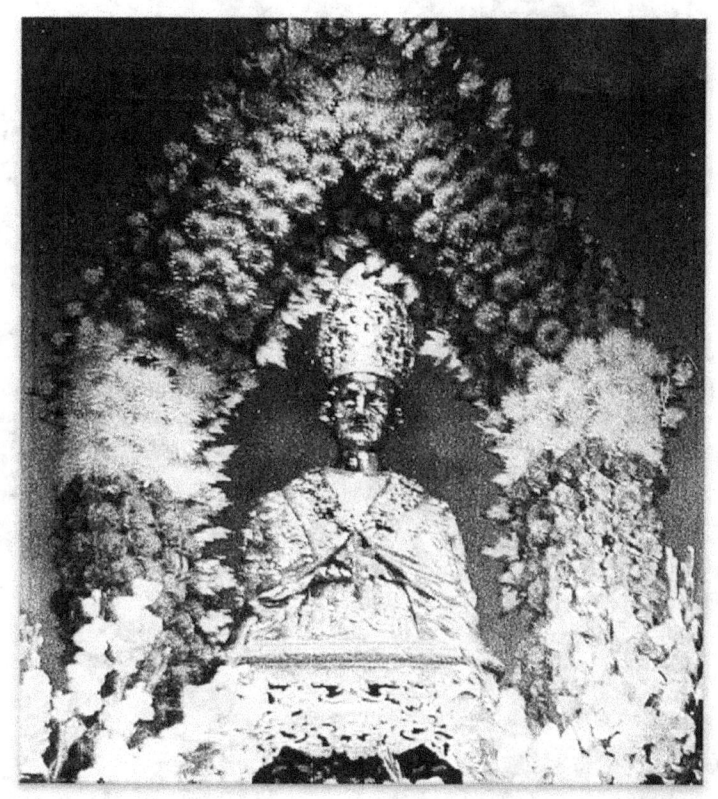

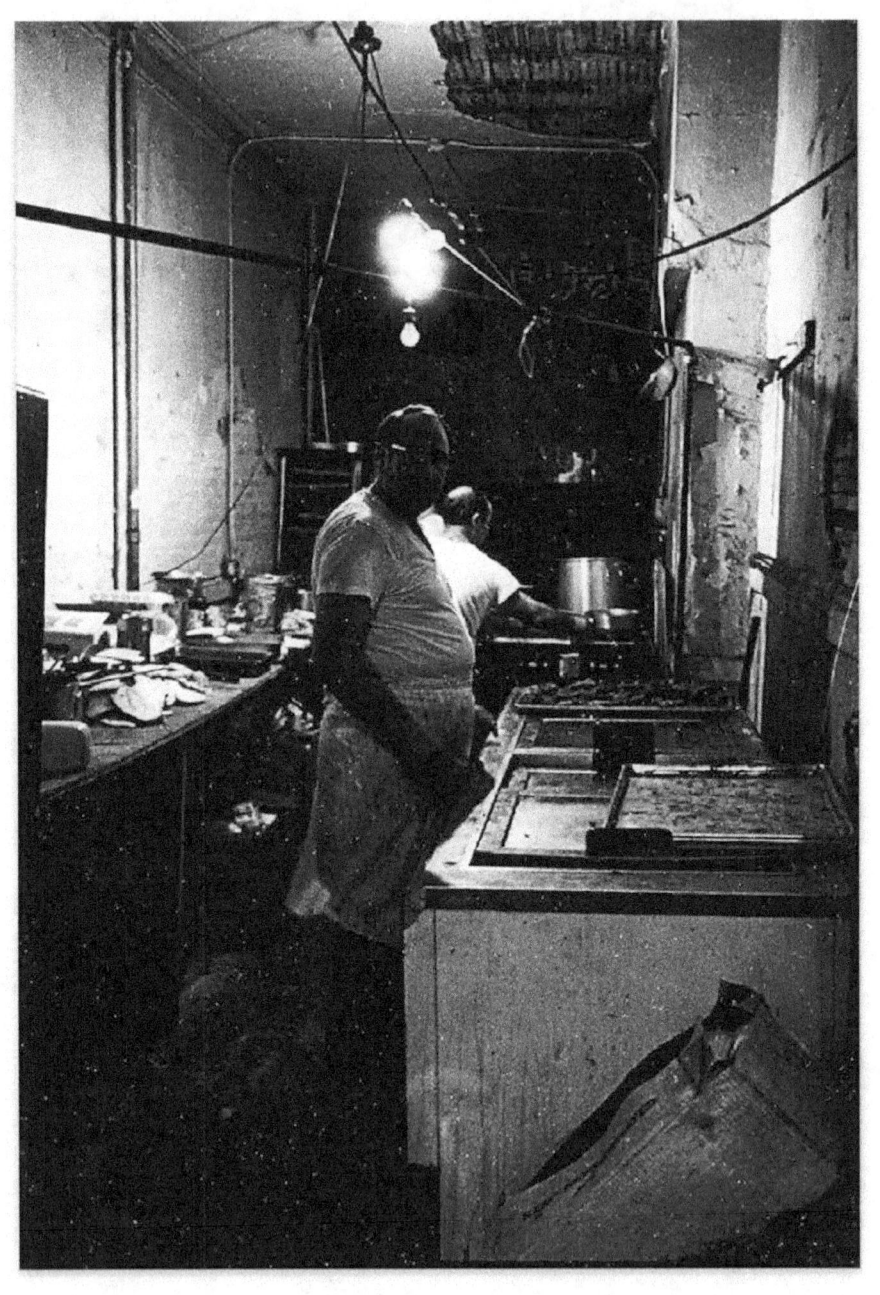

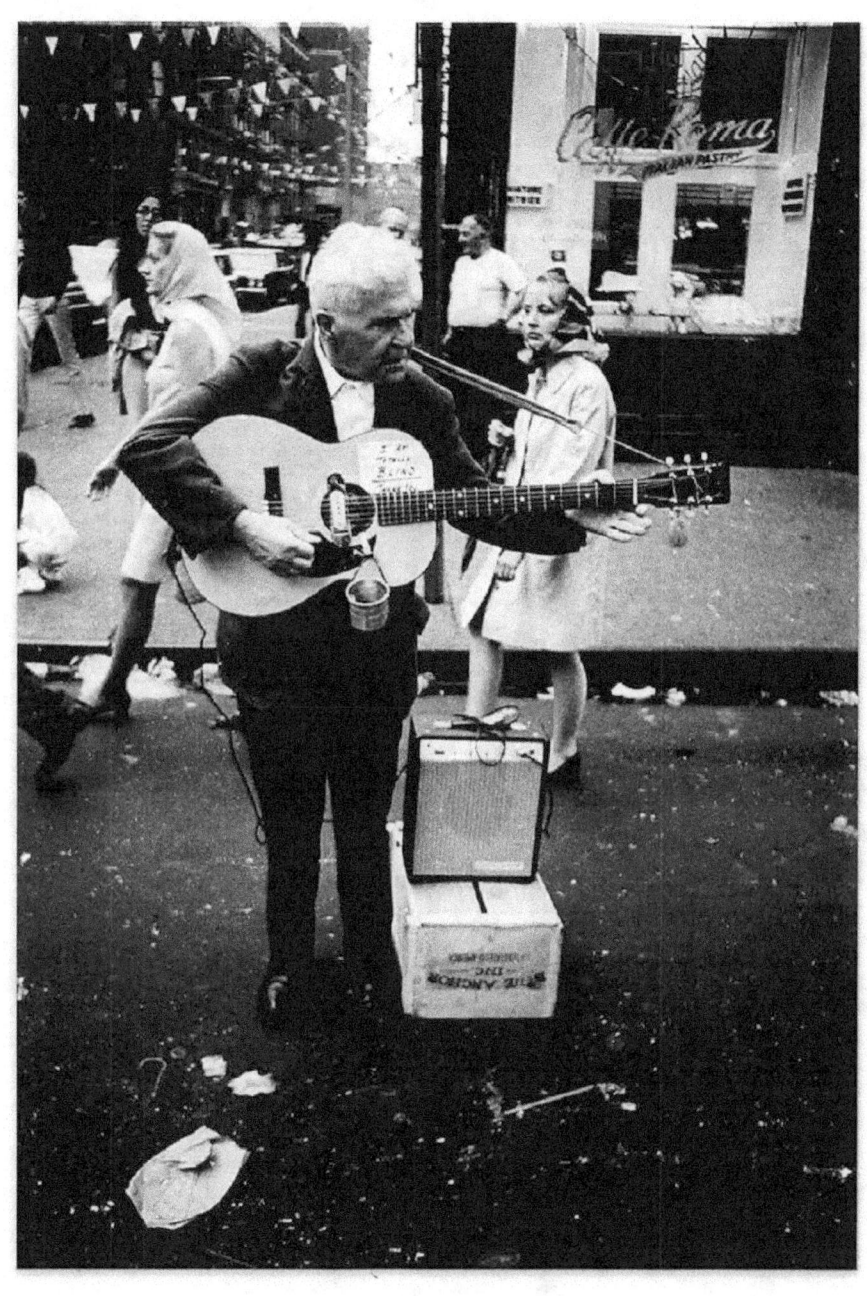

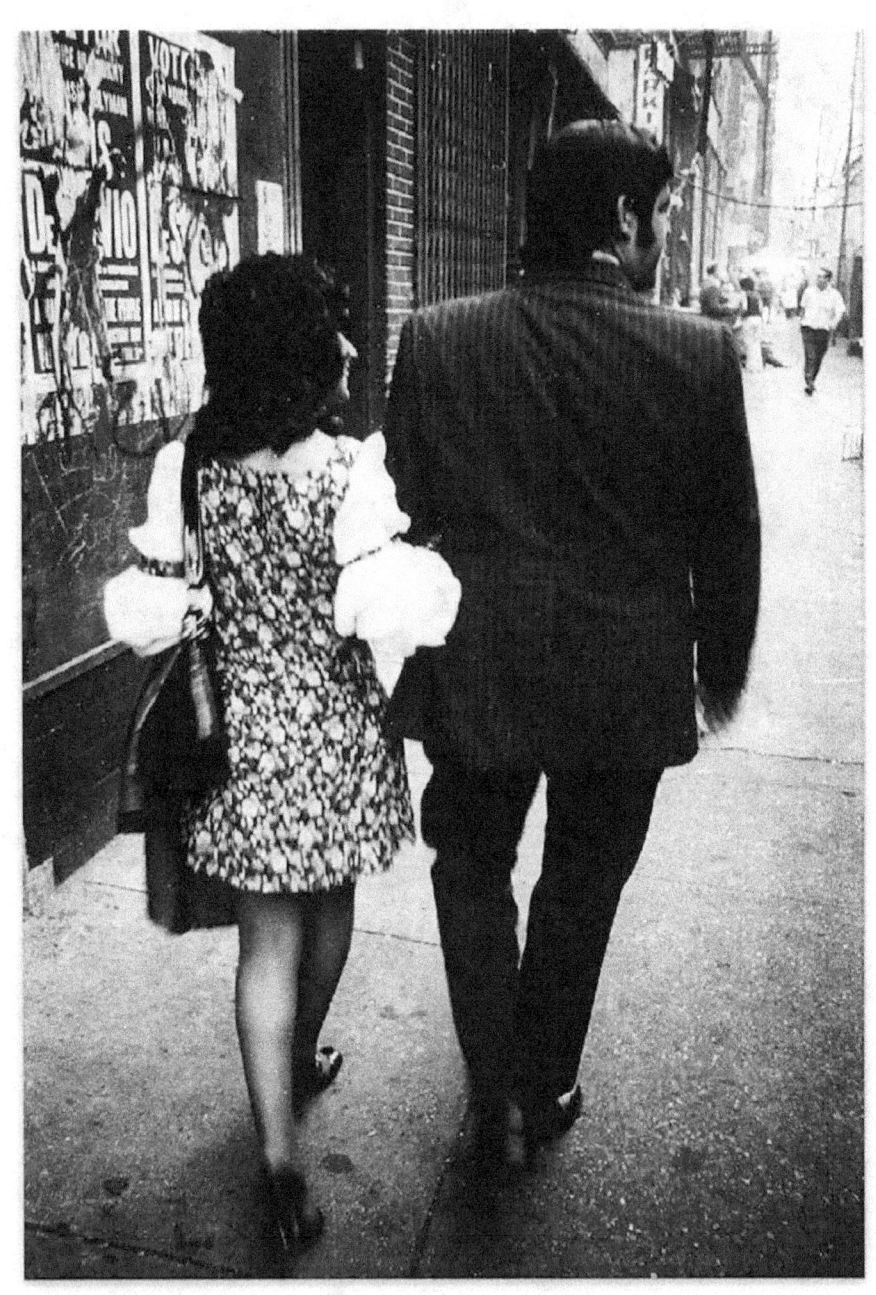

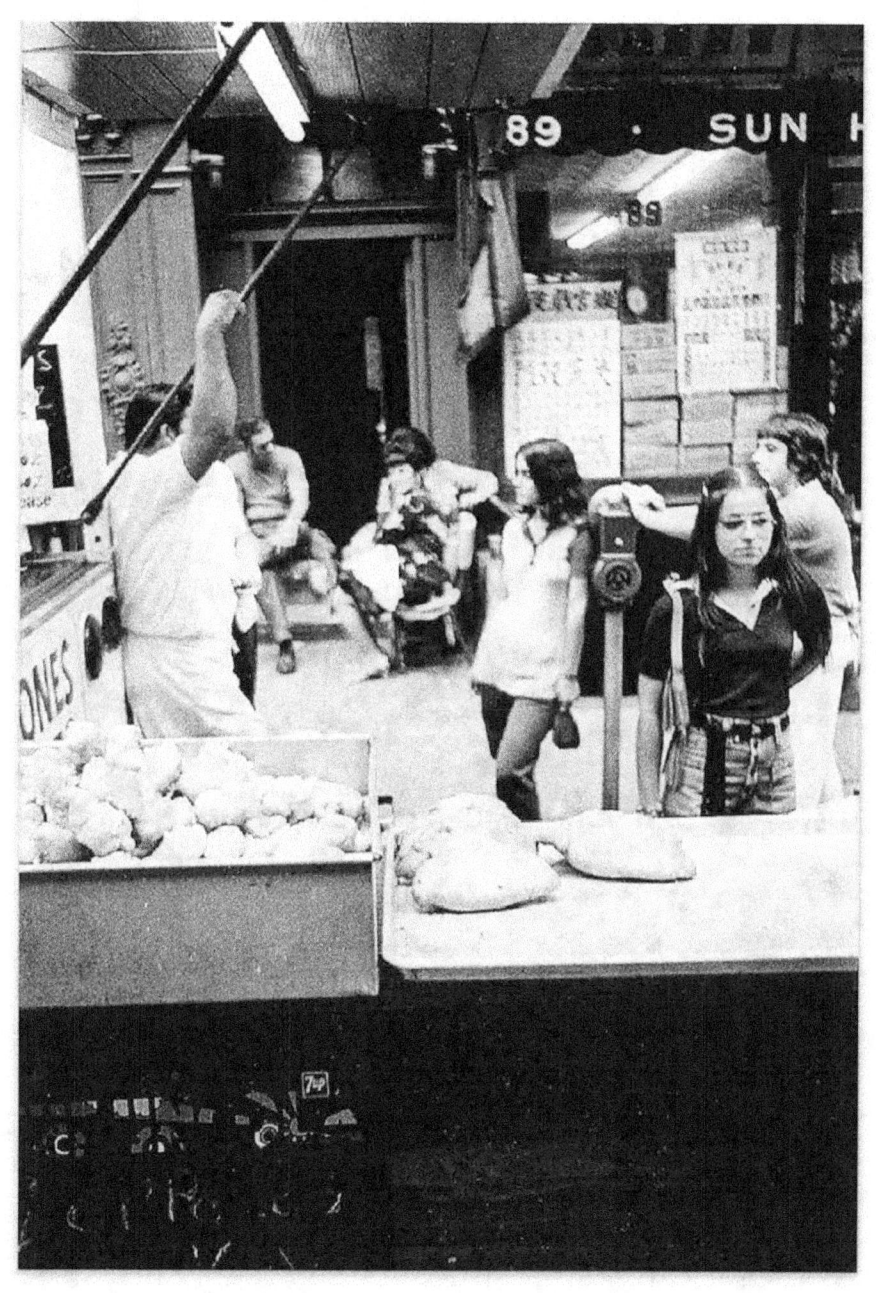

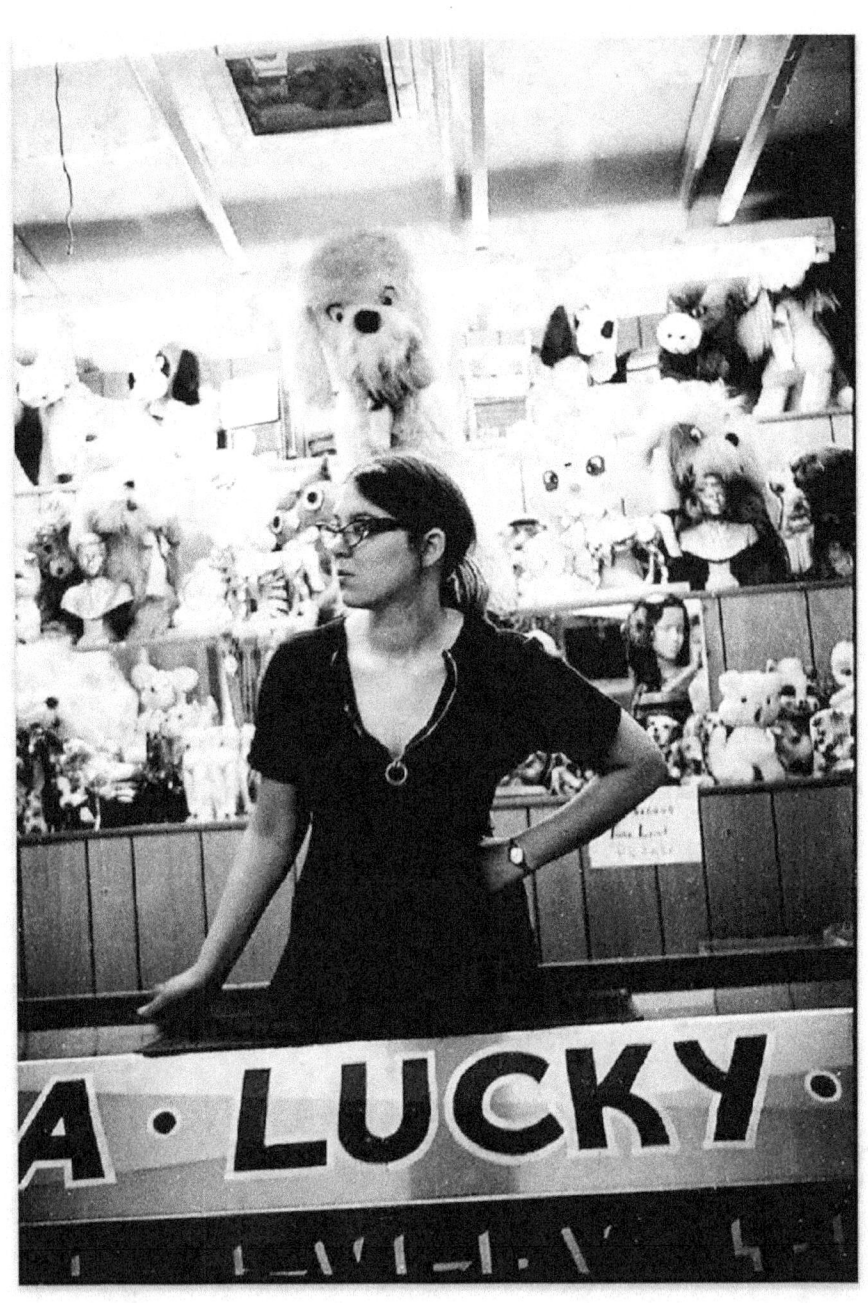

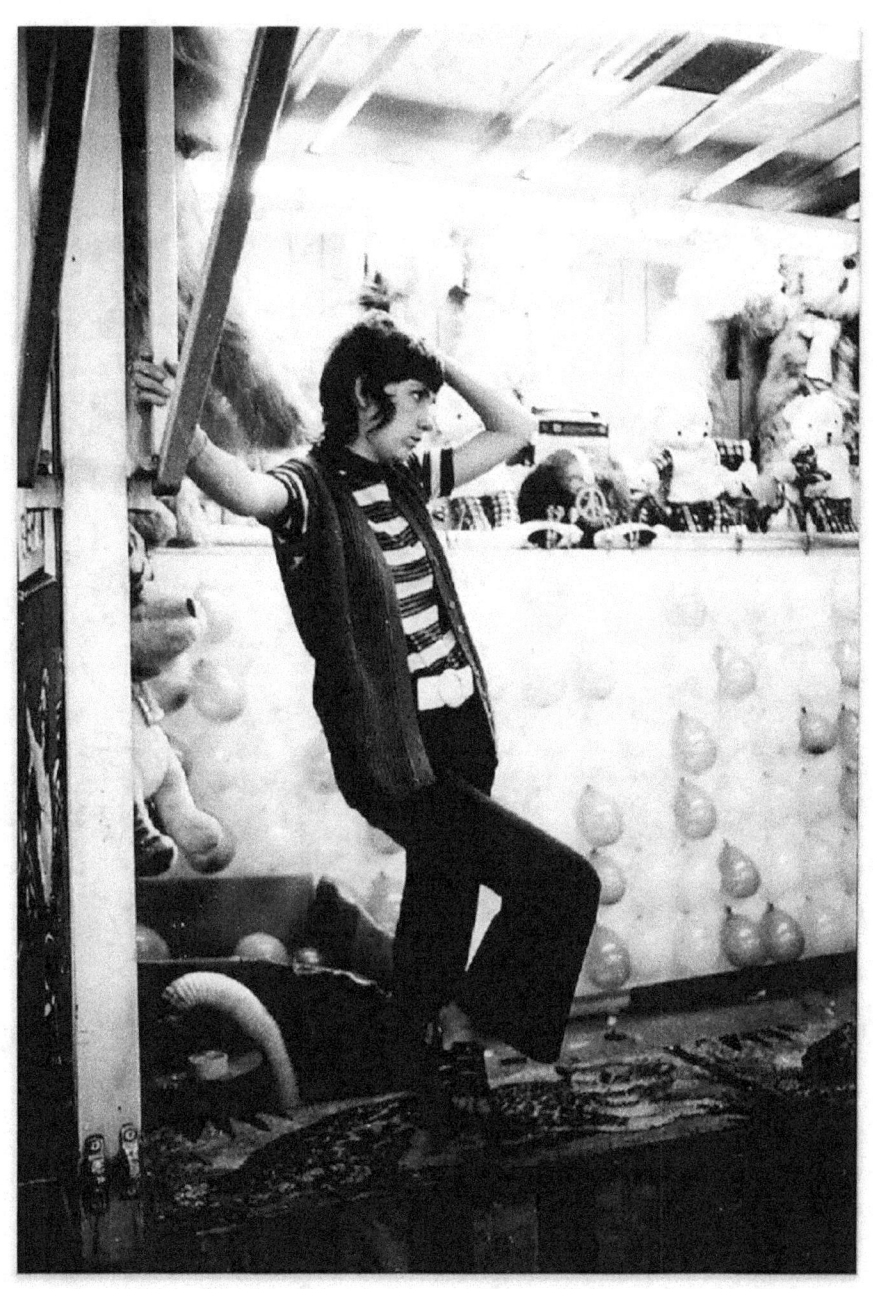

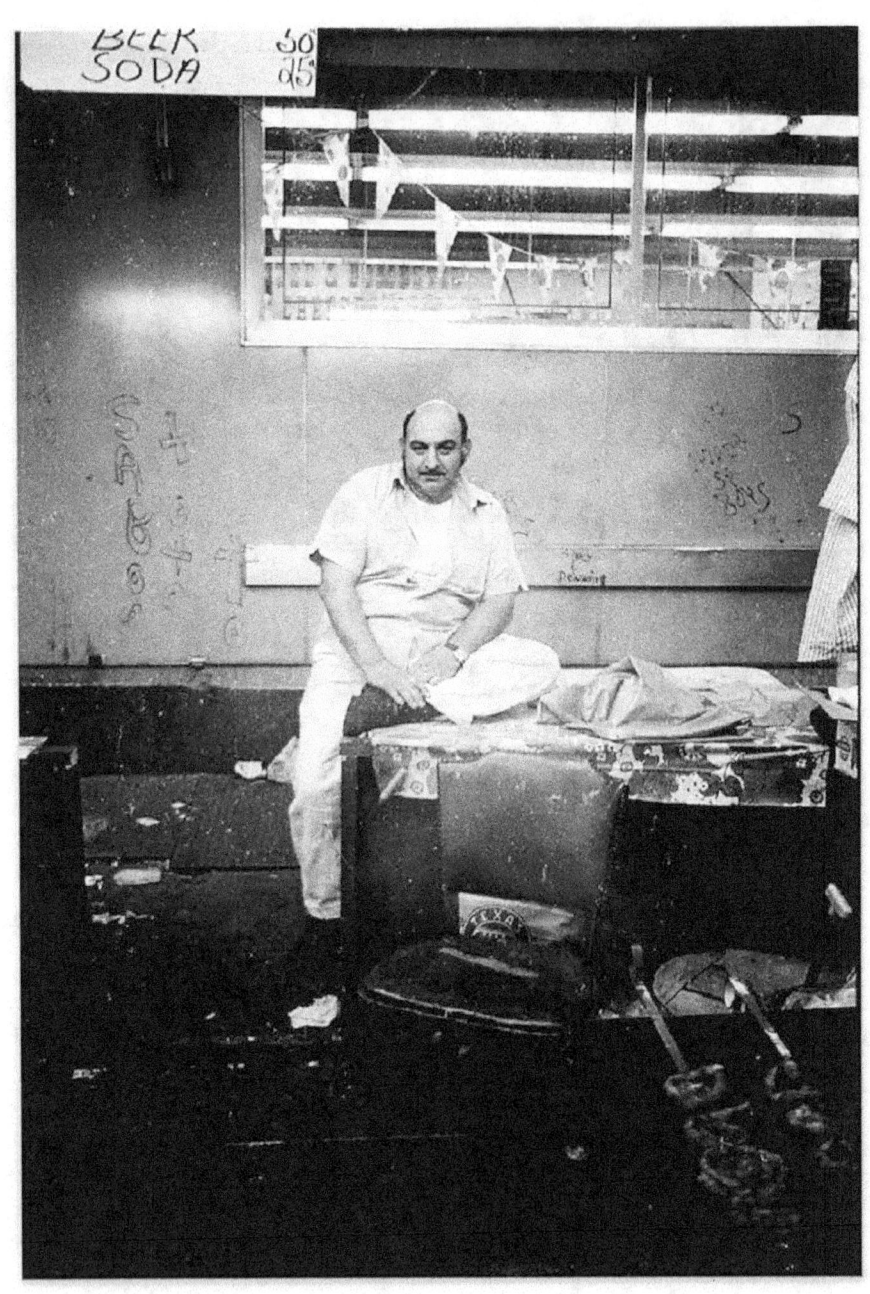

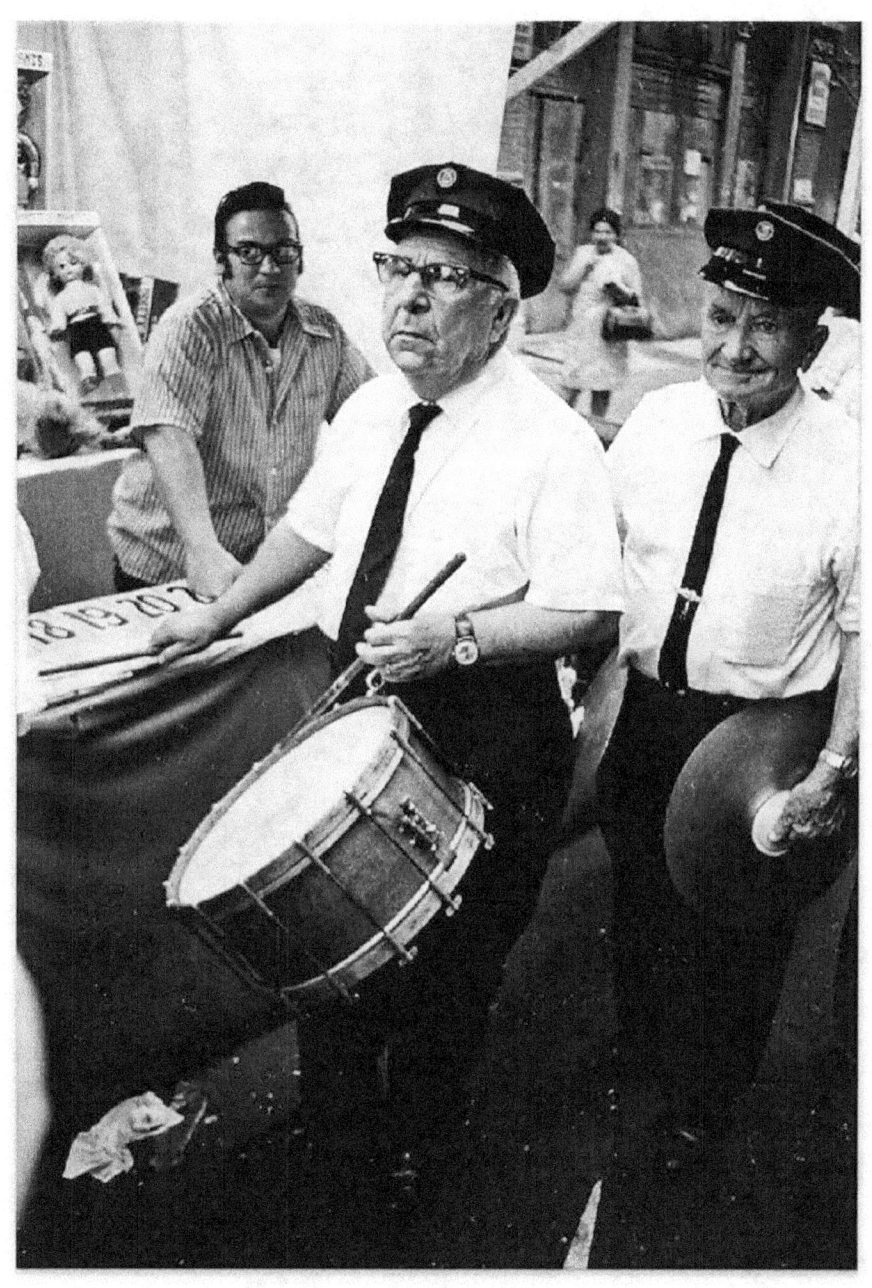

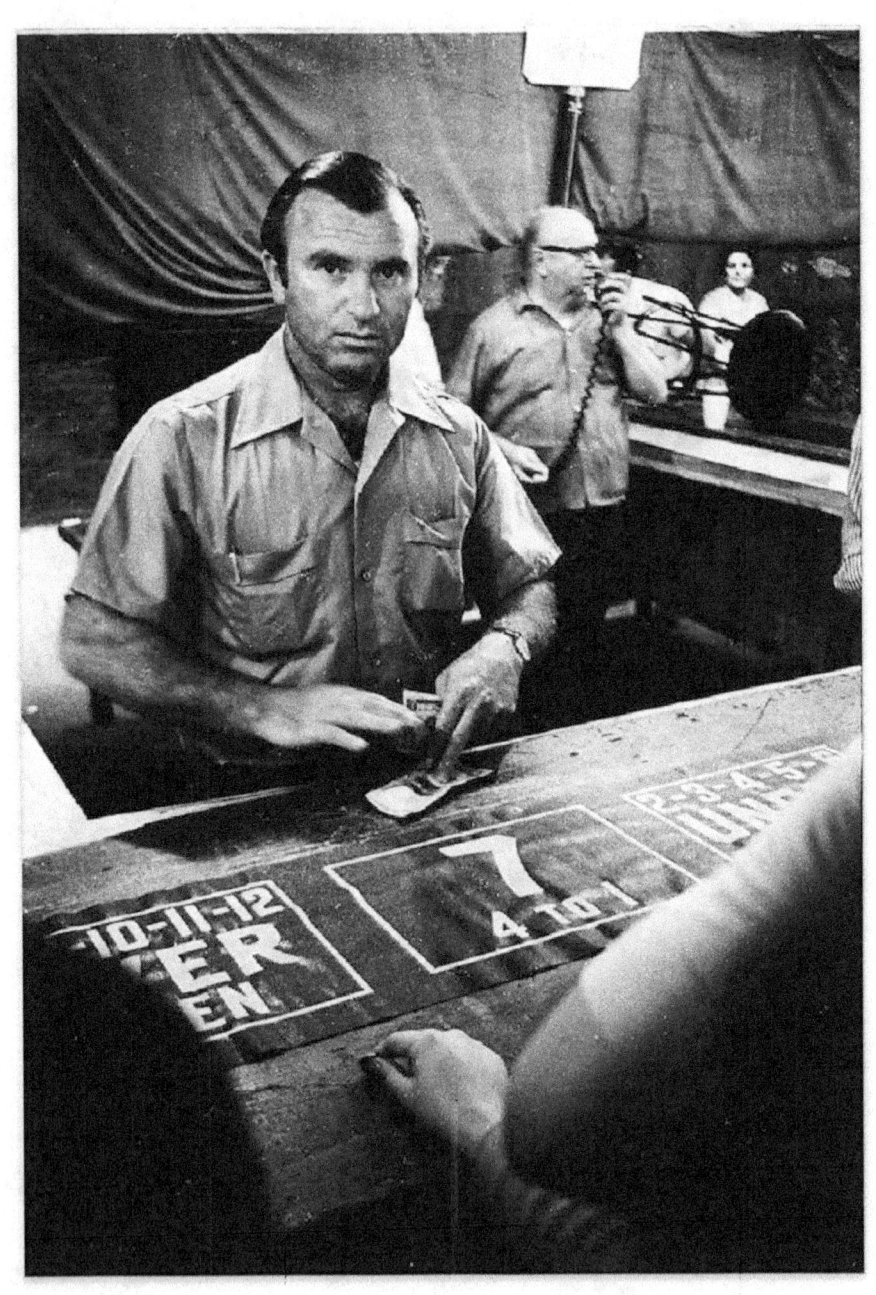

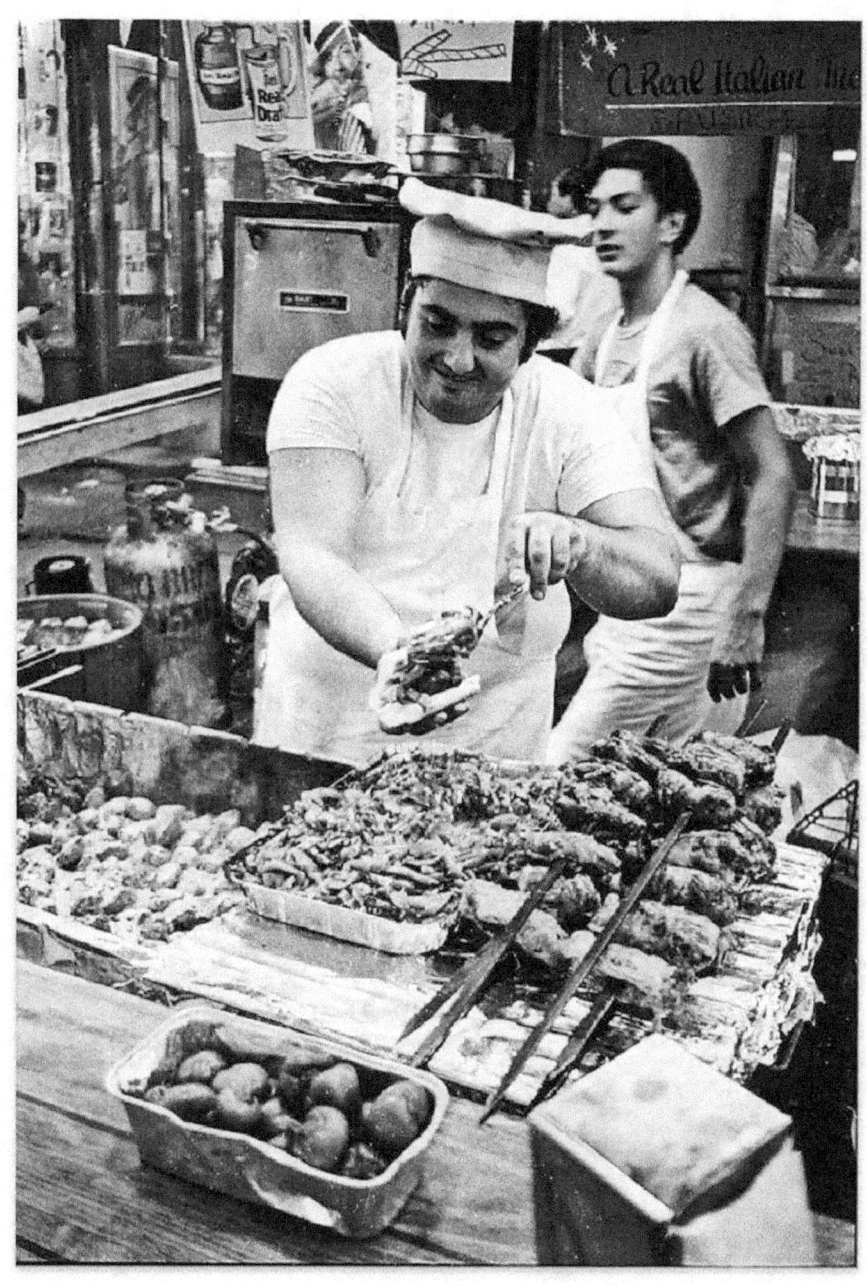

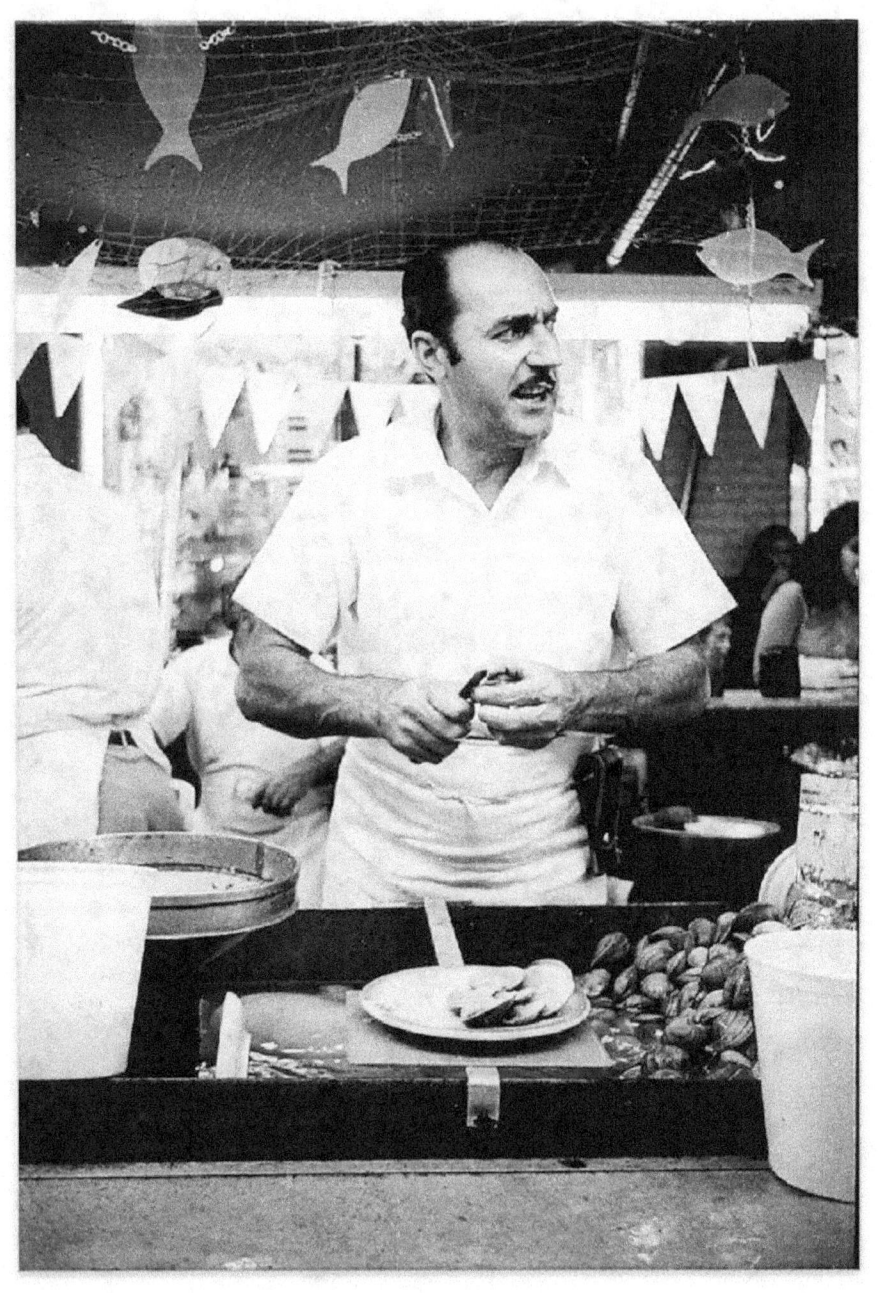

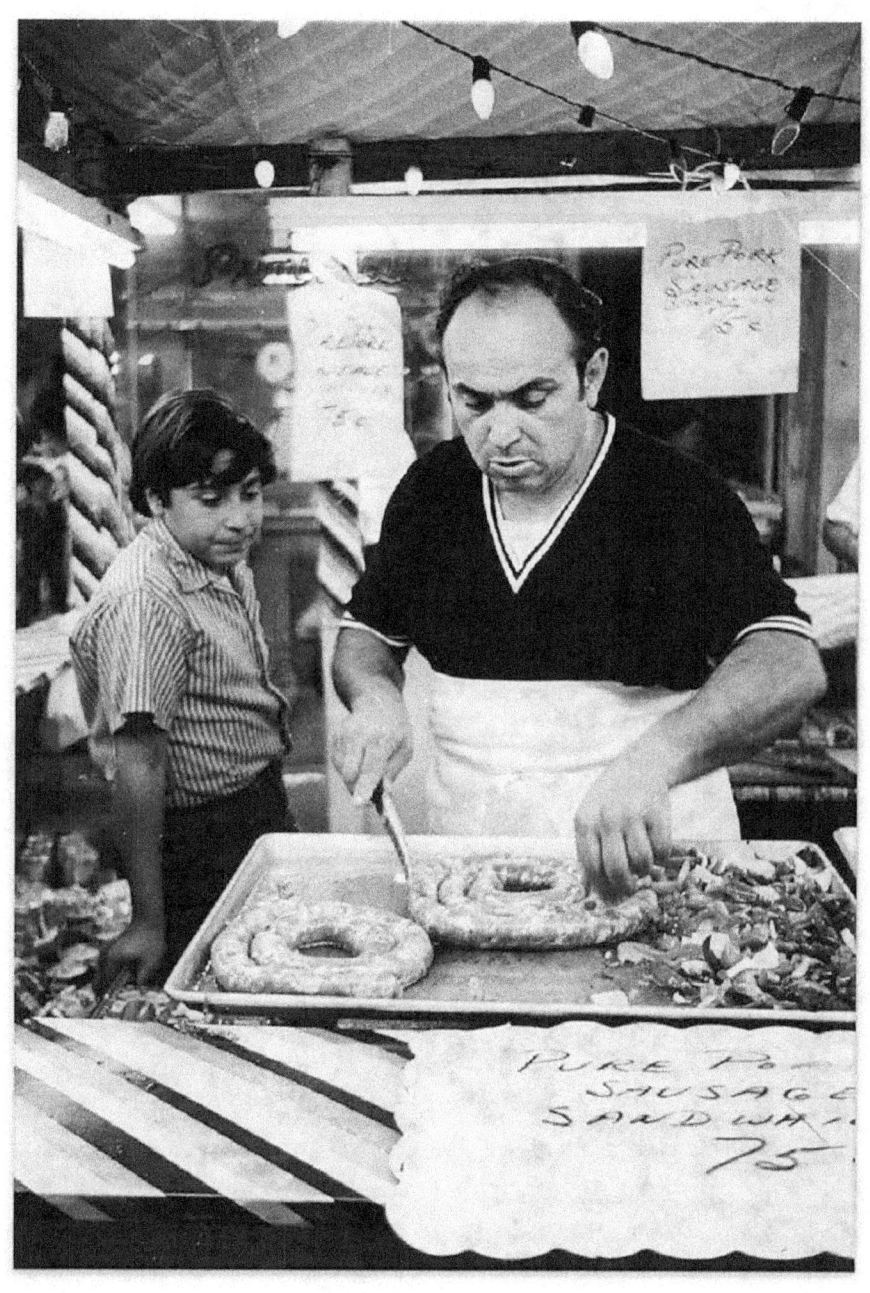

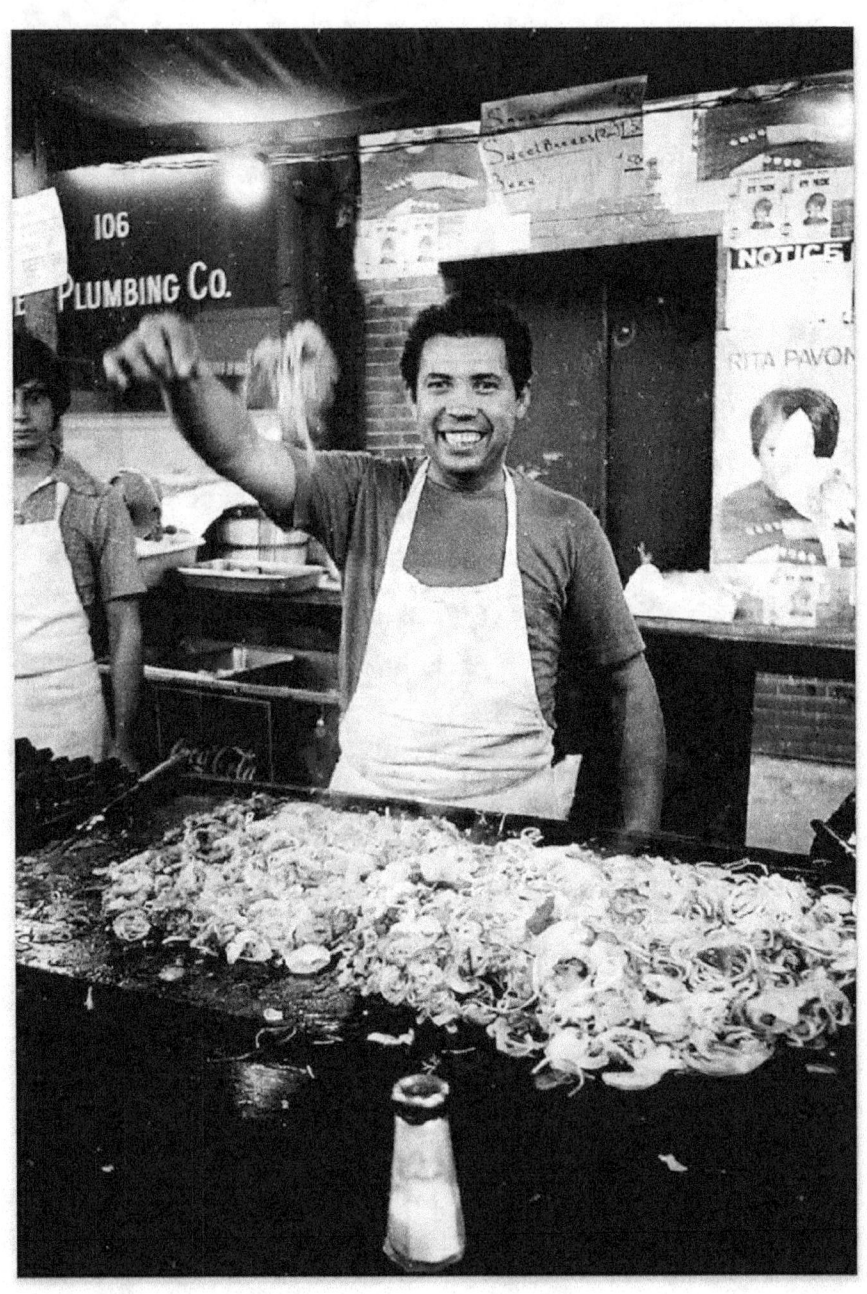

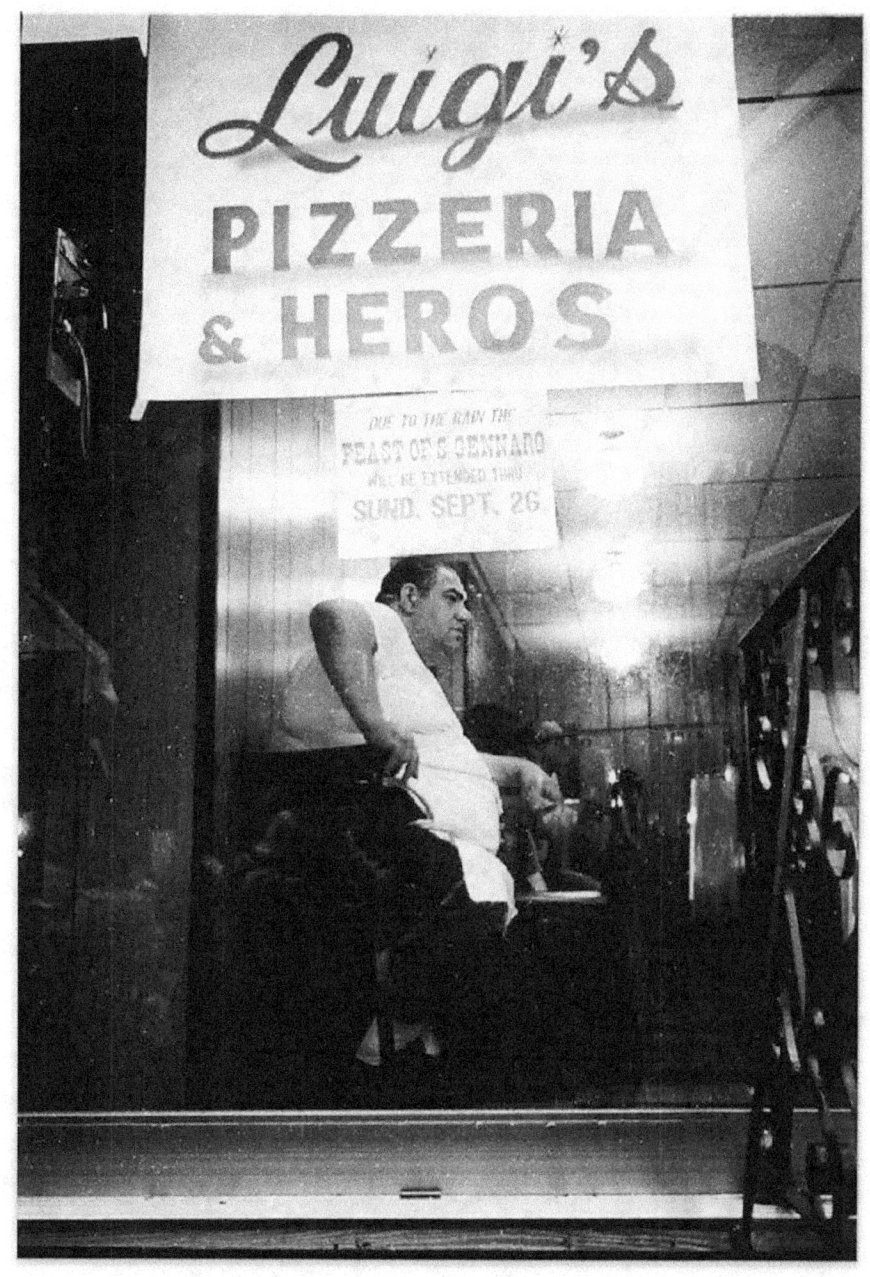

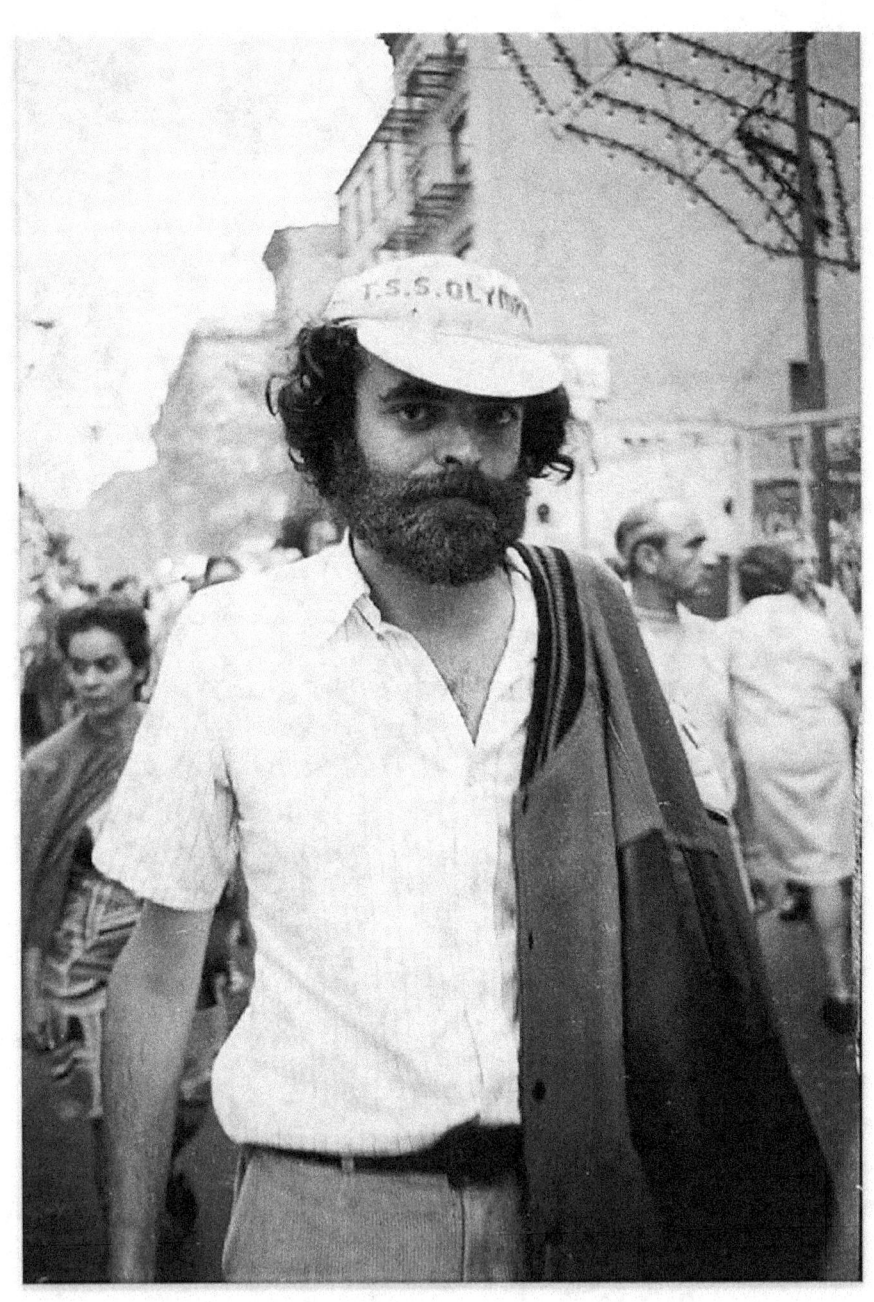

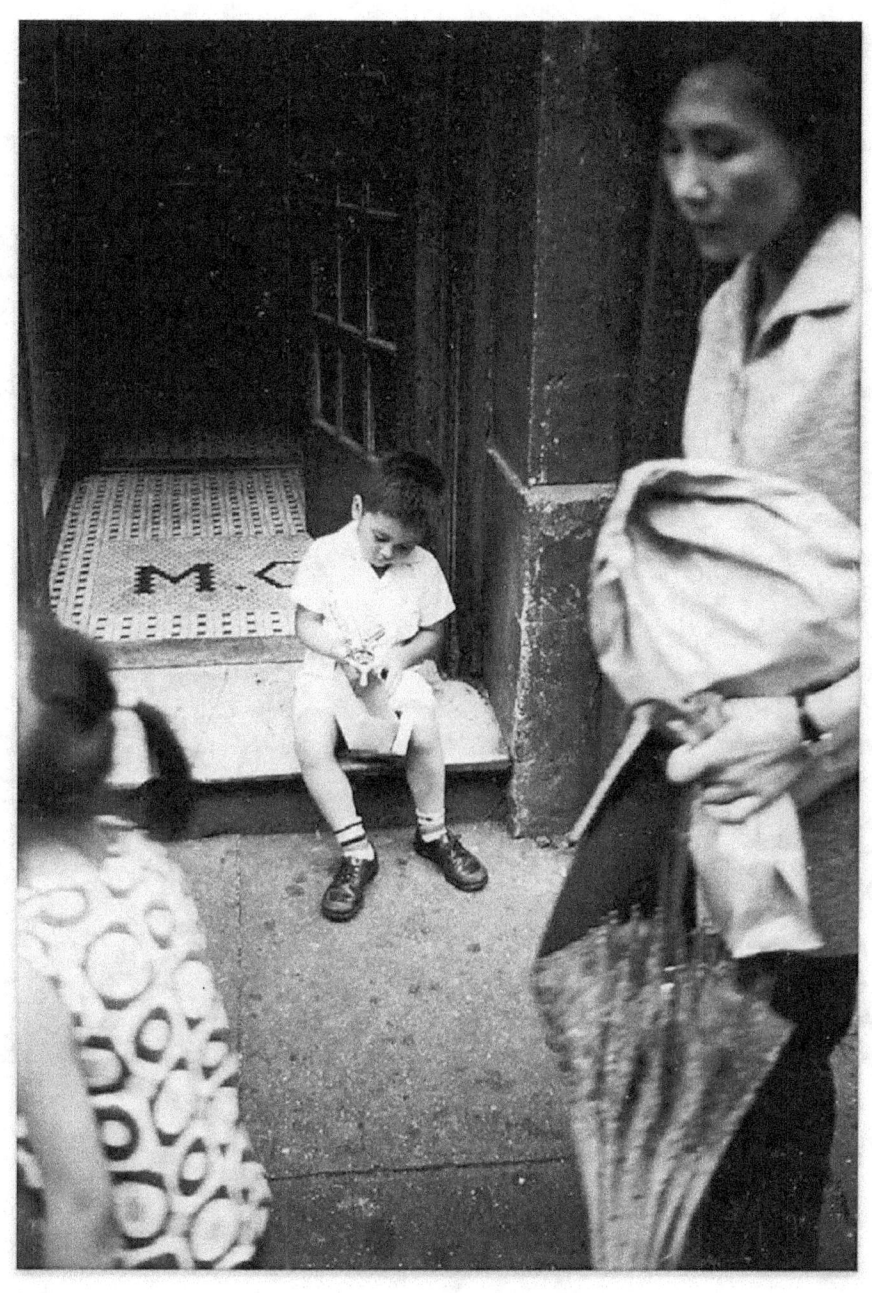

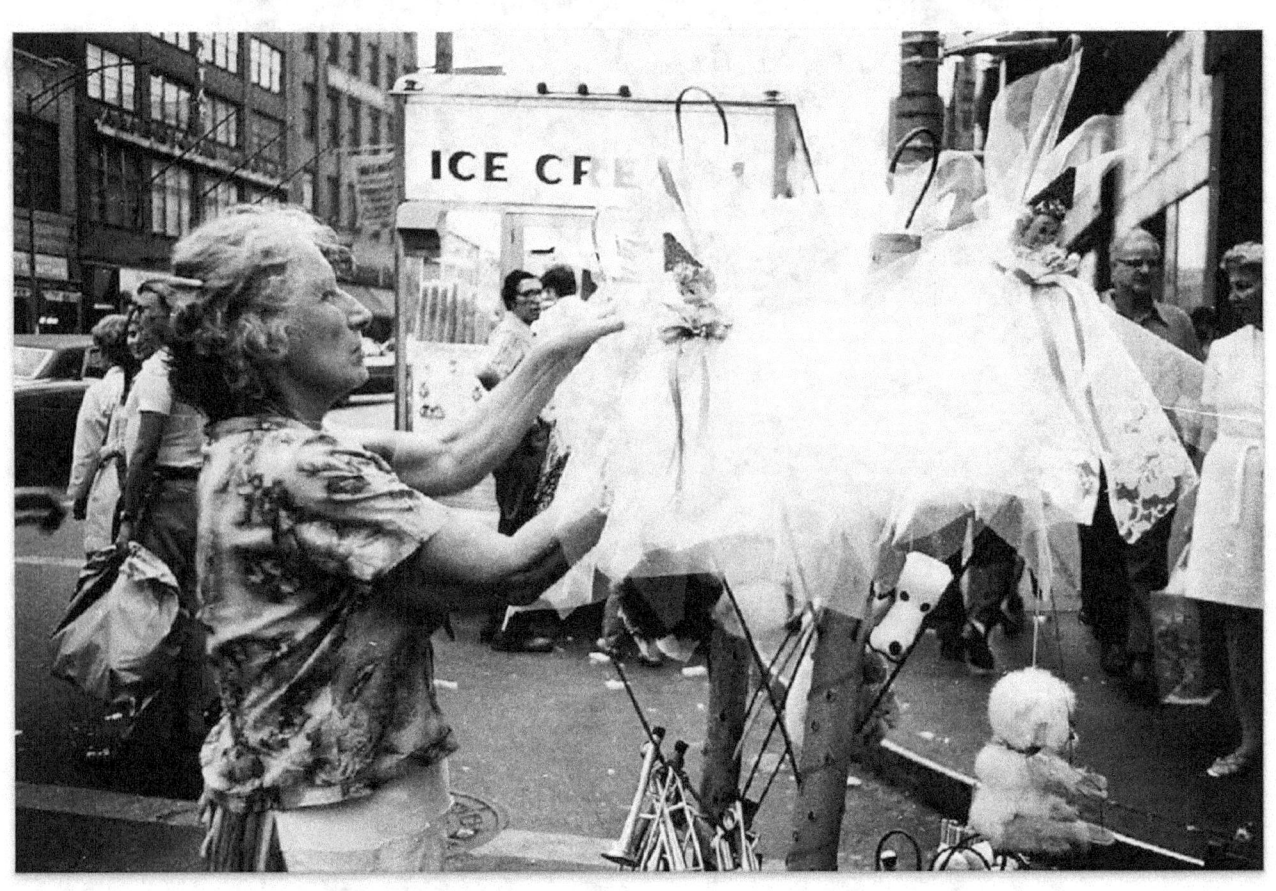

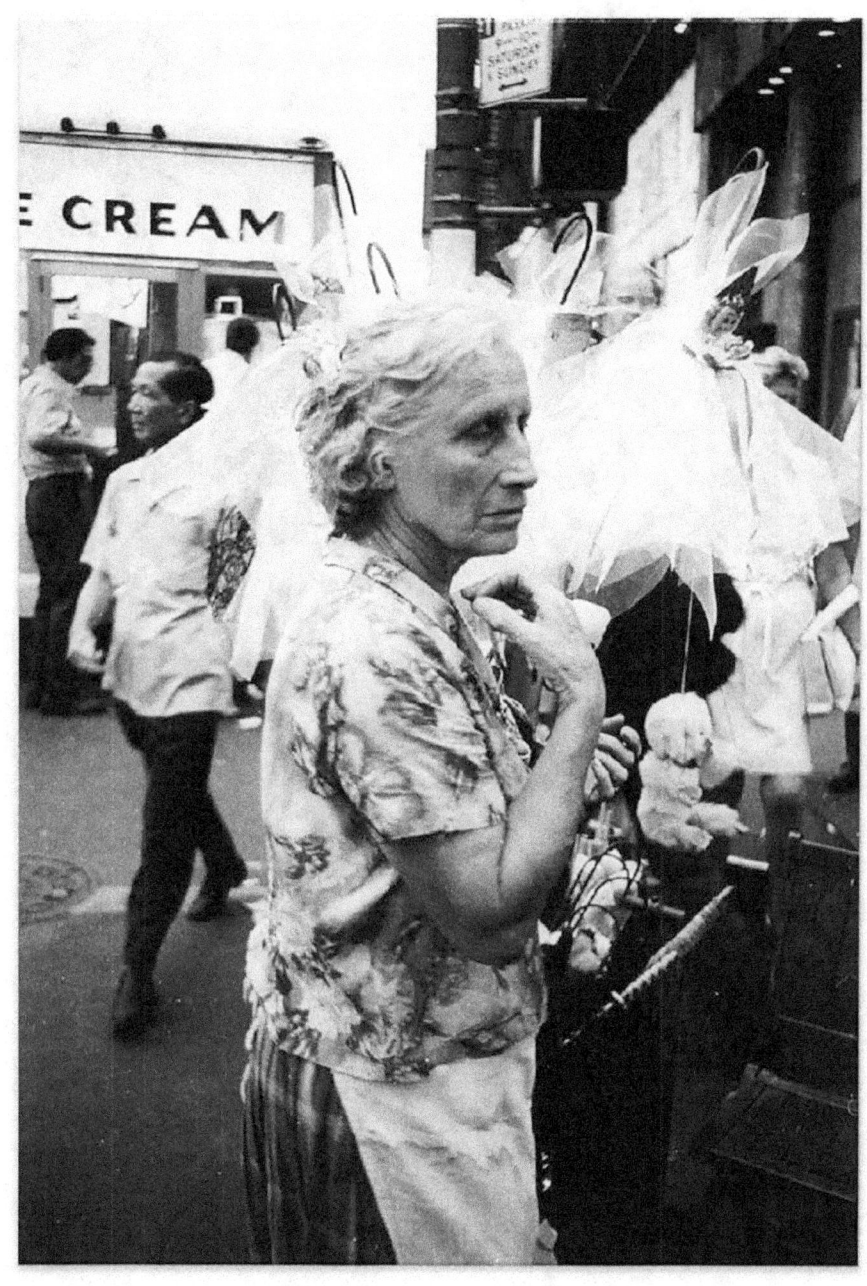

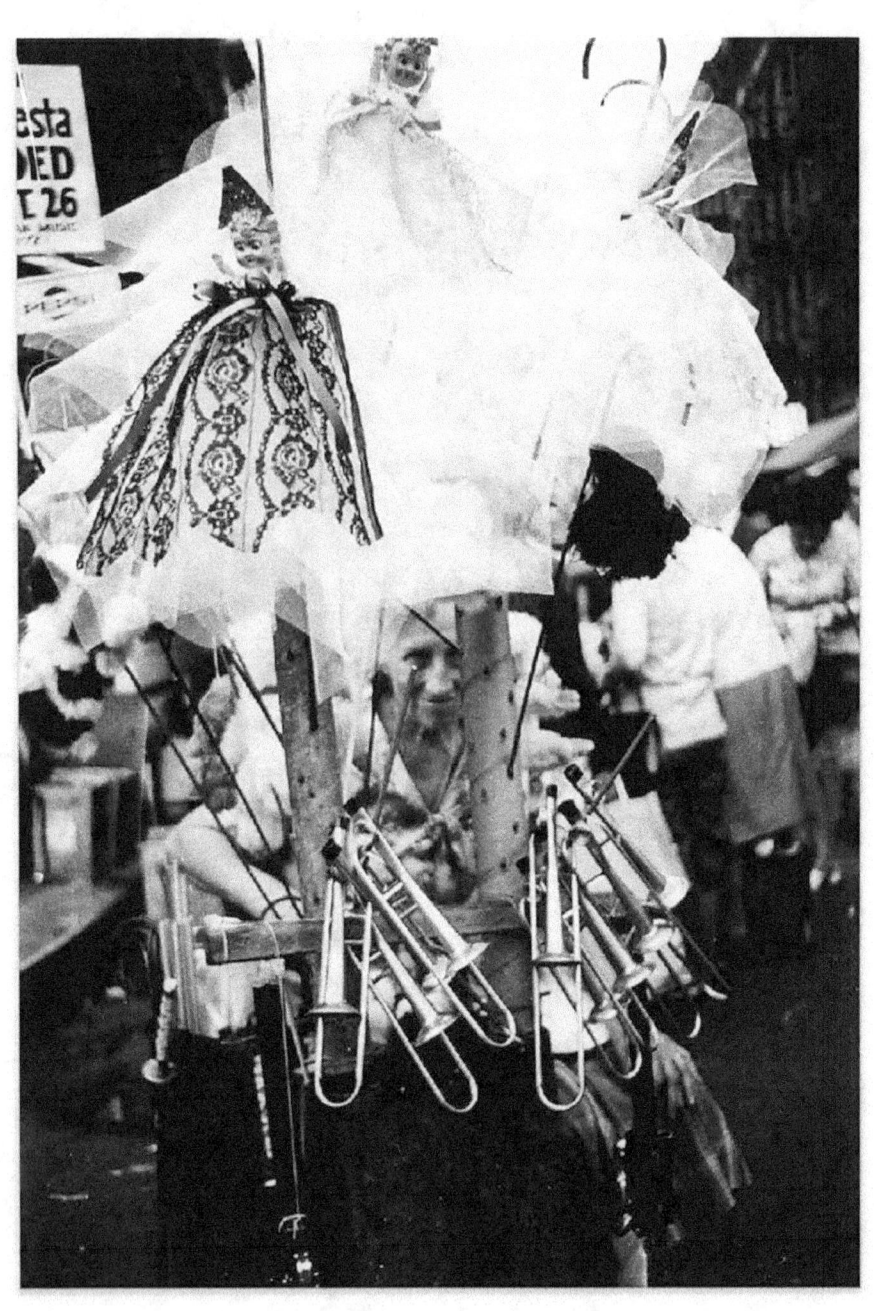

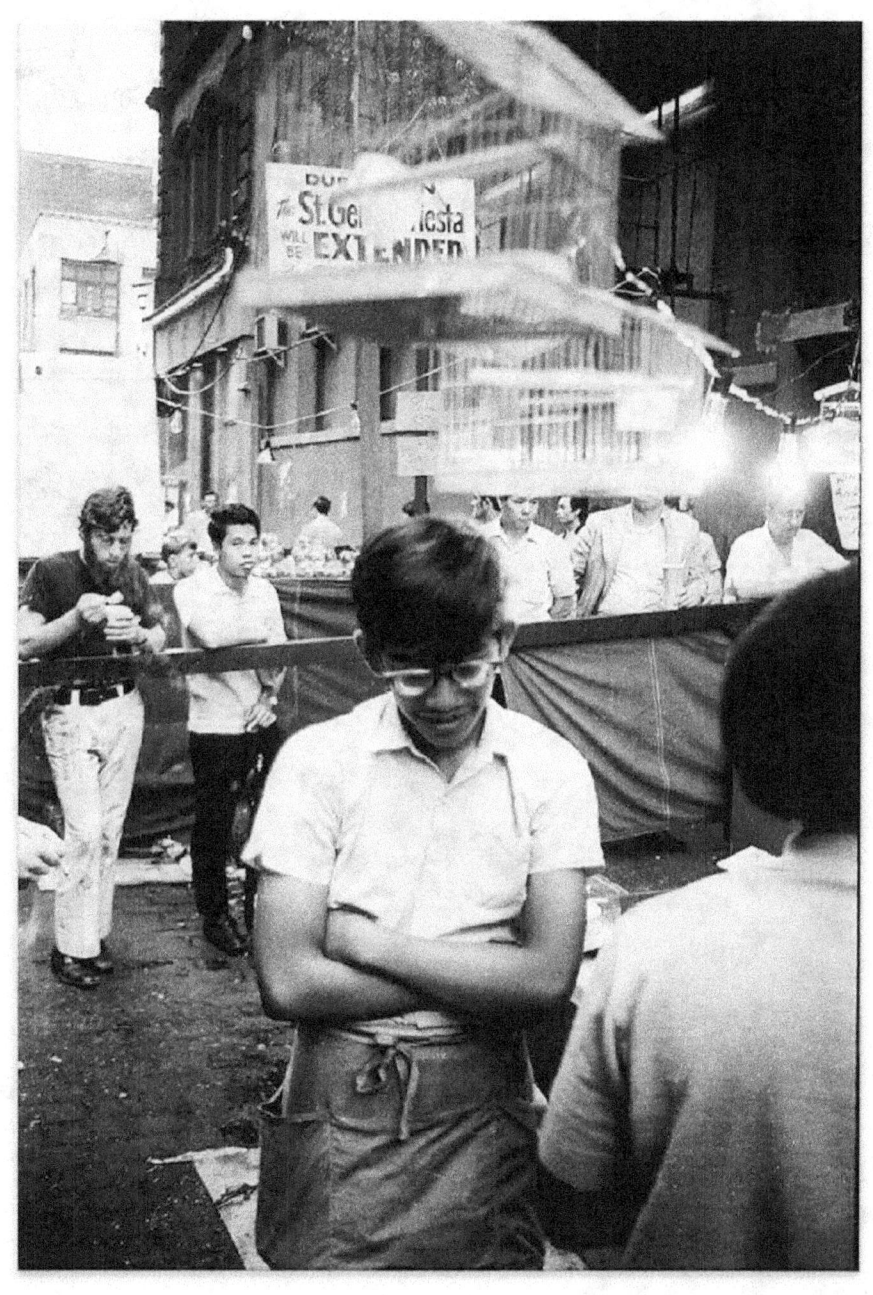

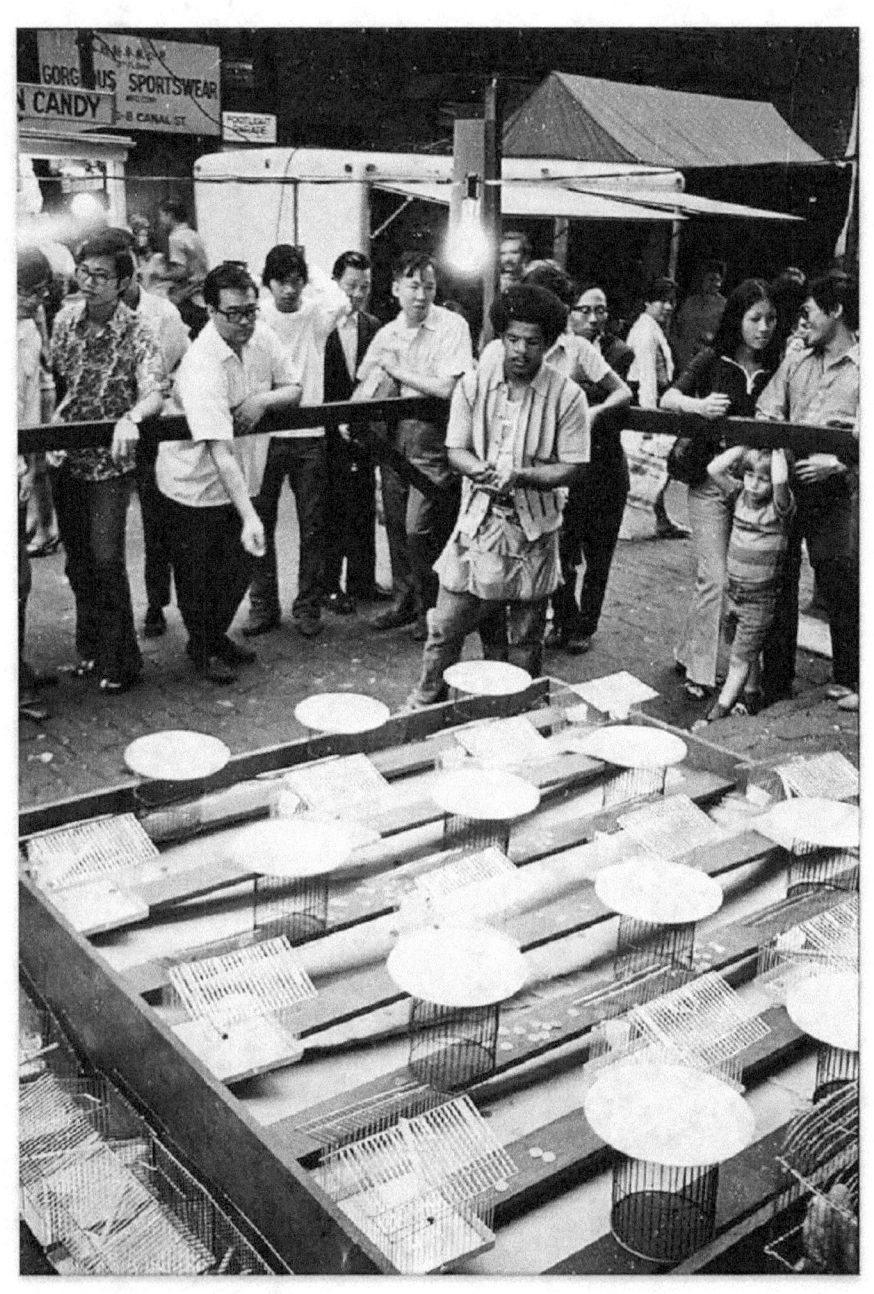

The Feast of San Gennaro, 1971

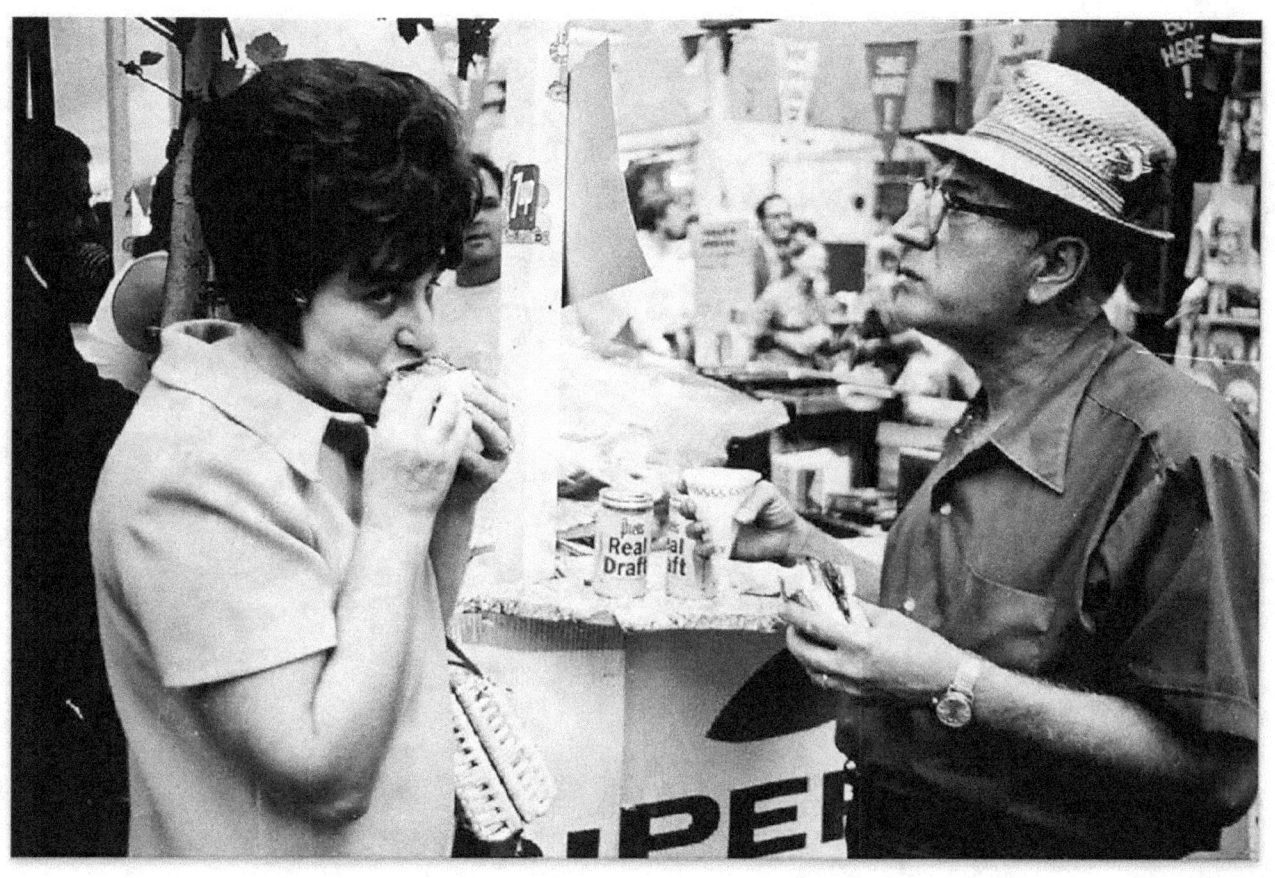

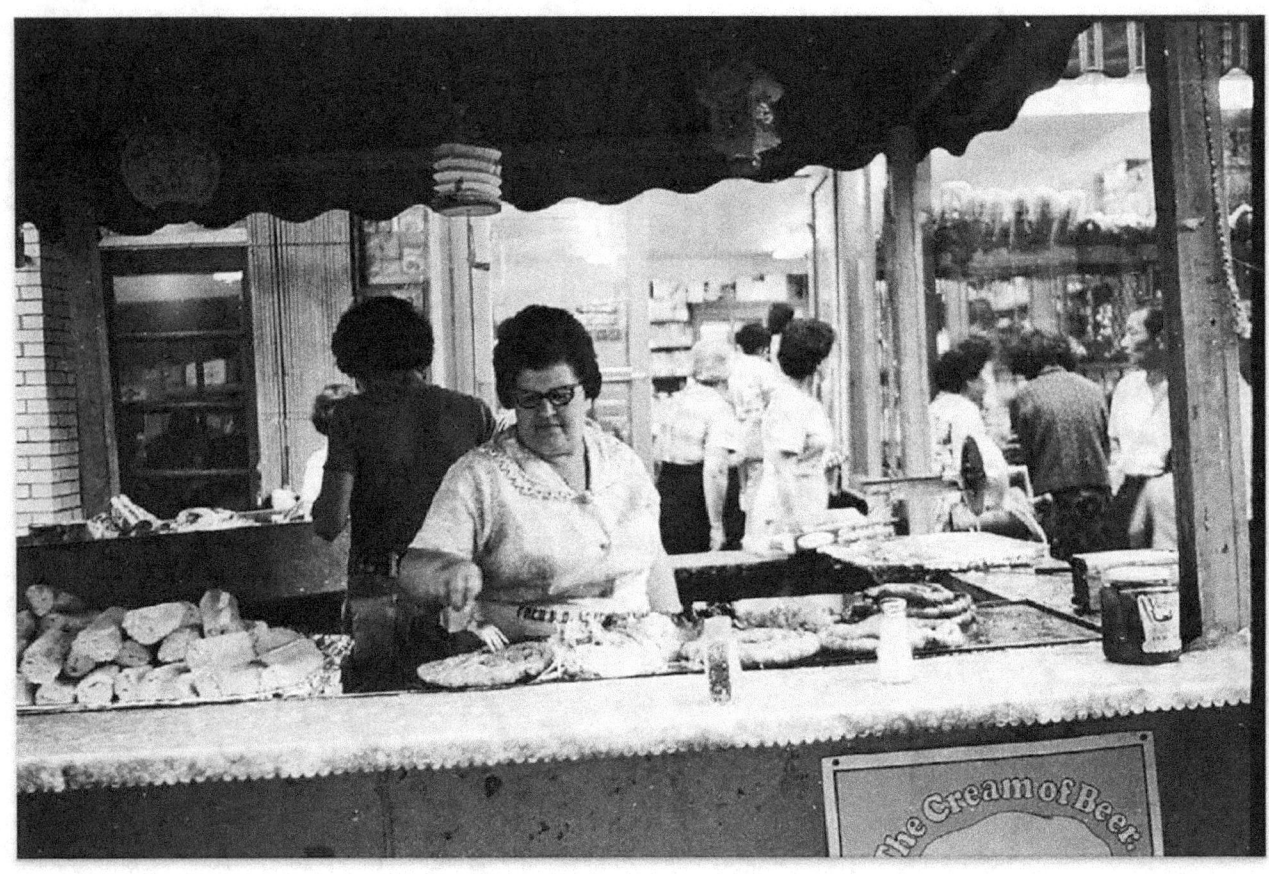

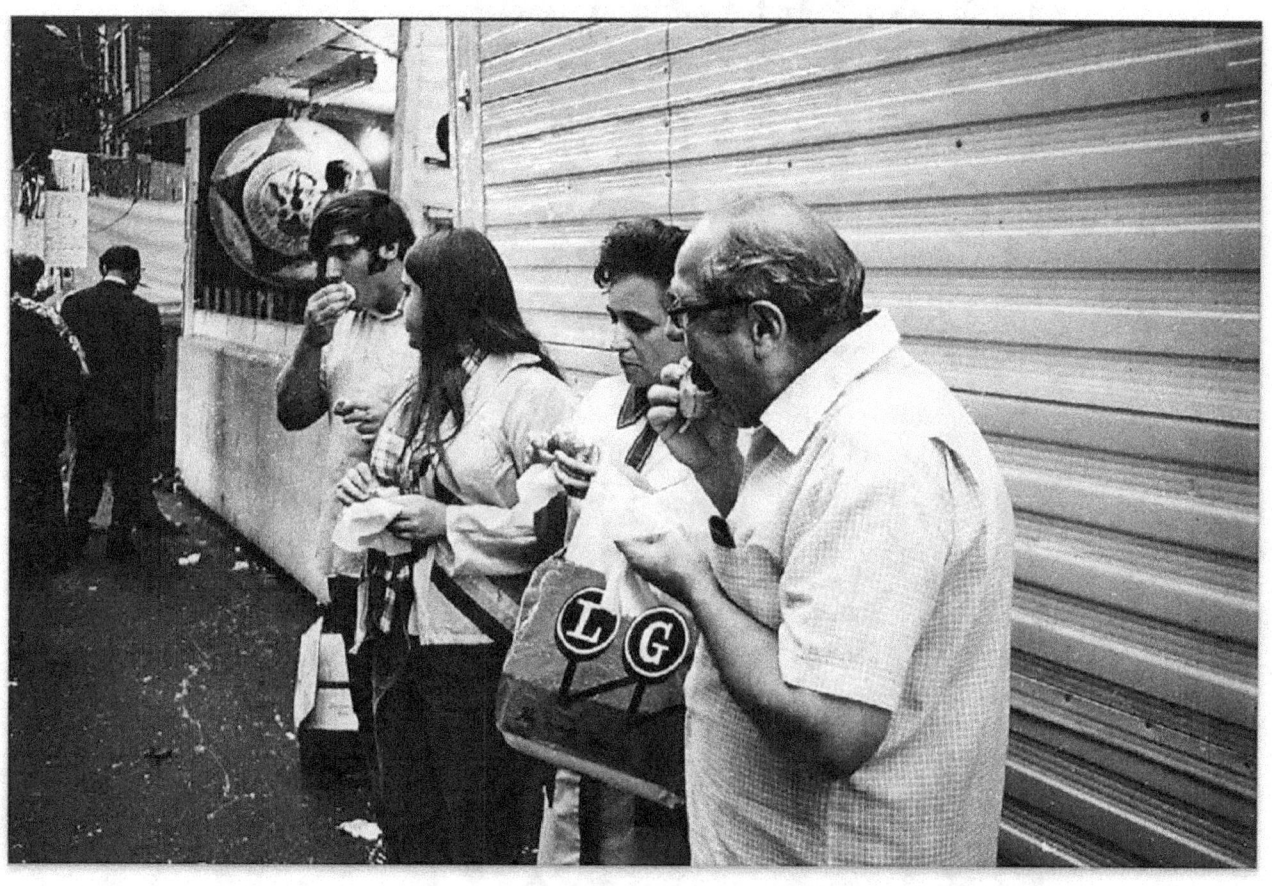

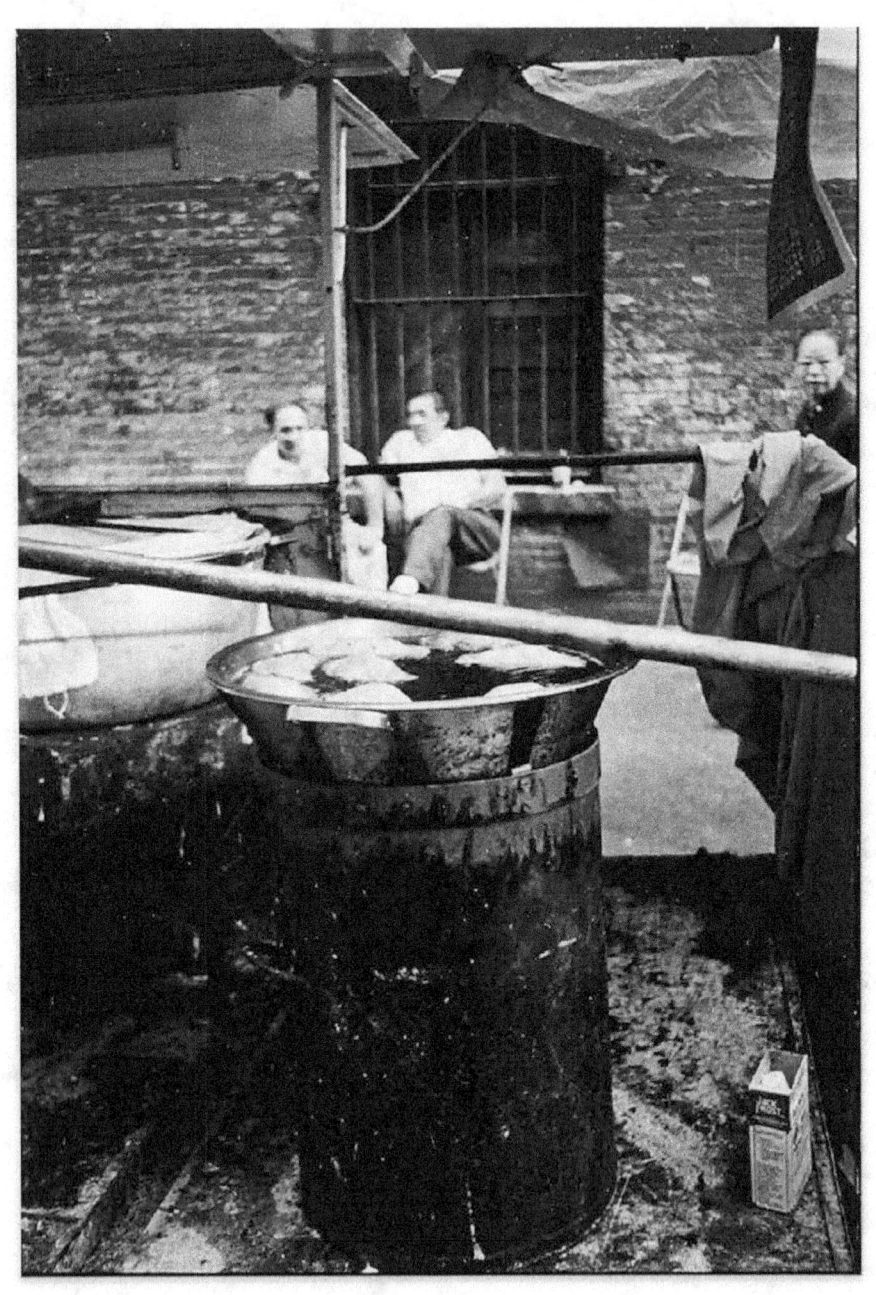

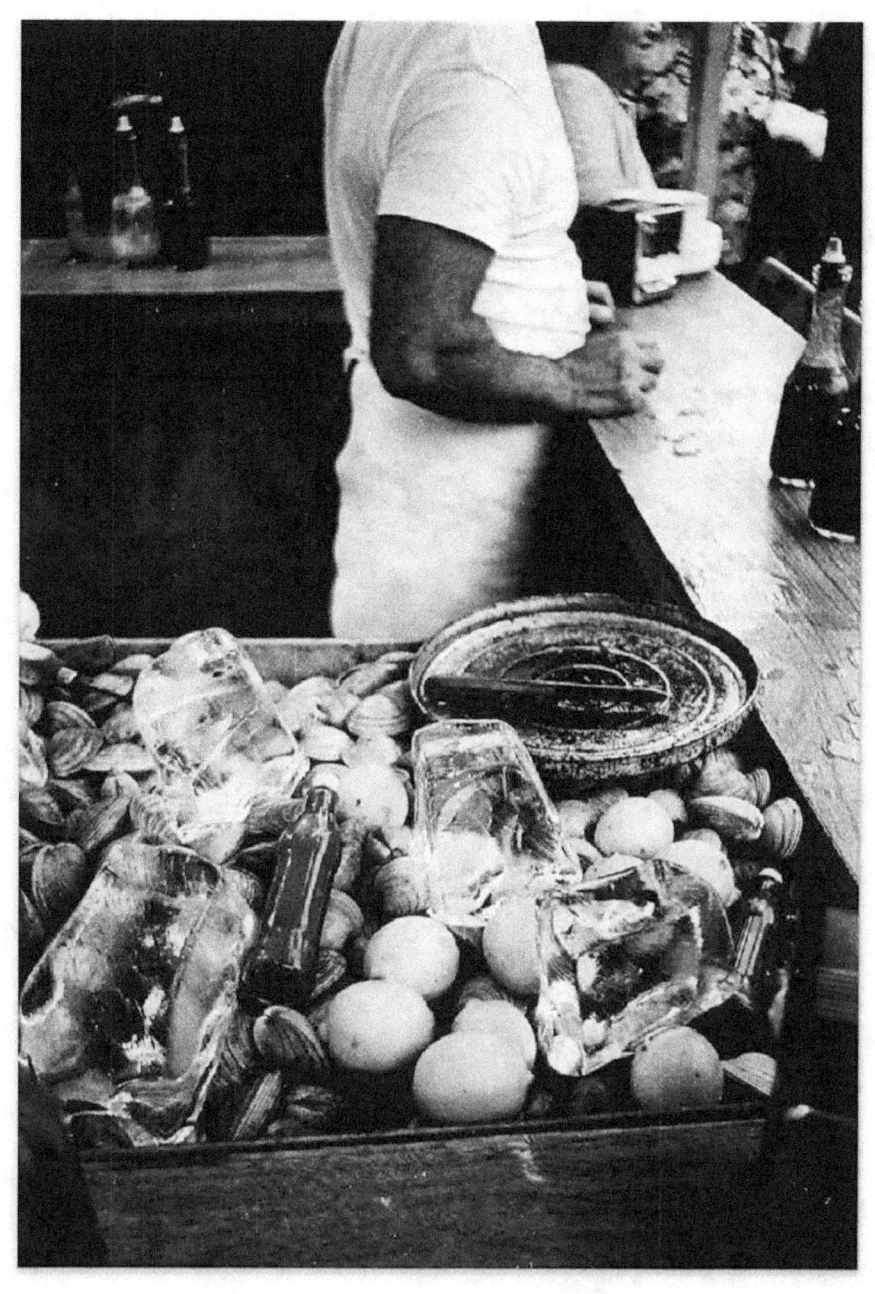

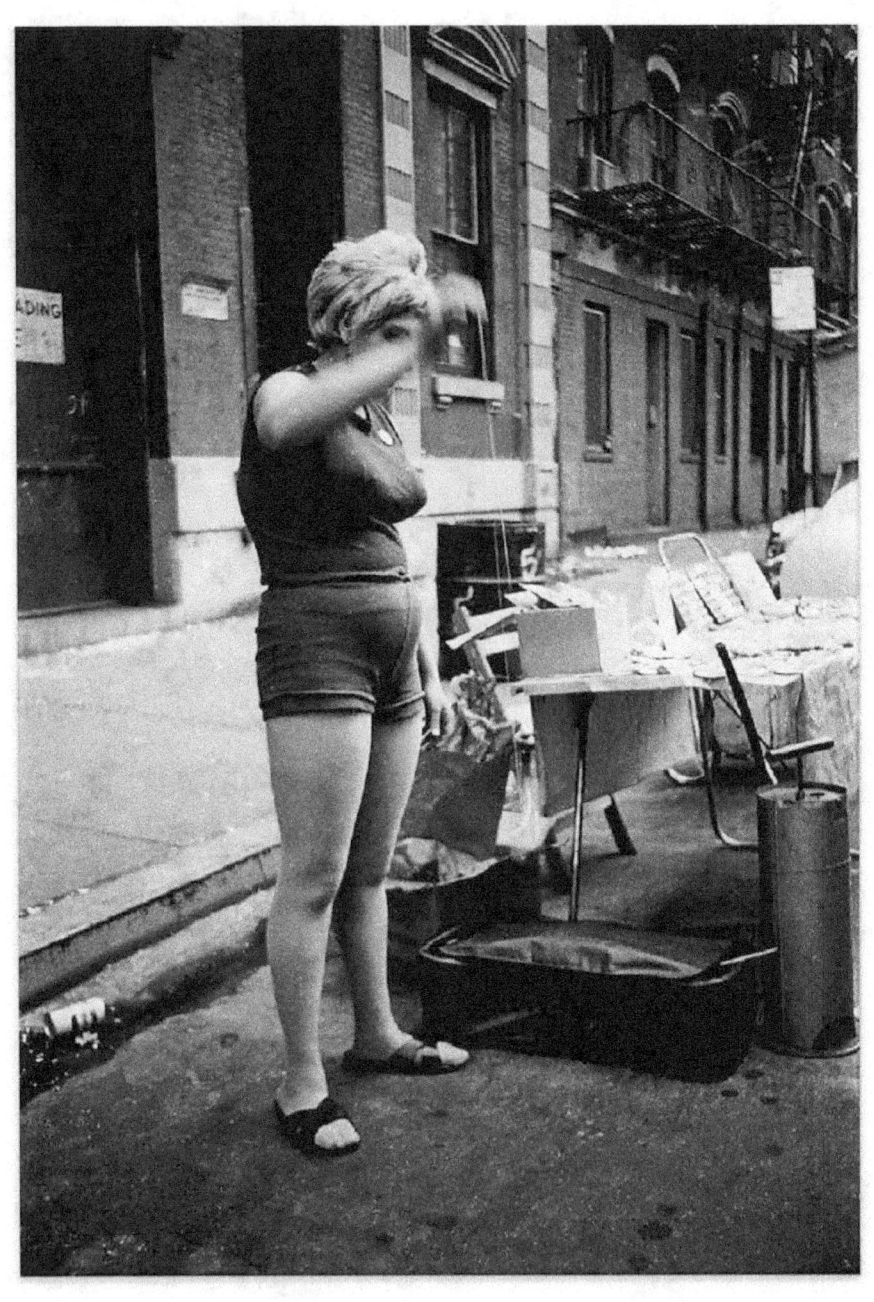

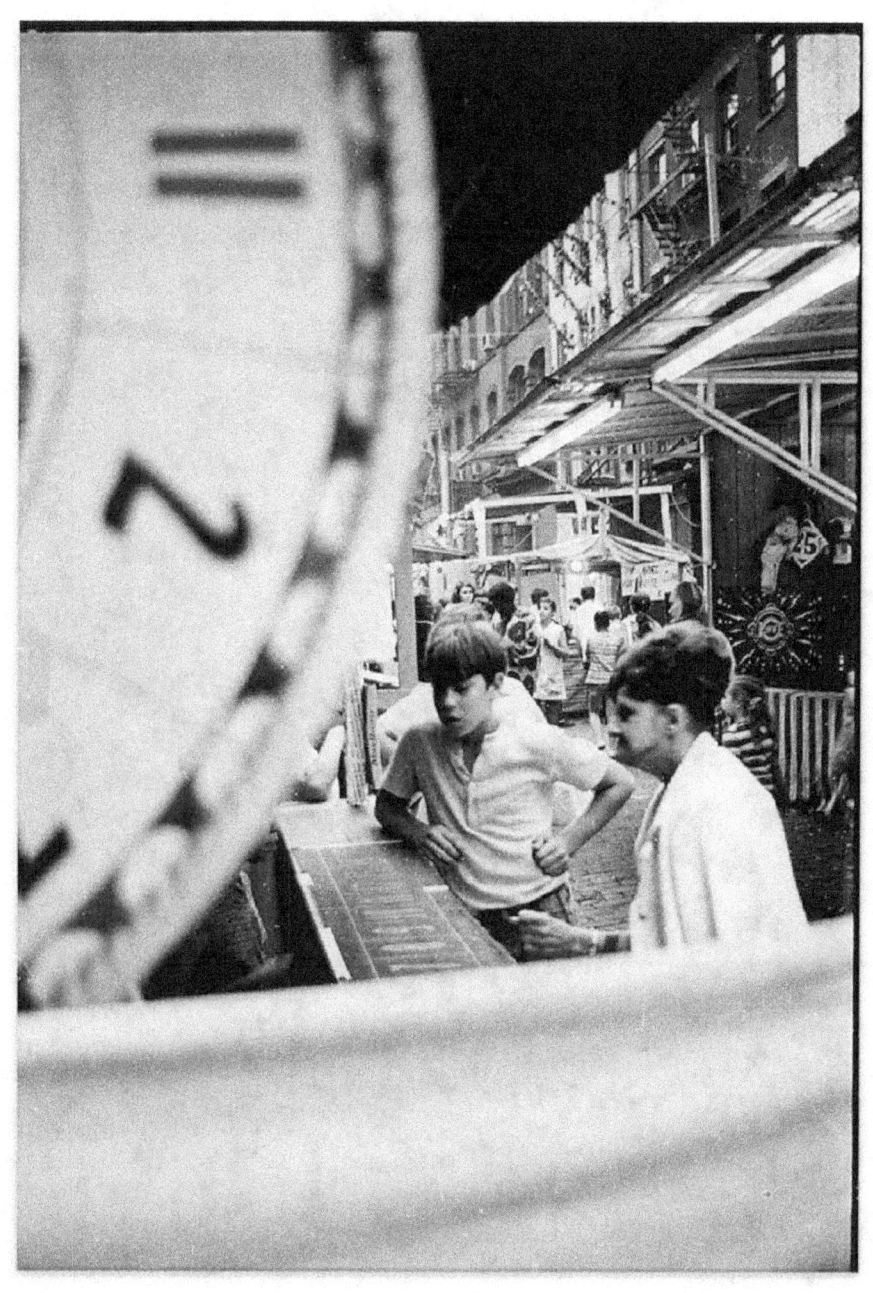

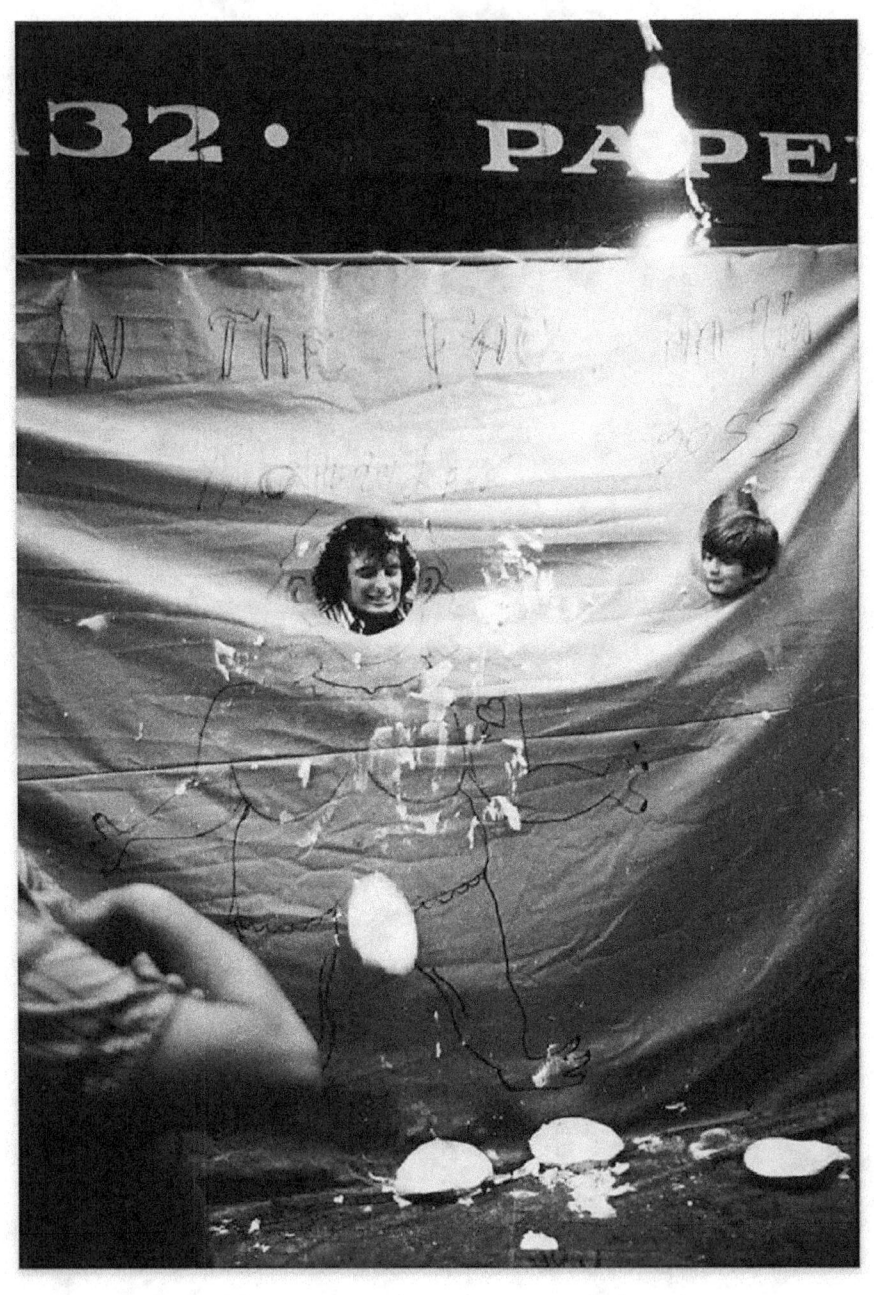

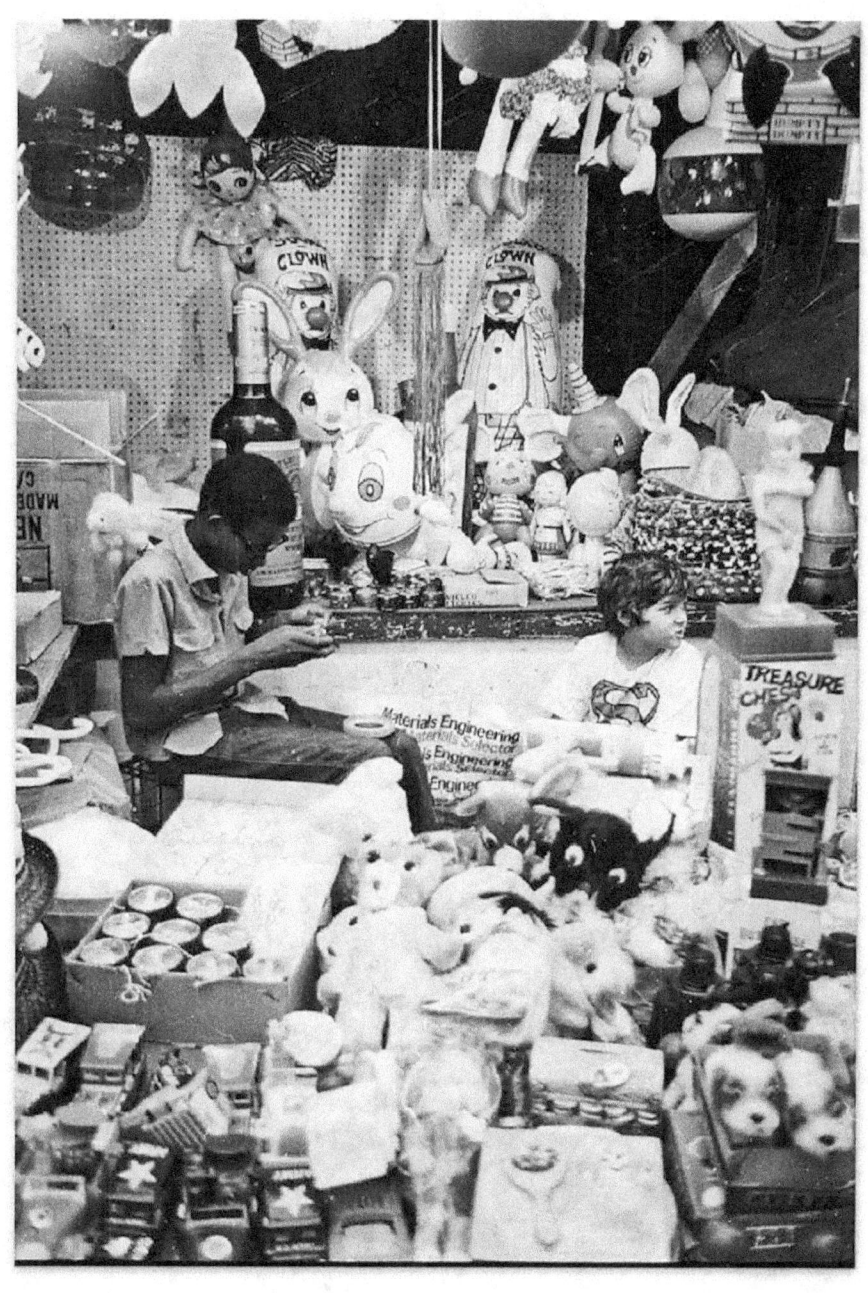

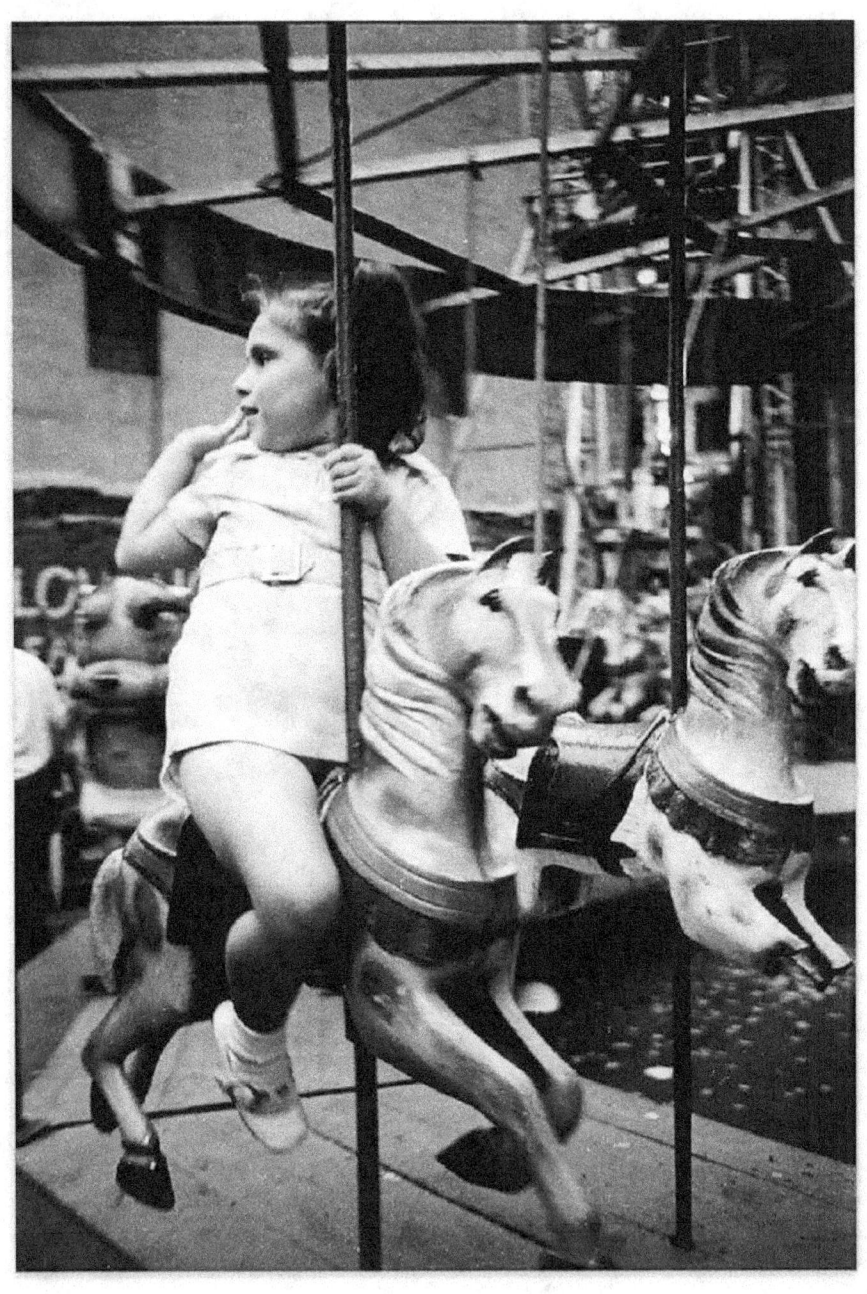

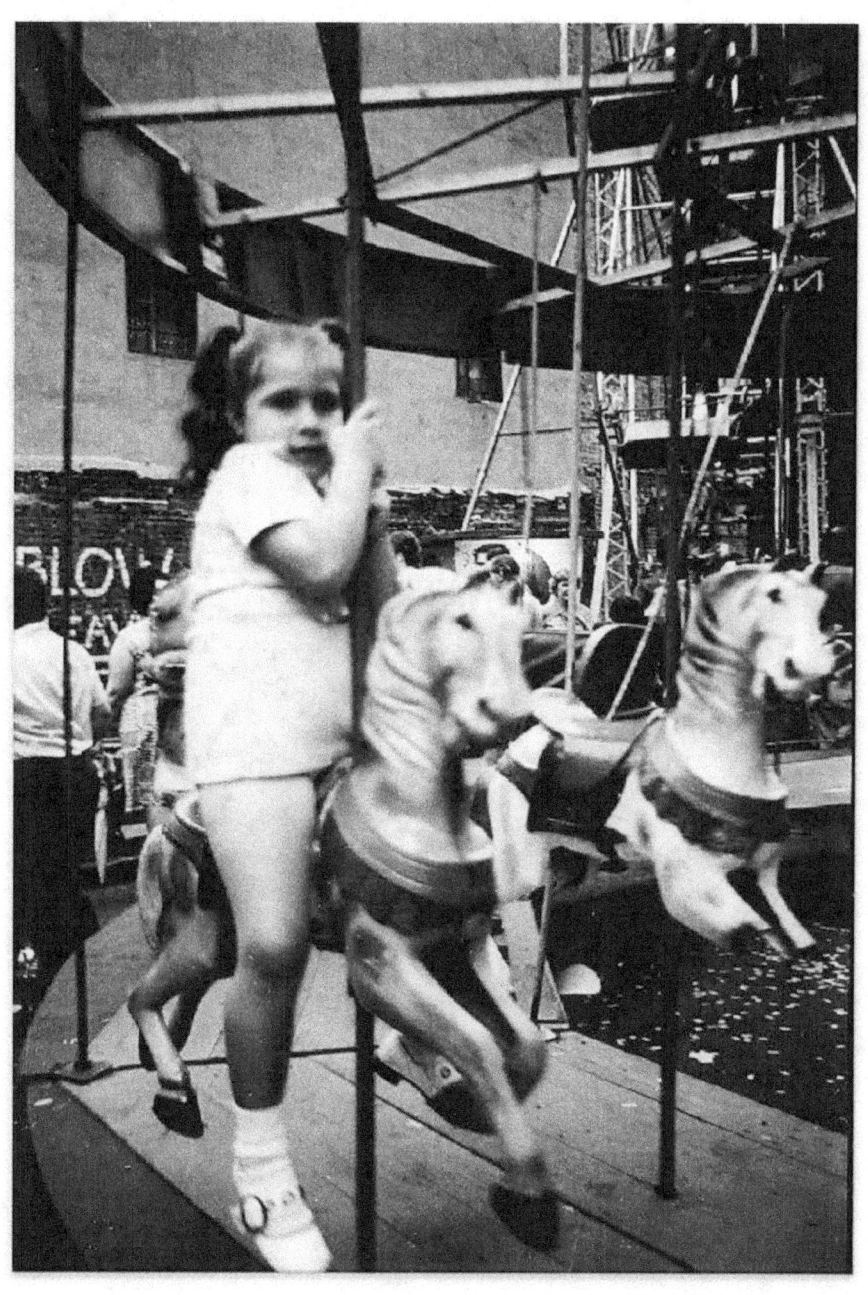

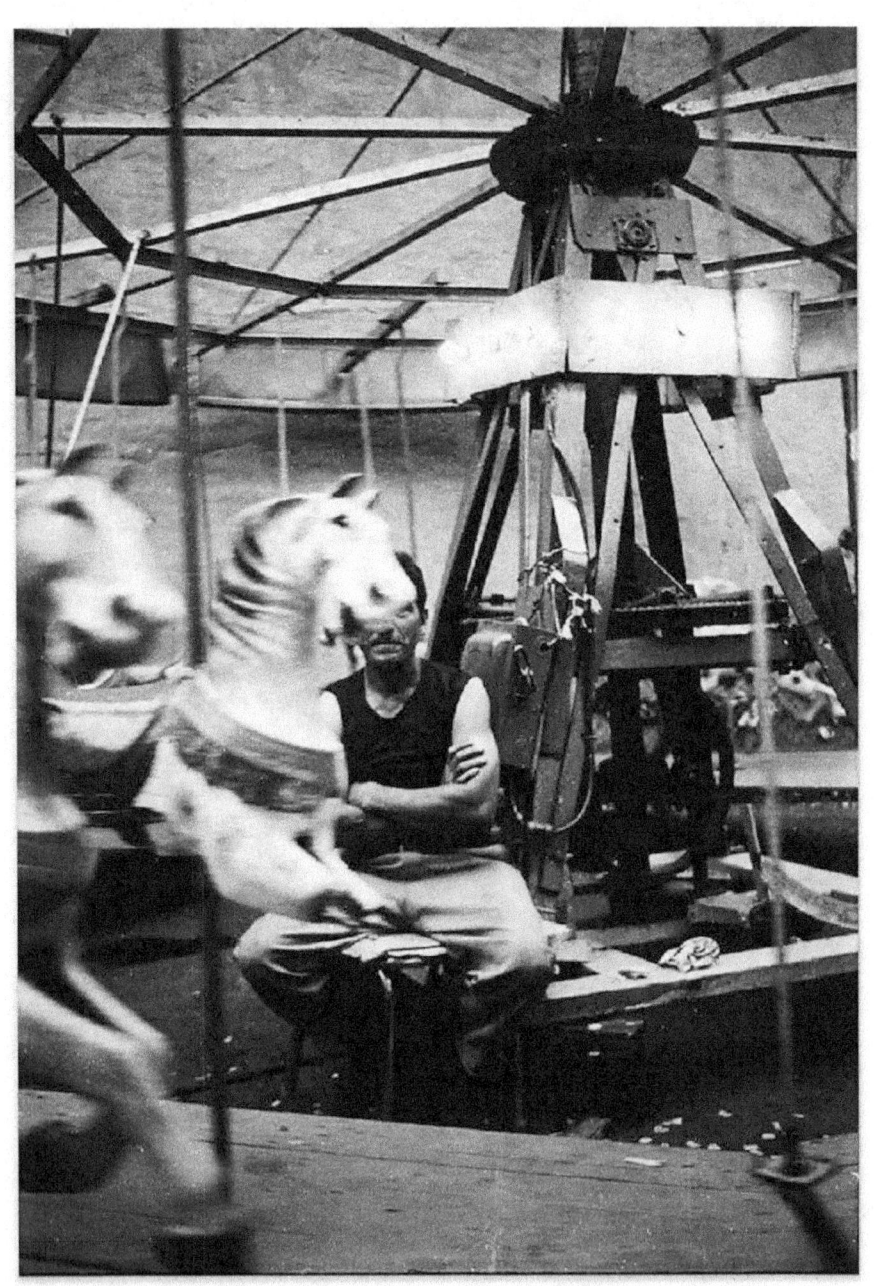

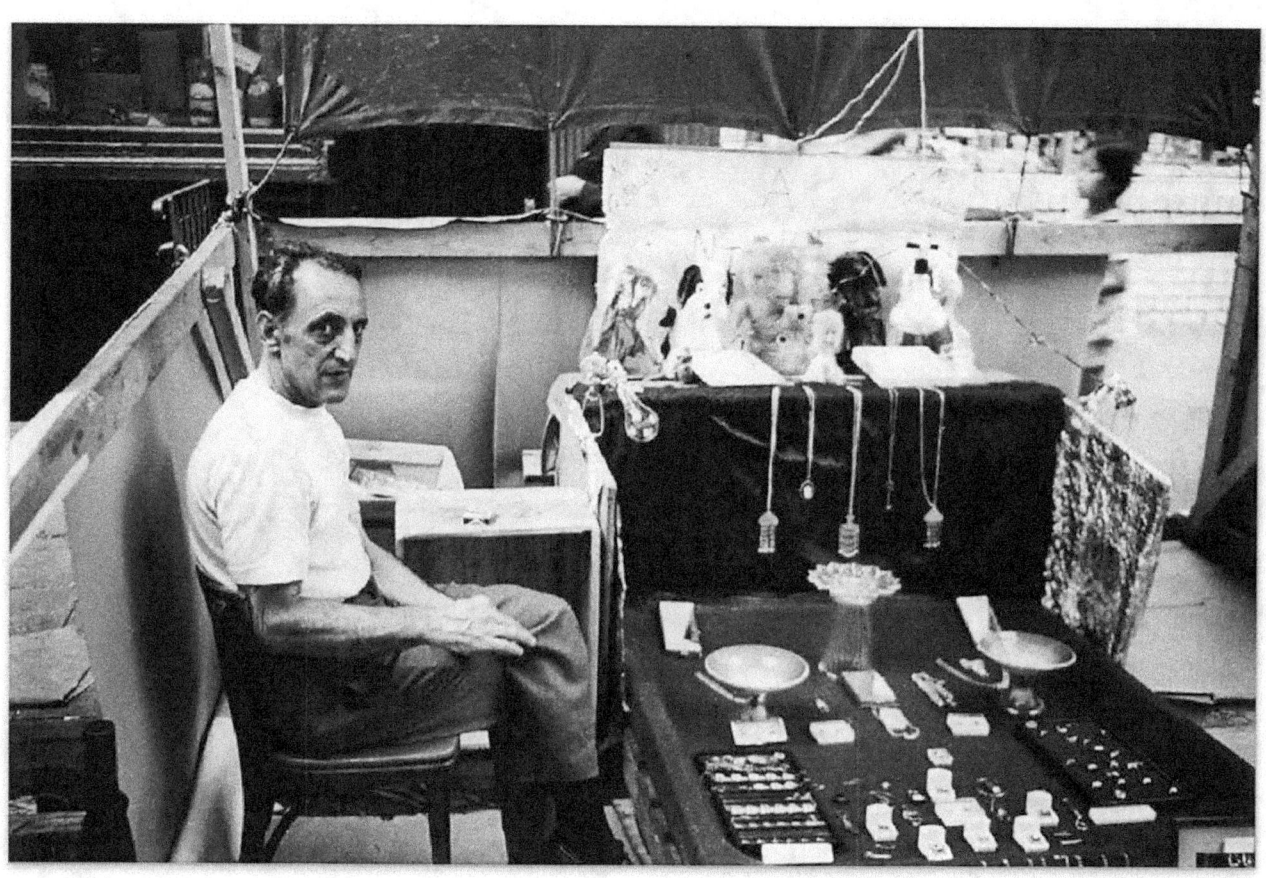

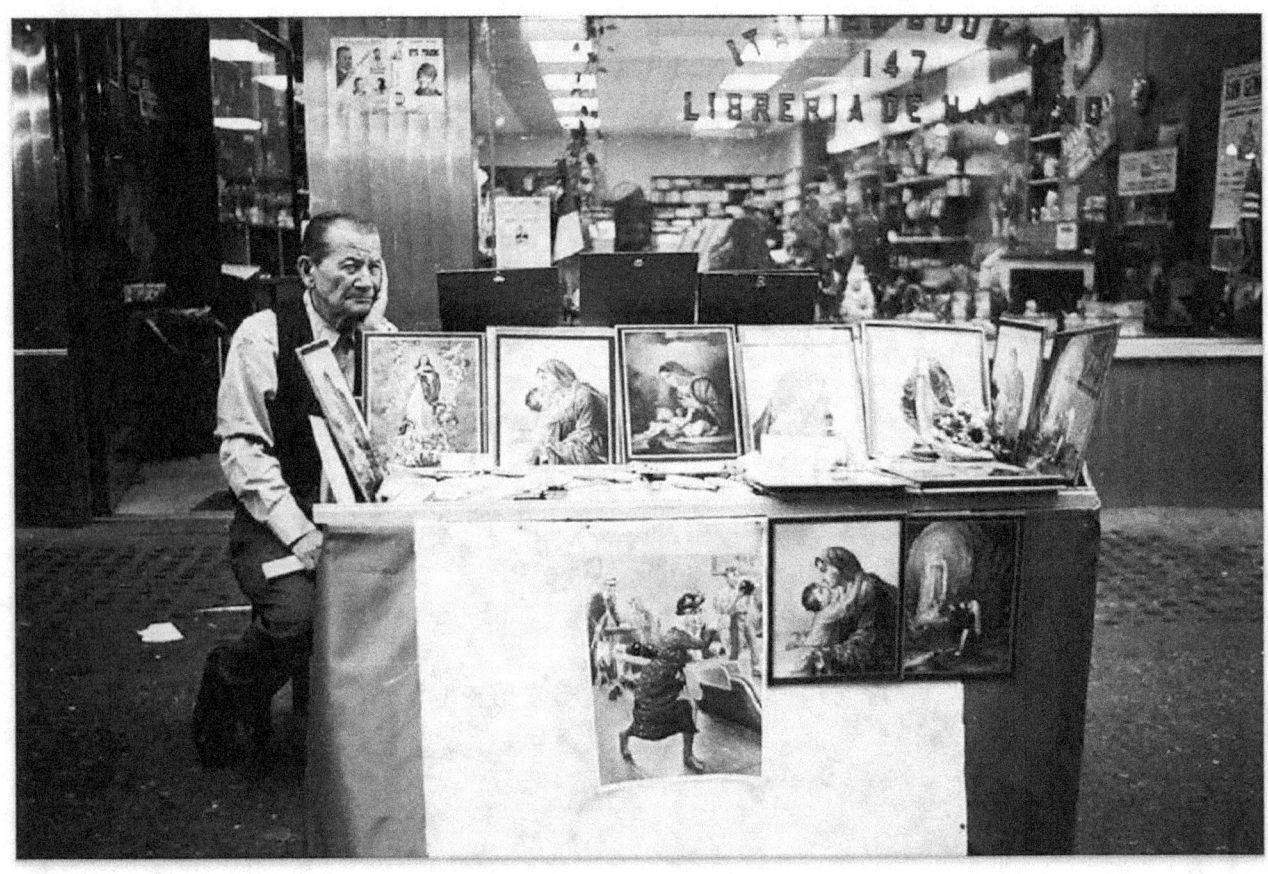

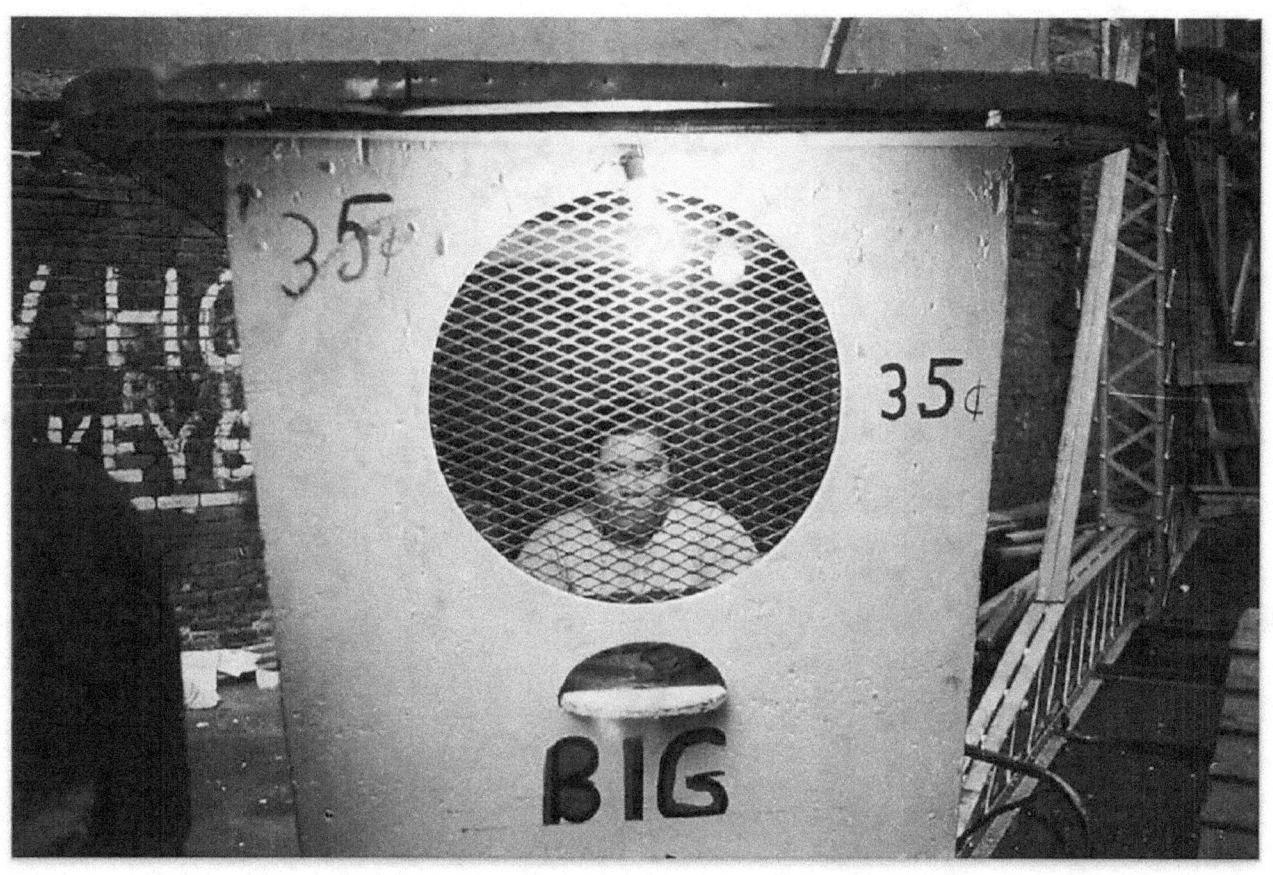

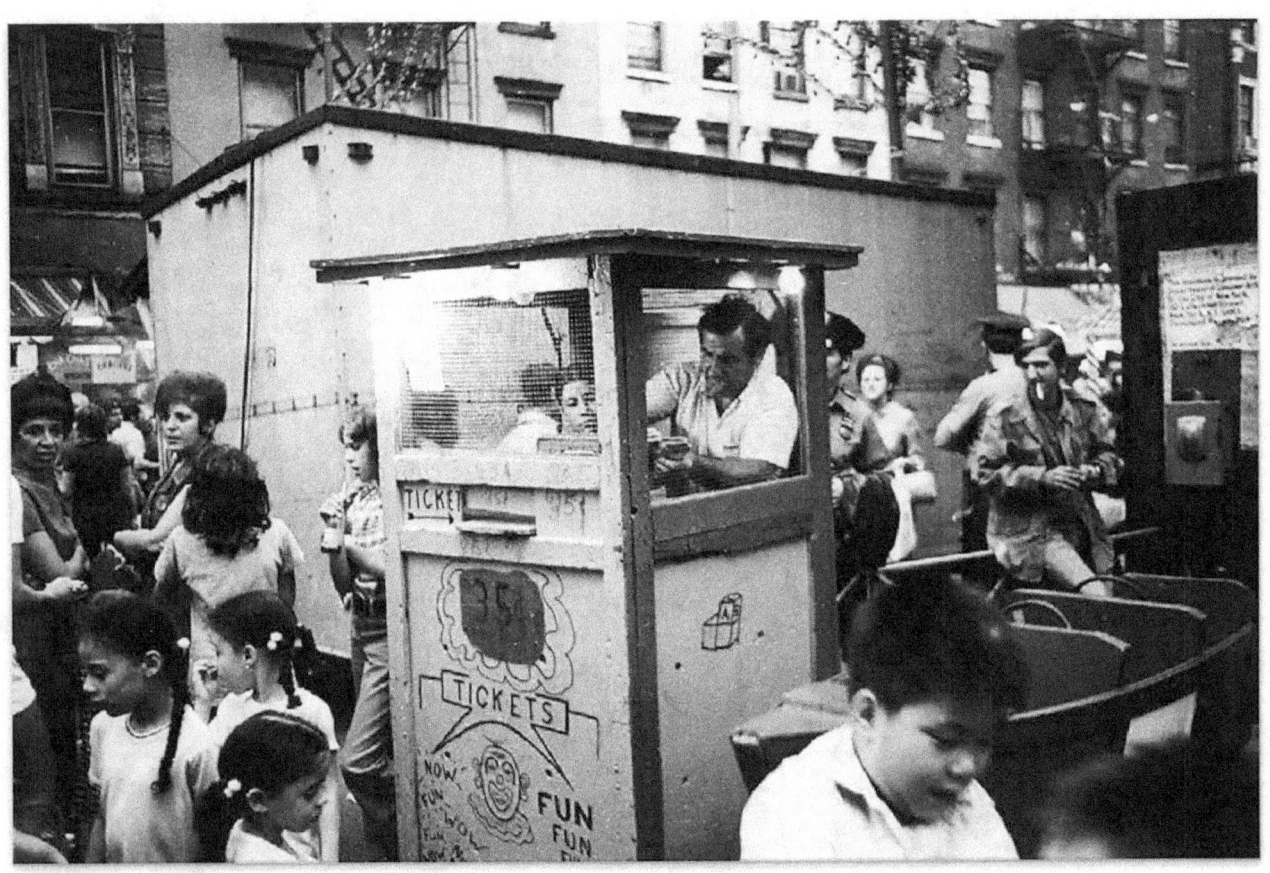

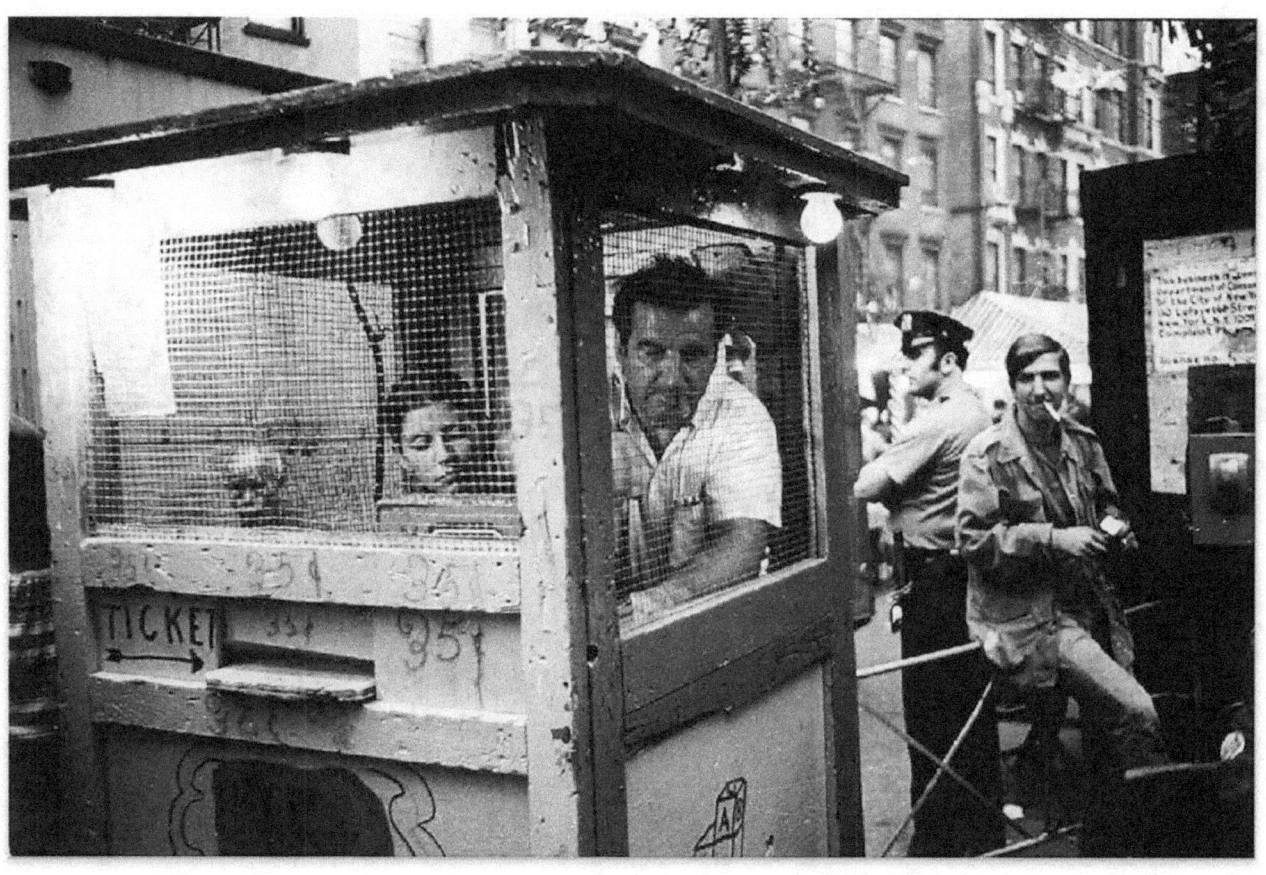

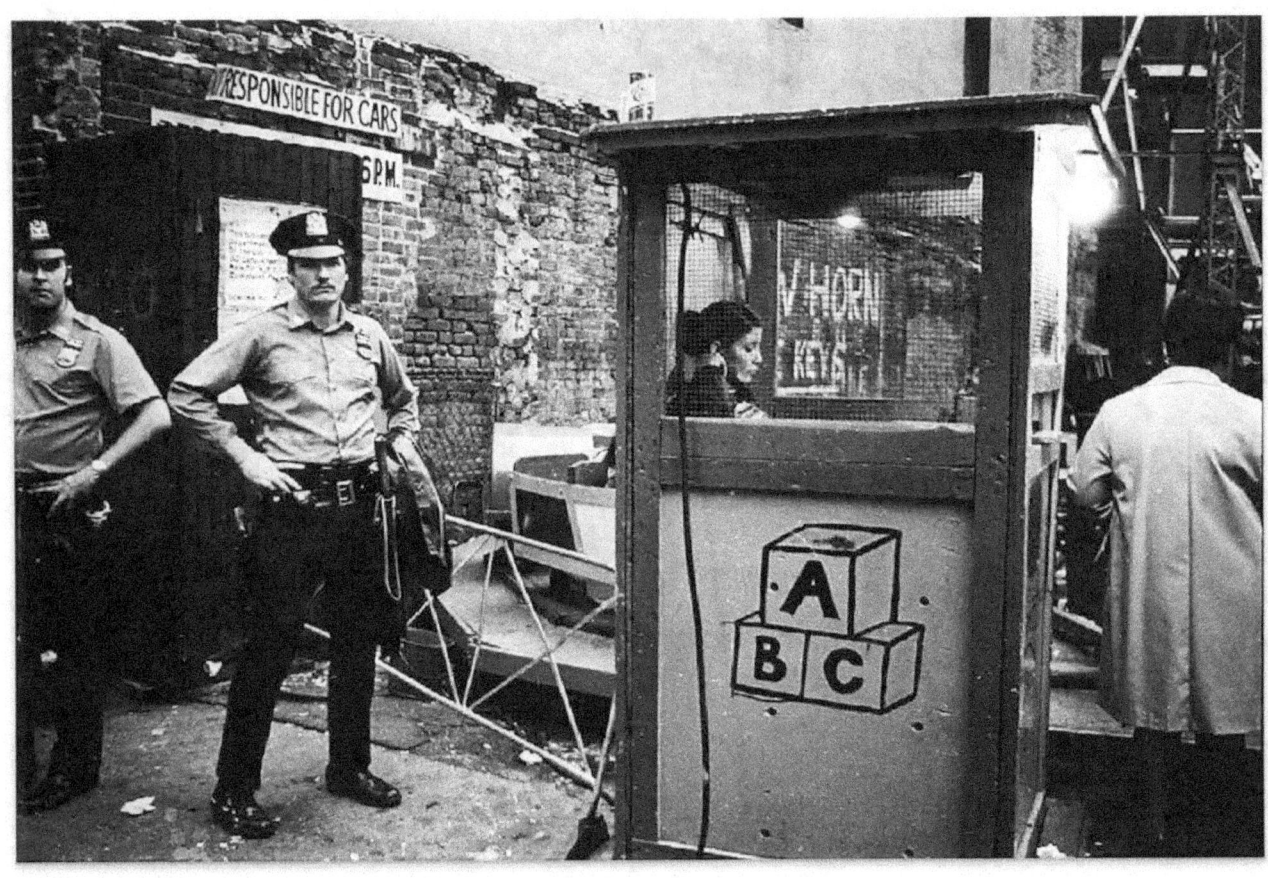

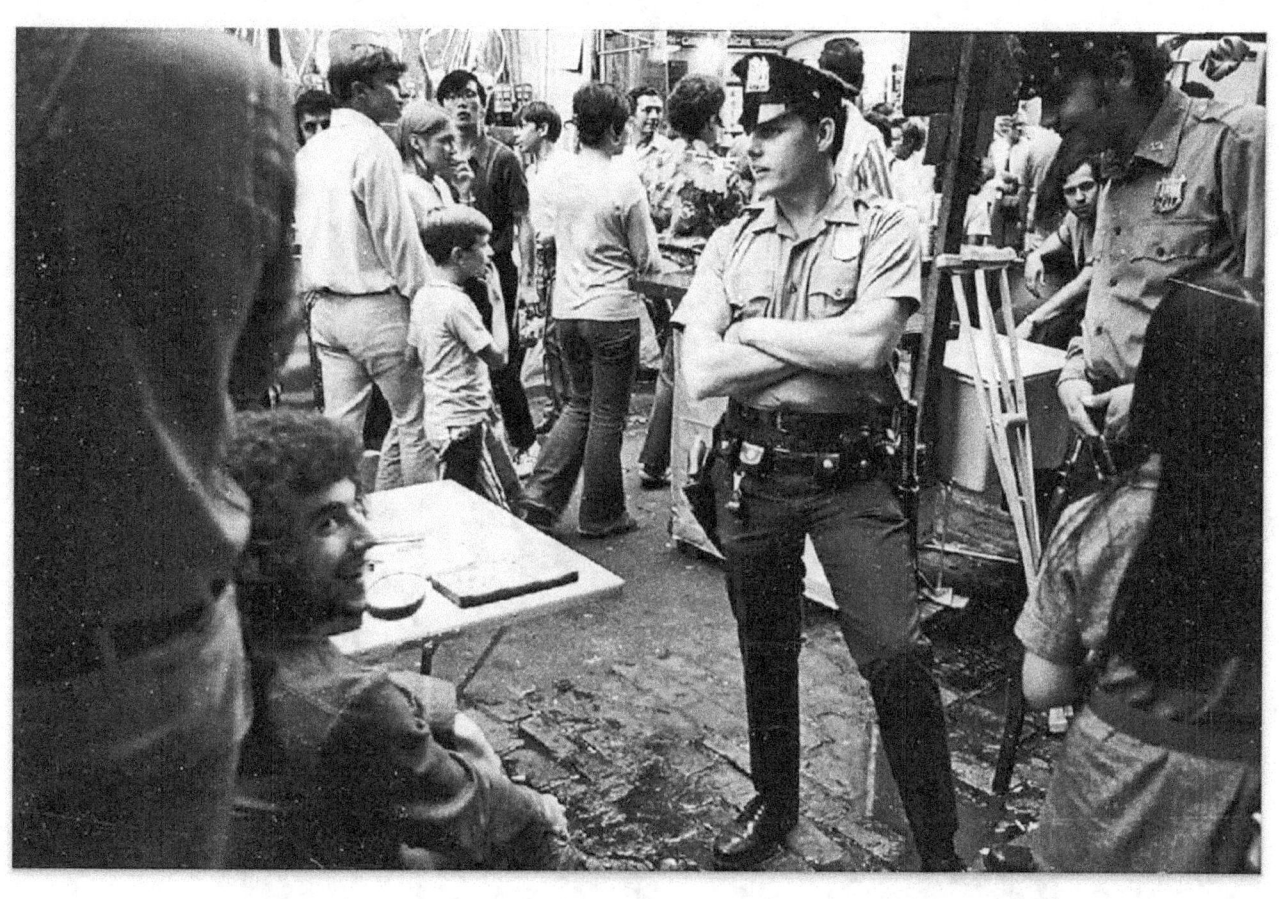

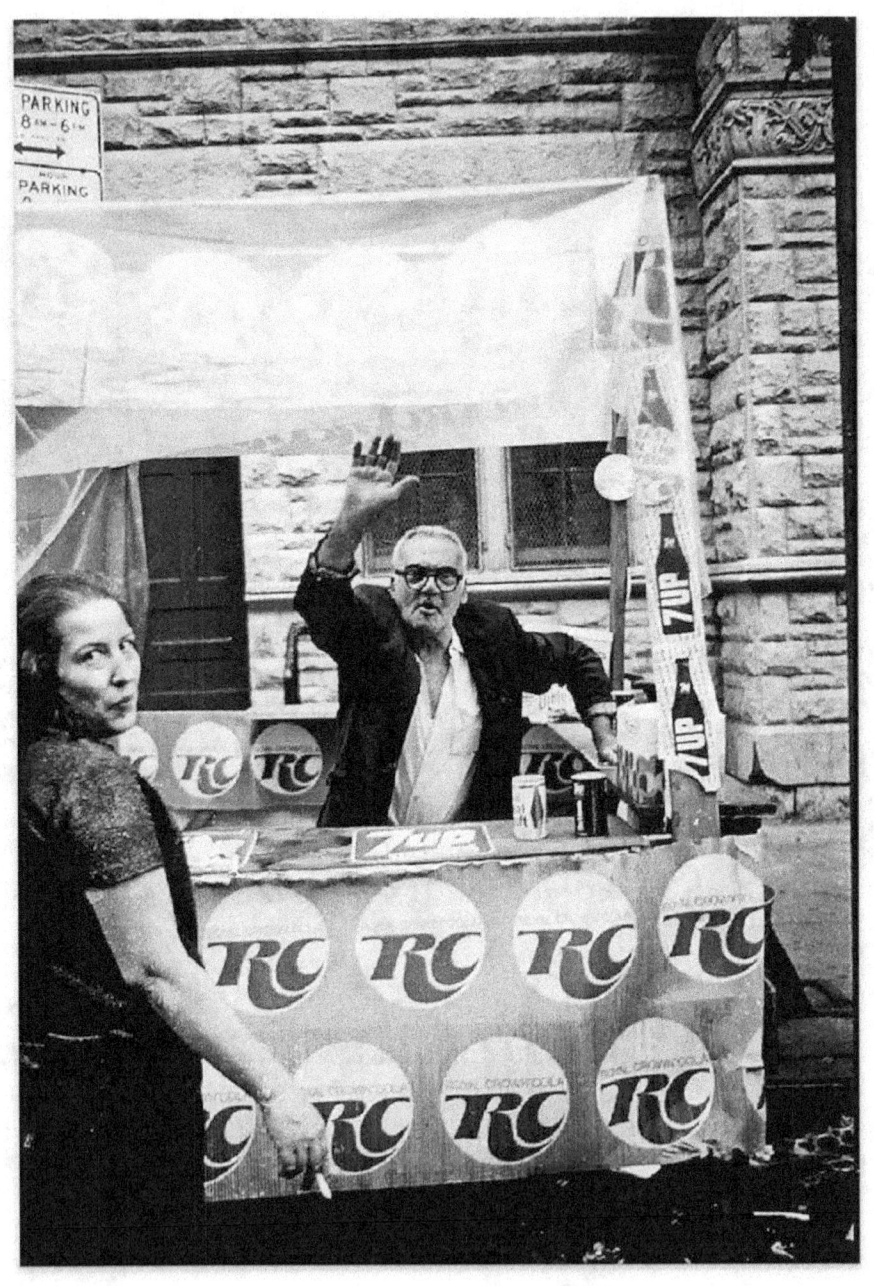

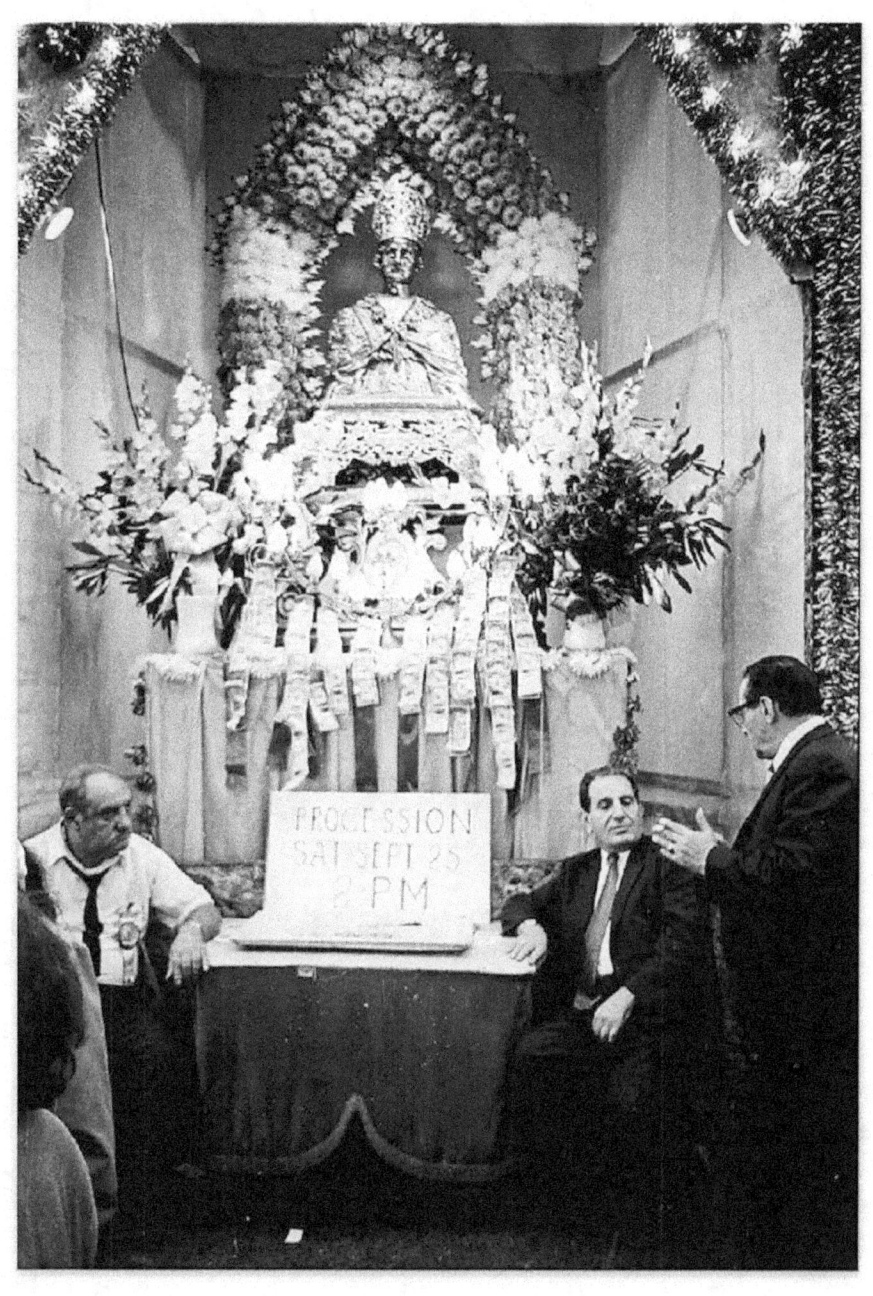

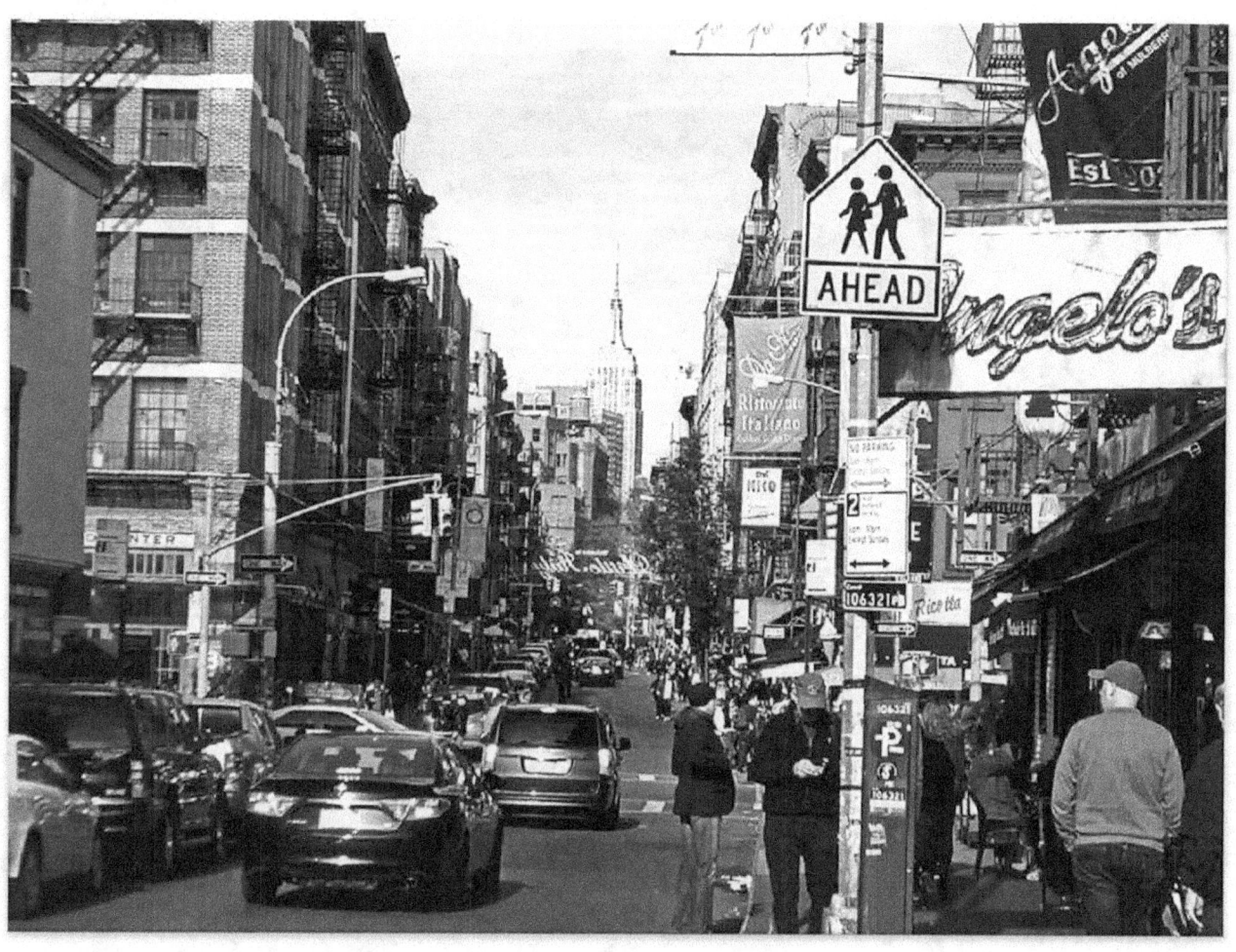

Mulberry Street, looking north, November 4, 2017.

Manhattan, Washington Heights, c. 1972

My parents lived a few blocks from where these photographs were taken, forty years before I did. They were musicians, and the northern reaches of Manhattan were of the more affordable areas on the island.

In 1972, I lived on Riverside Drive and 181st St. In some ways, this small section of Washington Heights was not what some might consider a neighborhood – lots of highways, few stores, no tree-lined streets. But it had an authentic feel to it.

The photographs are not a systematic documentation of the place or era. I photographed what visually attracted me, and selected ones I liked the most.

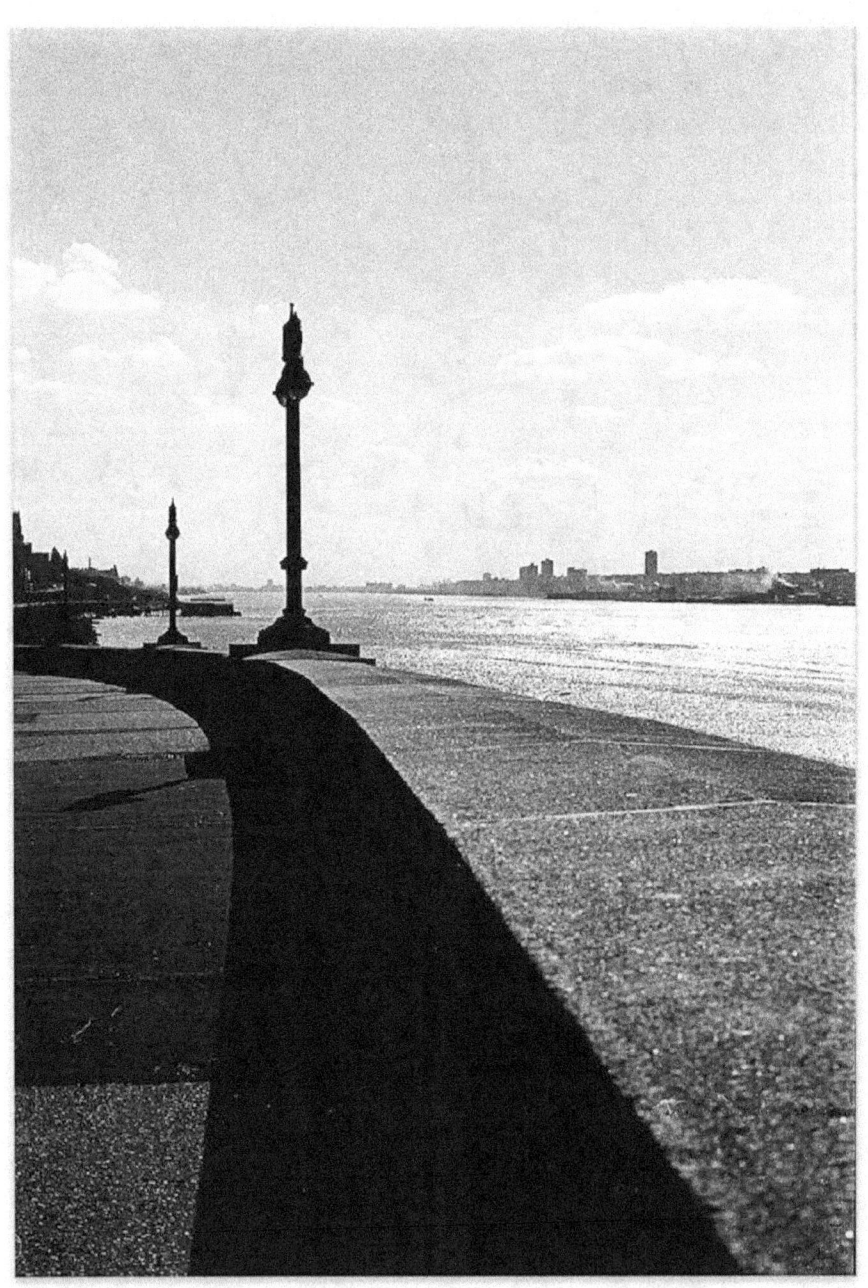

Riverside Drive and 158th Street, facing south, c.1972.

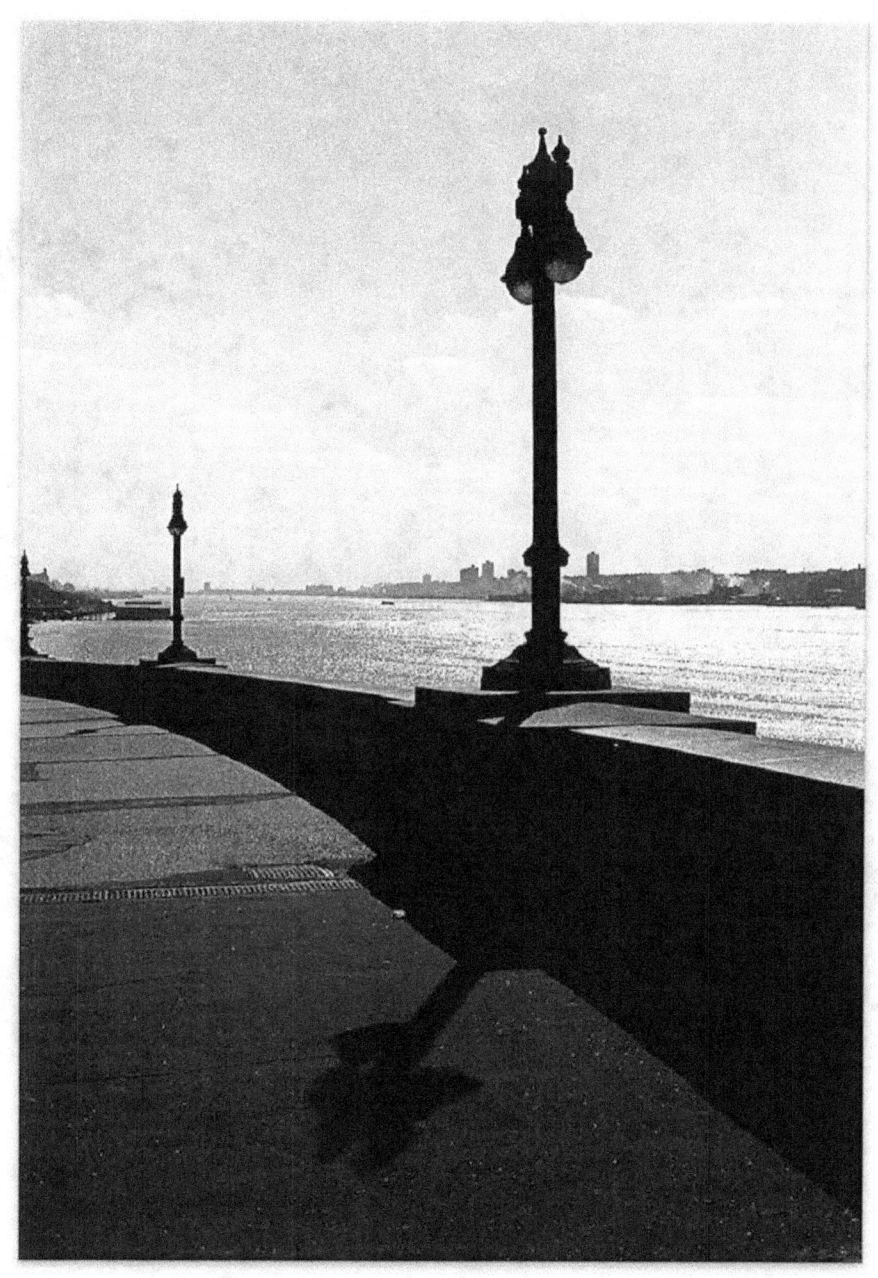

Riverside Drive and 158th Street, facing south, c.1972.

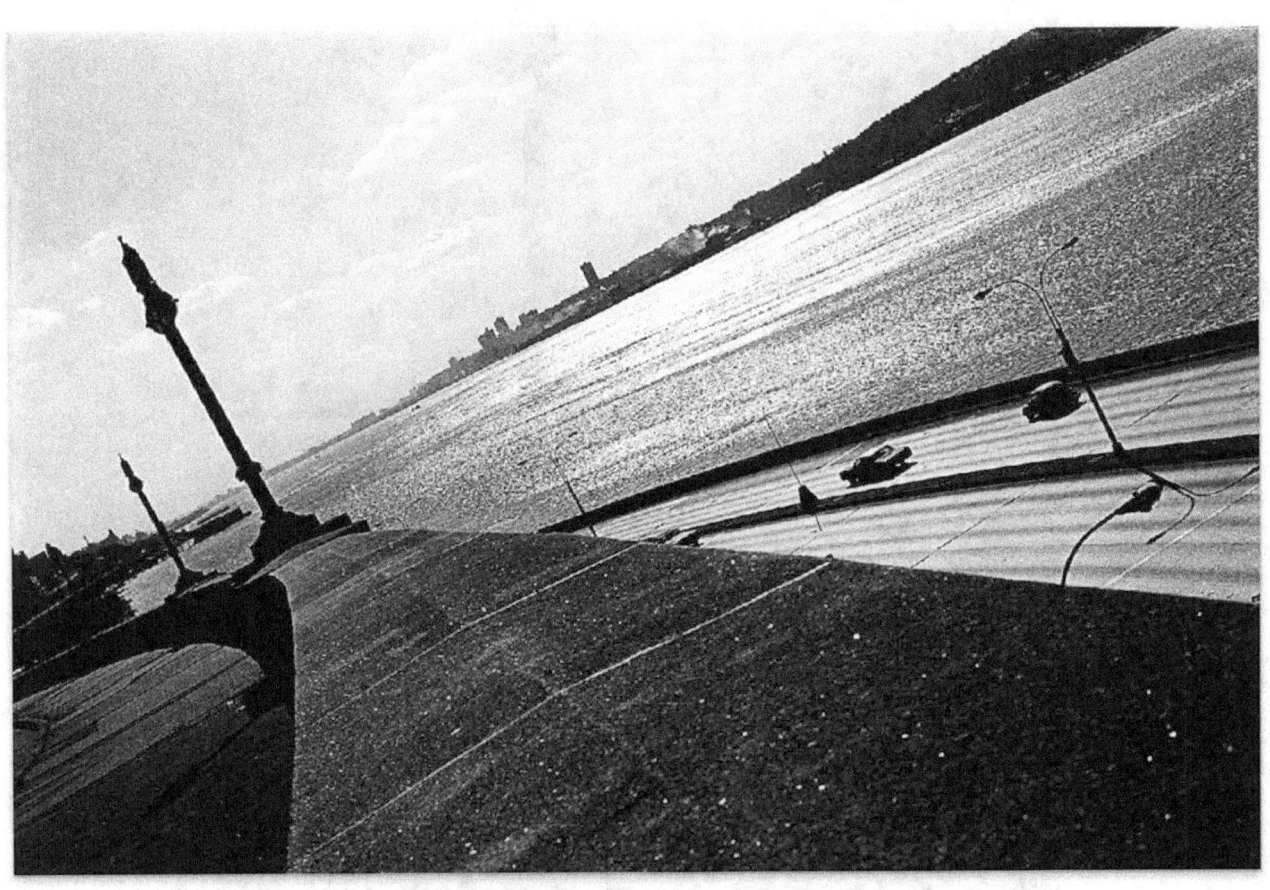

Riverside Drive and 158th Street, facing south,
Hudson River and West Side Highway below, c.1972.

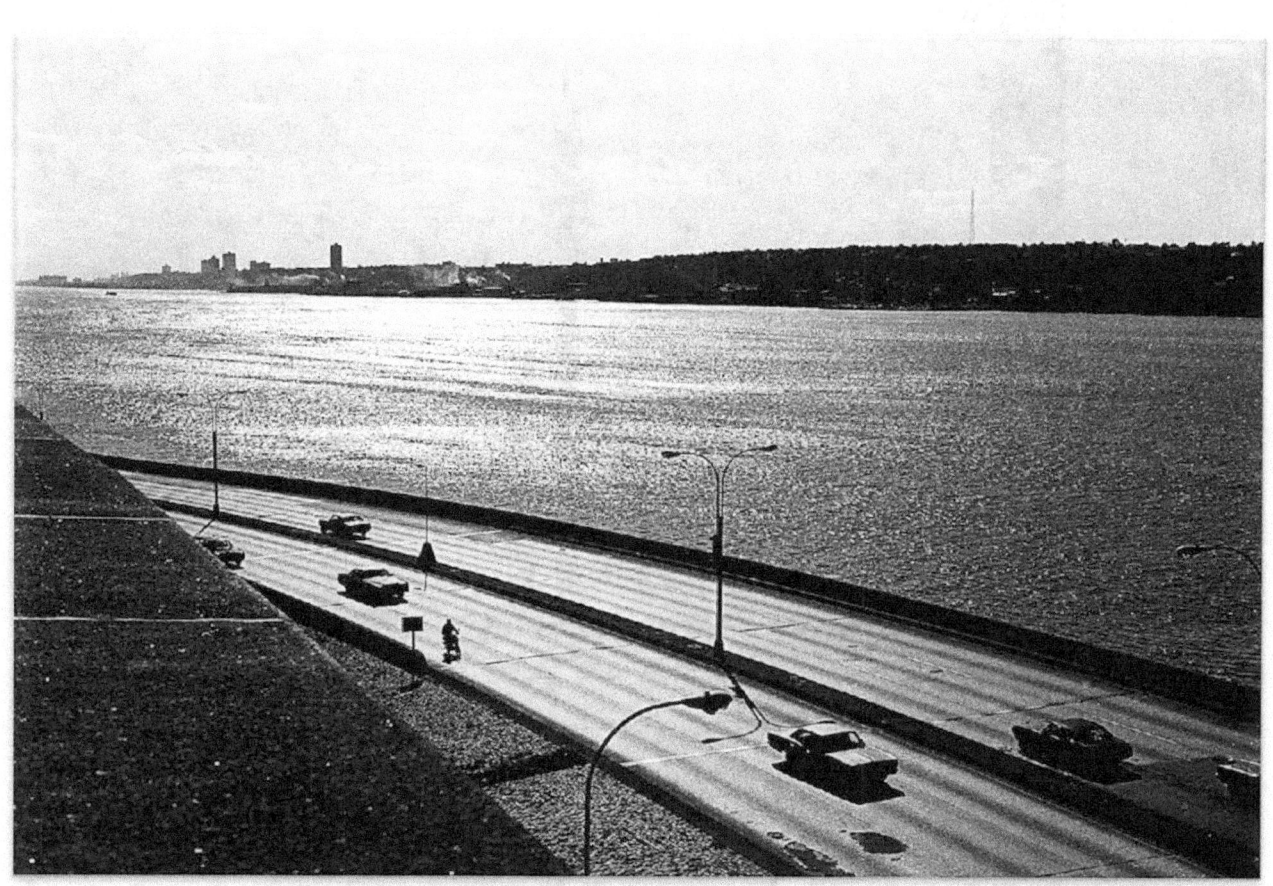

Riverside Drive and 158th Street, facing south,
Hudson River and West Side Highway below, c.1972.

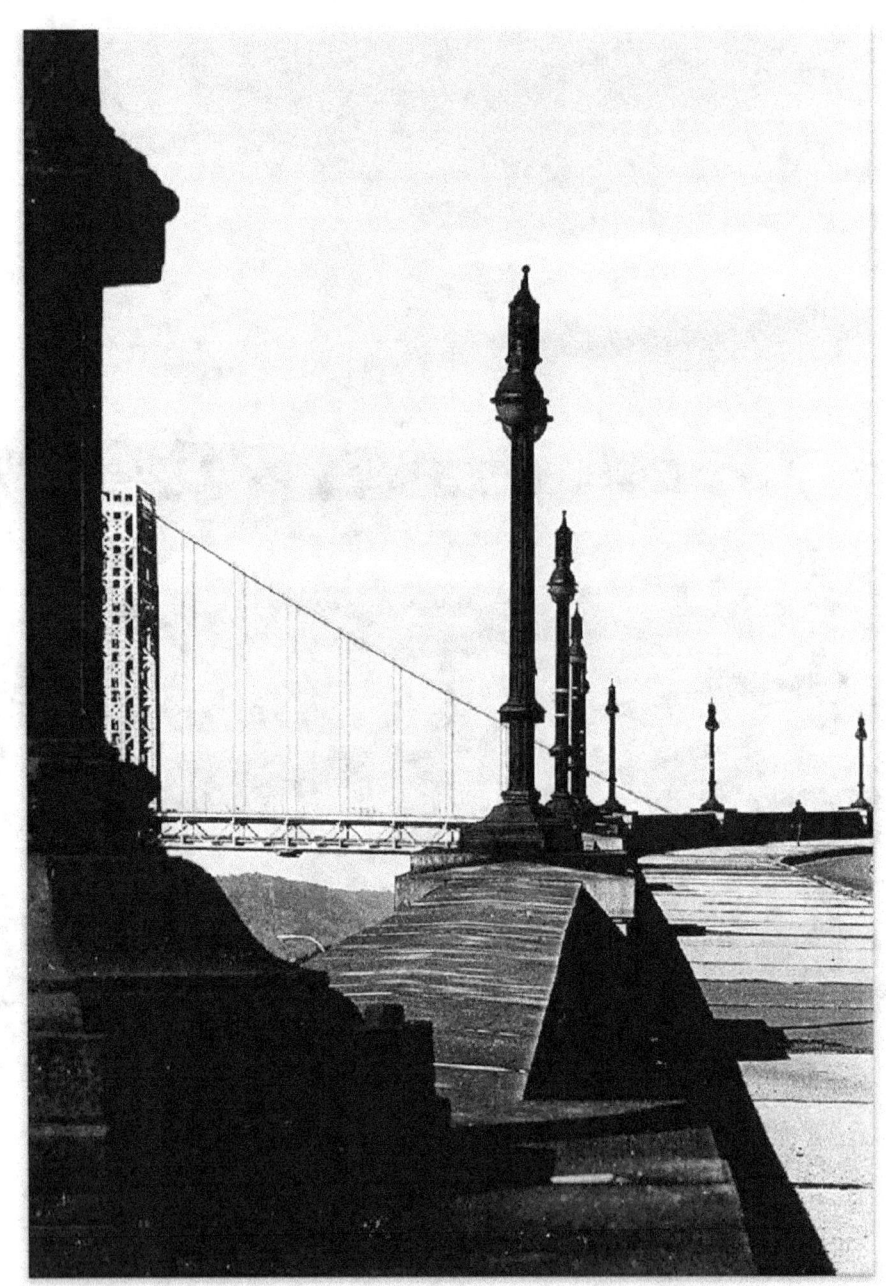

Riverside Drive and 158th Street, facing north,
George Washington Bridge, Palisades in distance, c.1972.

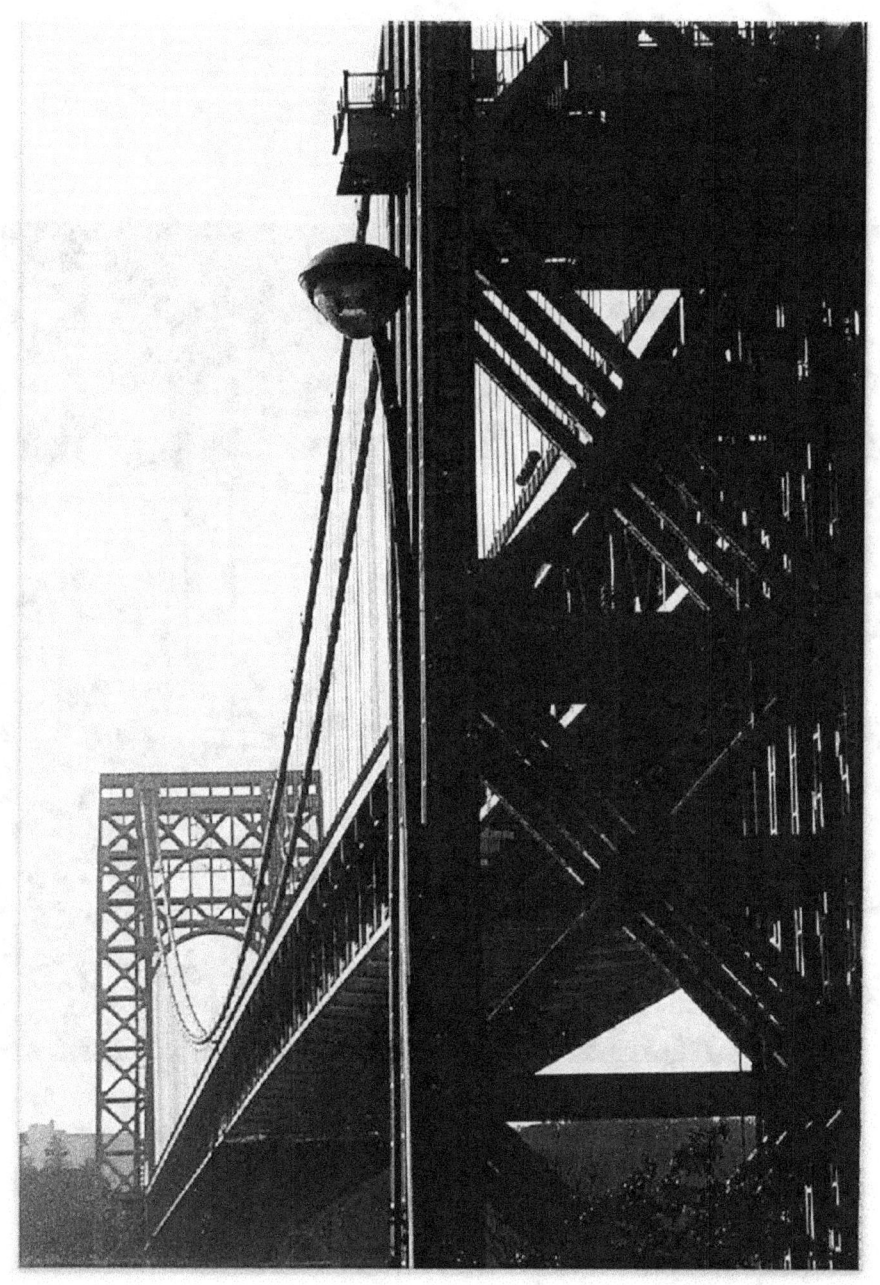

Fort Washington Park (Point), at the George Washington Bridge,
facing west, c.1972.

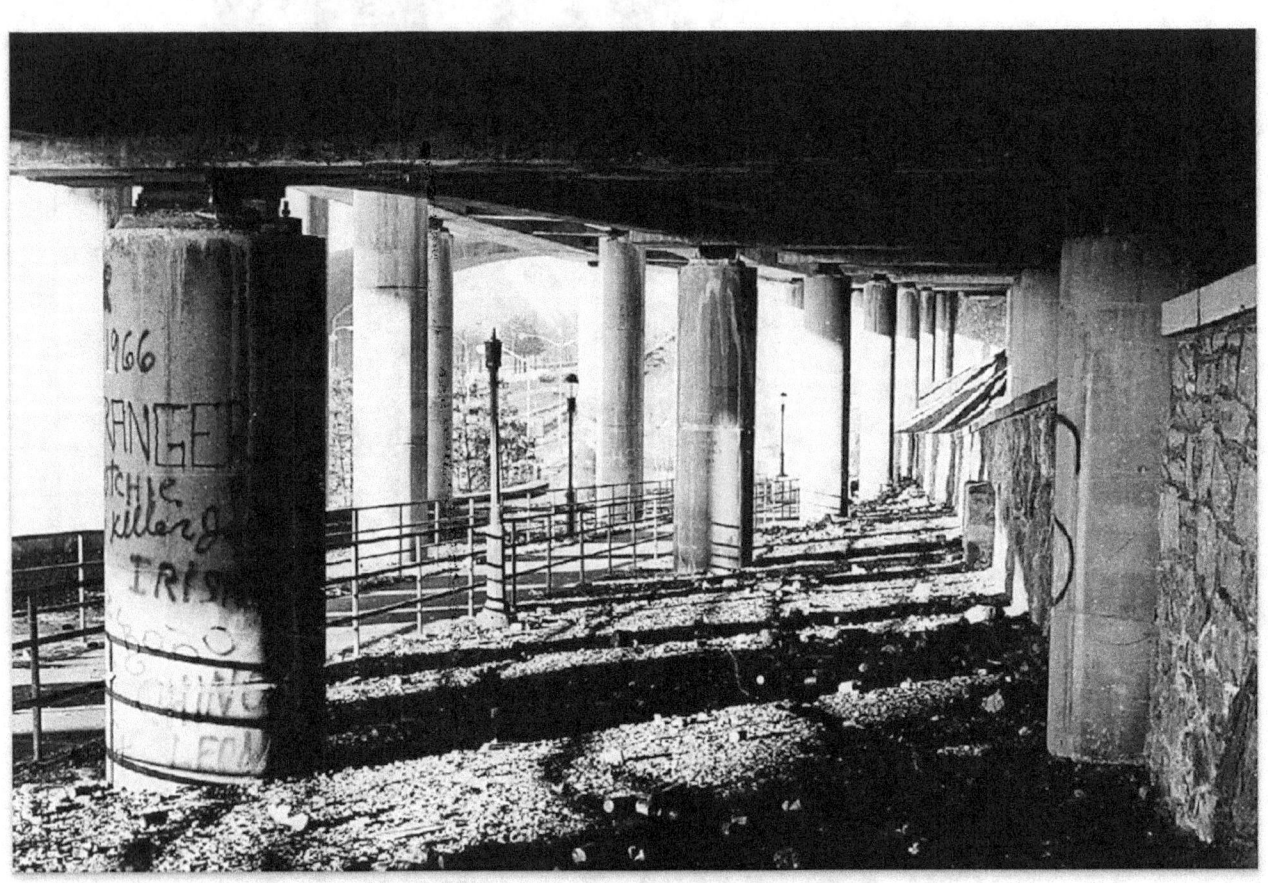

Below Riverside Drive exit ramp to 181 Street,
near the George Washington Bridge. c. 1972

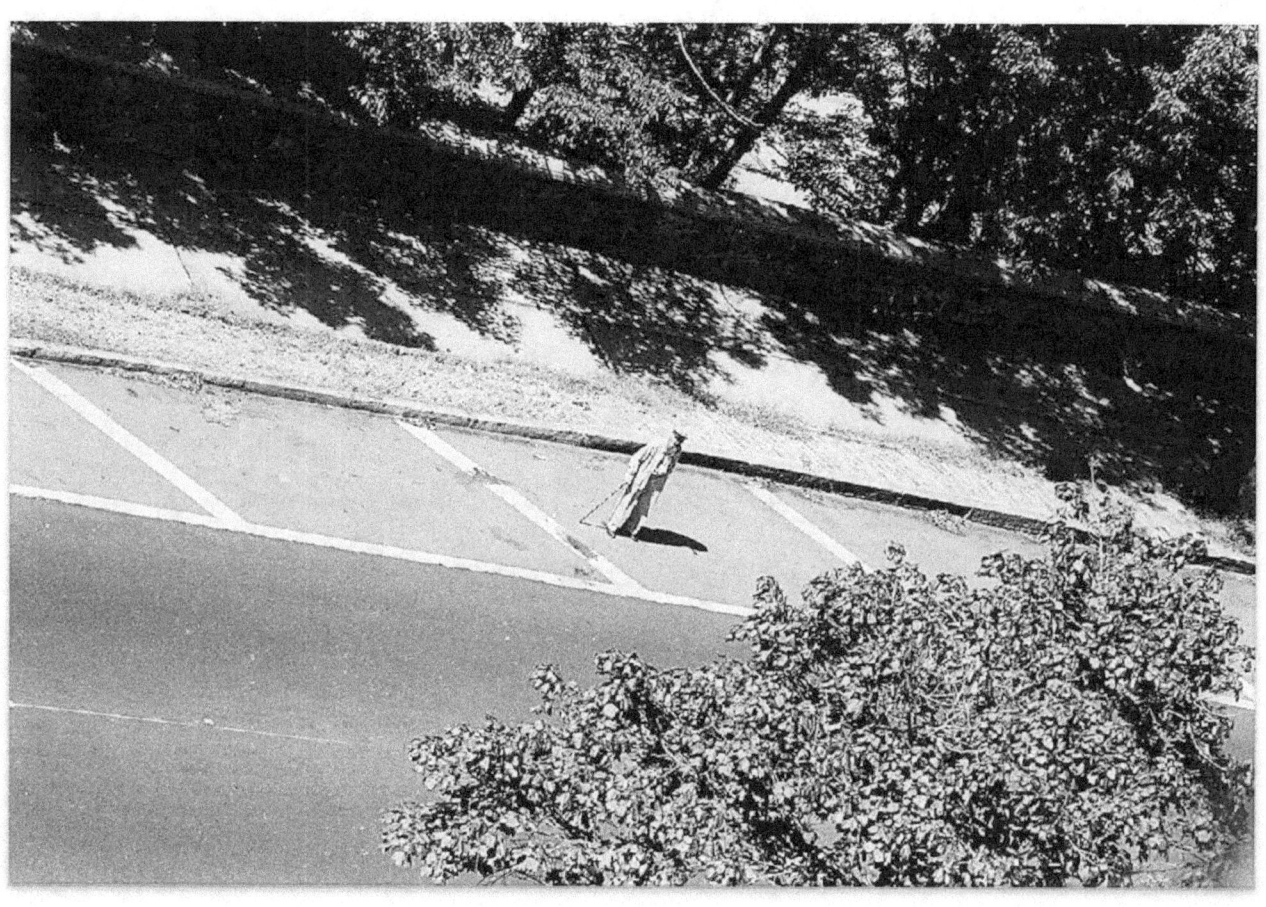

Man with cane, crossing Henry Hudson Parkway,
3 blocks north of the George Washington Bridge, c. 1972 (Technically not in Washington
Heights but Hudson Heights because it is just north of the George Washington Bridge).

Bellevue Hospital, 1982

I worked in Bellevue Hospital as a clinical engineer from 1979 to 1985. What's a clinical engineer? It's a subcategory of biomedical engineering and is concerned with the maintenance and general oversight of the medical technology used in a health-care facility. Often not very visible, engineers and technicians keep equipment functioning, address operational issues with medical staff, evaluate new devices, and assist in the implementation of new patient-care services.

Working in Bellevue was an adventure I can never forget. Bellevue is part of a network of New York City-owned hospitals and claims to be the oldest public hospital in America (established in 1736). It is a large teaching hospital with many departments: standard hospital services, a Level 1 trauma center, a prison medical holding area, and a psychiatric facility. My position provided me with a unique view of patient care, as well as a first-hand experience of the functioning of a large institution.

One year, an associate director of nursing asked me to contribute photographs for the 1981-1982 Bellevue School of Nursing Bulletin. Some of the photographs shown here are from that project; others I took on my own. I knew most of the people I photographed.

All photographs were taken with a medium format, 2 ¼ camera, and are presented here full-frame and without manipulation.

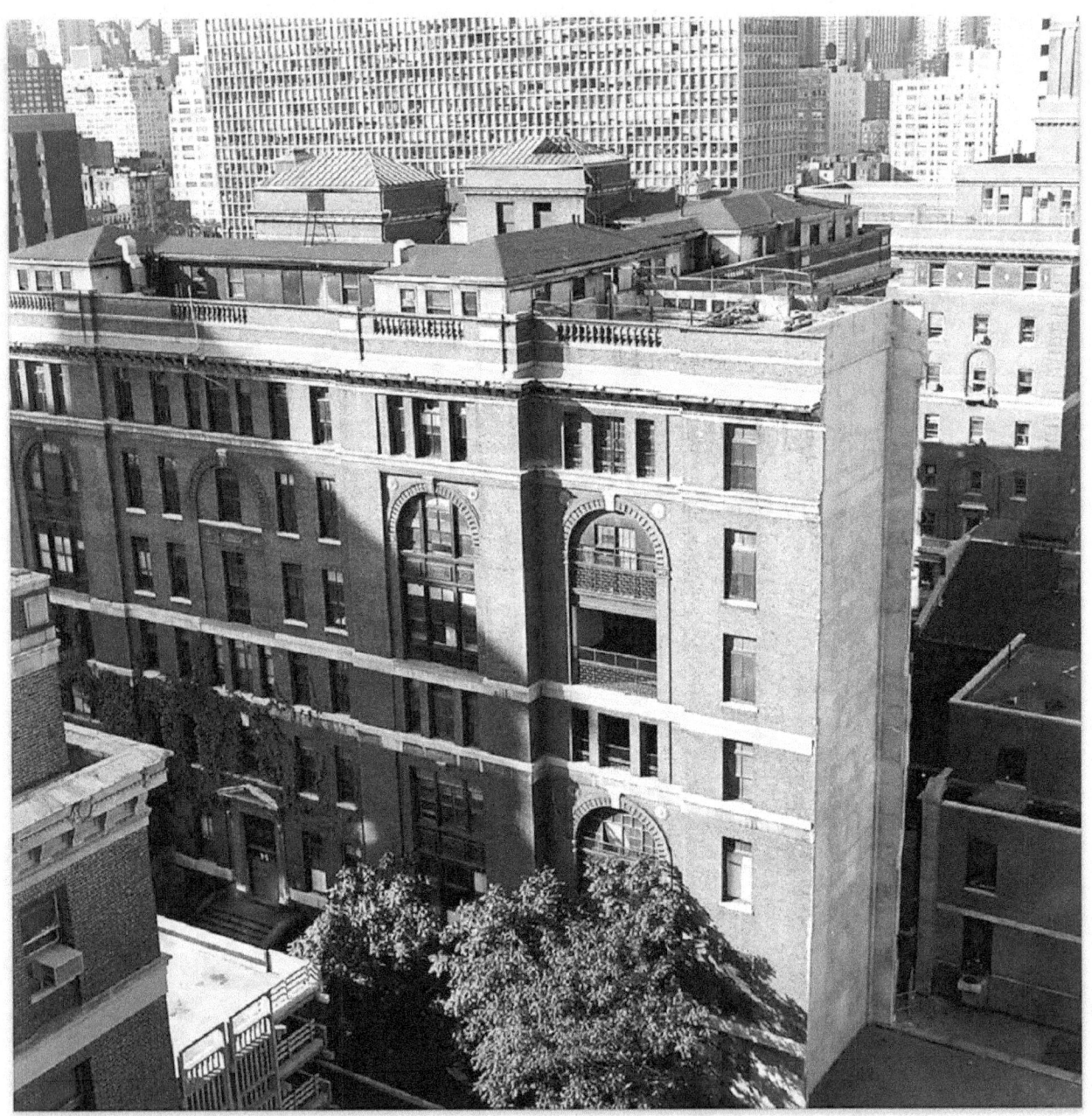

R&S Building, built in 1910, pathology department and male staff dormitories listed State and National historic preservation site, currently used for children in crisis care.

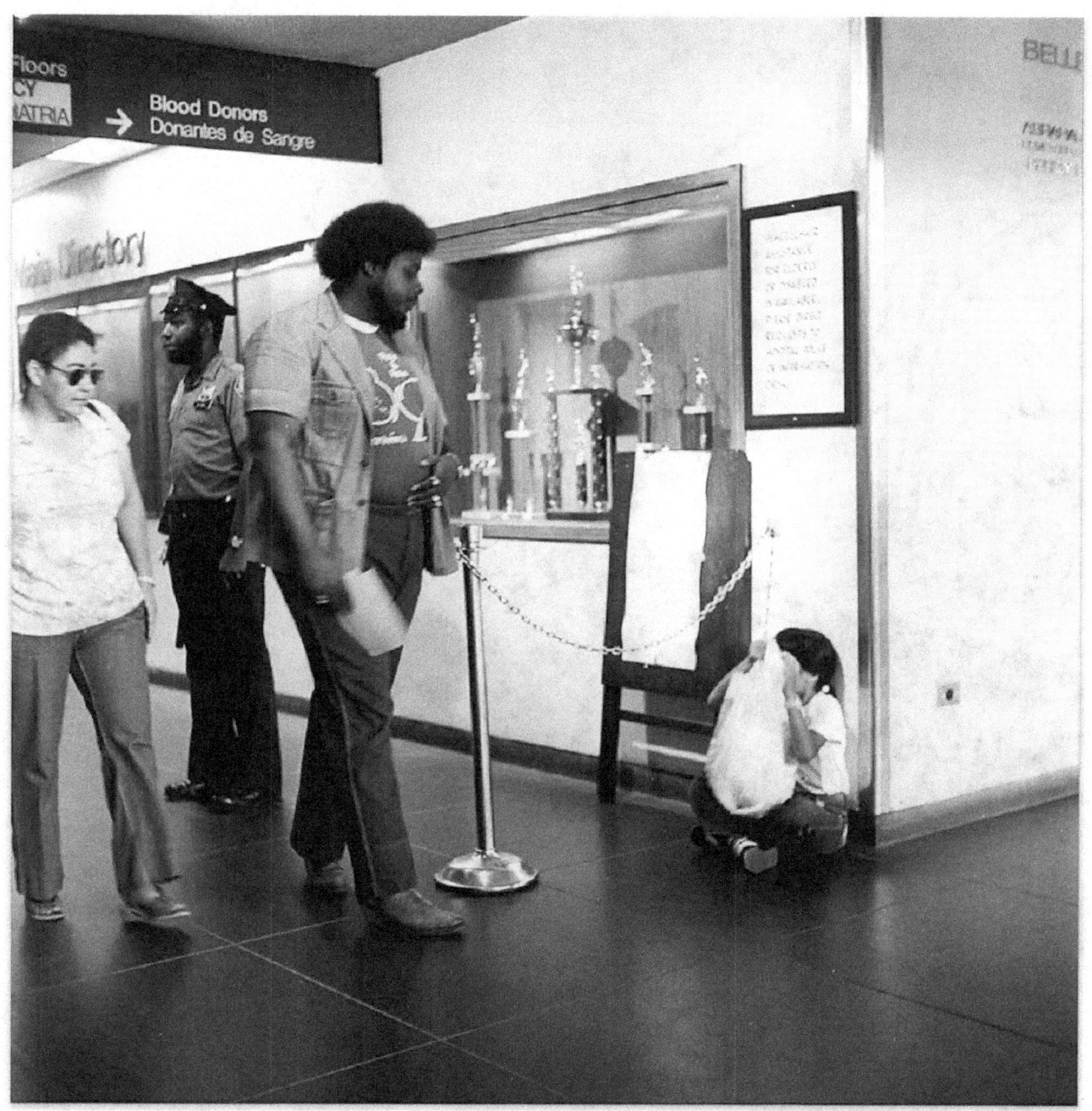

Visitors entrance, main lobby, "New Building" (completed in 1974).

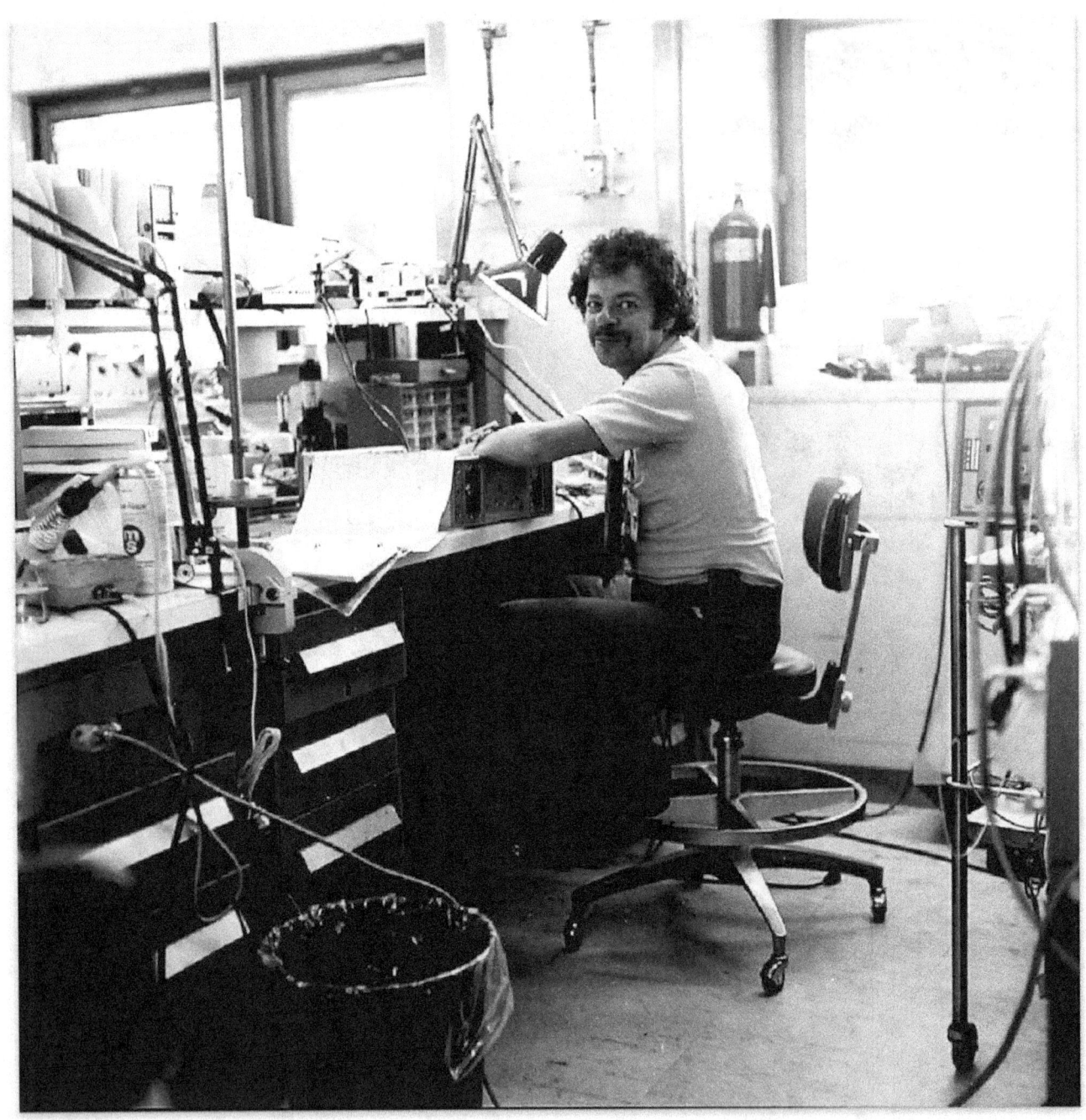

Director, Biomedical Engineering Department.

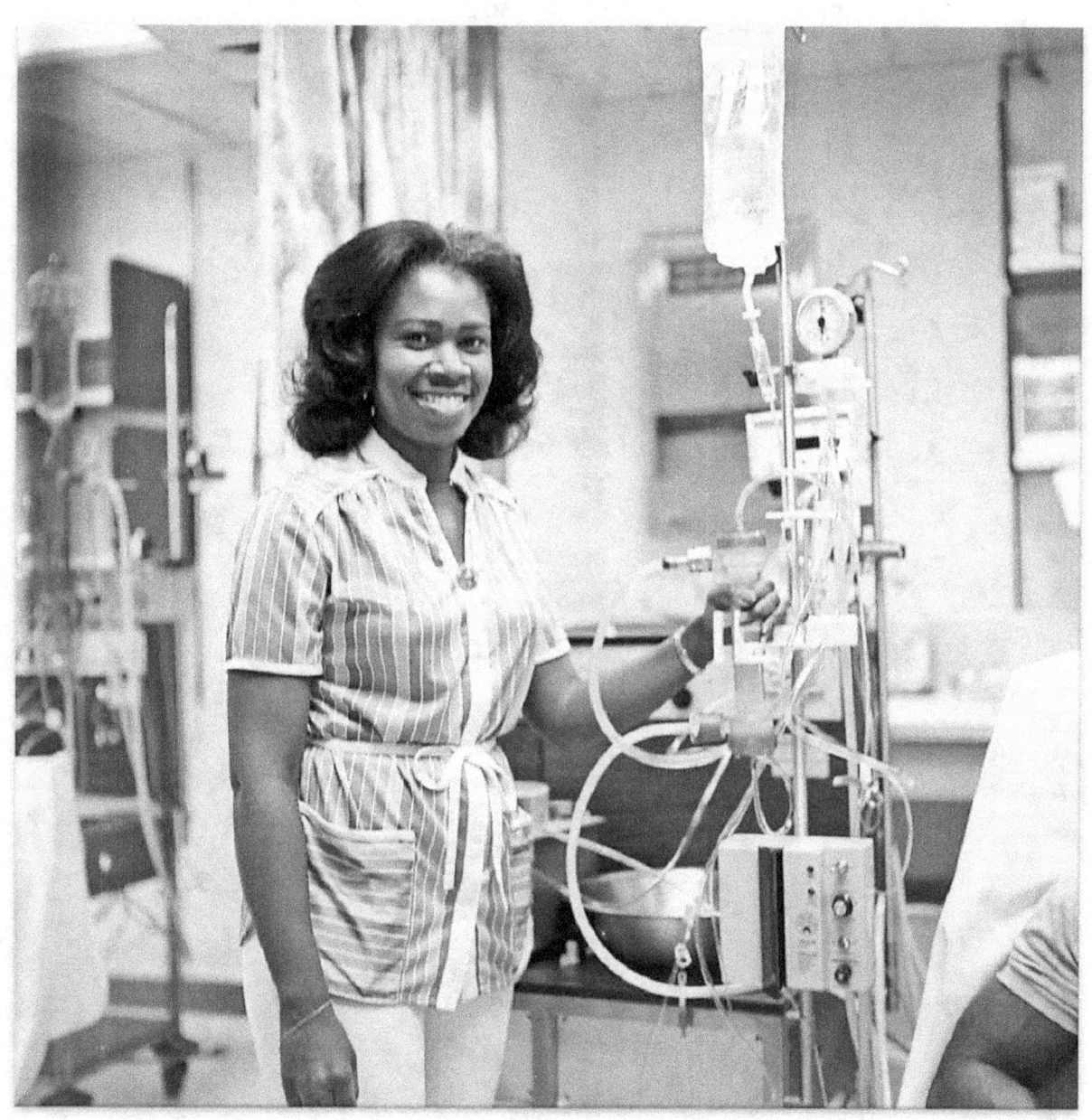

Nurse, Dialysis Unit.

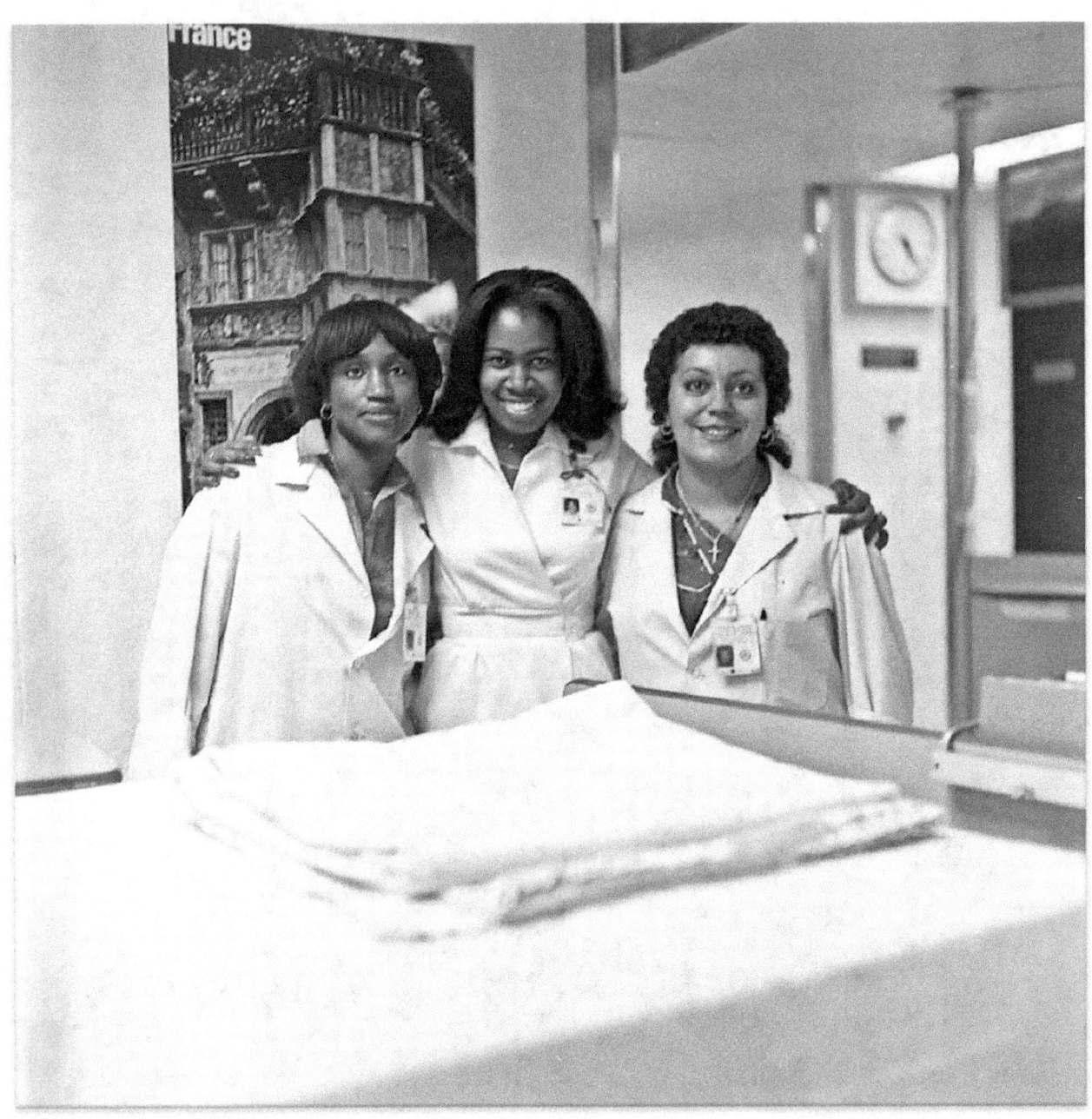

Nursing staff, Dialysis Unit.

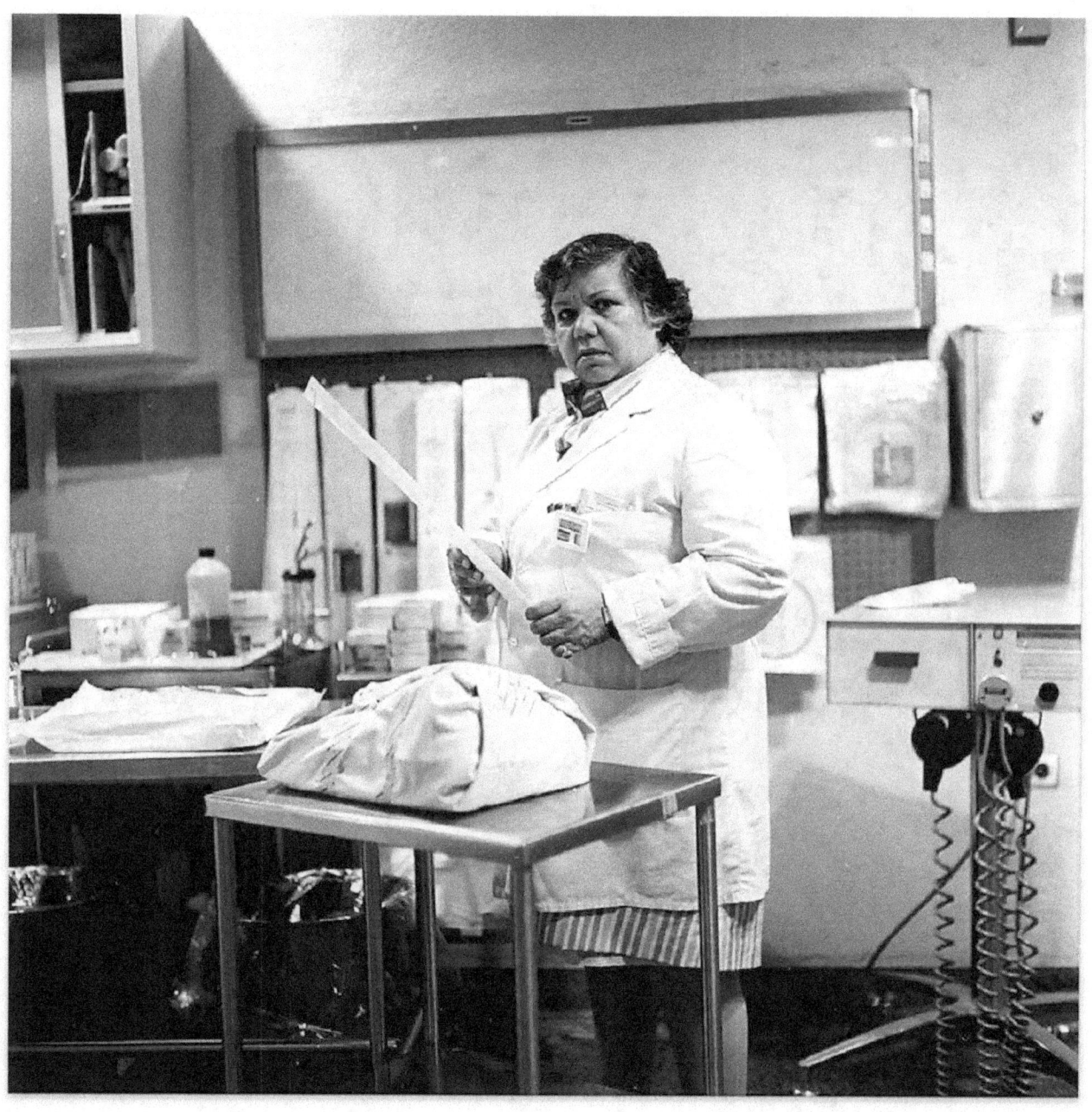

Nurse, Cardiac Catheterization Lab.

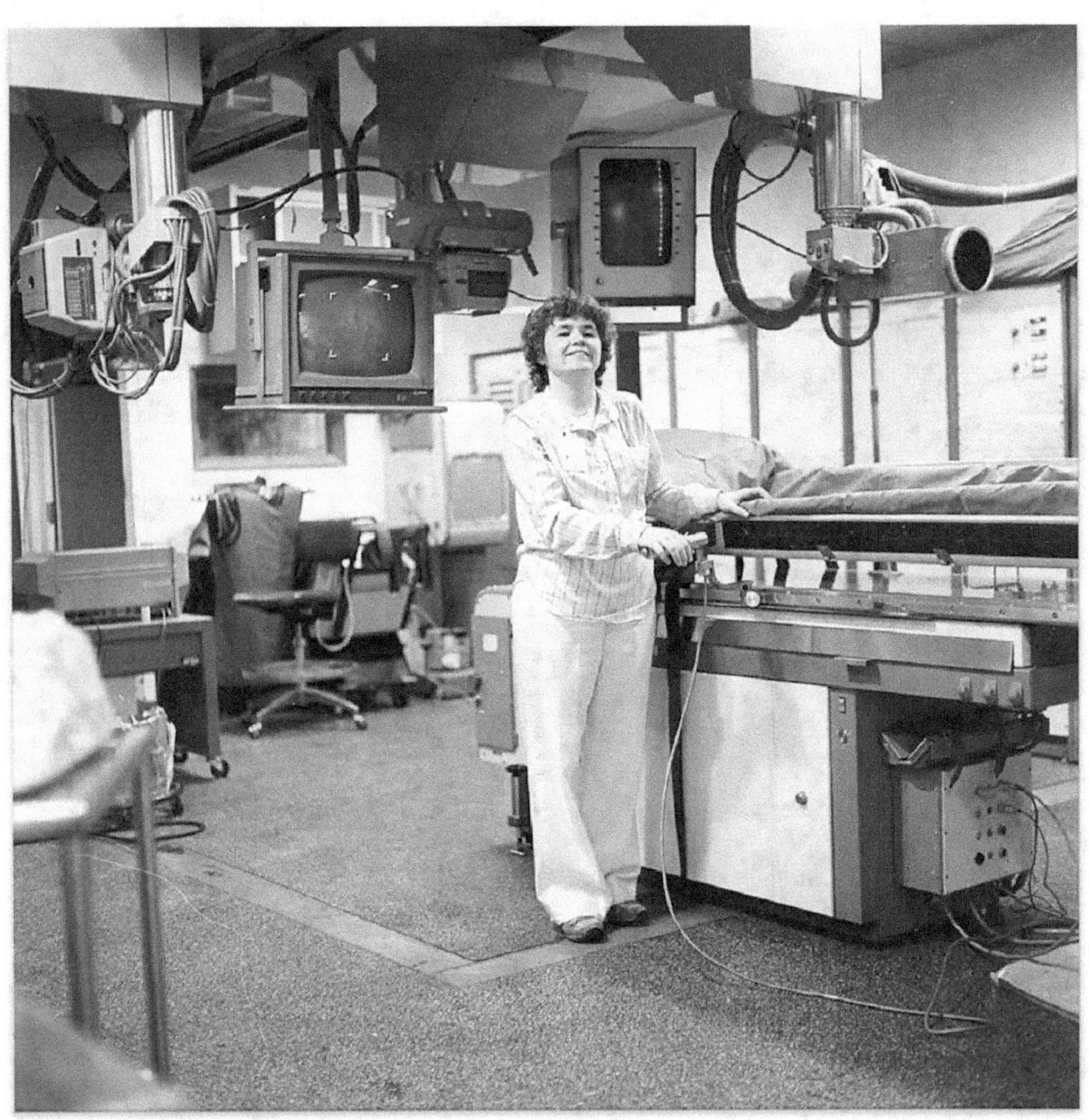

Nurse, Cardiac Catheterization Lab.

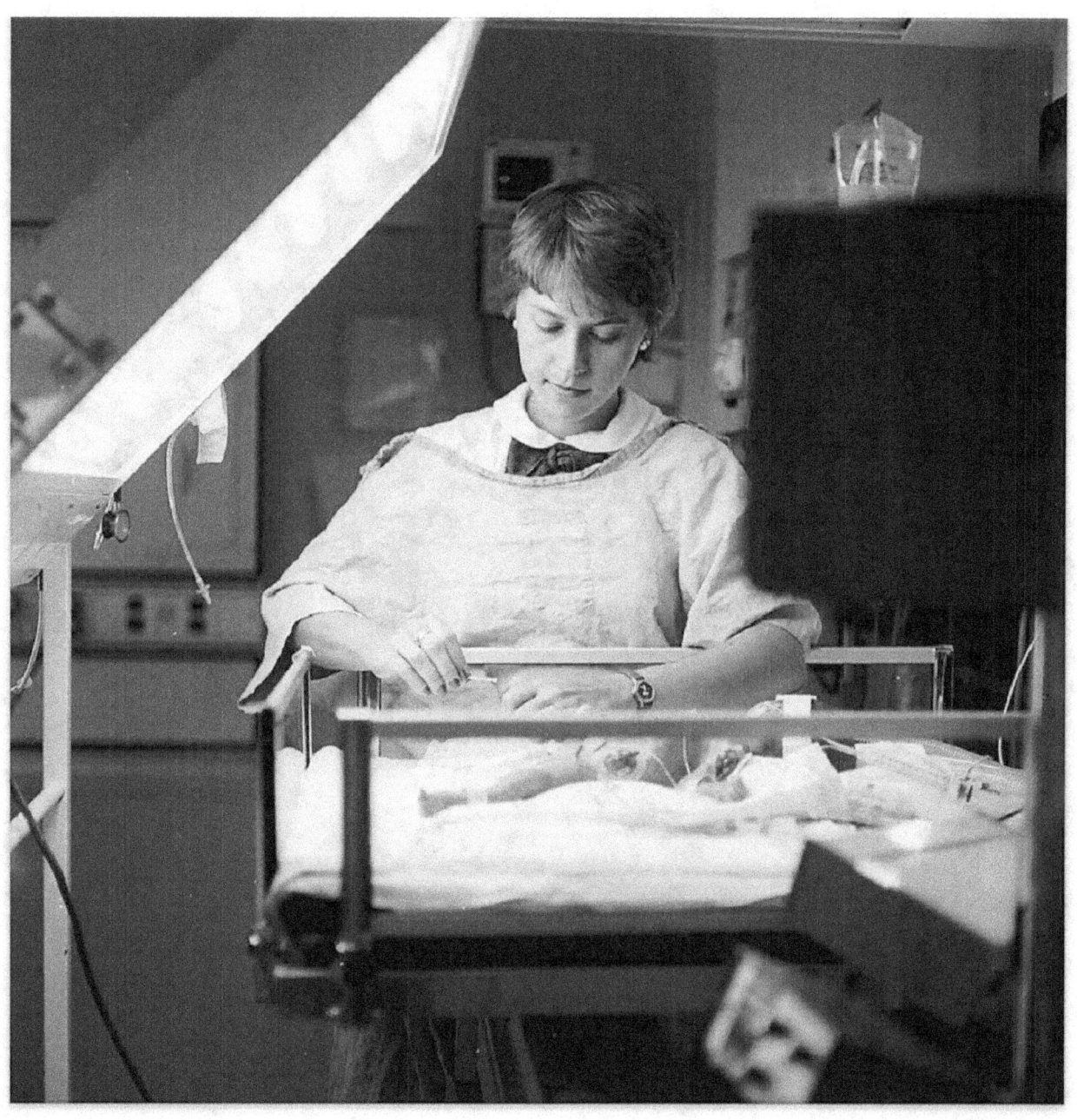

Nurse, Neonatal Intensive Care Unit.

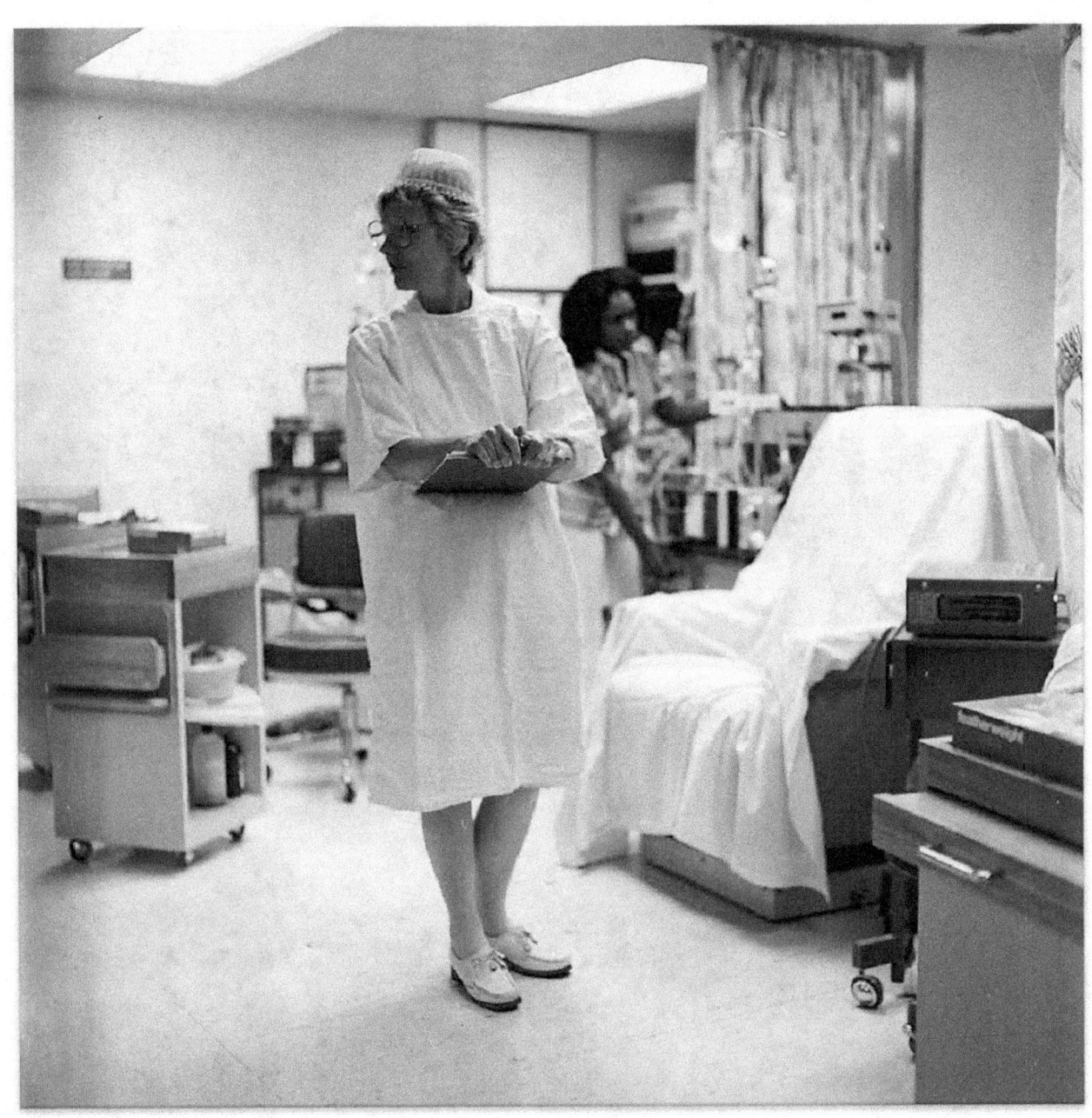

Nurse, Dialysis Unit.

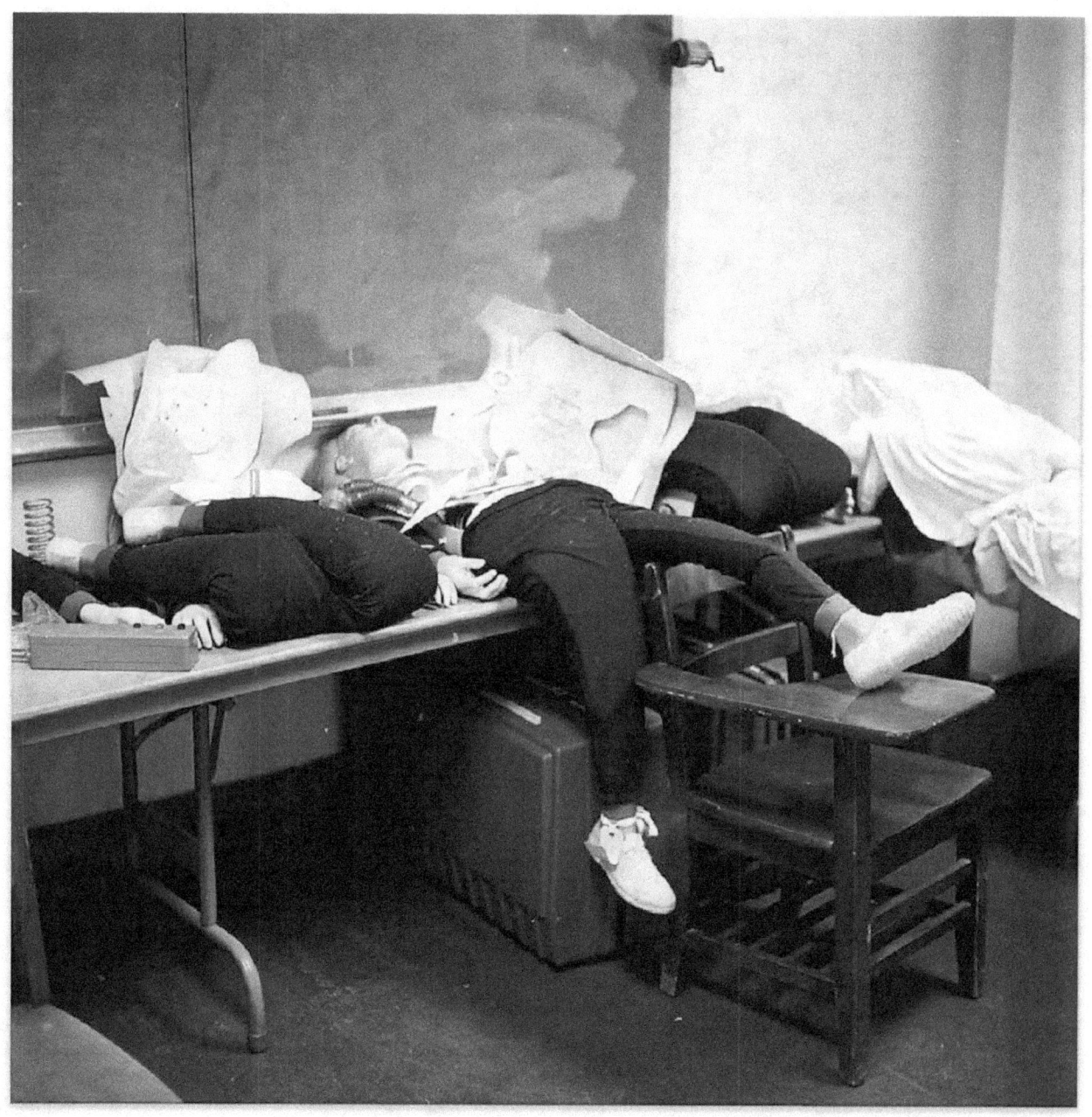

Resusci Anne (resuscitation practice devices).

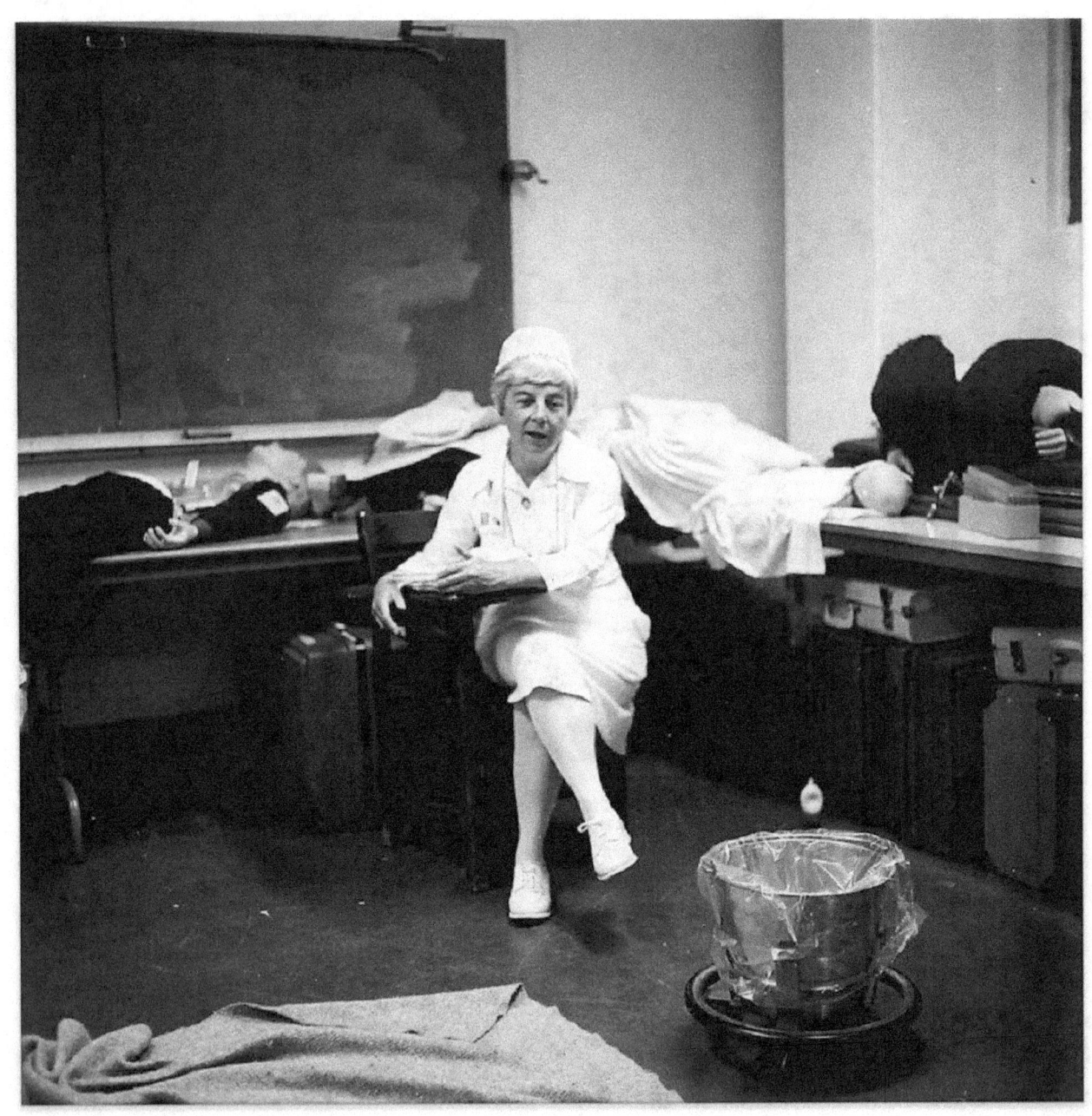

A Director of Nursing.

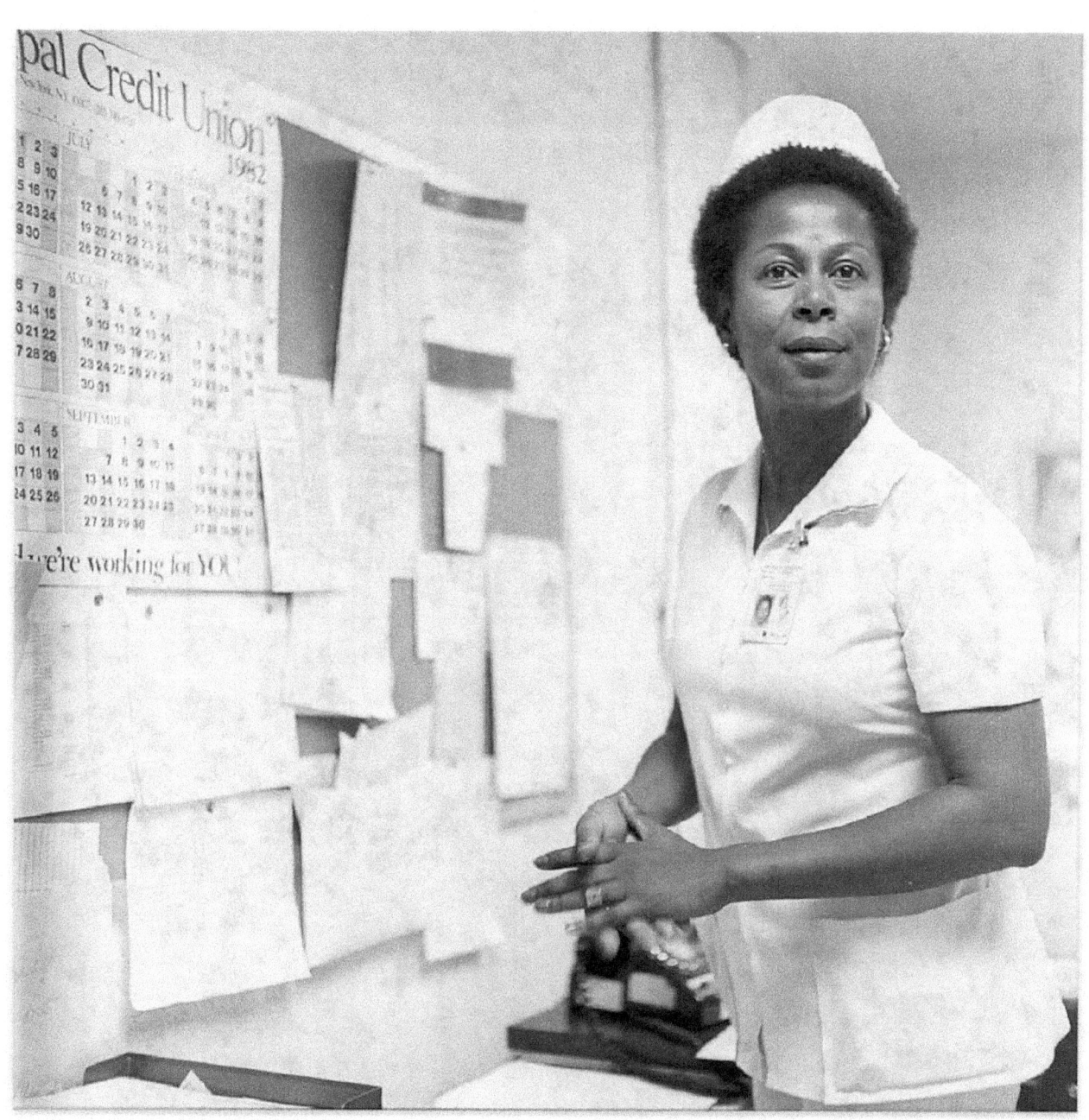

Nursing Supervisor.

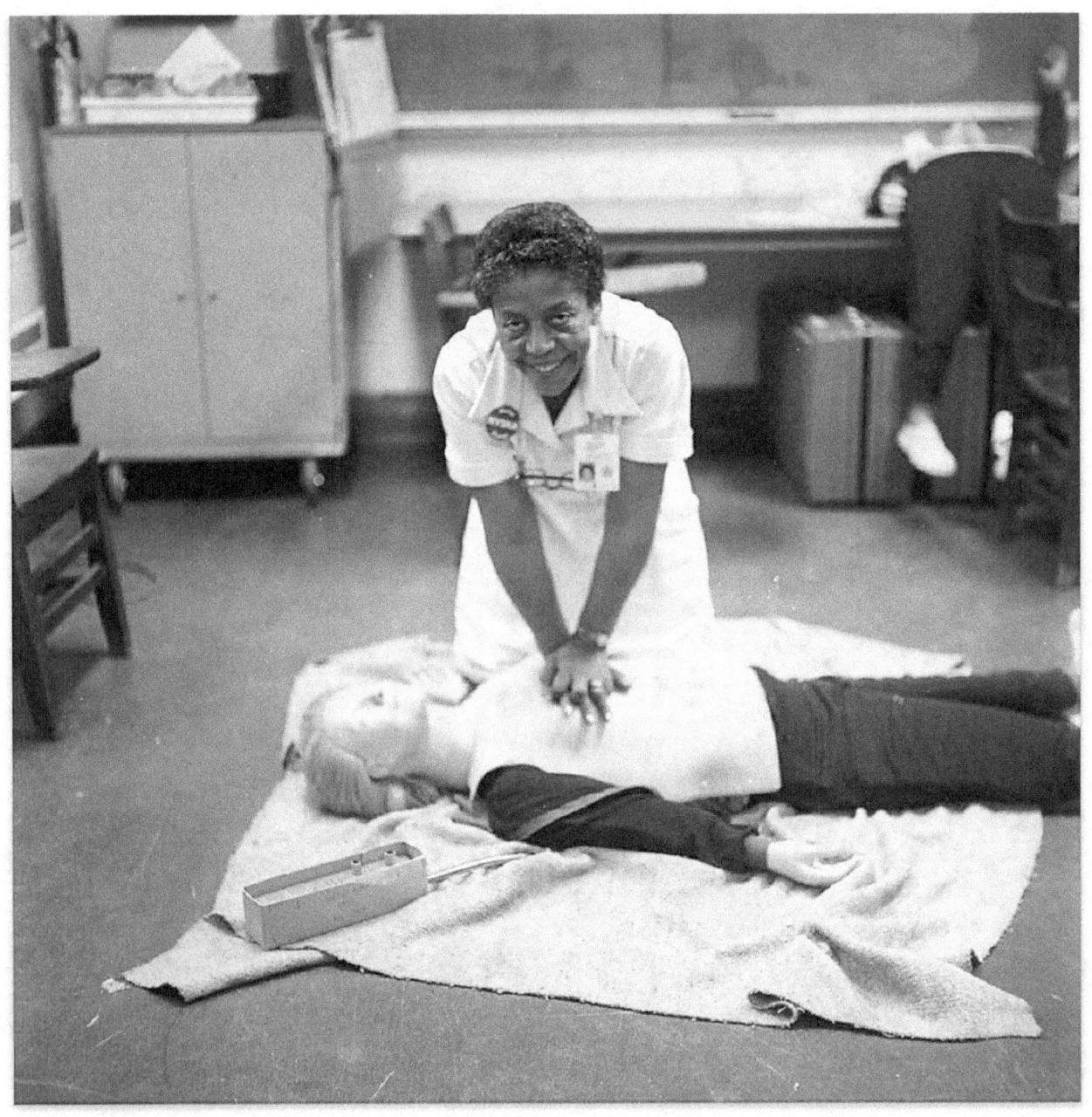

Practicing CPR on a Resusci Anne.

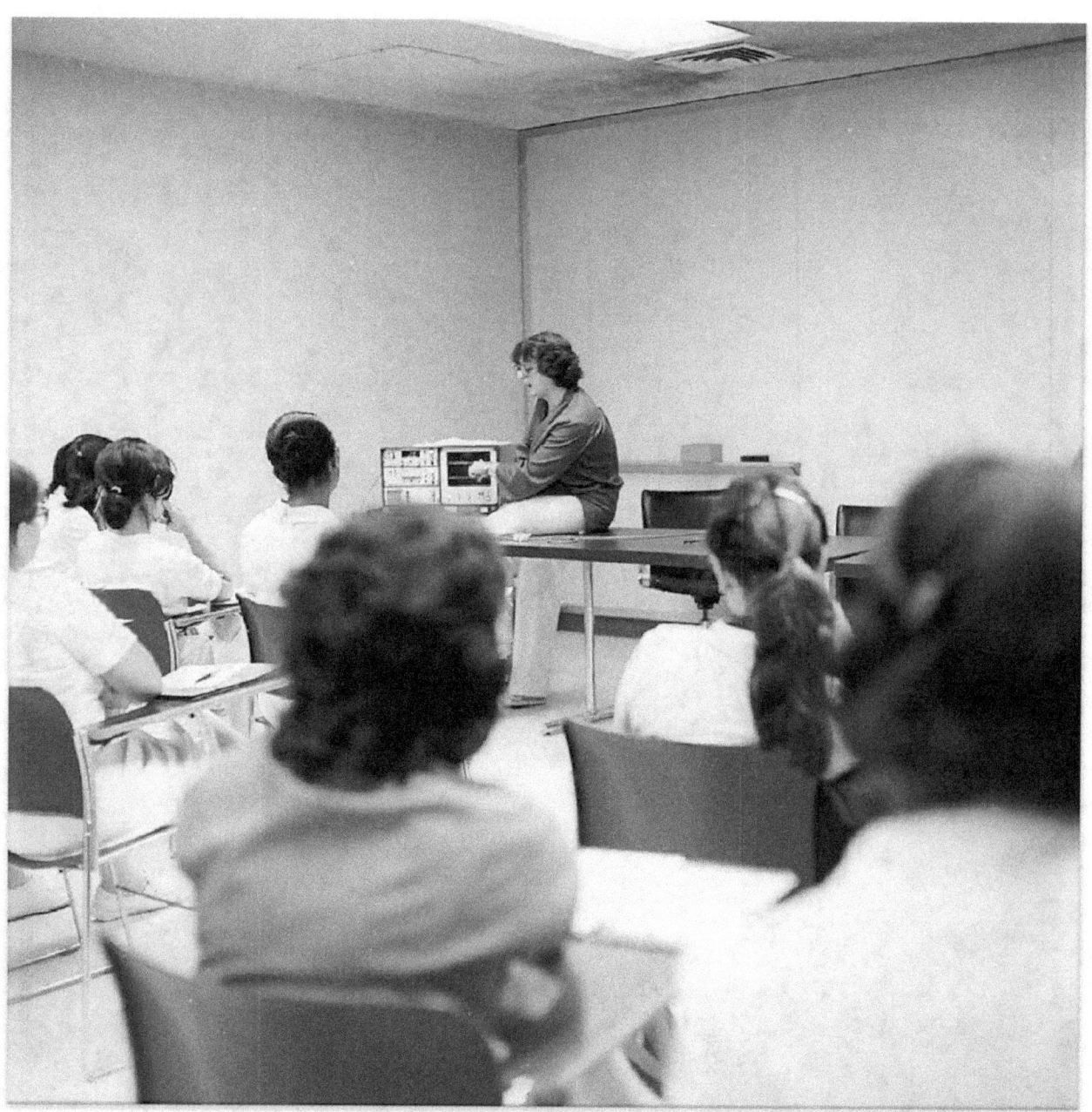

Service Education Instructor, demonstrating a new generation of cardiac monitor.

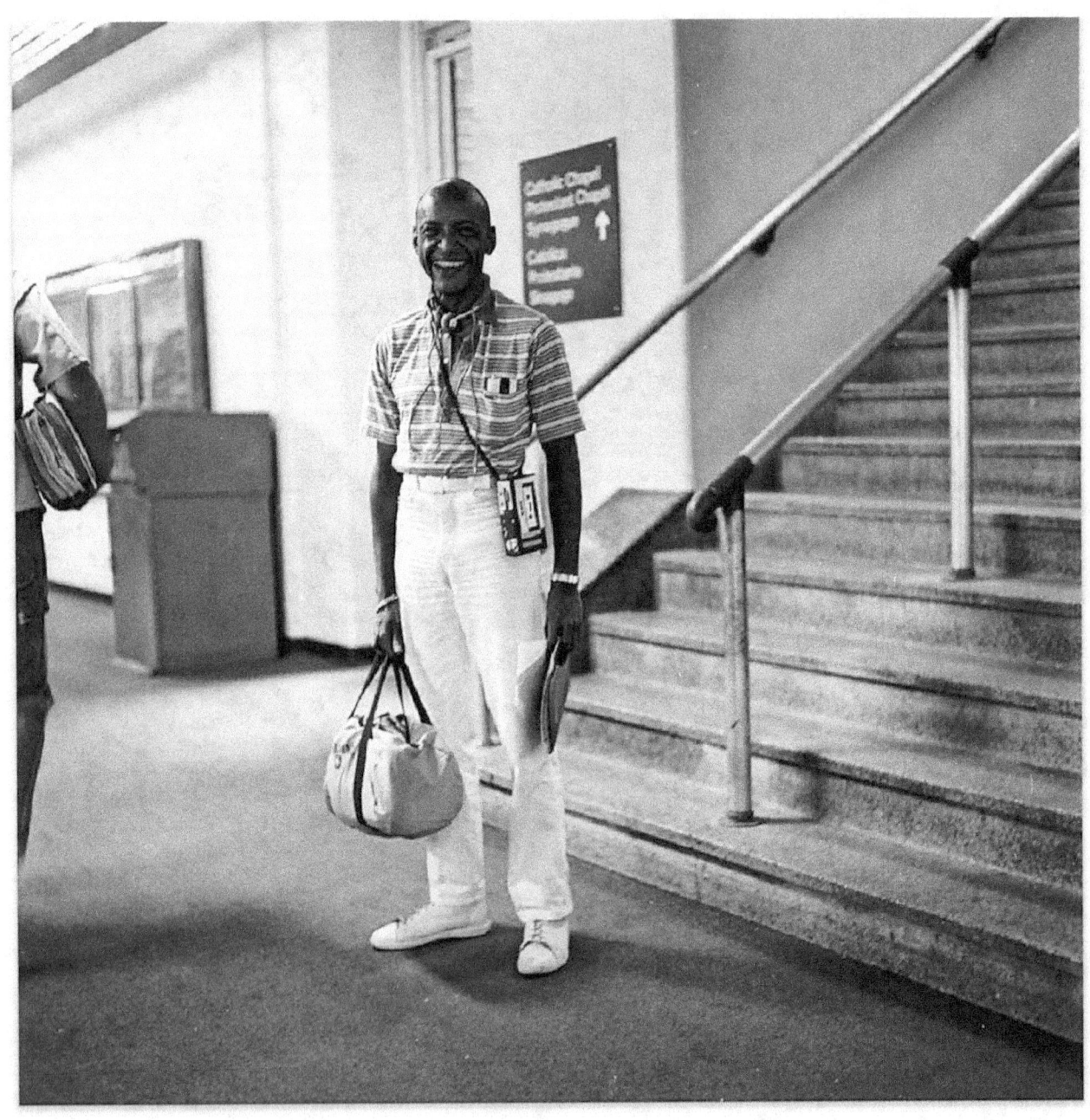

Nursing student.

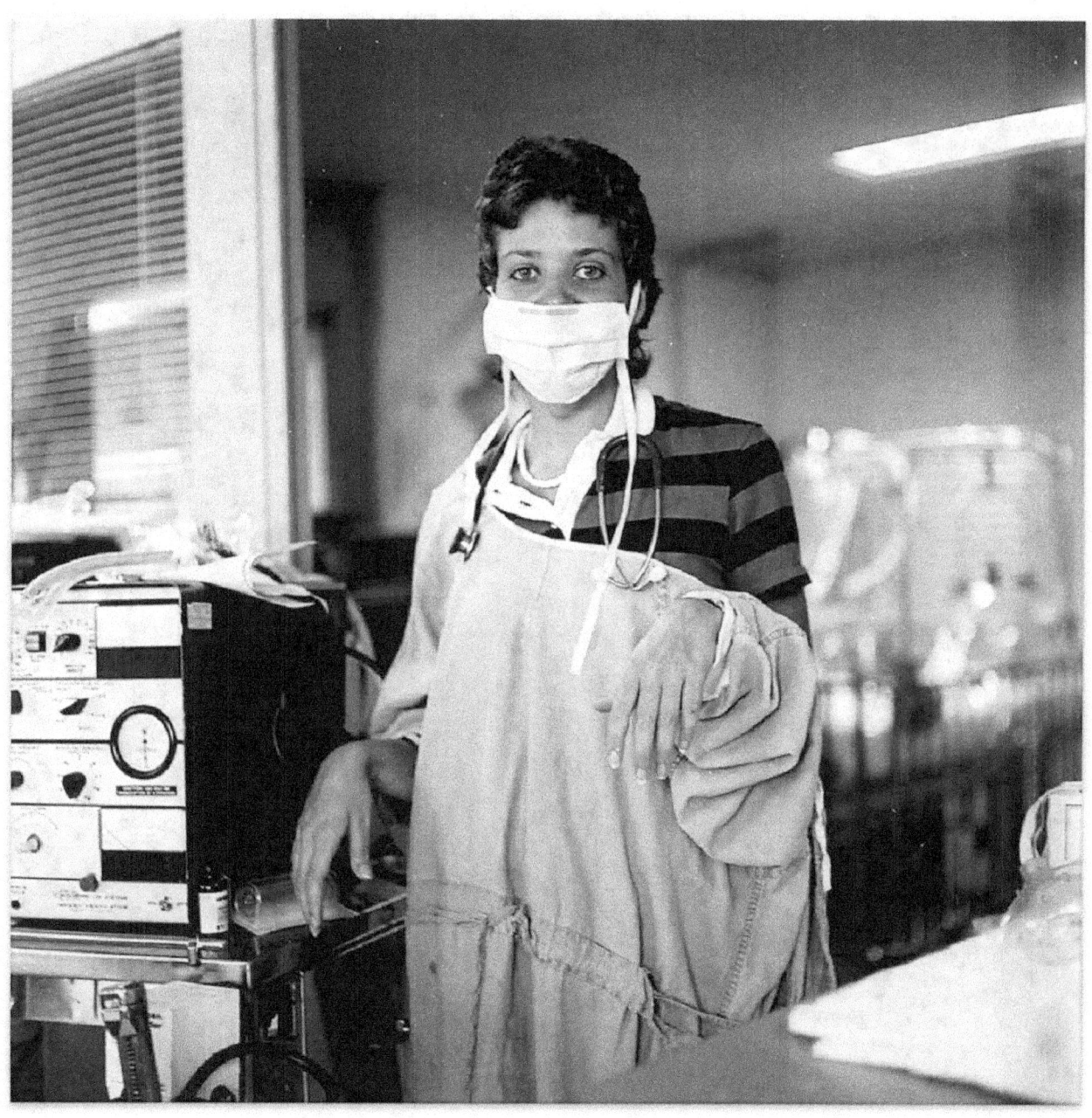

Neonatal nurse, next to ventilator.

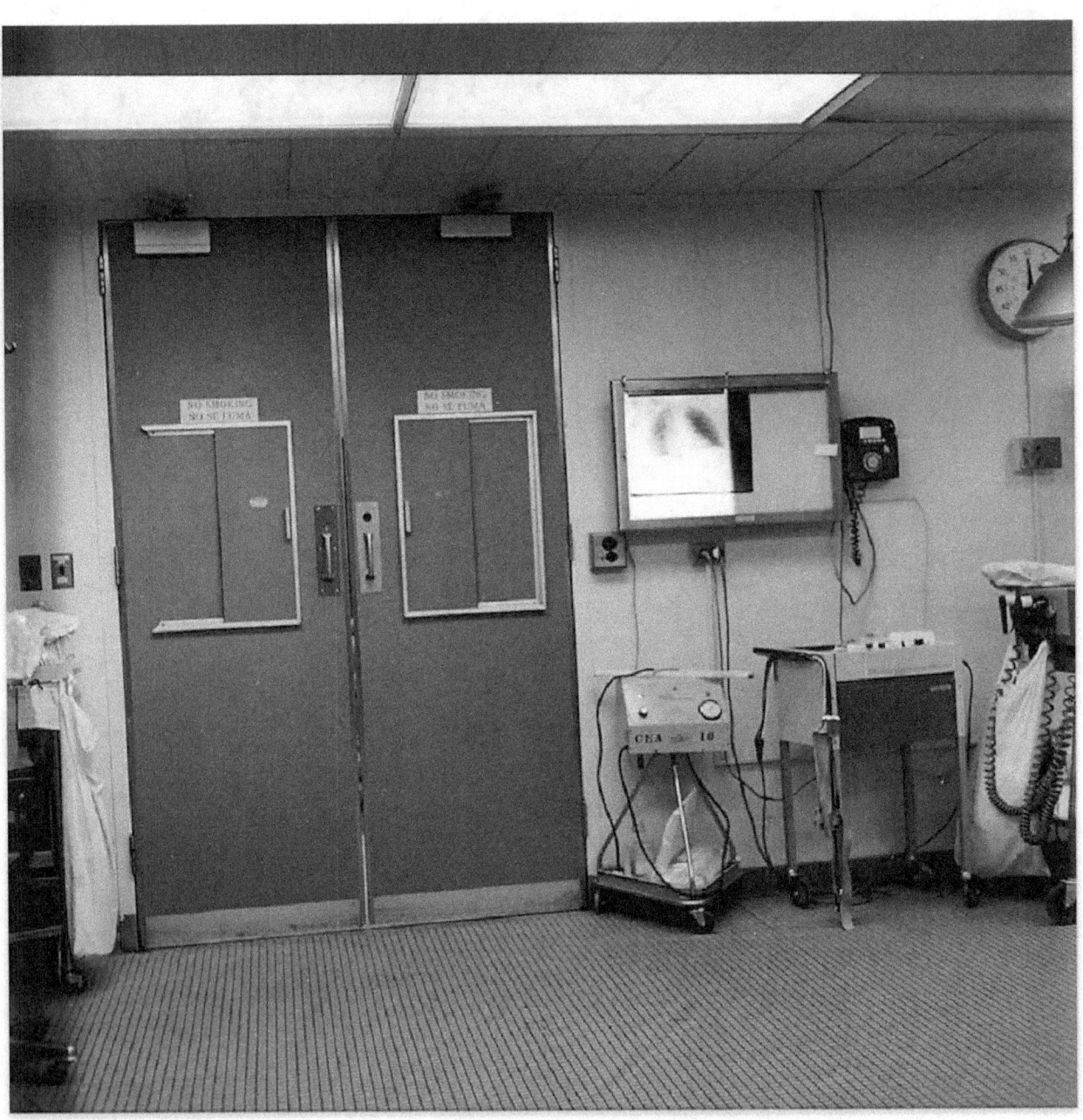

Emergency Department, (surgical) trauma room.

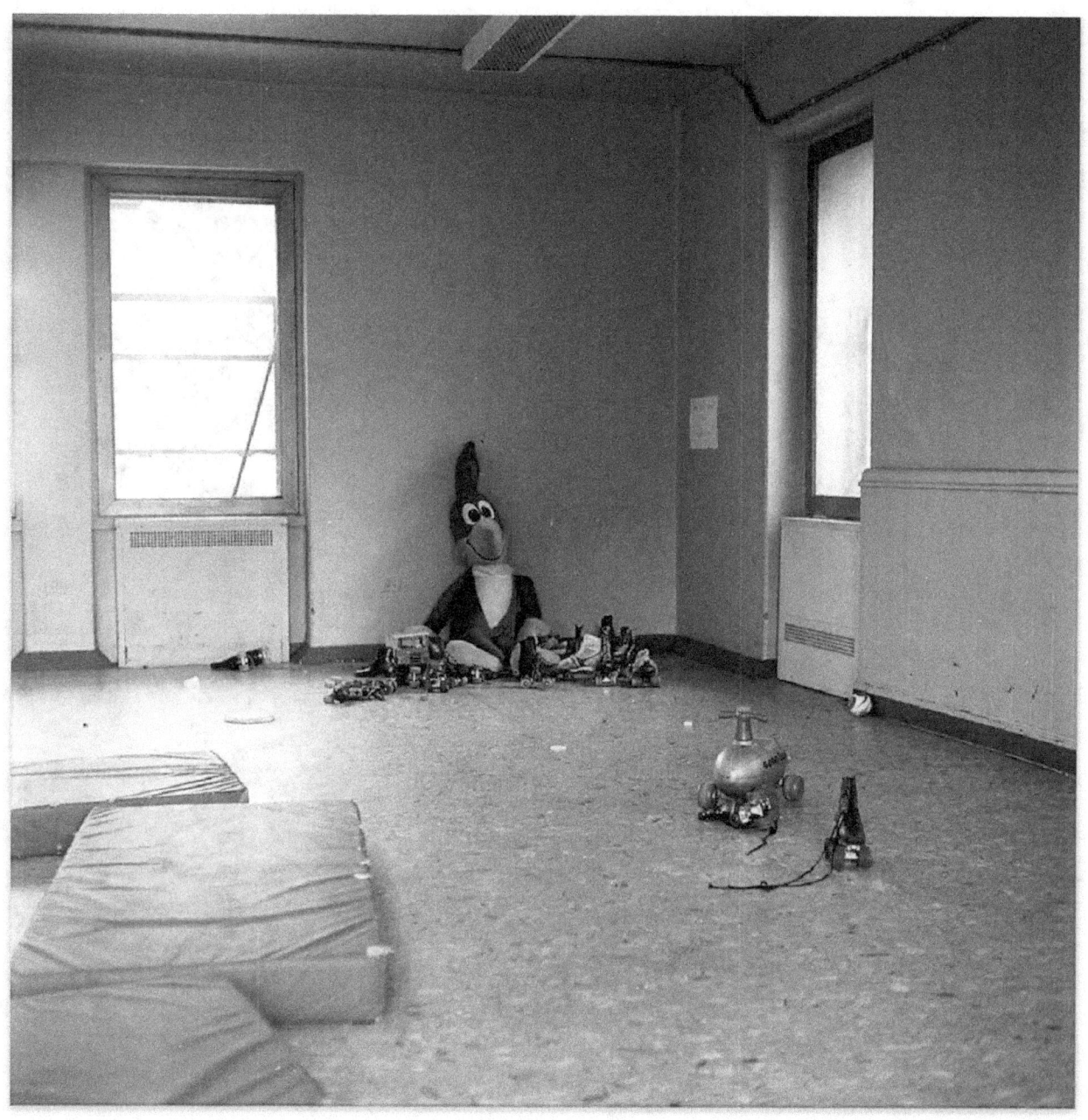

Pediatric Psychiatric Ward, play room, with roller skates.

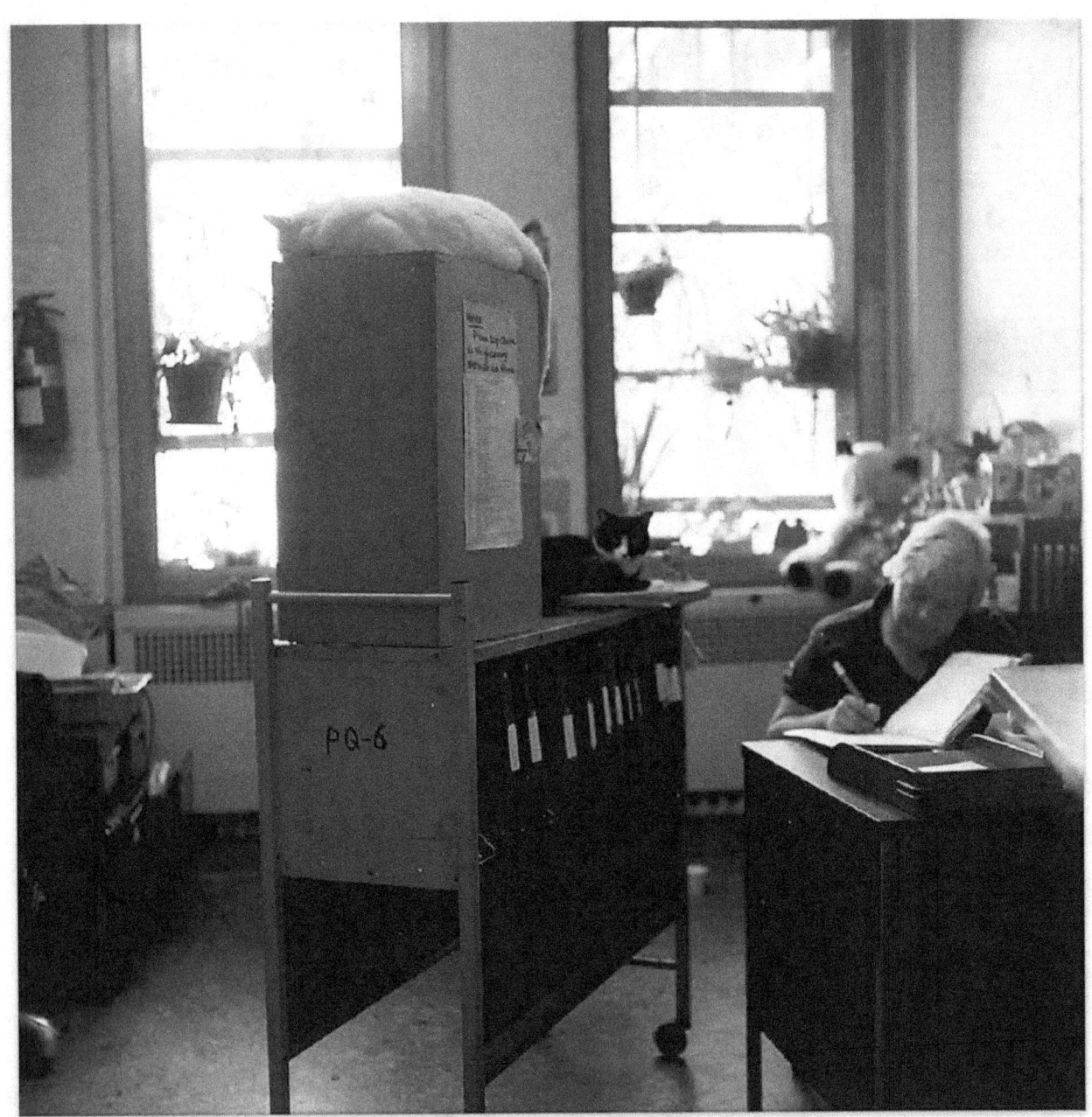

Pediatric Psychiatric office, and play therapy cats.

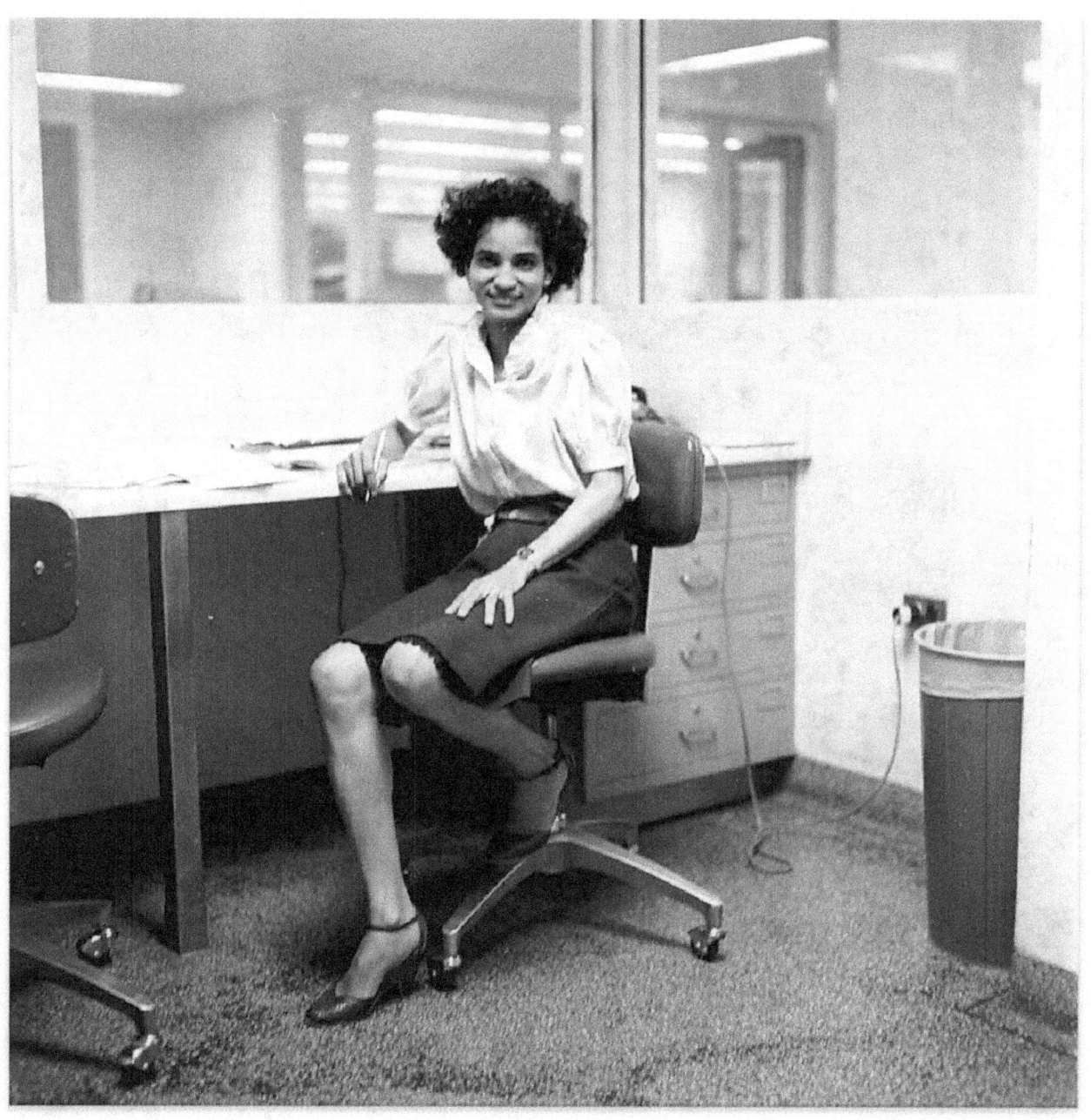

Administrative office.

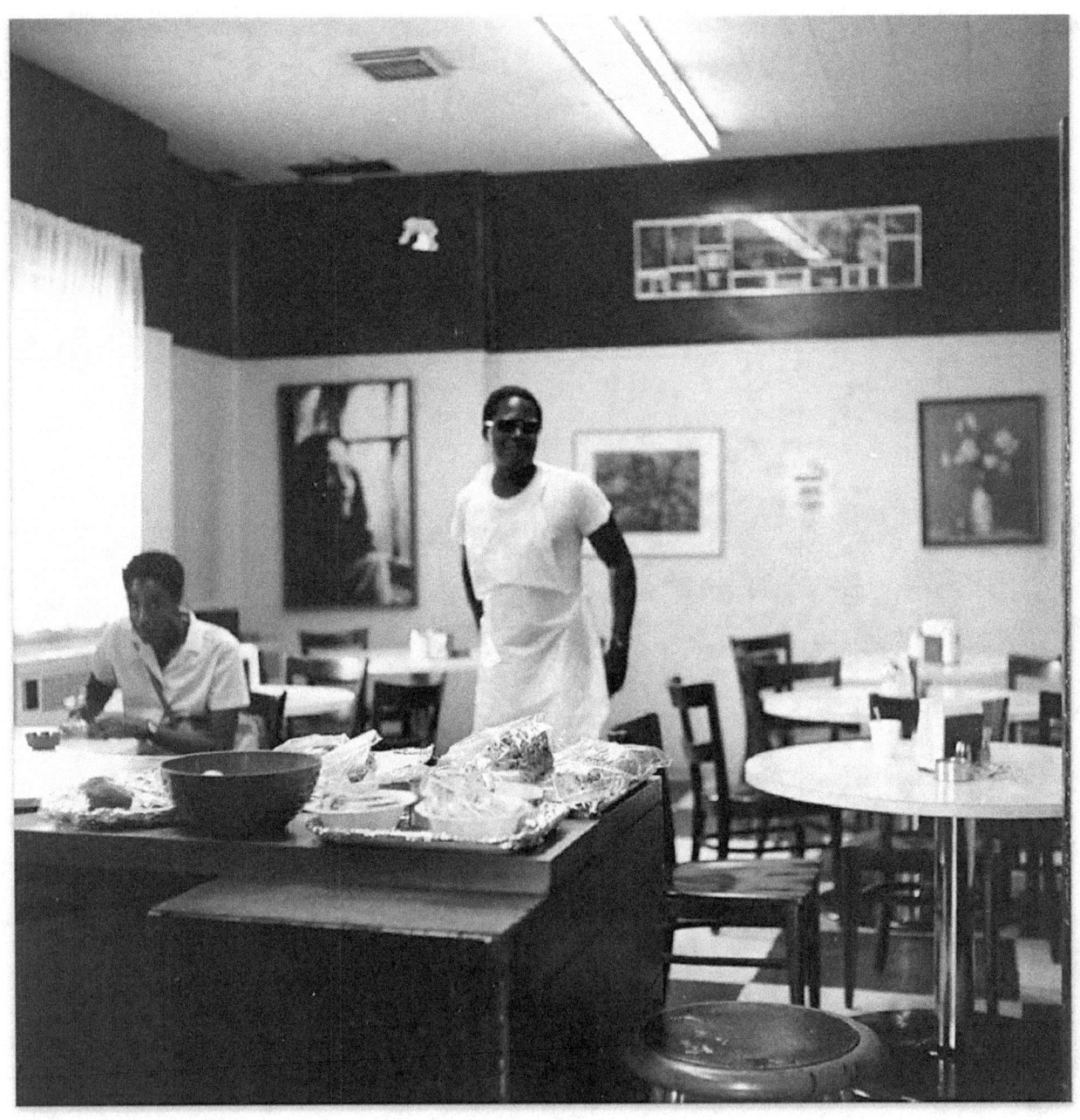

Staff cafeteria.

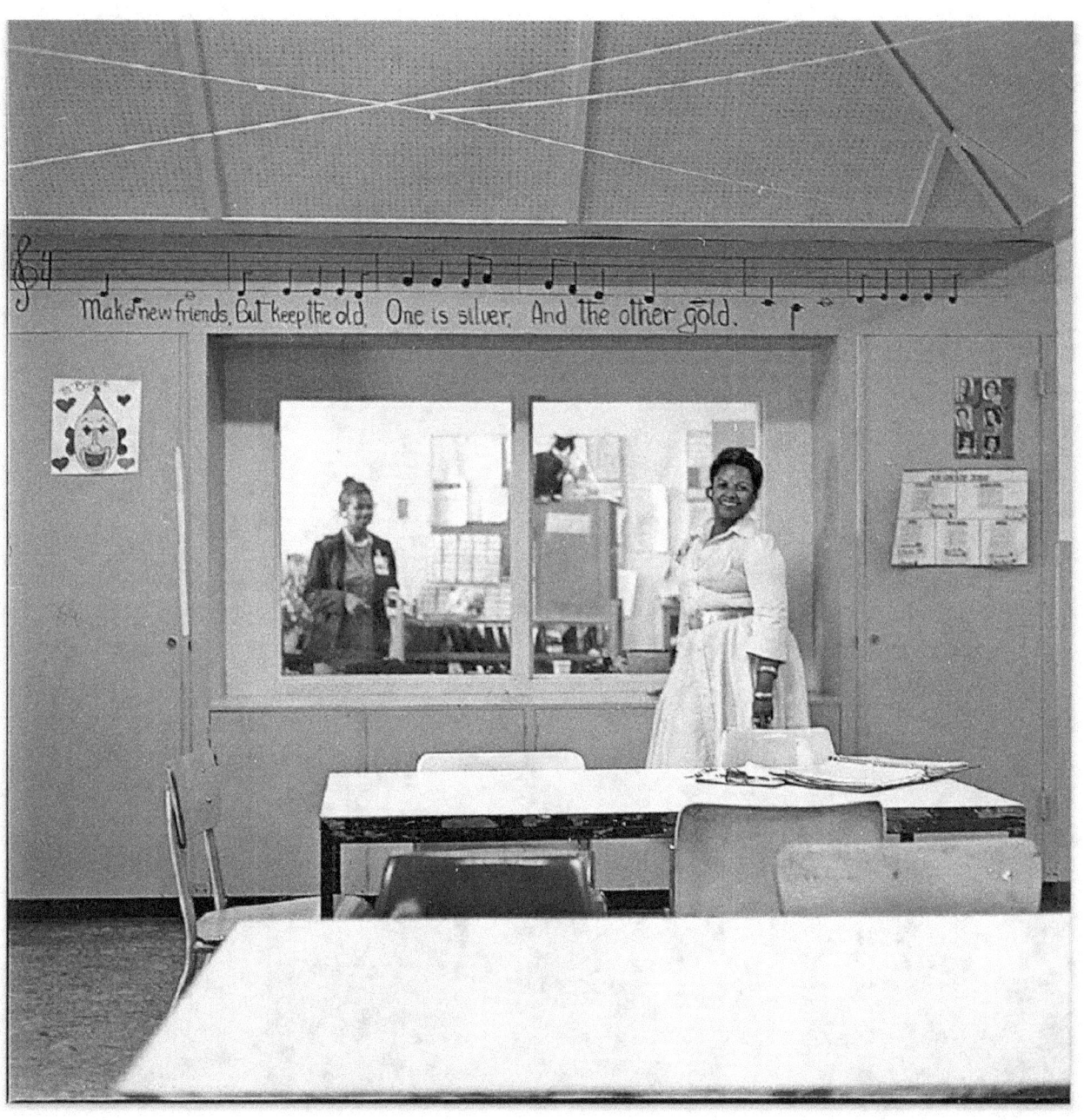

Psychiatry. Sign says: "Make new friends. But keep the old. One is silver, and the other gold."

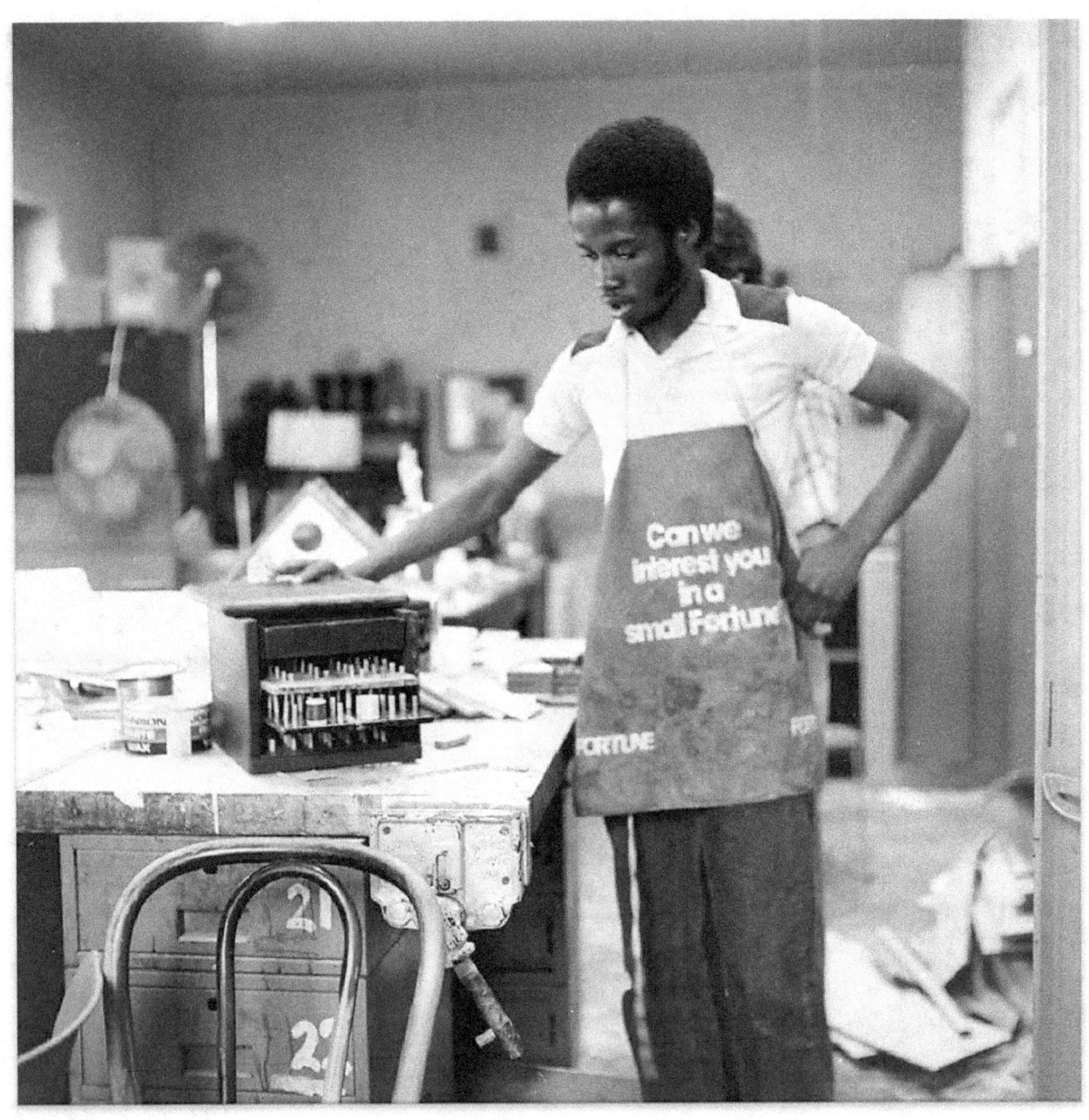

Woodworking shop for In/Out patient use.

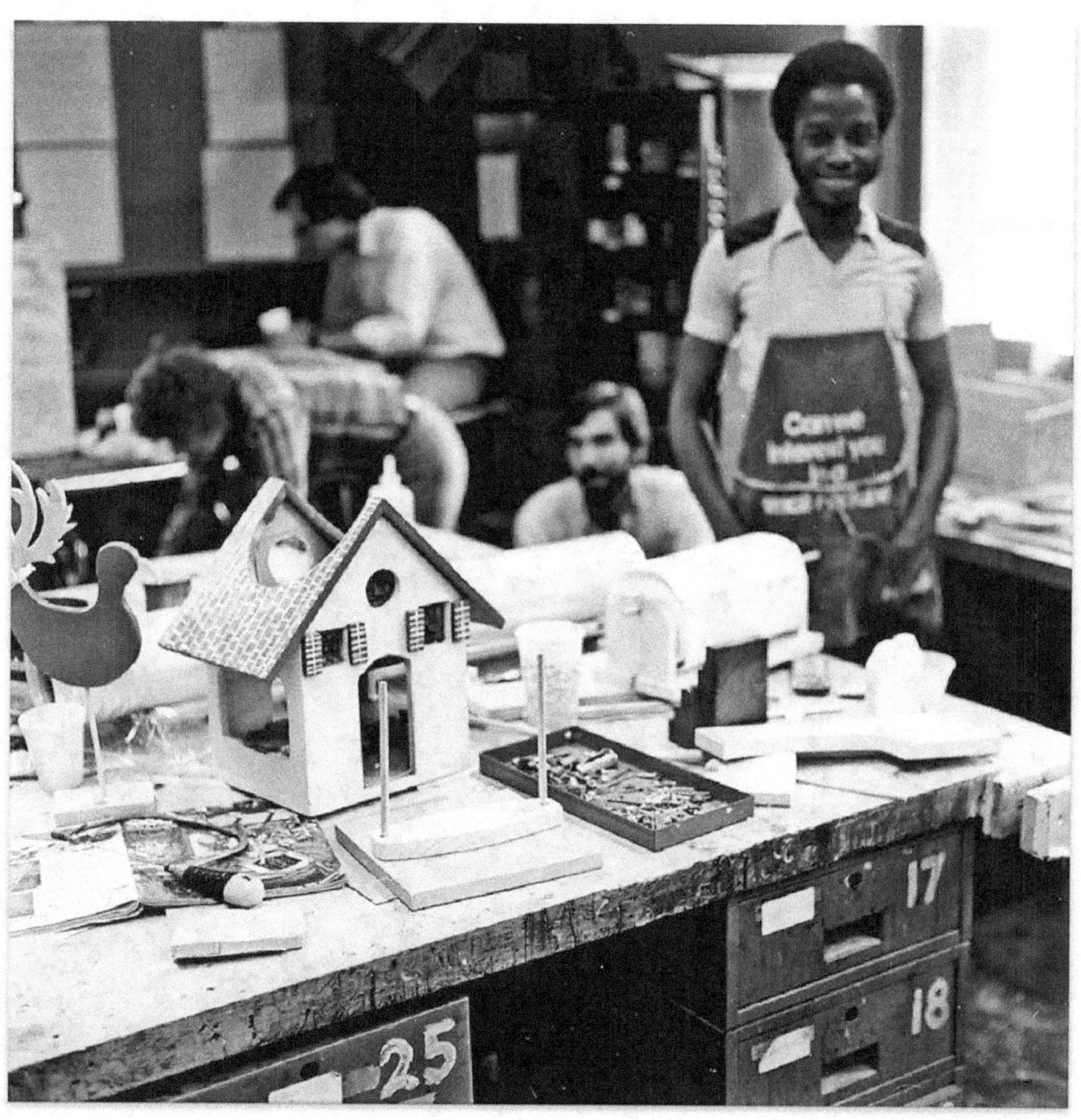

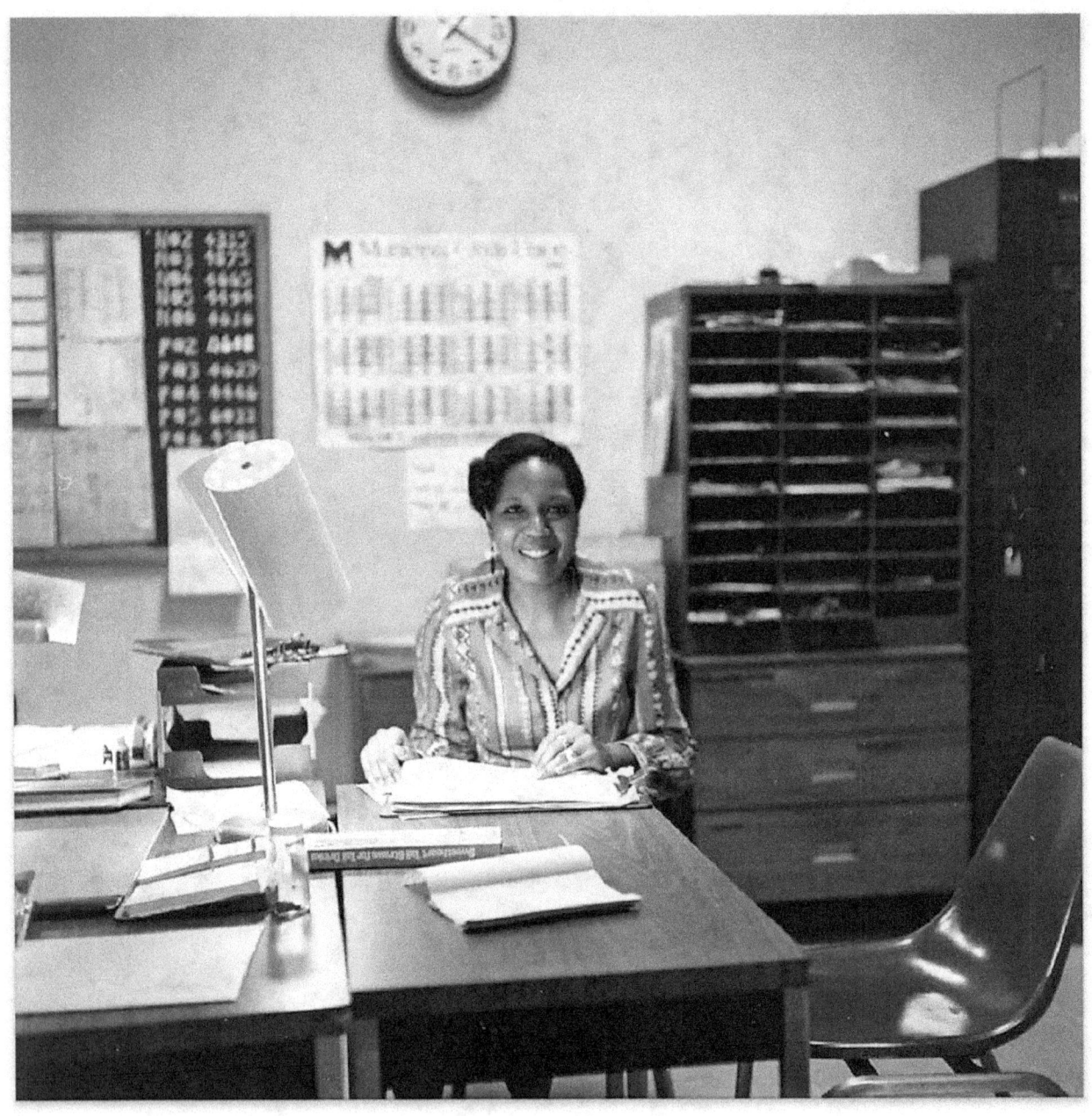

Nursing Supervisor.

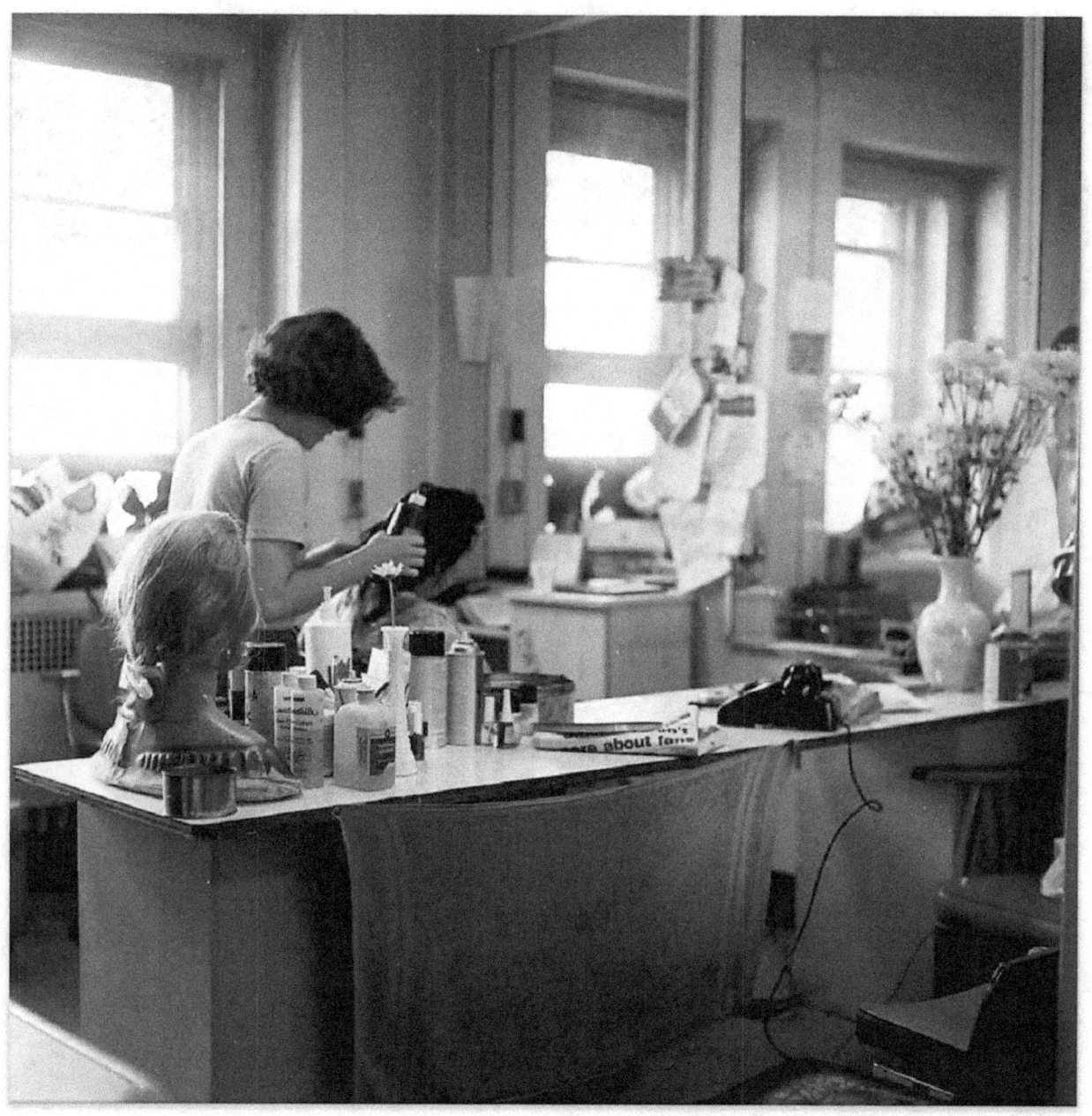

Beauty salon for patients.

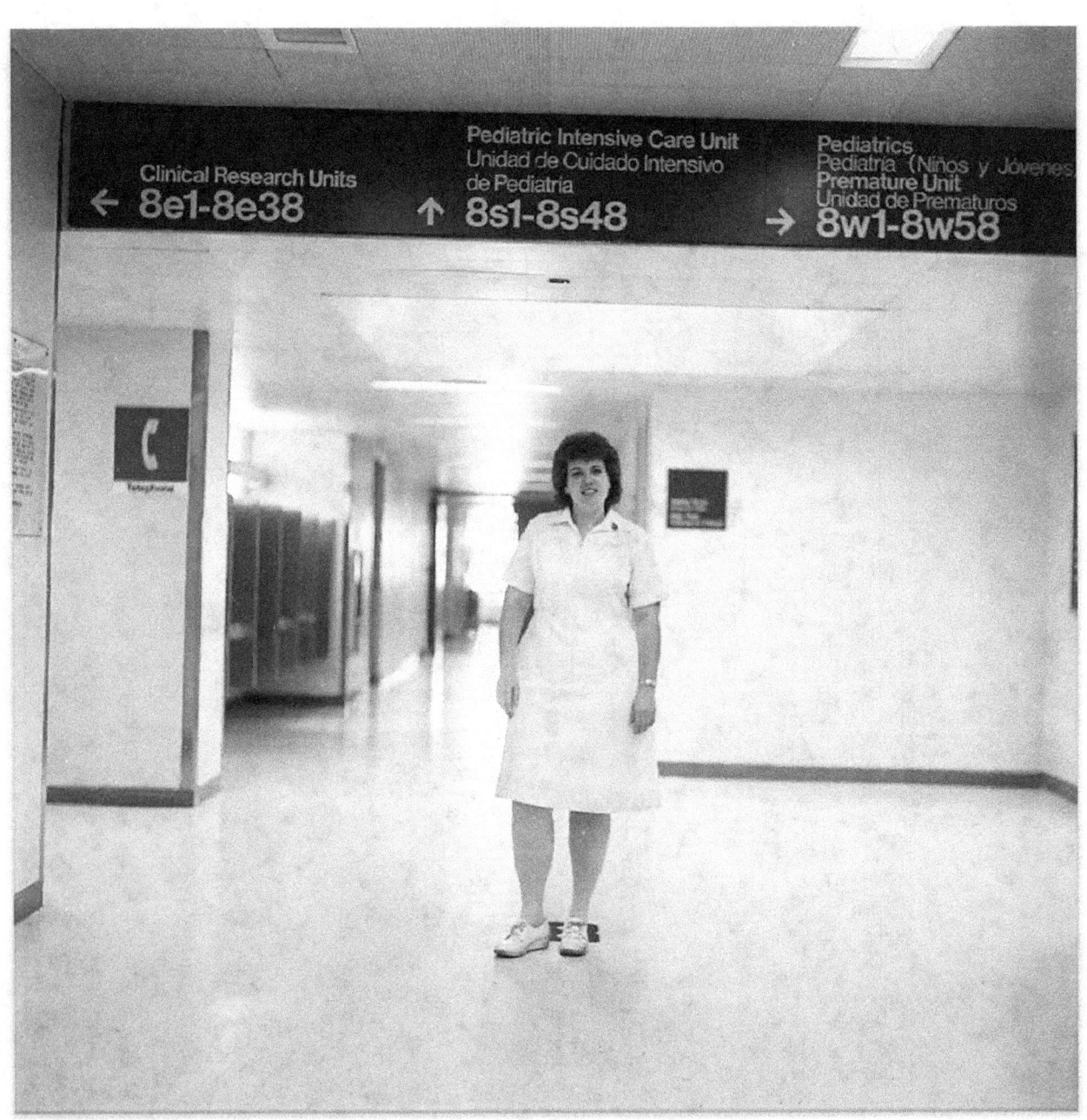

Nurse.

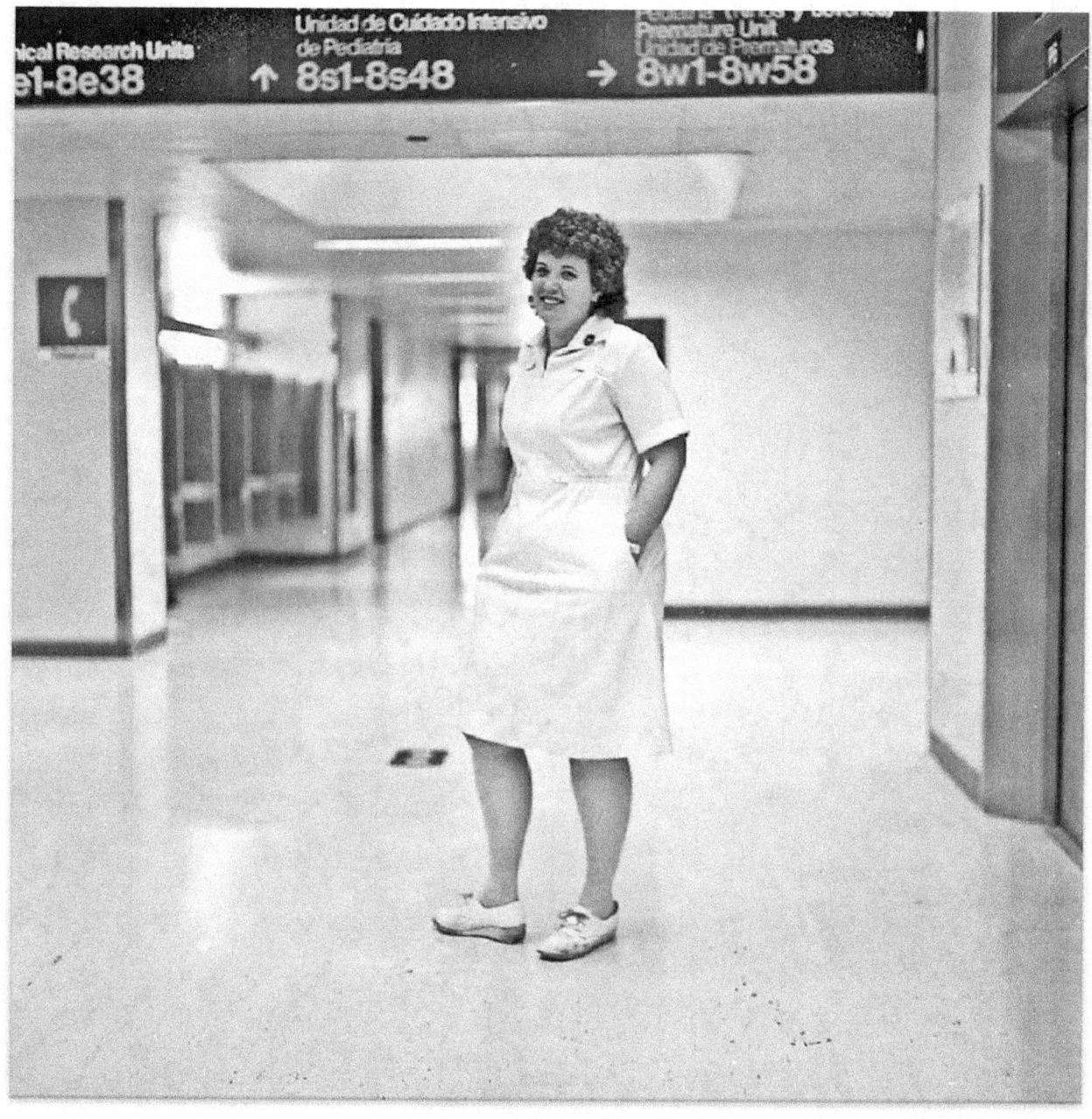

Times Square from a Bus, 2000

It is the summer of 2000, a warm evening, and I am returning home from work riding in a New York City Metropolitan Transportation Authority (MTA) bus. I have the good luck of finding a corner seat at the rear of the almost empty bus and I've got a window that I can slide open. Back then, it was still possible to find sliding windows. Tonight an open window means I can take photos through air, not through dirty glass.

This series was photographed in the time it took the M104 Broadway bus to travel through the Times Square area, down 7th Avenue, and then making the turn east onto 42nd Street. Today, 2018, a portion of the Times Square area is a pedestrian walk-way, and another change, the M104 bus no longer turns east onto 42nd Street, but continues down 7th and then west onto 41st. Even so, the same vantage points are still possible.

I was using an inexpensive early digital camera, and the light was just perfect.

Just plain good luck.

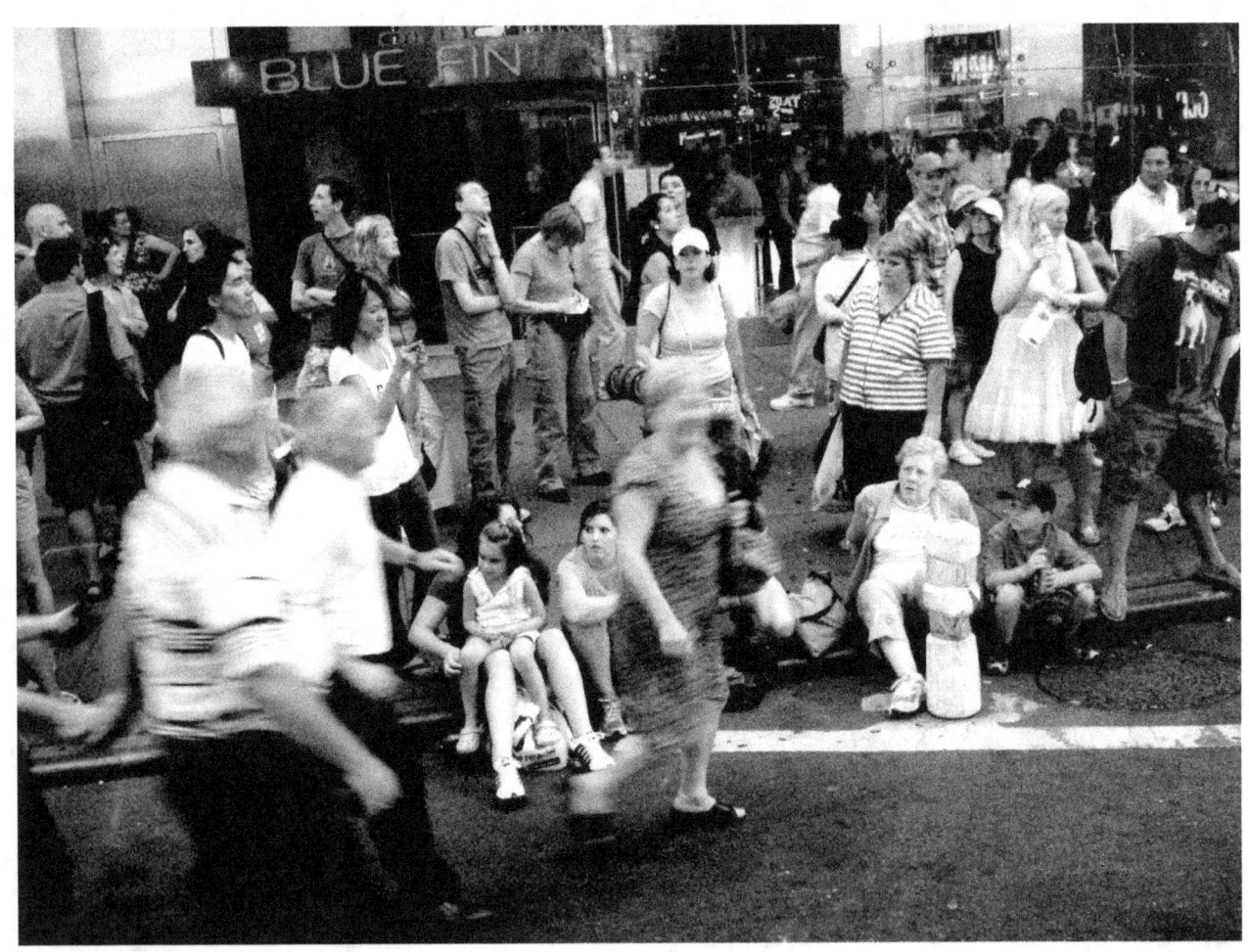

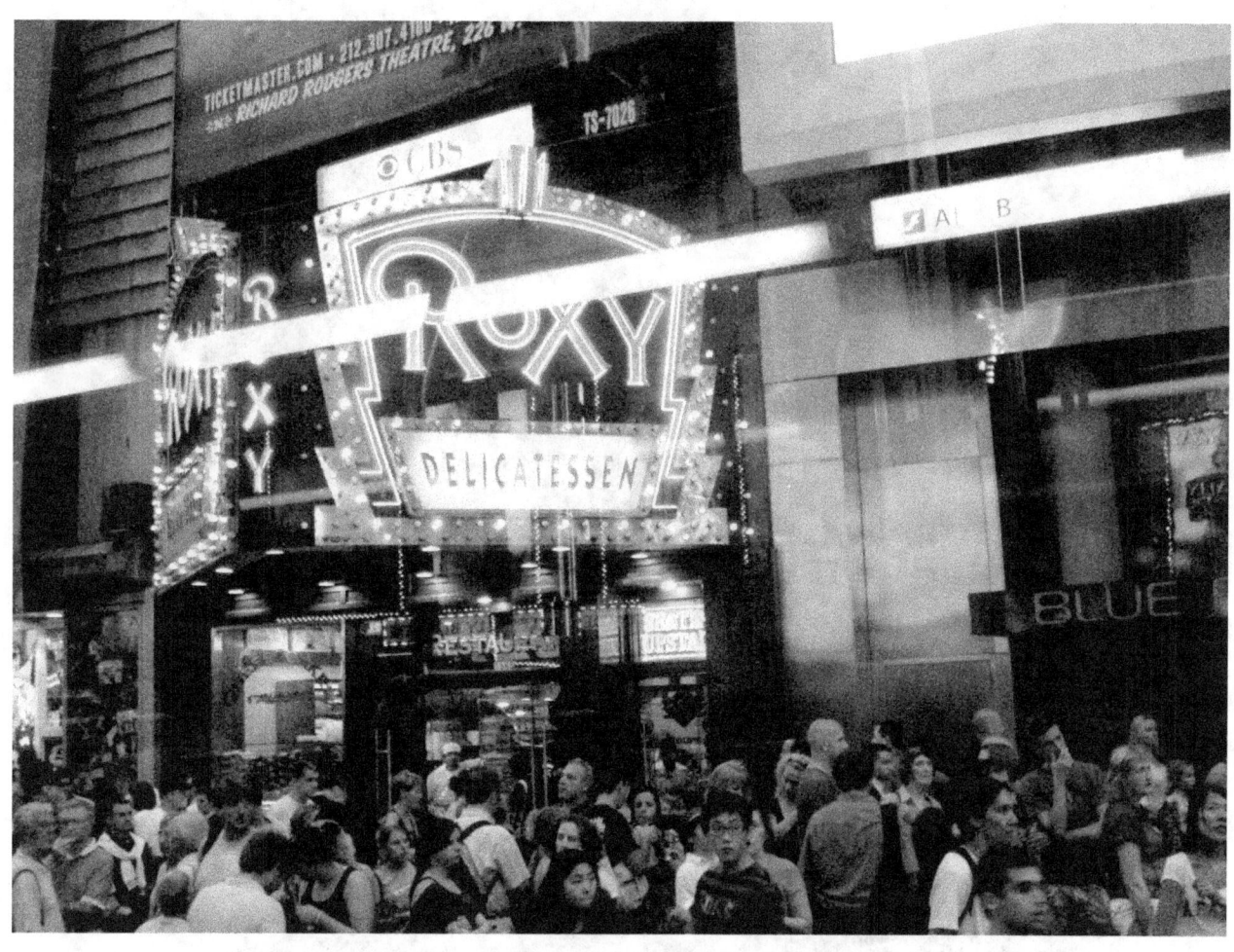

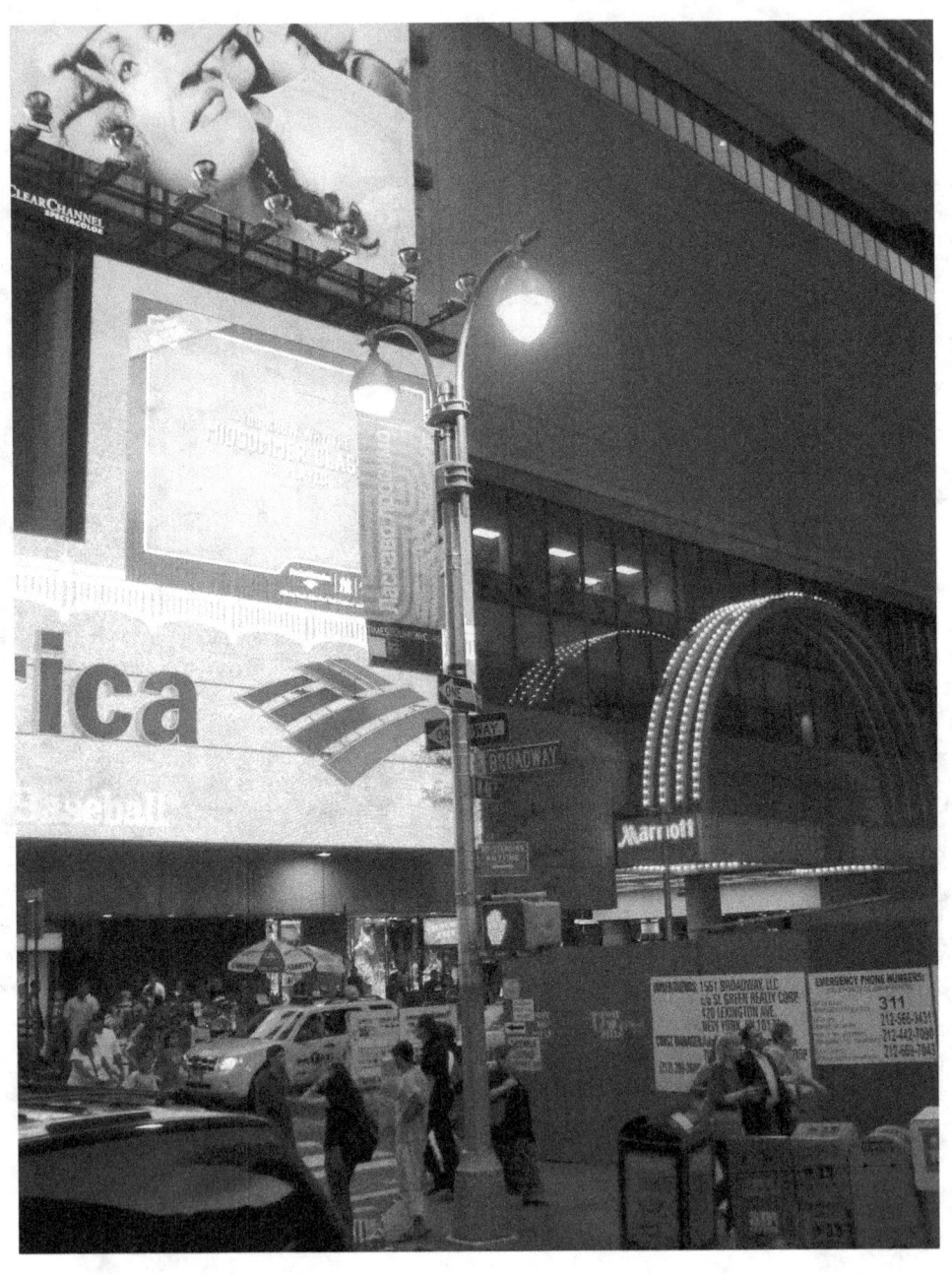

Times Square from a Bus, 2000

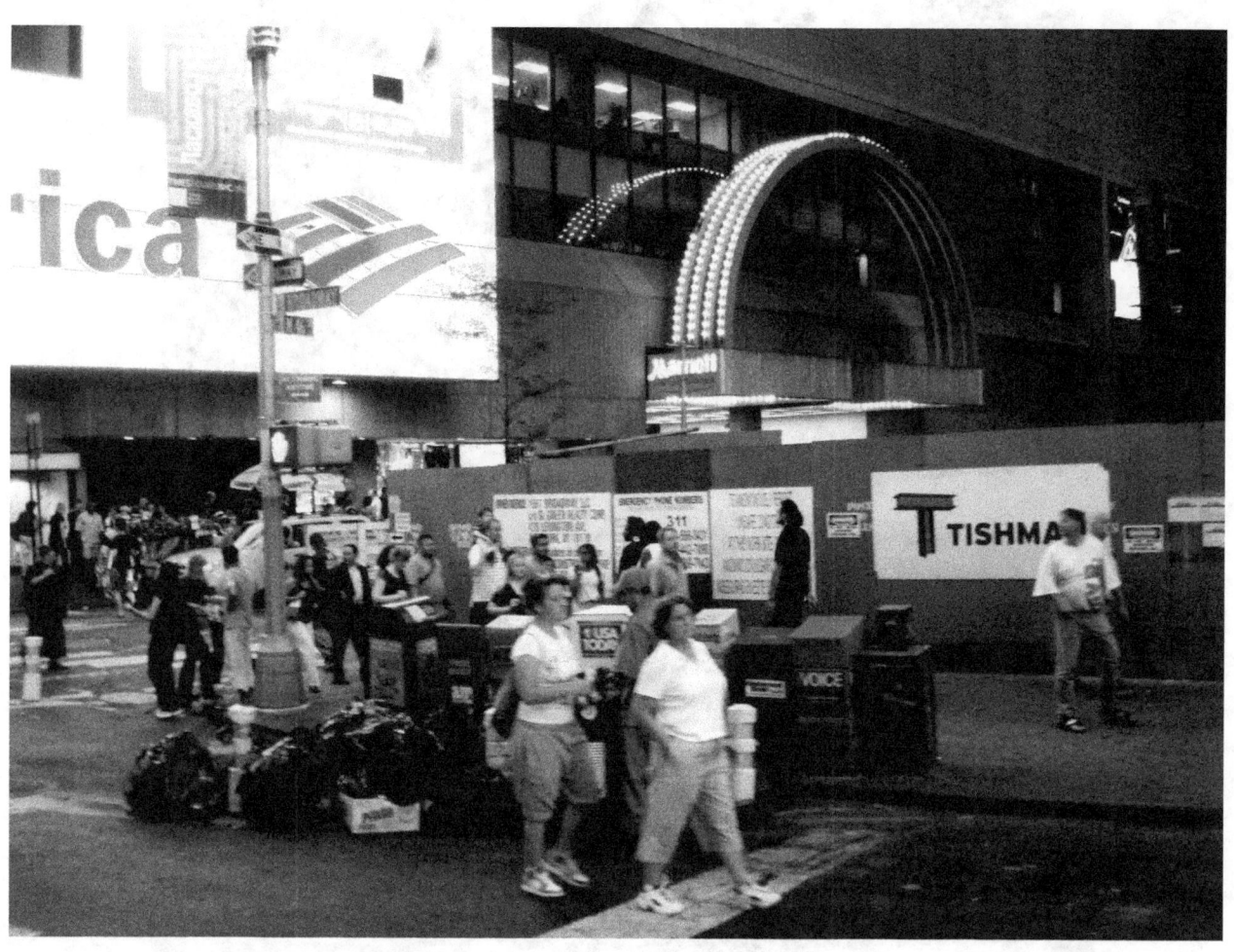

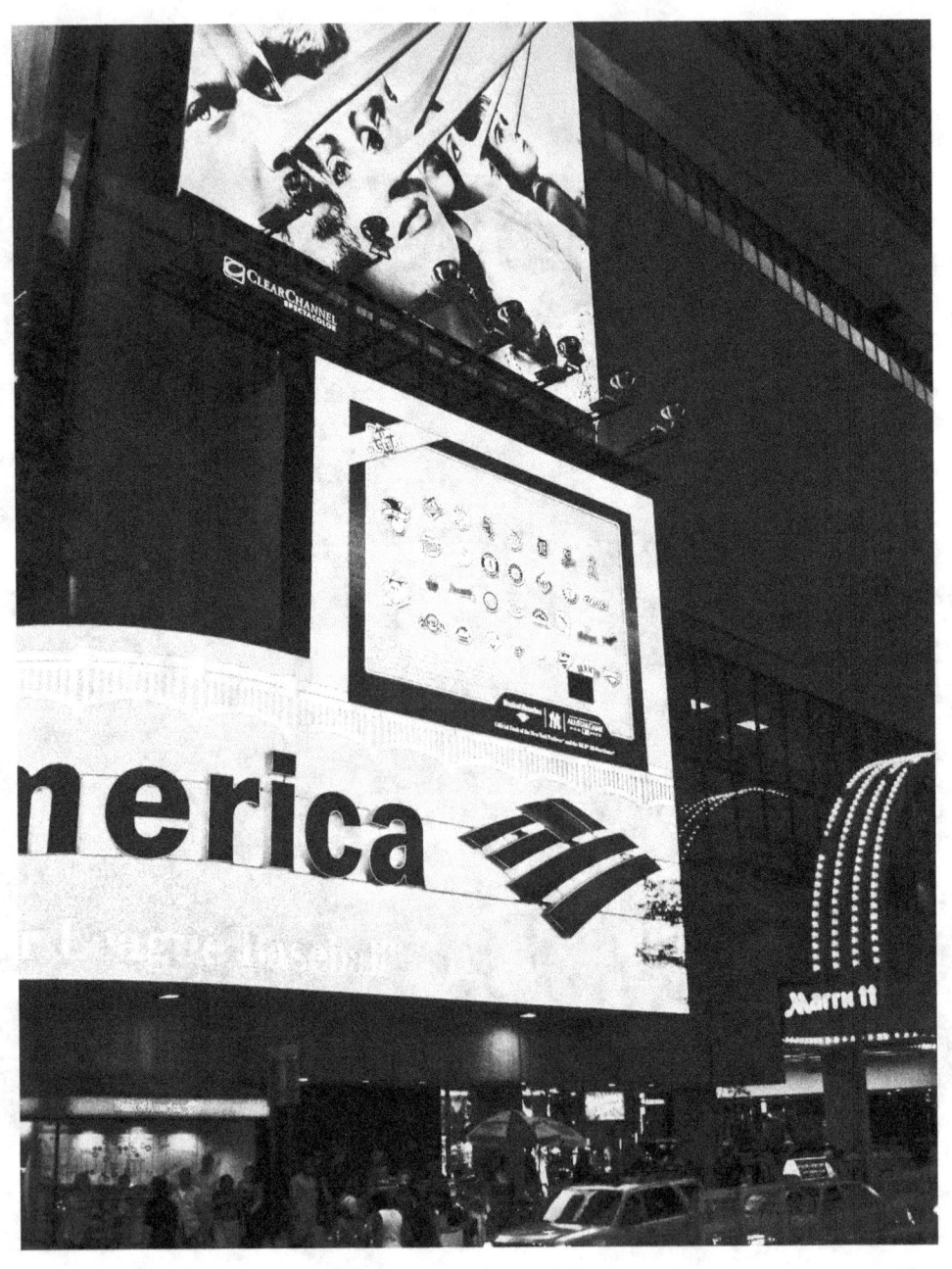

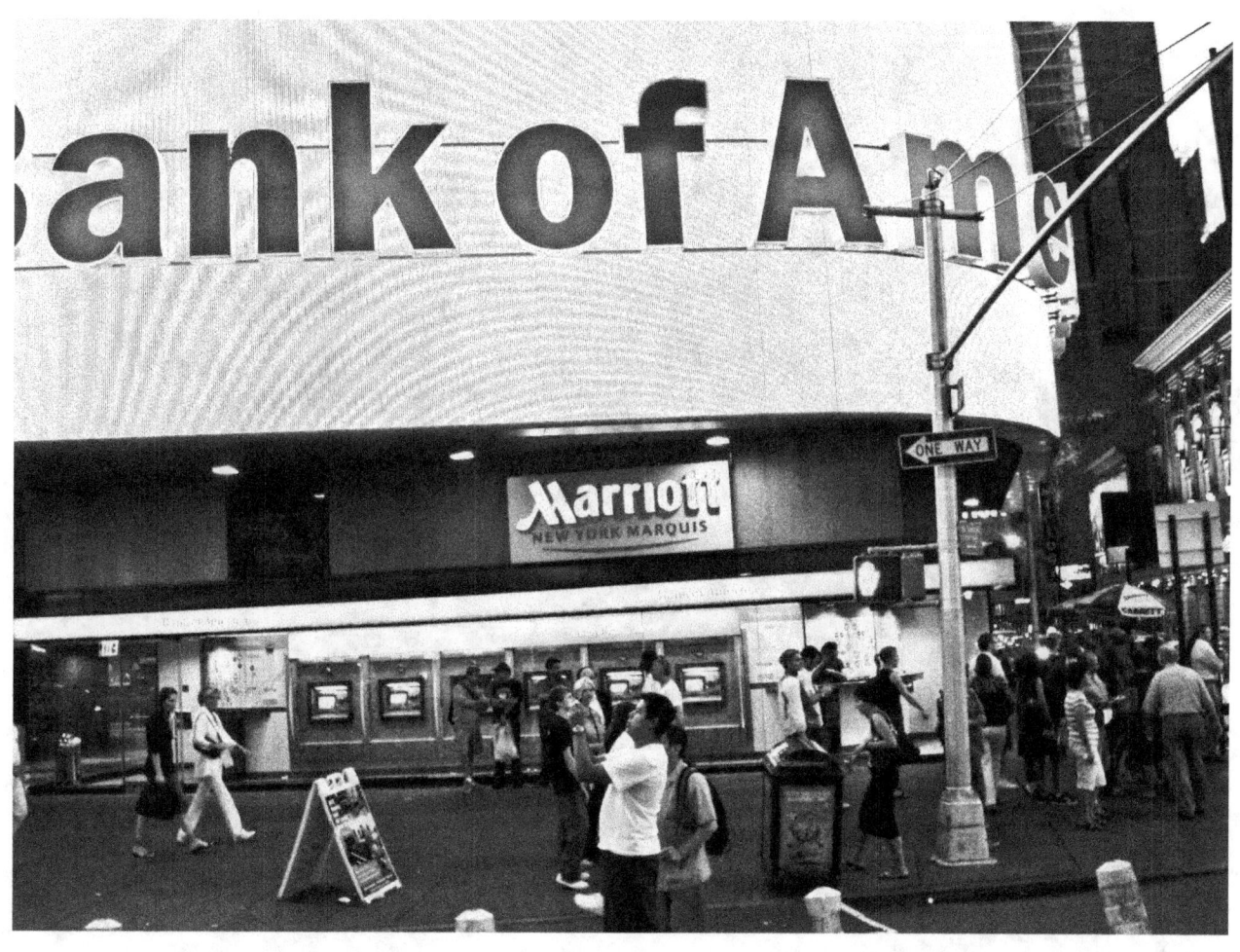

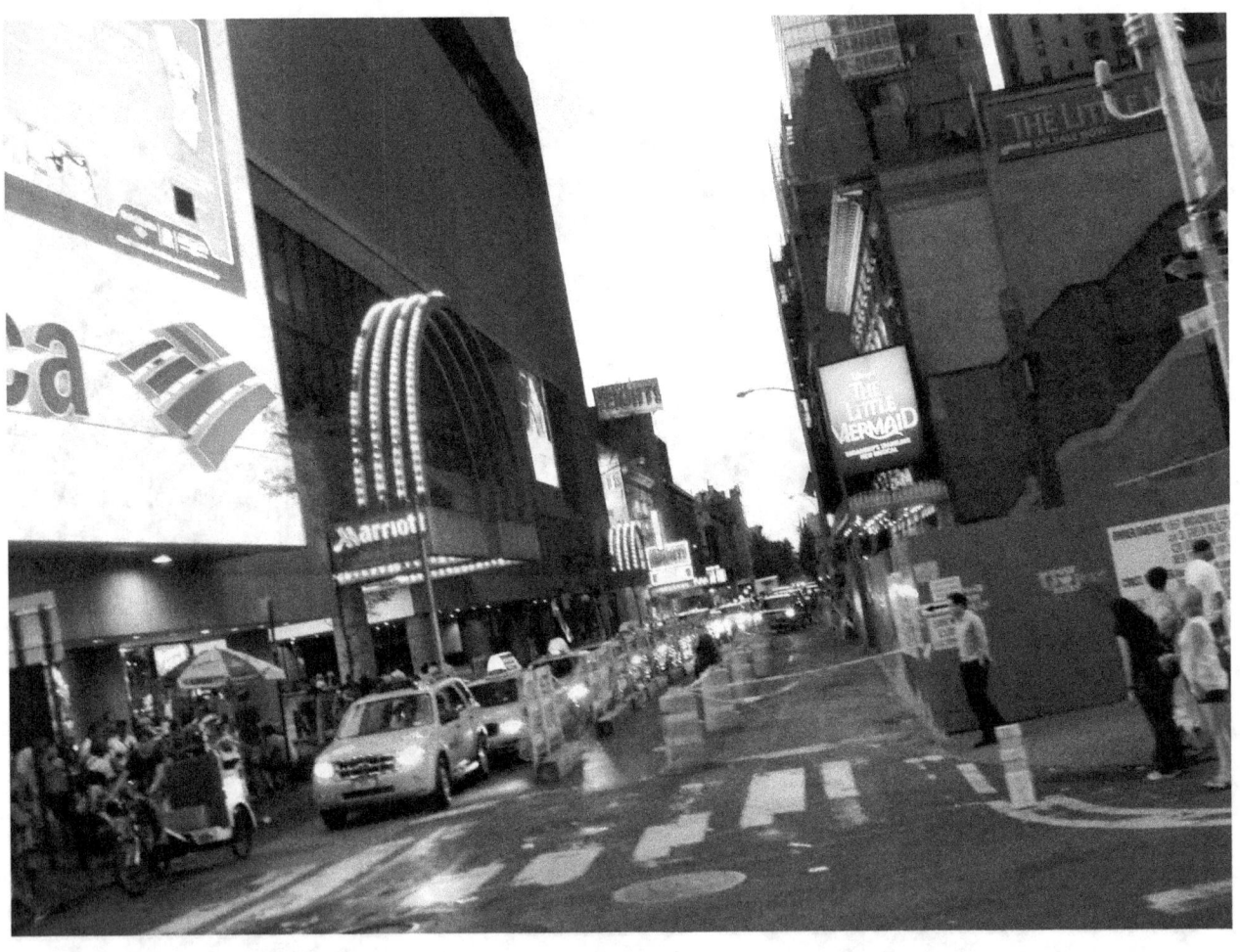

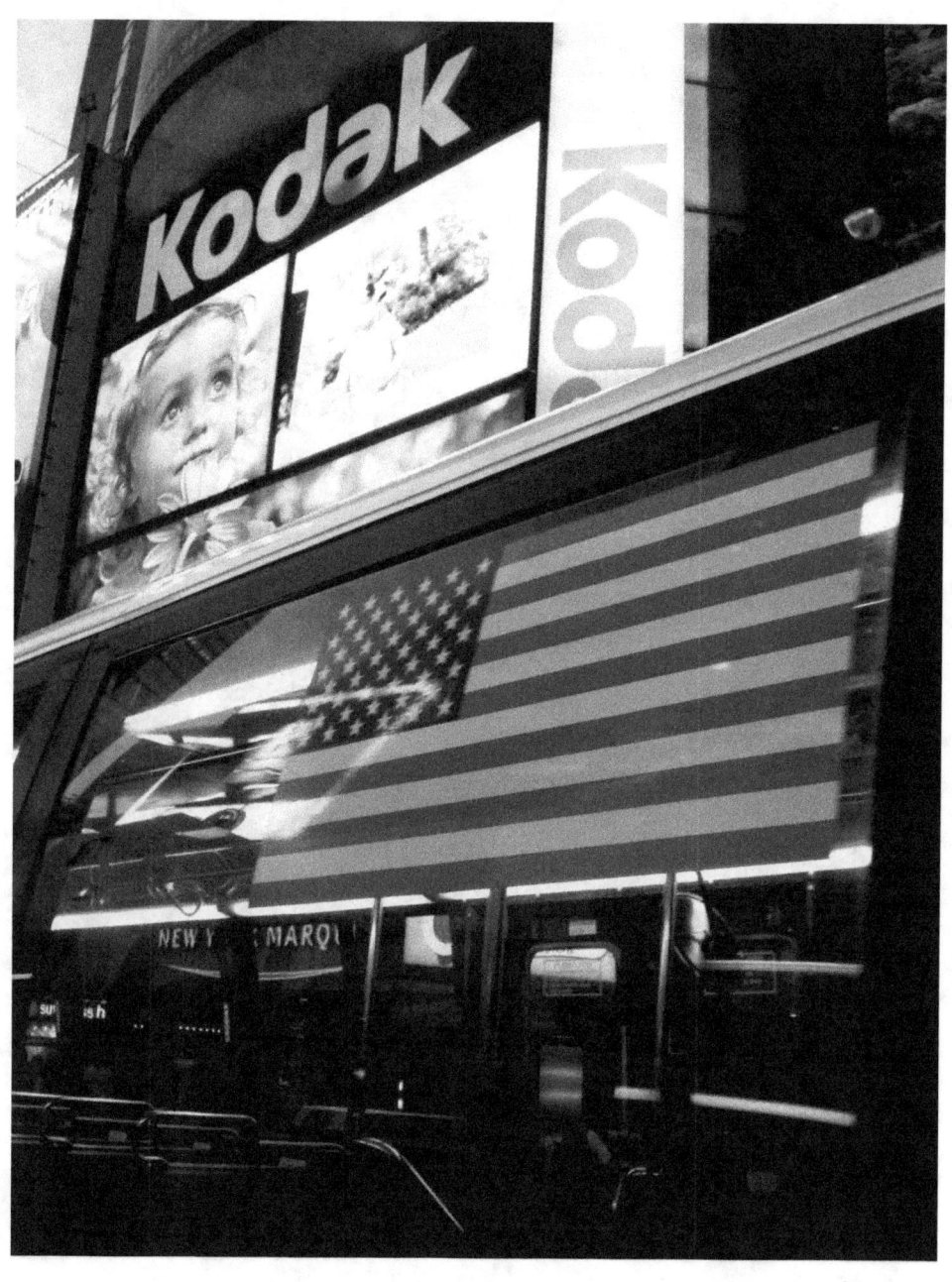

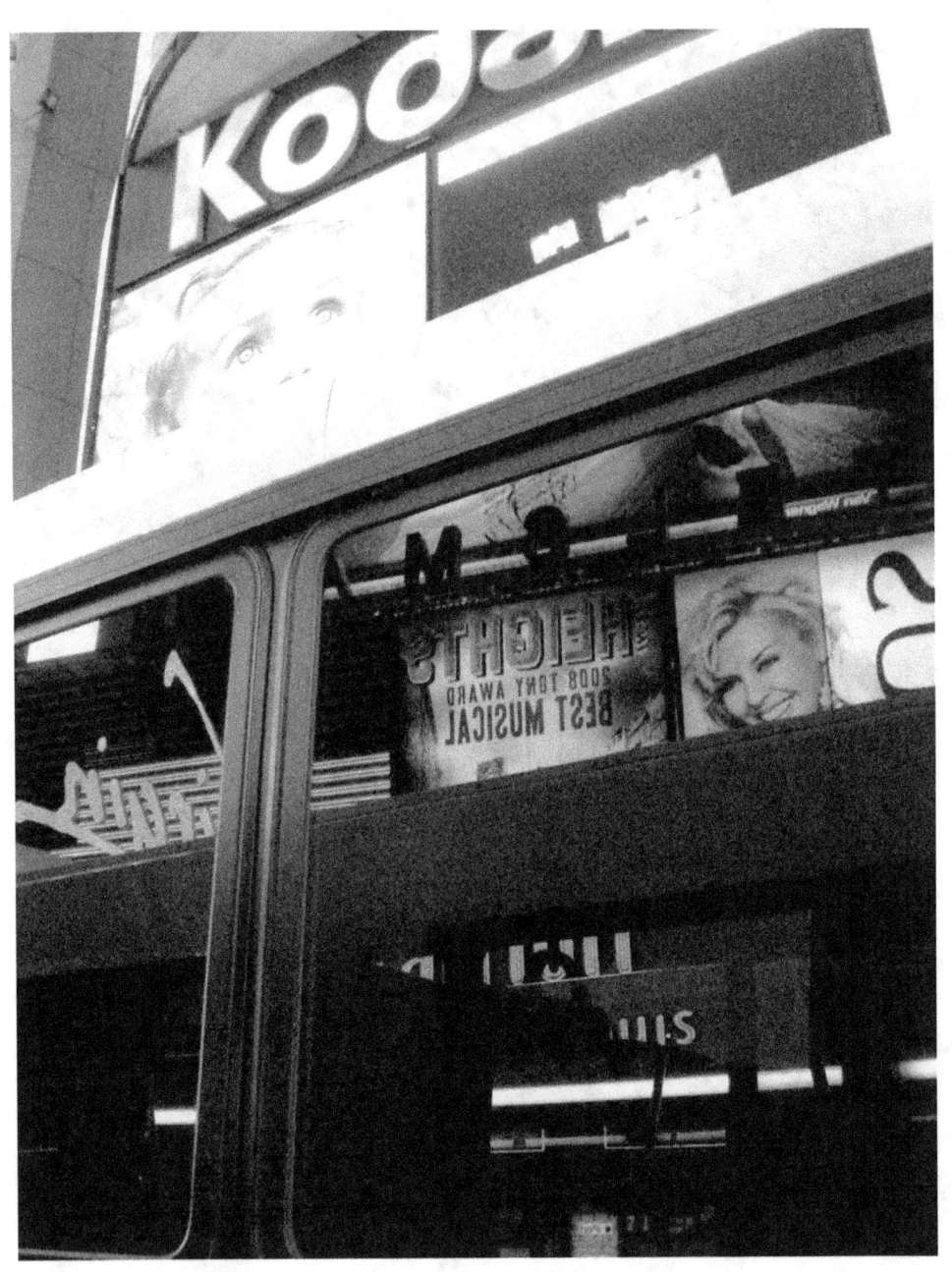

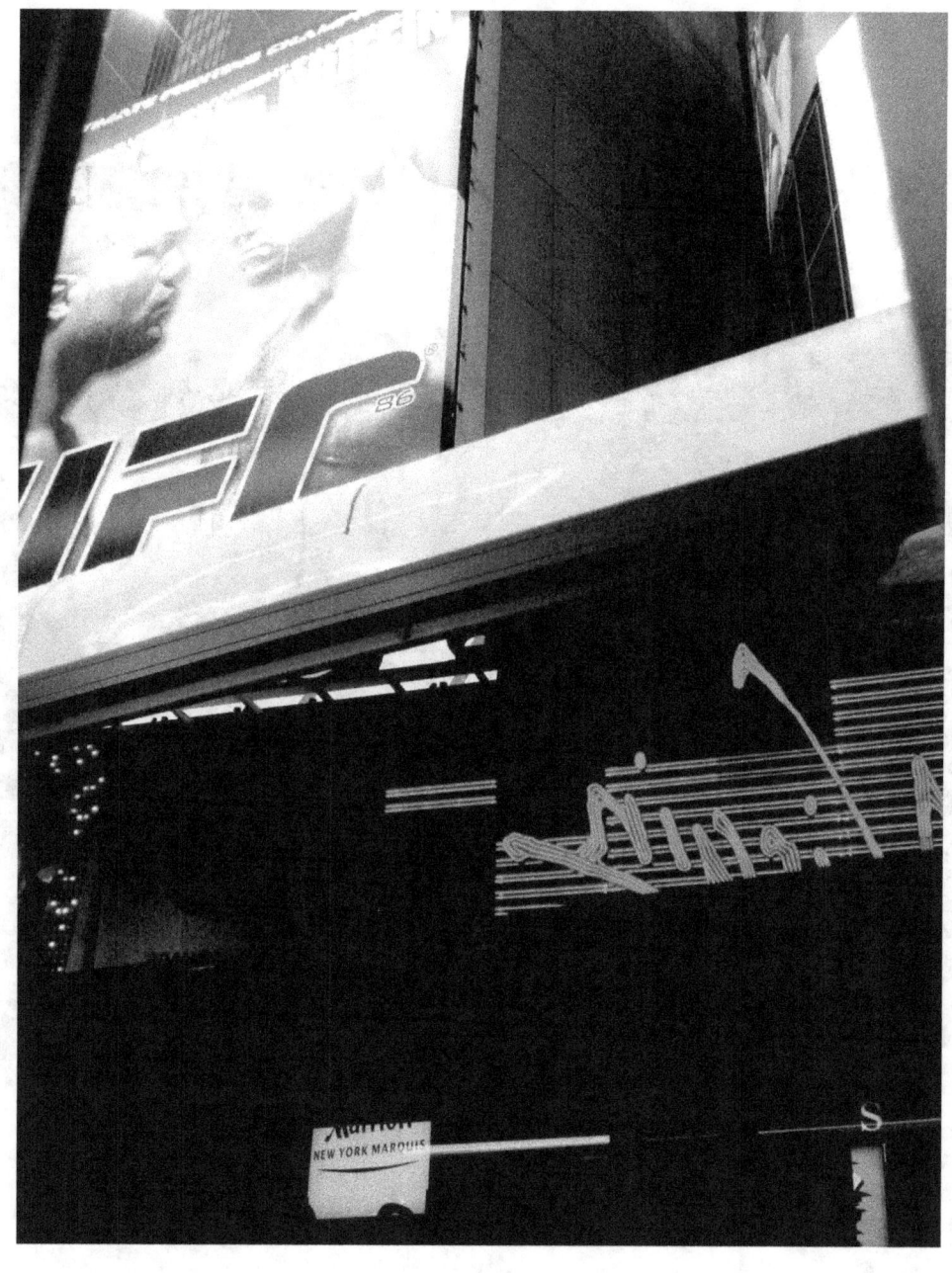

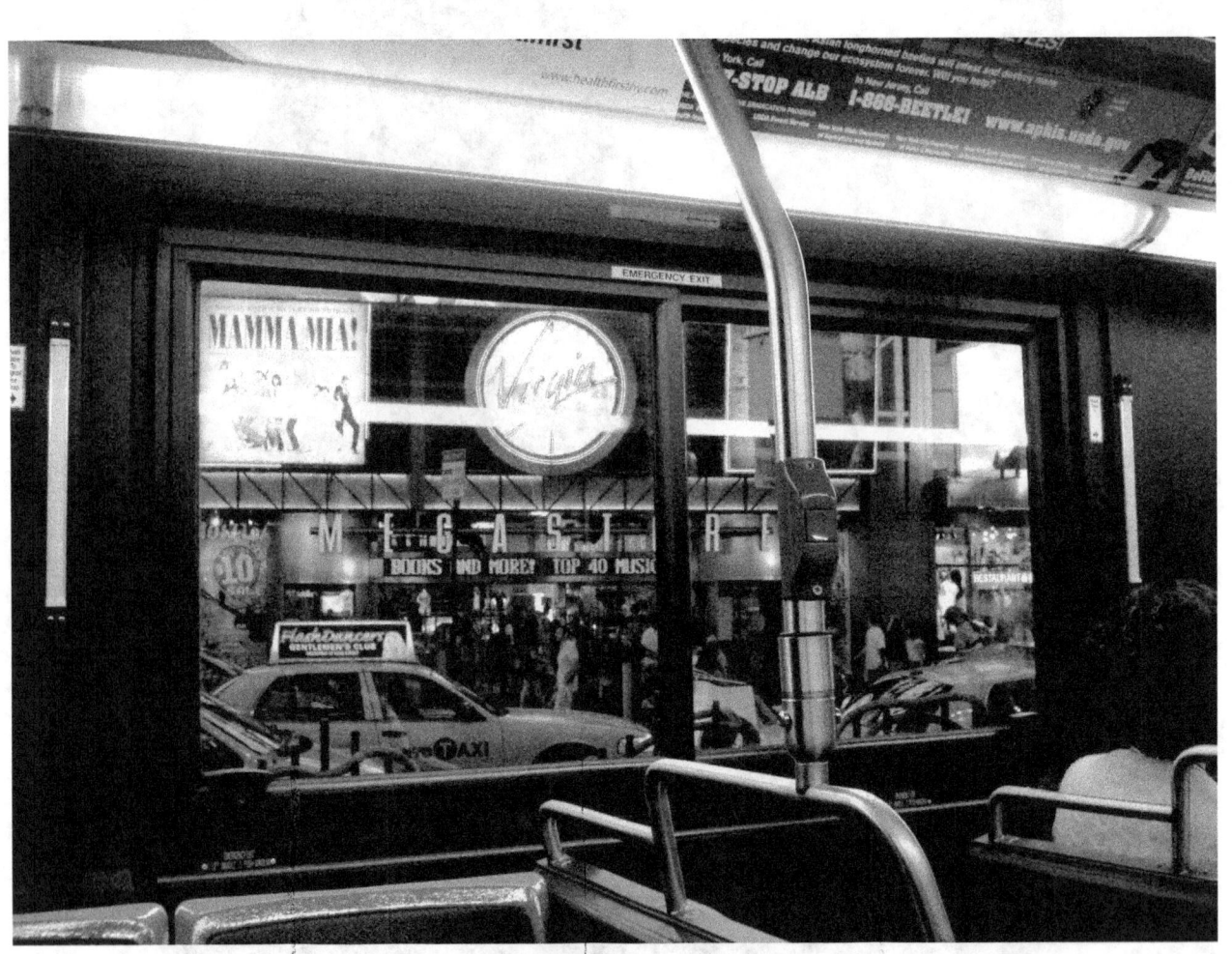

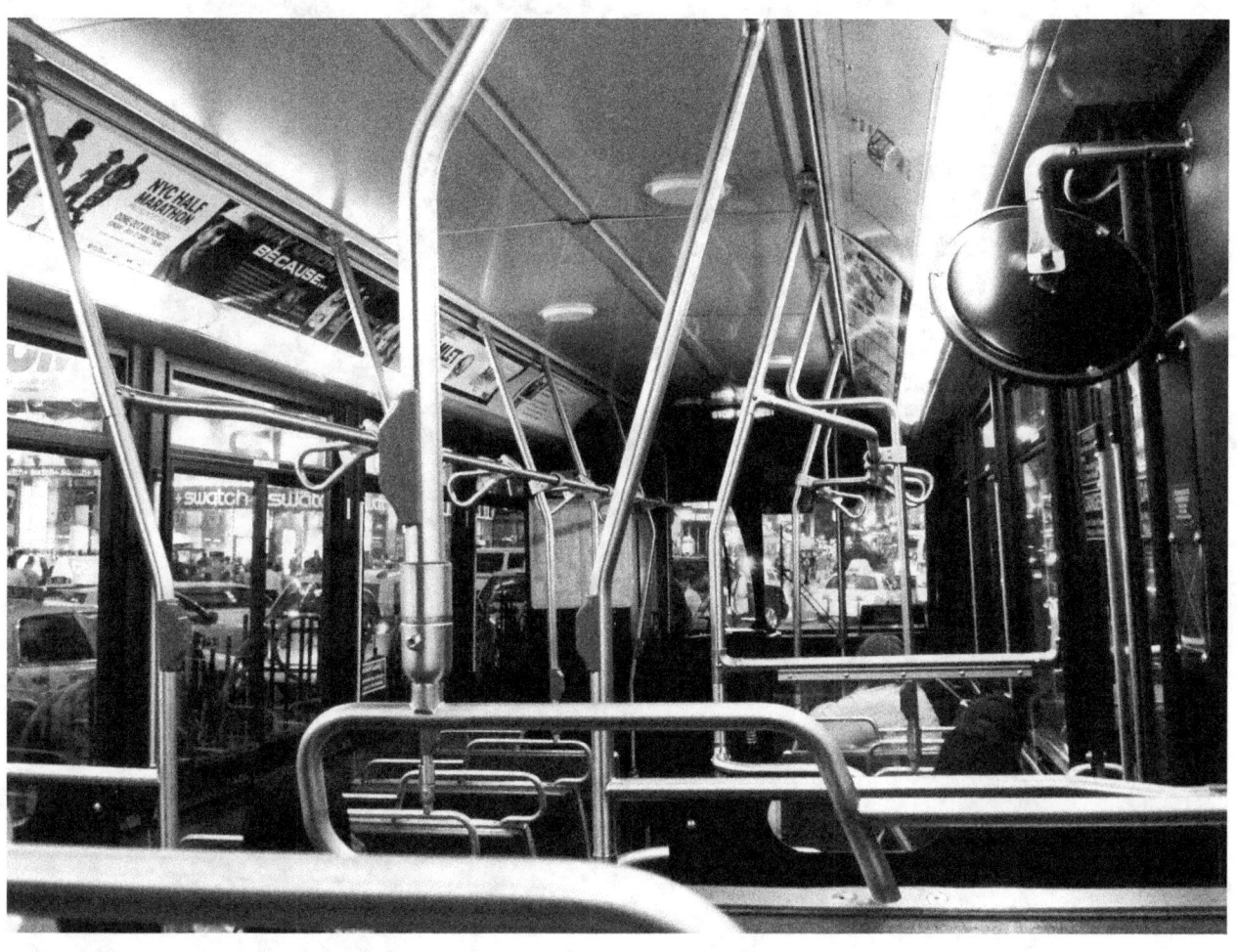

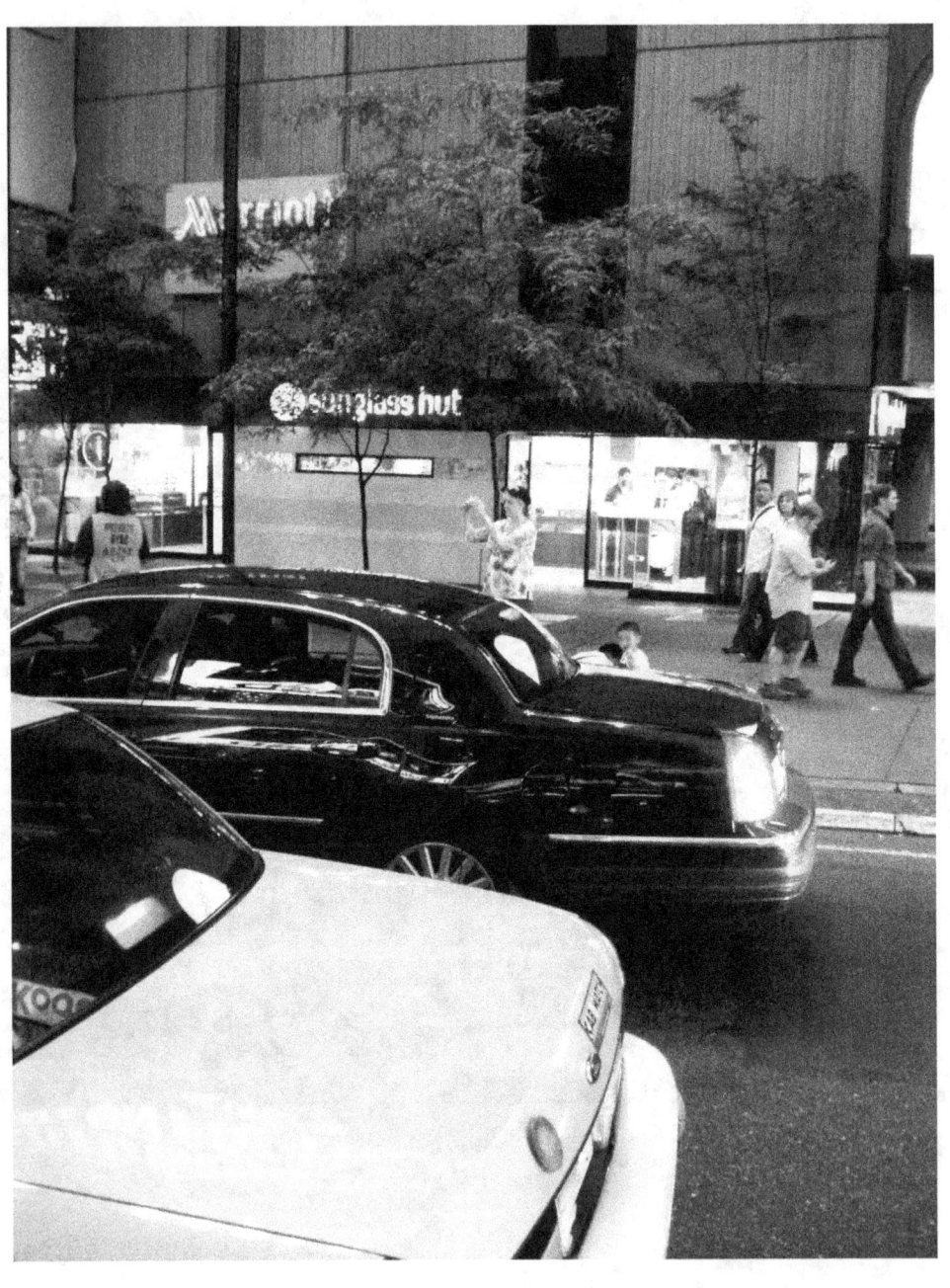

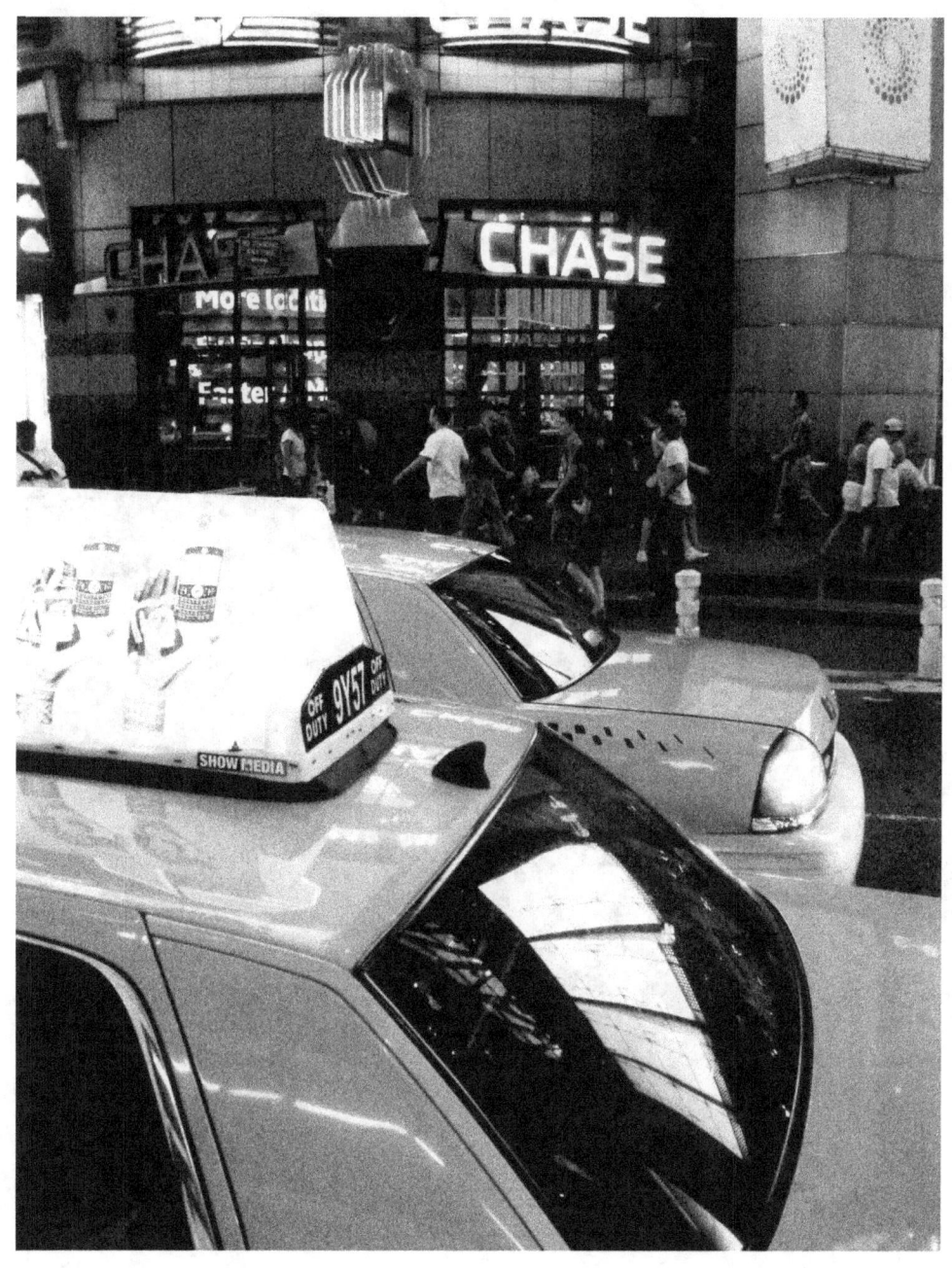

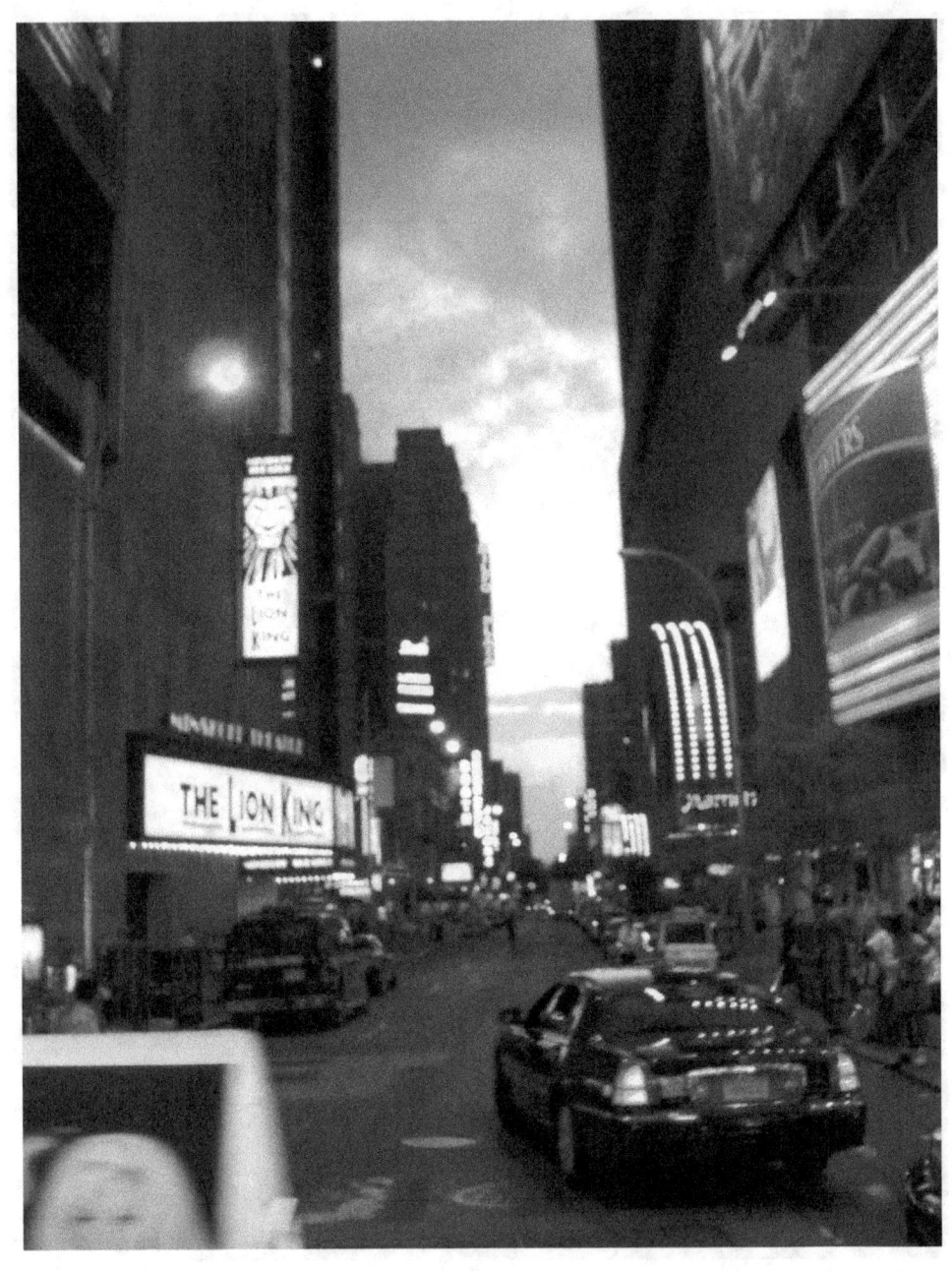

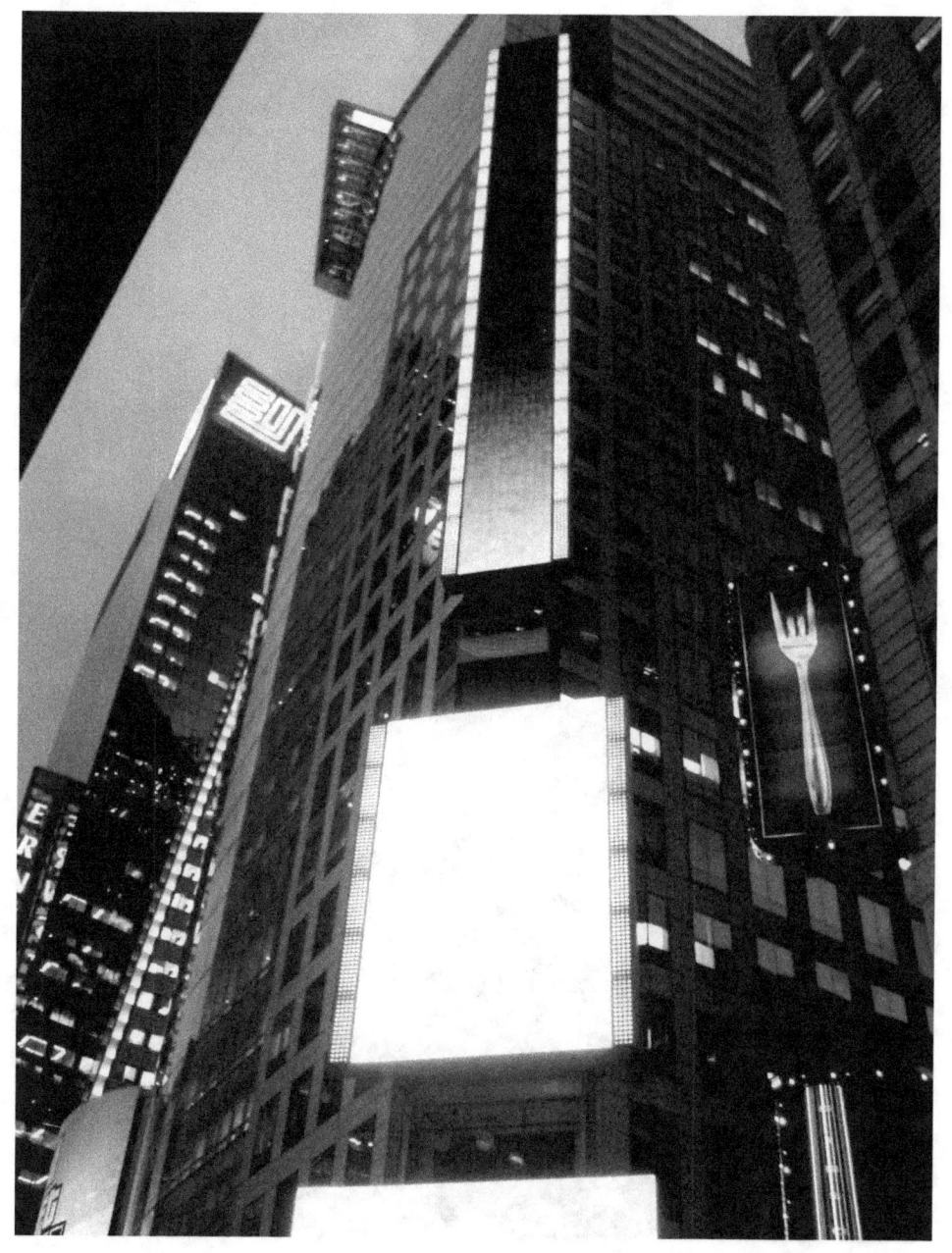

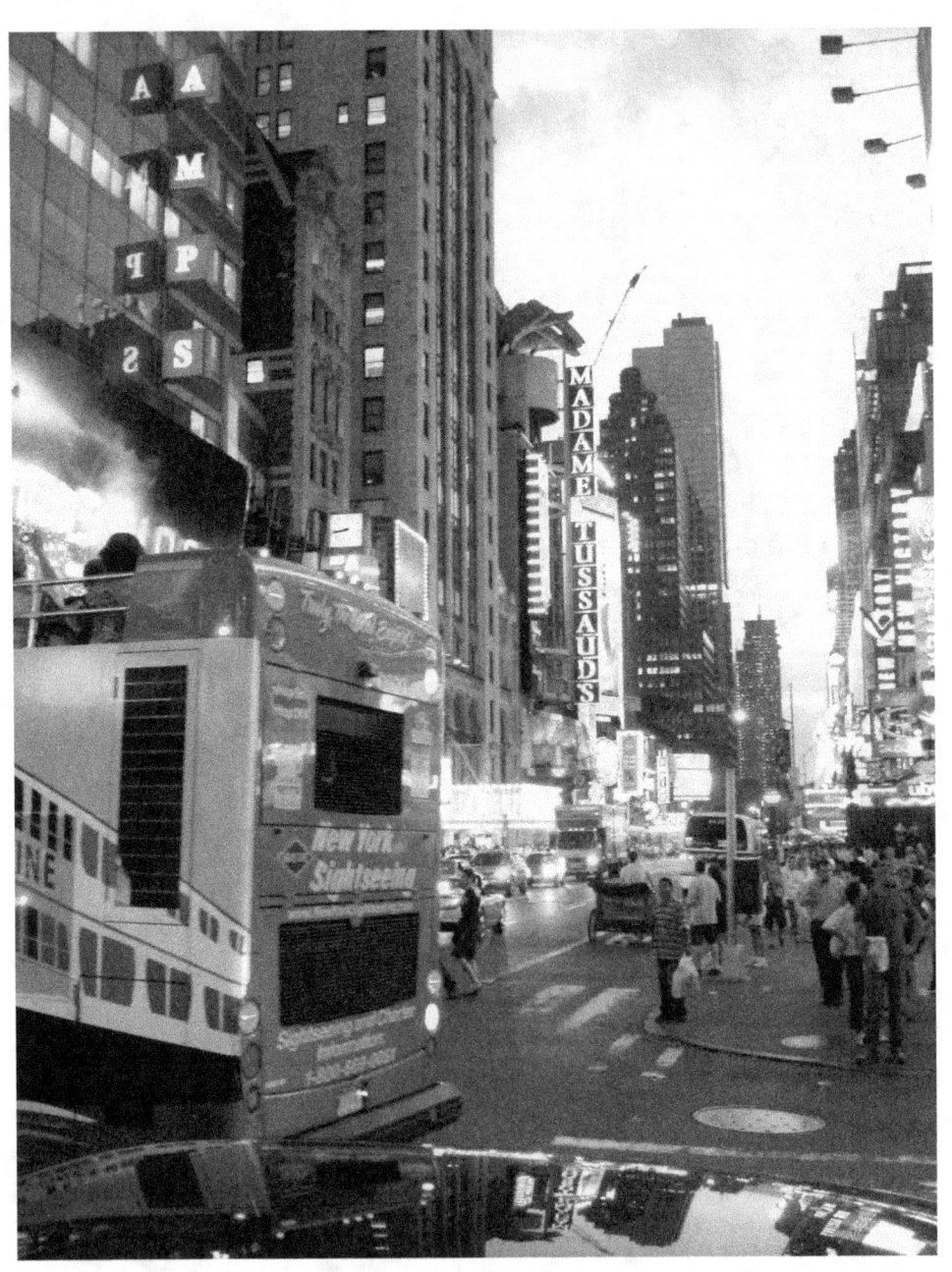

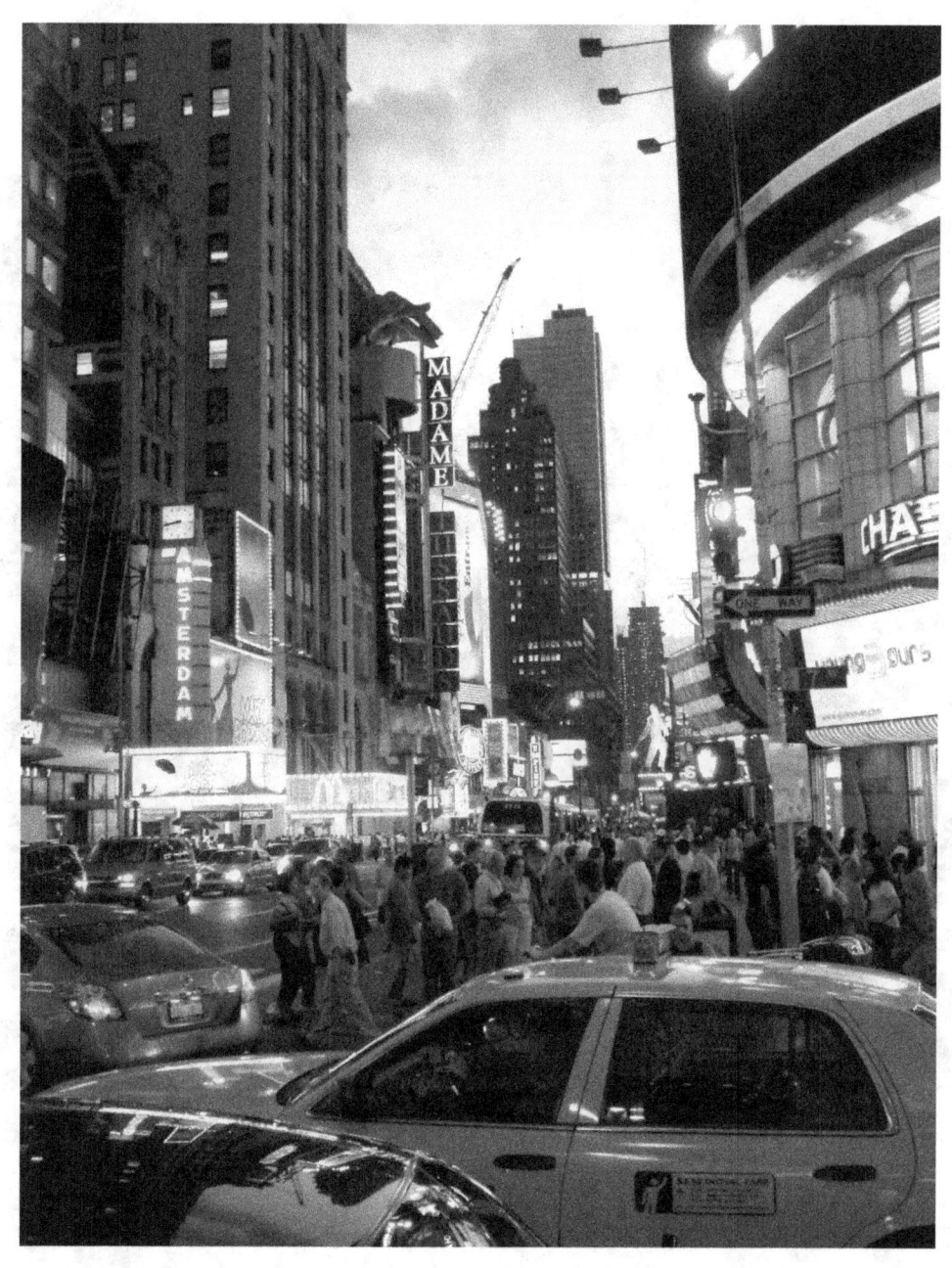

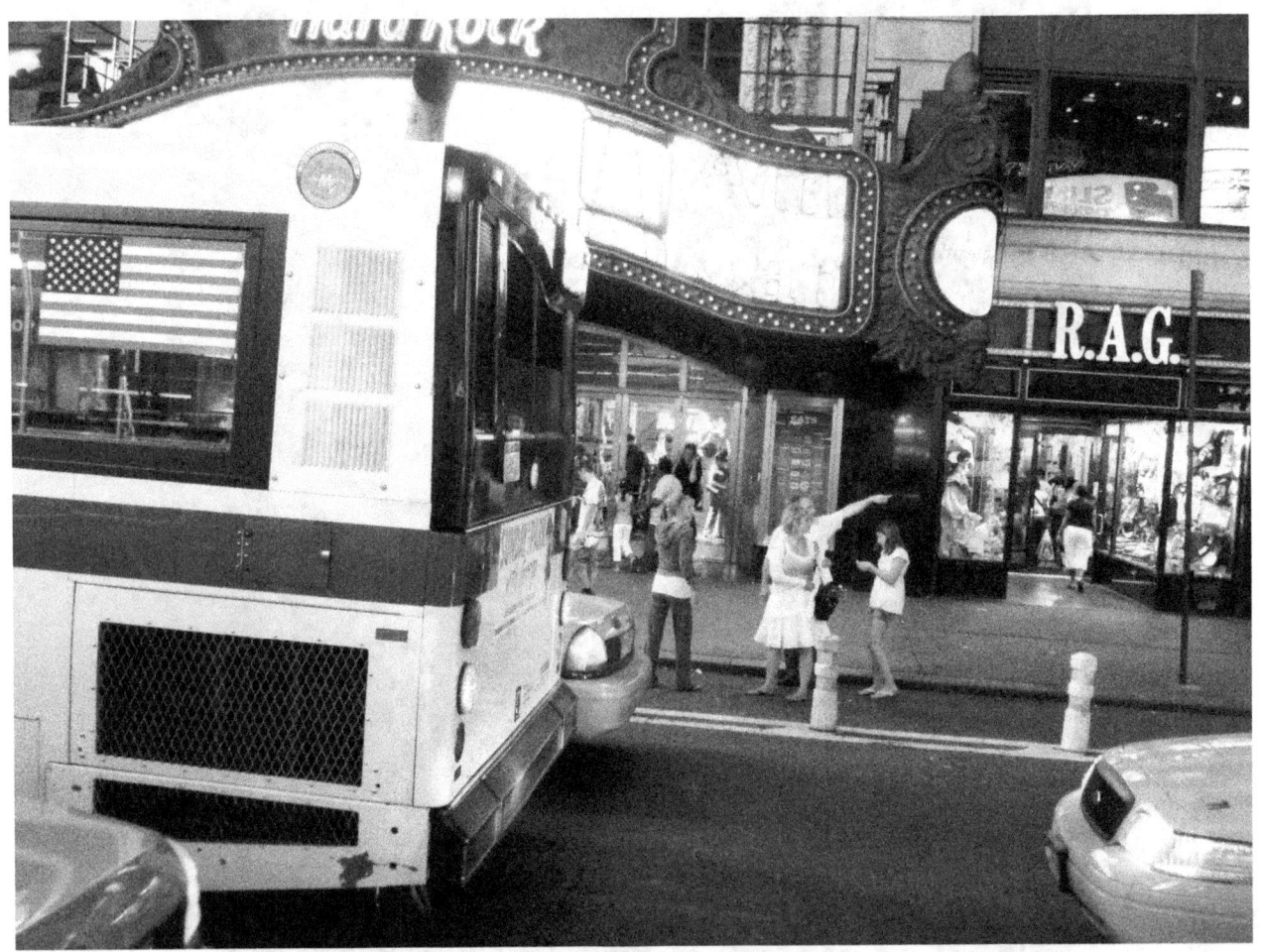

Times Square from a Bus, 2000

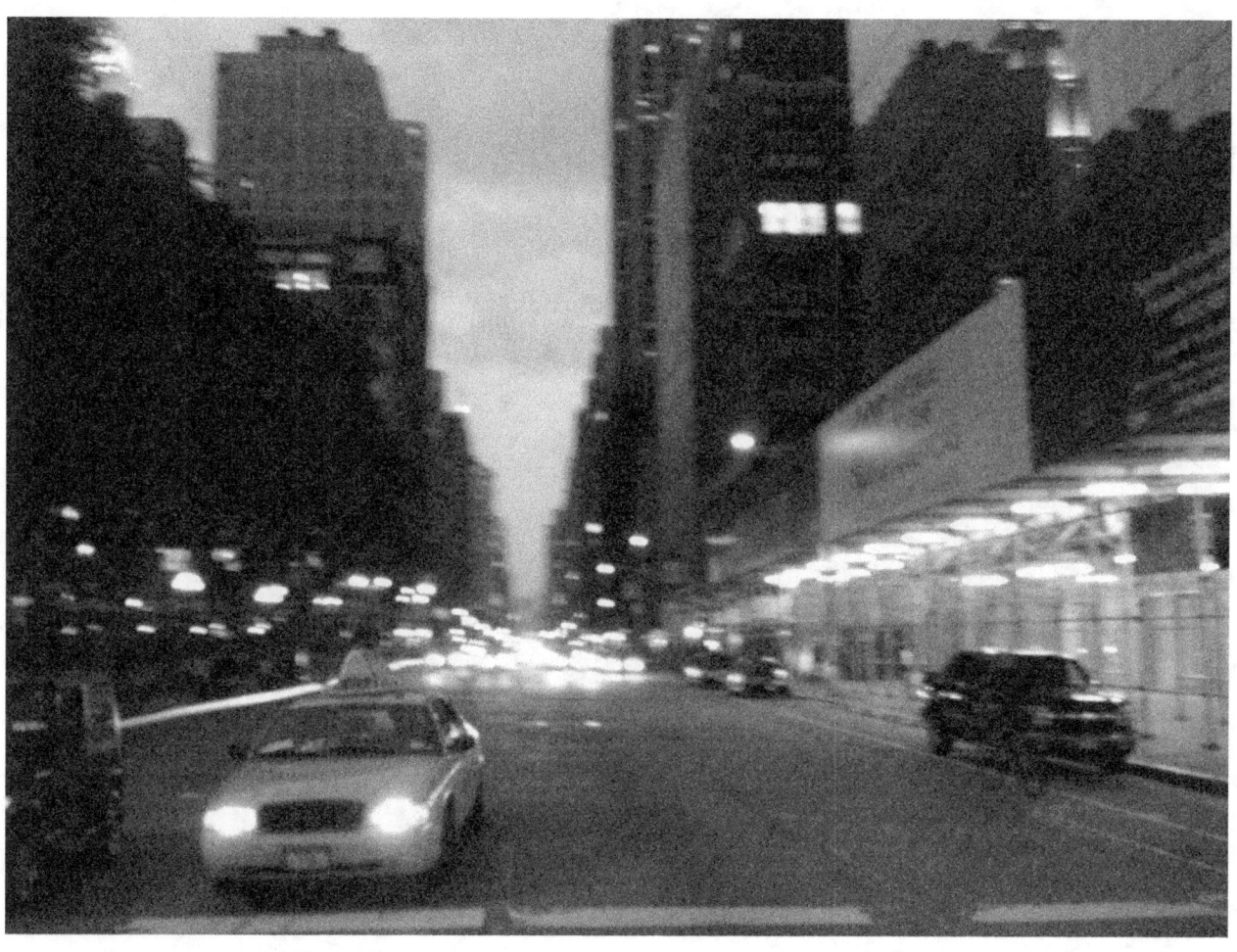

NYC Outtakes

These can't really be outtakes when they are included in the book. However, they don't fit neatly into a specific category, even though they all belong to New York City and to a phase of my life. Almost all of these photographs were taken during the early years of picture taking, and, of course, they represent a very different landscape from what New York is today (Perhaps less today, but back then, Manhattan was often referred to as simply, New York, and in other boroughs, might be called, "the city," as in, "Are you going to the city tonight?")

From the Staten Island Ferry, to Riverside Drive, and the George Washington Bridge, this part of New York City, for me, has the overall feel of a favorite shirt: threadbare, but you still want to wear it. And for me, black-and-white photos of this period suit the times: I actually don't remember many things in color from that time, photos or otherwise. That's not to say the city was not colorful. It certainly was, but it seemed to have less of a commercial glow, or glare, to it.

Compared with New York in the twenty-first century, the seventies presented a far less manicured image to the eye. I think it's safe to say that, generally speaking, people had more opportunities to look at and speak with other people rather than communicating electronically. There was greater casualness about contact, including how one moved about, whether walking down Fifth Avenue, or attending a street fair or festival.

Of all these "outtakes," the most unusual experience for me is represented by the two pictures taken in the Bronx Psychiatric Center. I was in my early twenties and through some very early computer dating service, I met a nurse who worked at the Center. We never dated but learning of my interest in photography, she invited me to offer an instruction class at the Center (pictured are two from that class). It turned out that an instruction class wasn't the most important thing I could offer.

I only learned while doing research for this book that this Center was unique in how they managed those psychologically compromised (New York Times, *The Patients Can Walk Out At Any Time at Bronx State Mental Hospital*, By ROBERT CLURMAN, APRIL 2, 1972.). Except for a few locked floors, patients had free access within the grounds as well as to the outside world. They could go where they wanted. As I recall, the unit I was involved with was a locked floor, but the staff did permit me on several occasions to leave with a patient for a picture-taking field trip.

The weekly meetings continued for several months and included slide show presentations, camera functions and basic techniques, an attempt at some darkroom work, as well as the field trips. Though often difficult to relate to many in my group, I could see how learning to relate to photographs offered a unique and useful way of looking at life, as well as giving a sense of control in taking pictures. It all worked out just fine.

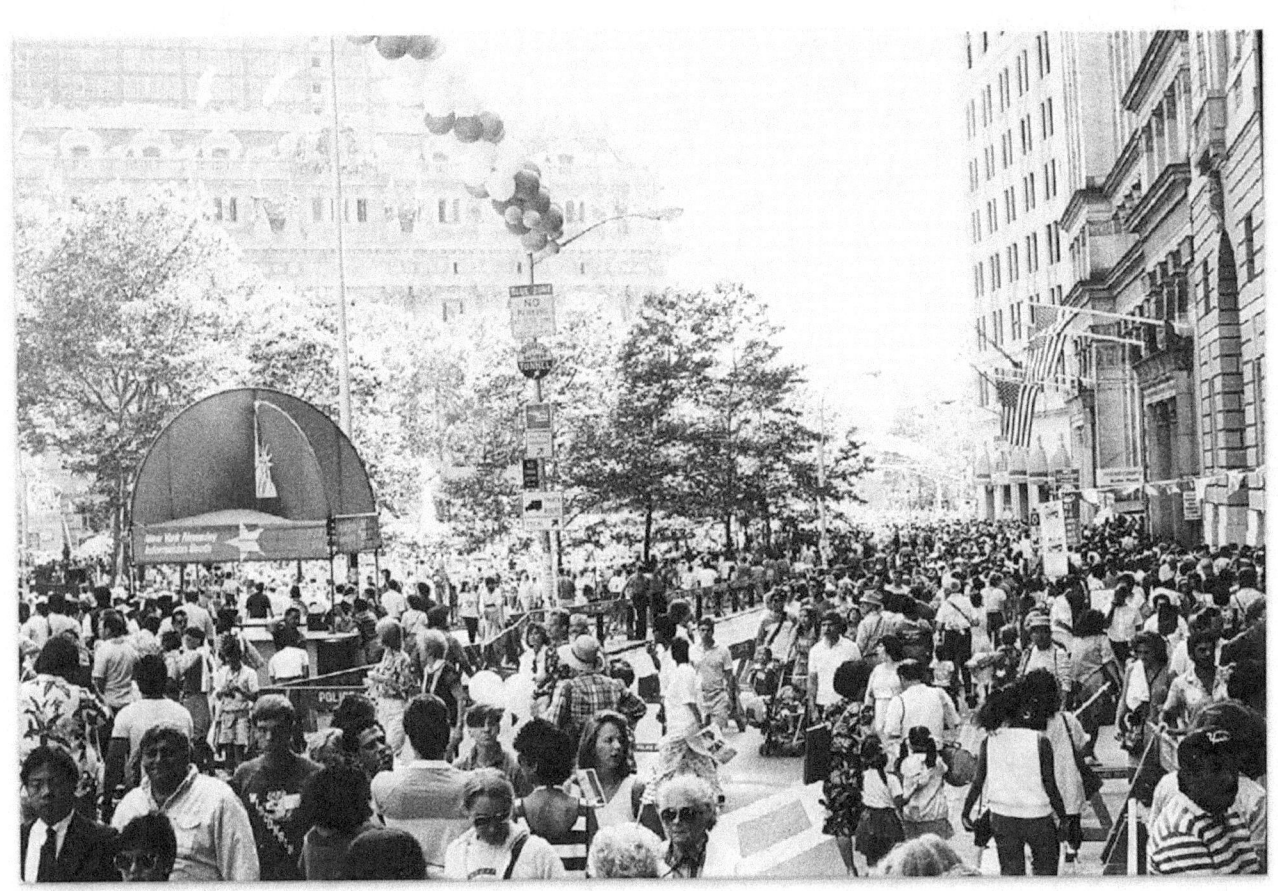

Earth Day event, c. 1970, Battery Park, lower Manhattan.

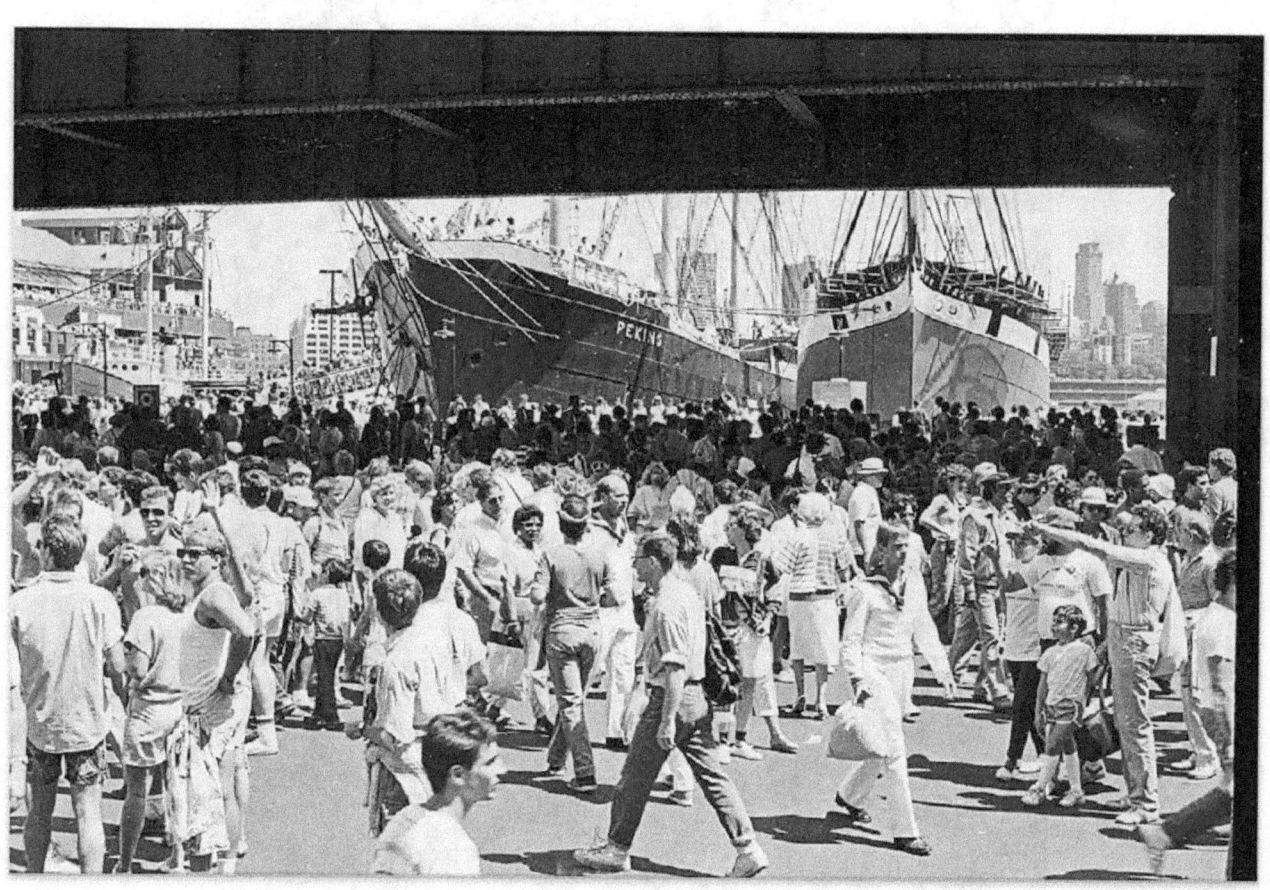

Earth Day event, c. 1970, South Street Seaport, lower Manhattan.

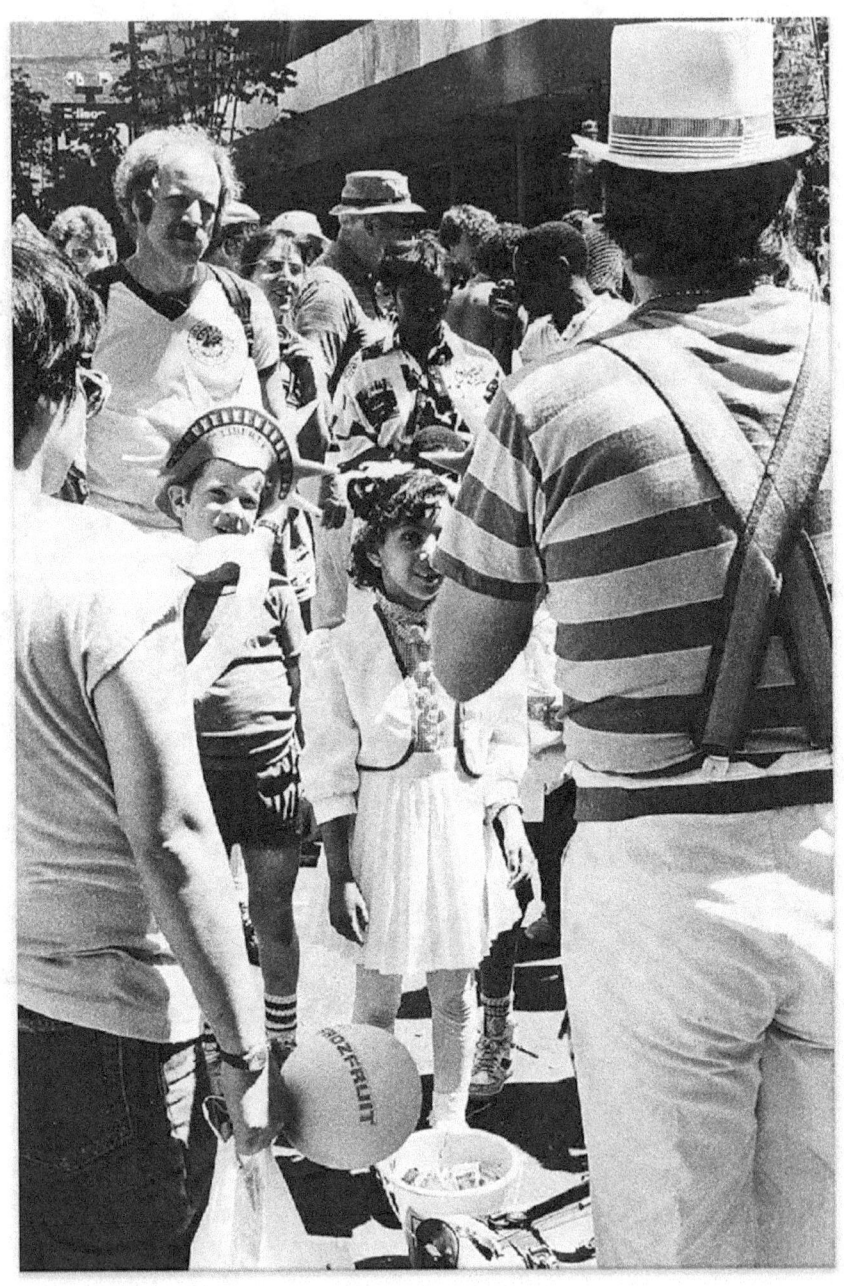

Earth Day event, c. 1970, Battery Park, lower Manhattan.

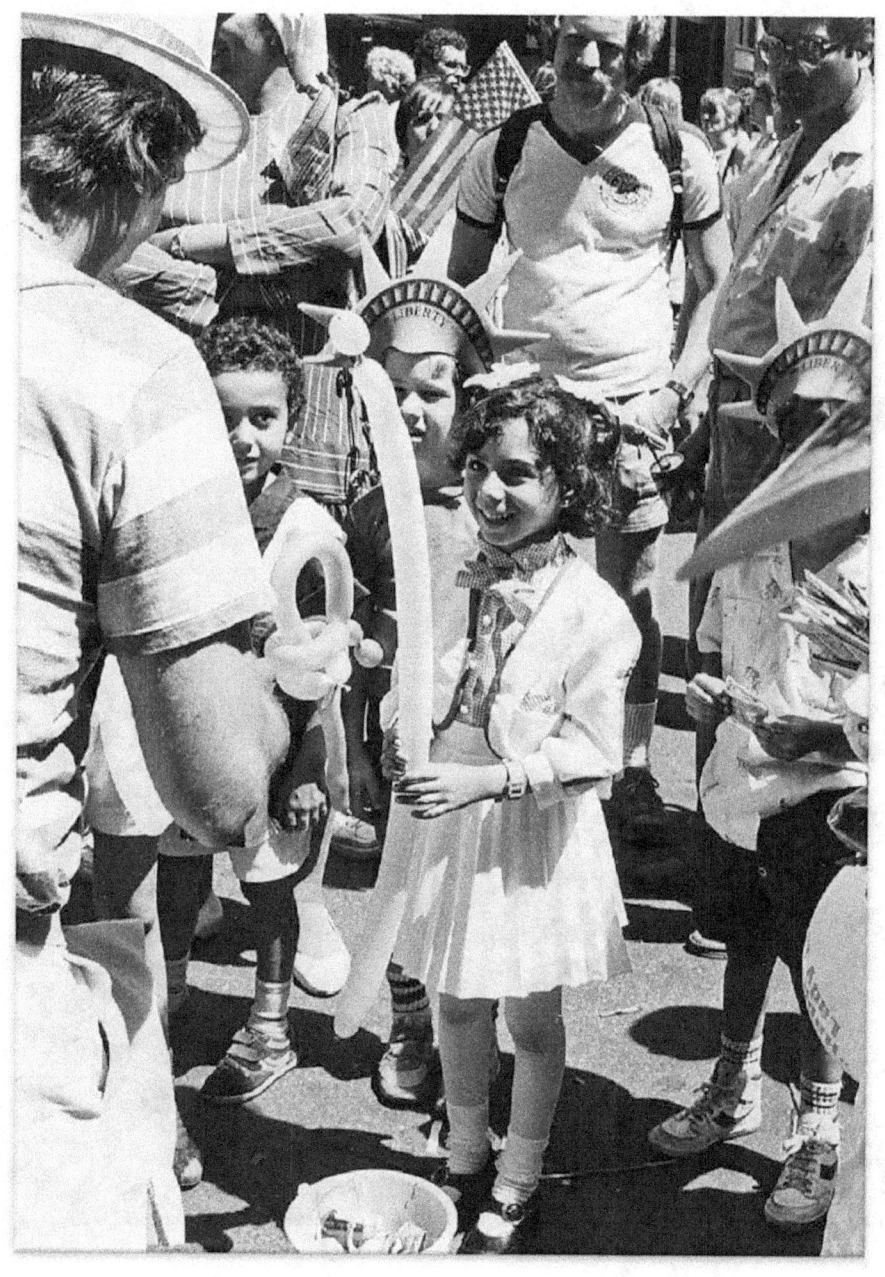

Earth Day event, c. 1970, Battery Park, lower Manhattan.

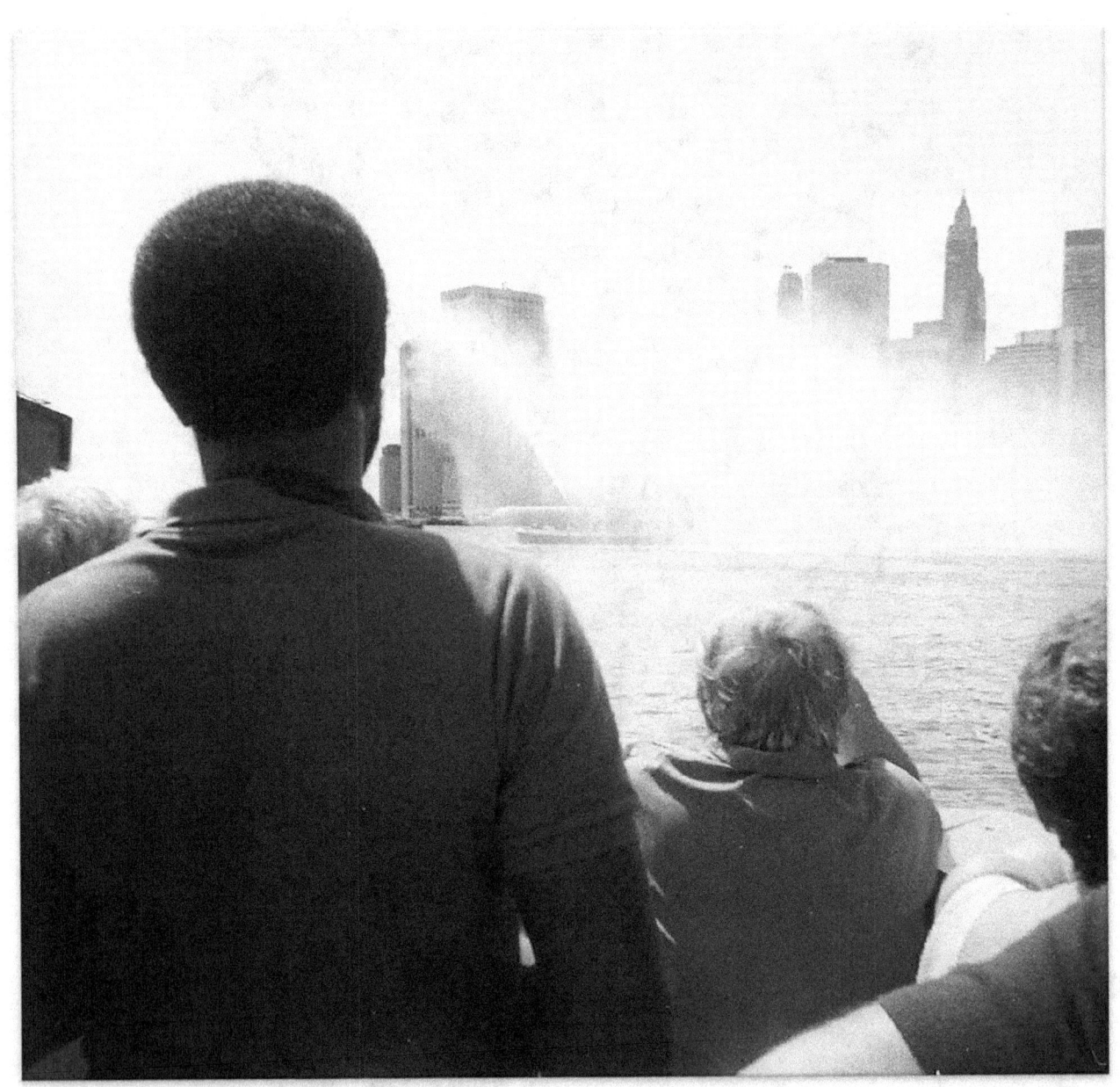

East River, fireboat display, c. 1970.

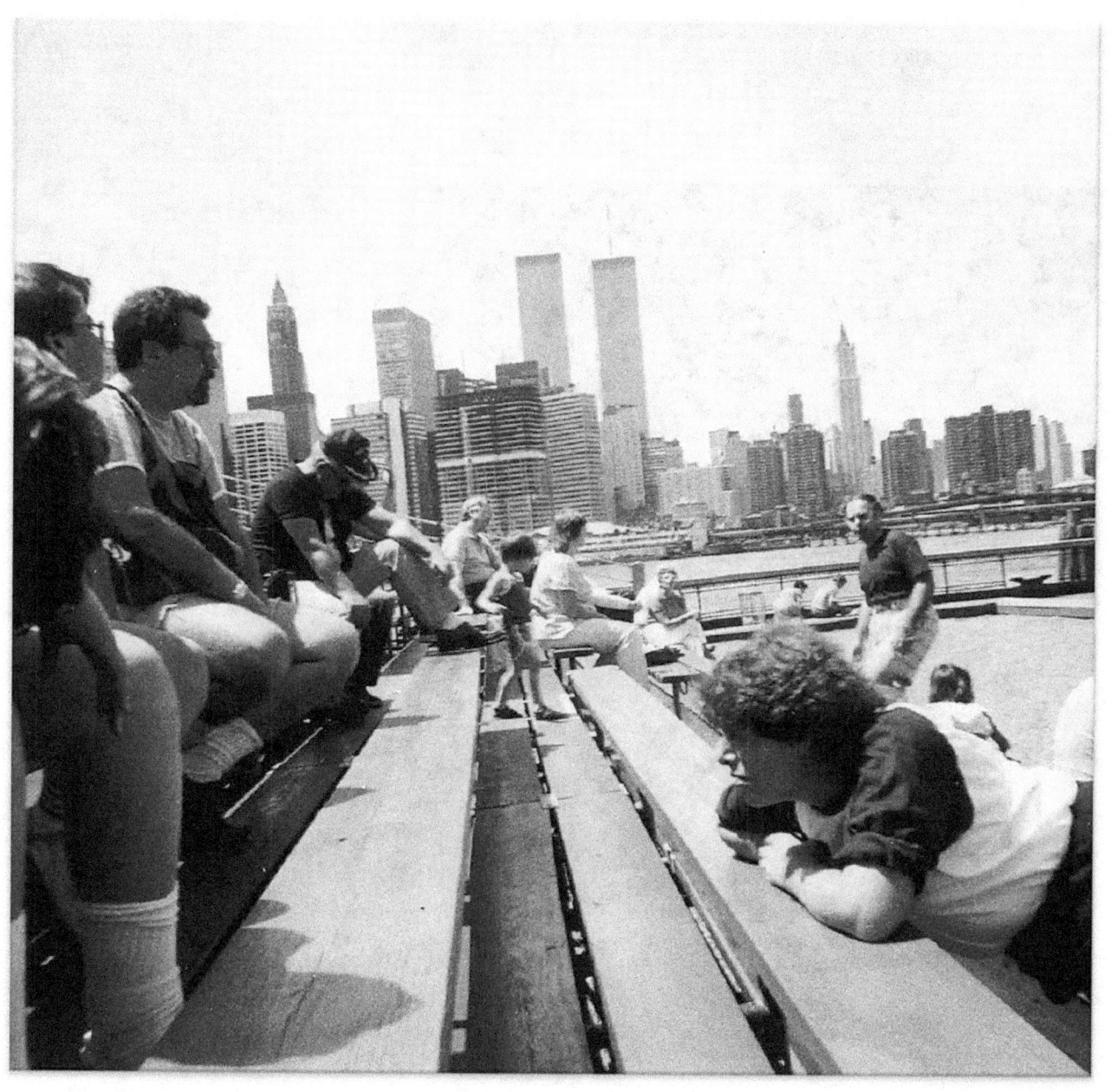

Brooklyn Bridge Park, looking west towards Manhattan and World Trade Center, c. 1974.

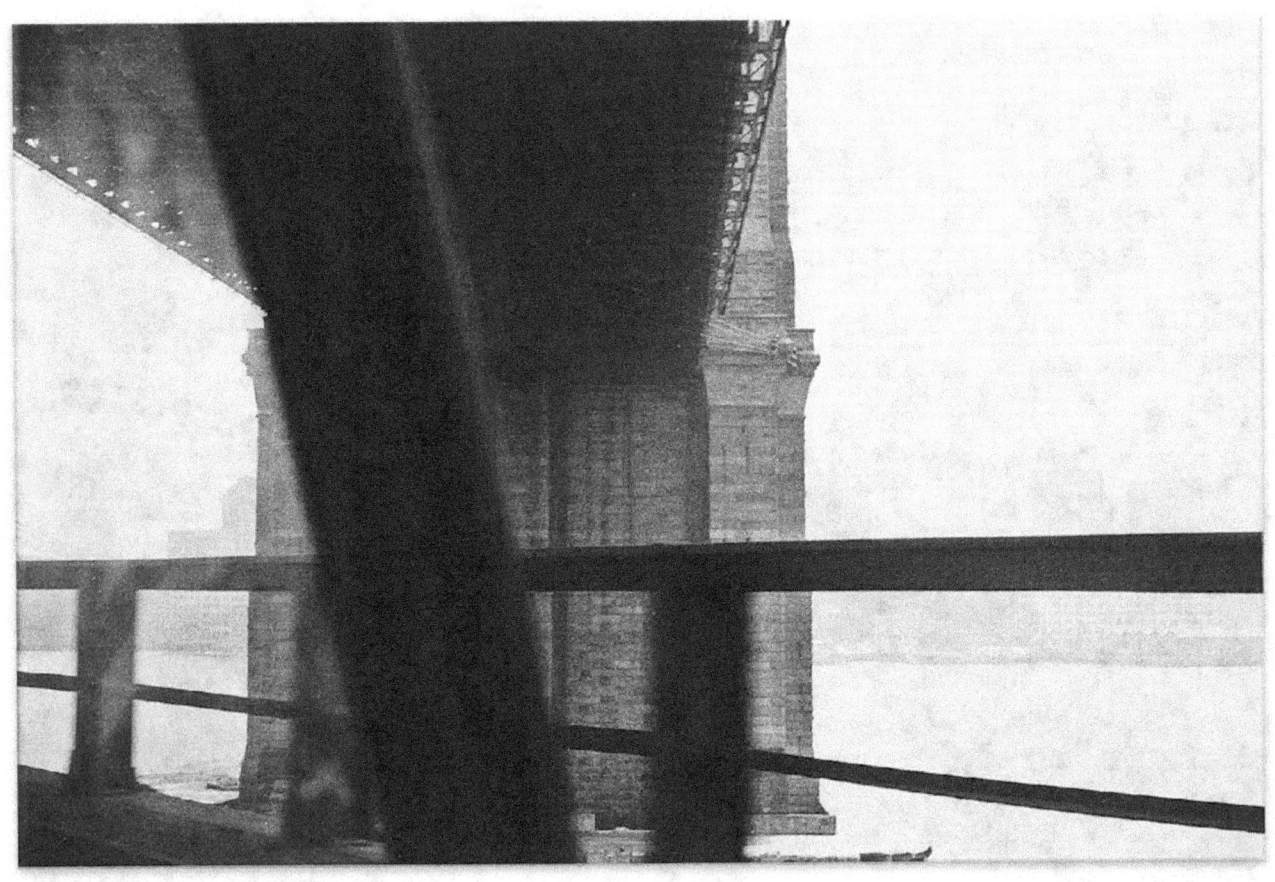

Brooklyn Bridge, FDR Drive ramp, looking toward Brooklyn, c. 1970.

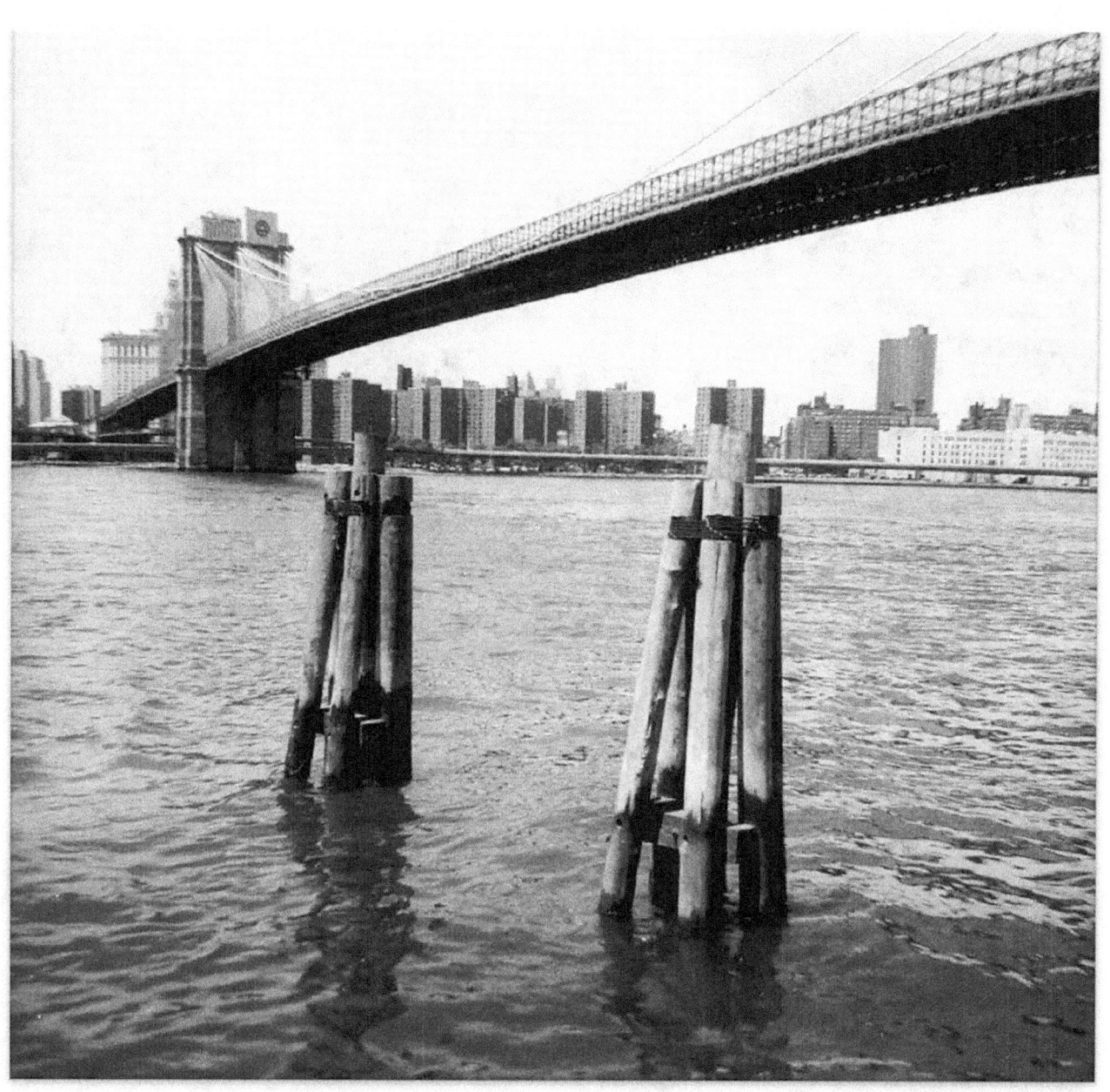

Brooklyn Bridge, from Brooklyn looking west, c. 1974

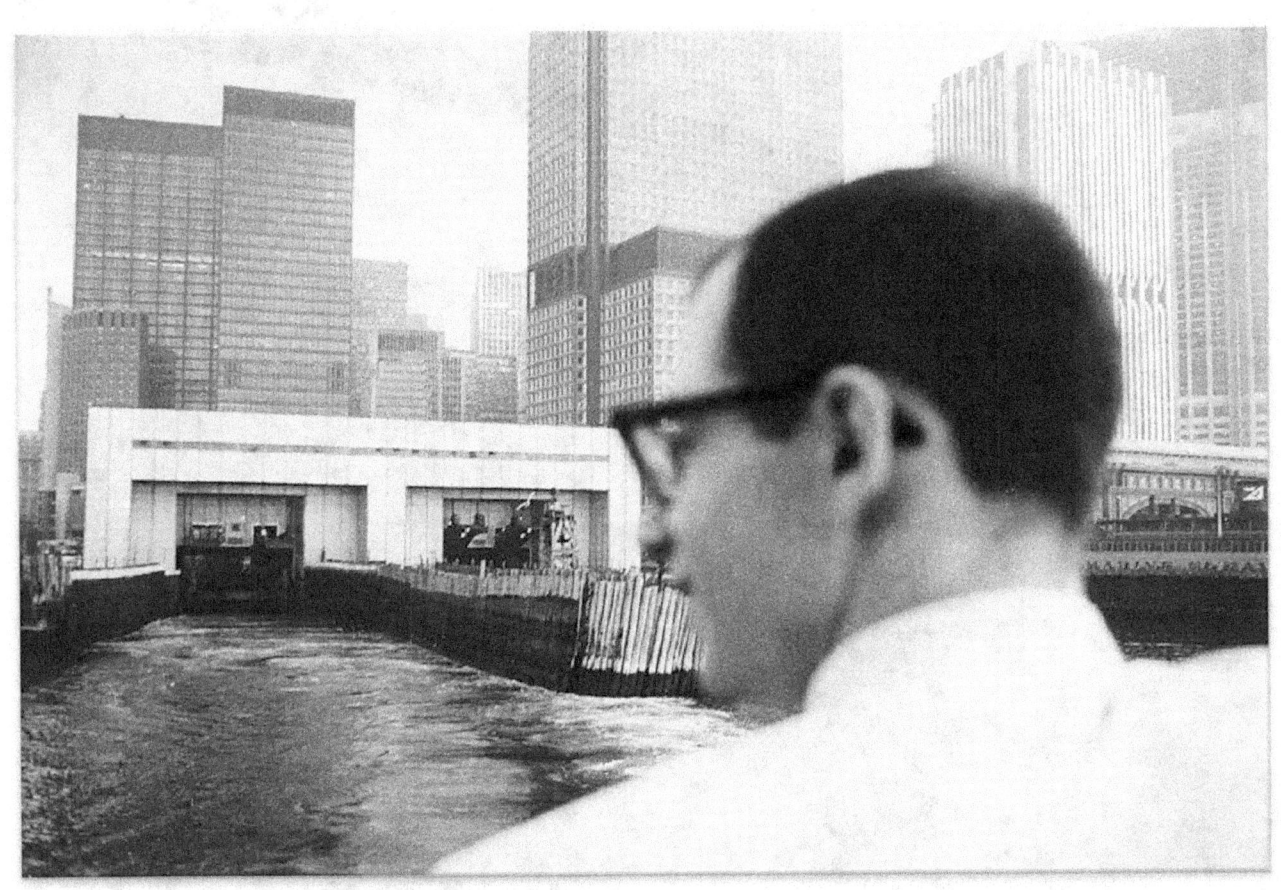

Staten Island Ferry, approaching Manhattan, c. 1974.

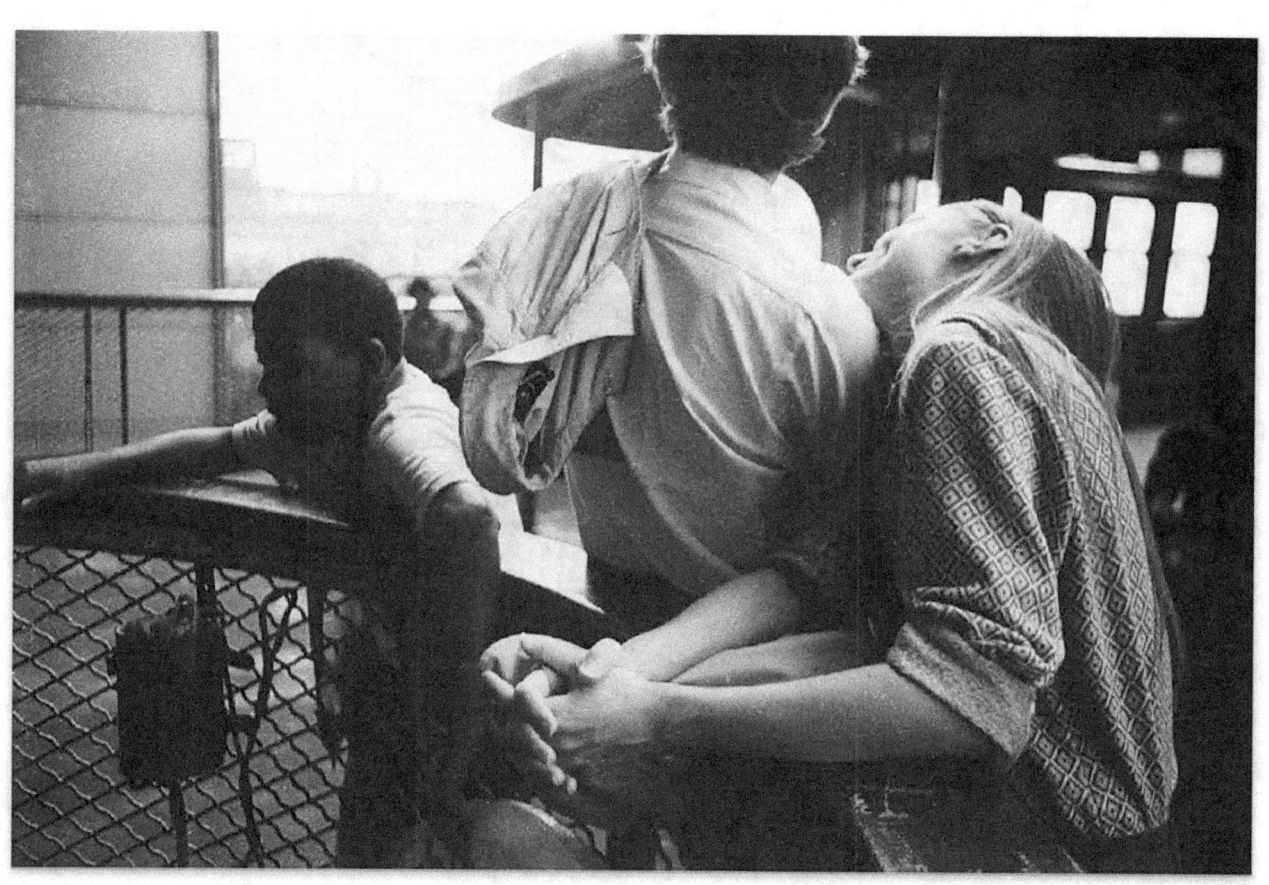

Staten Island Ferry, approaching Manhattan, c. 1974.

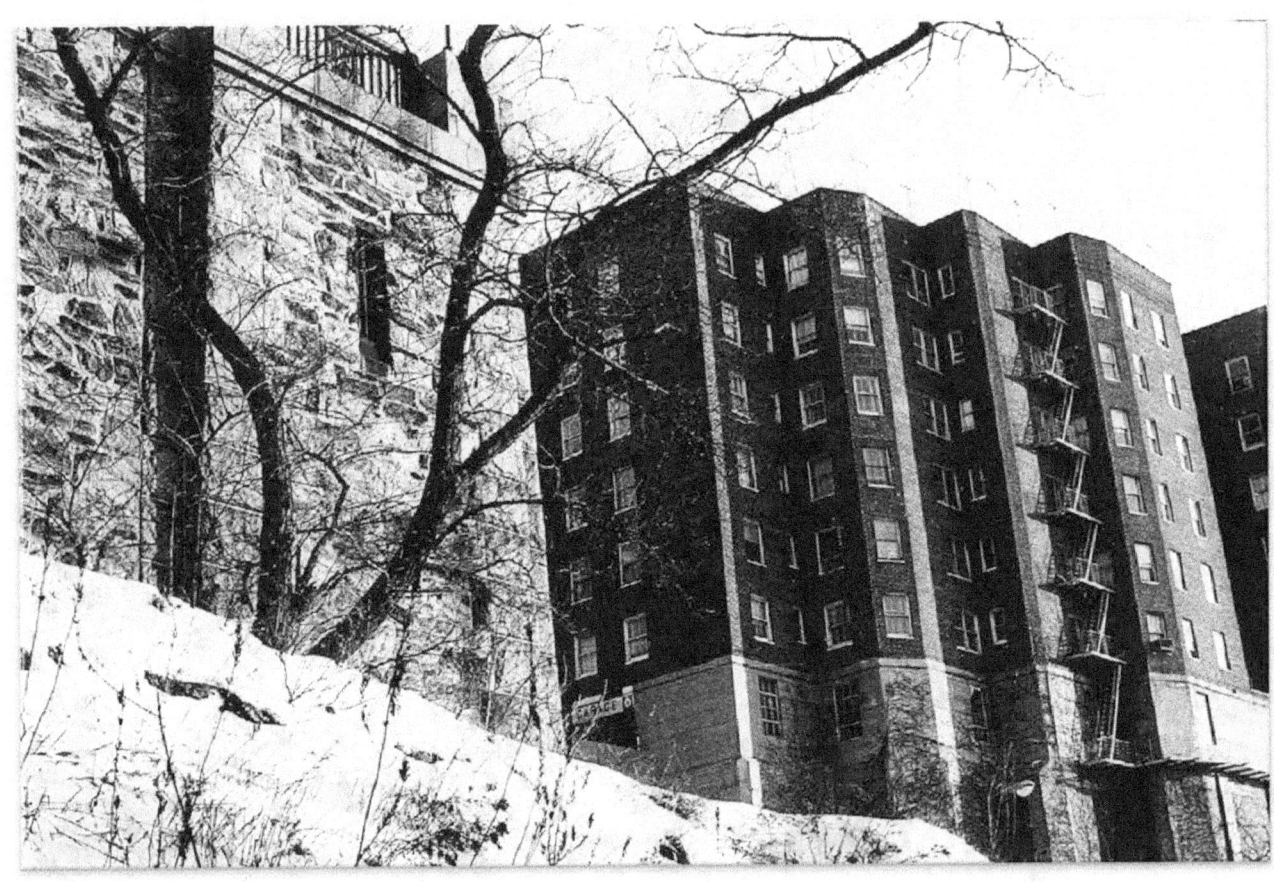

End of Riverside Drive around 184th Street, eastward view, c. 1973.

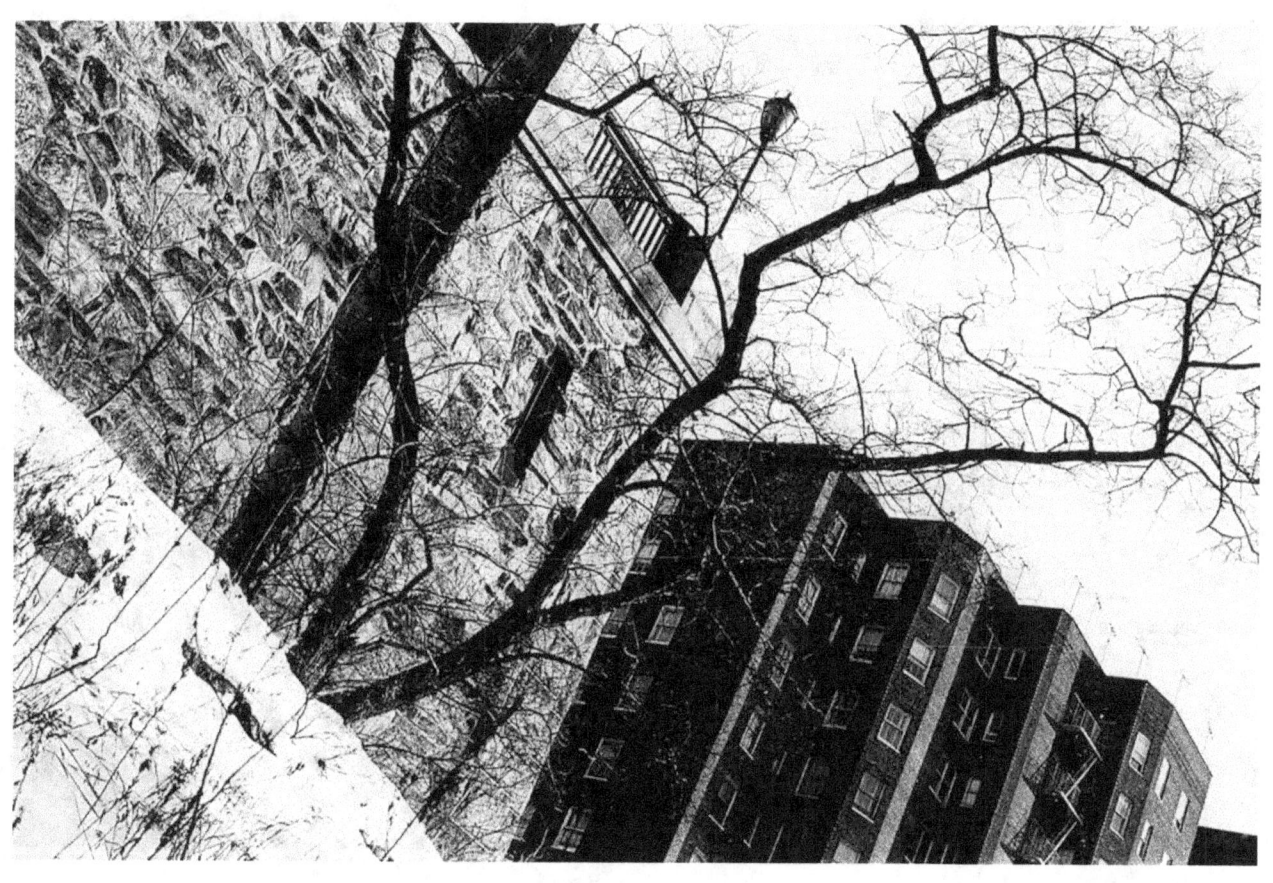

End of Riverside Drive around 184th Street, eastward view, c. 1973.

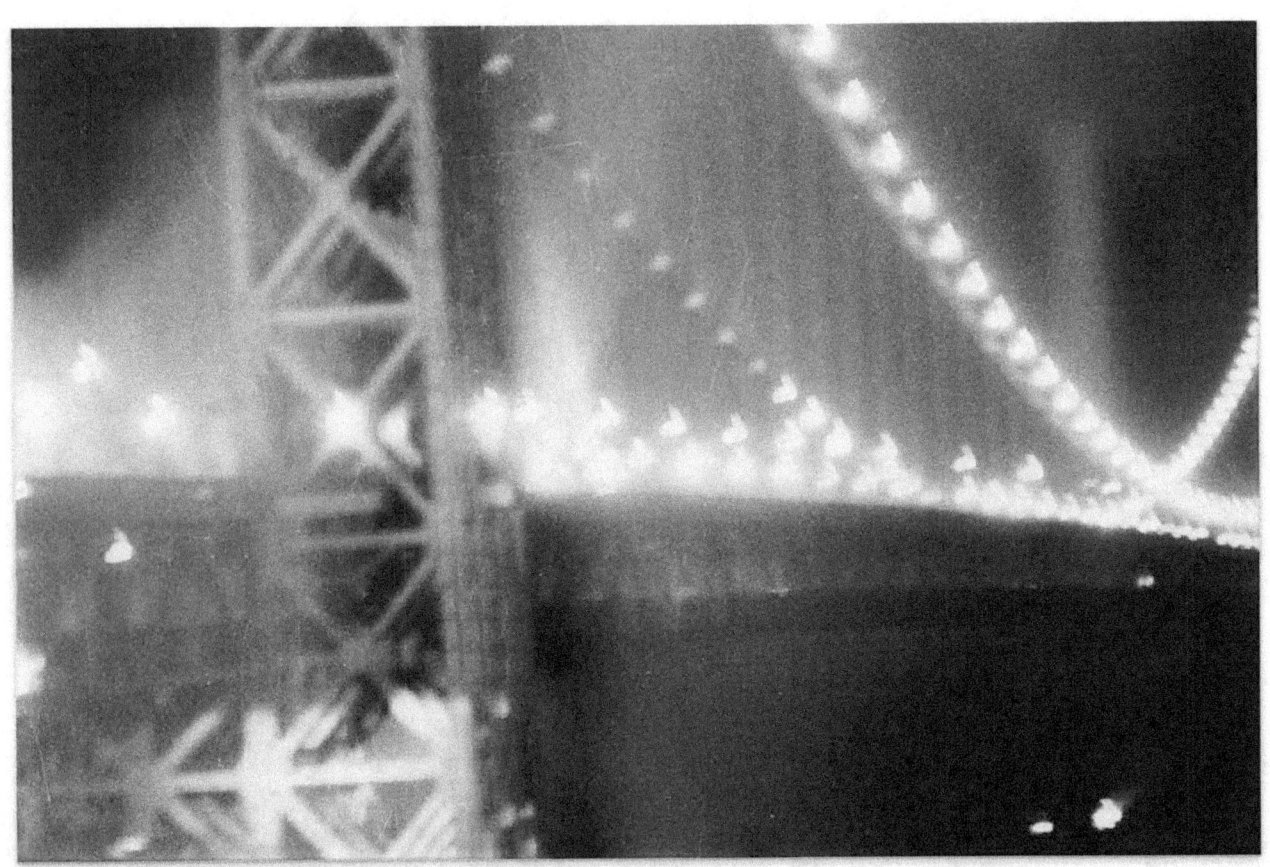

George Washington Bridge, from 5th floor window, 181th Street, Riverside Drive, c. 1973.

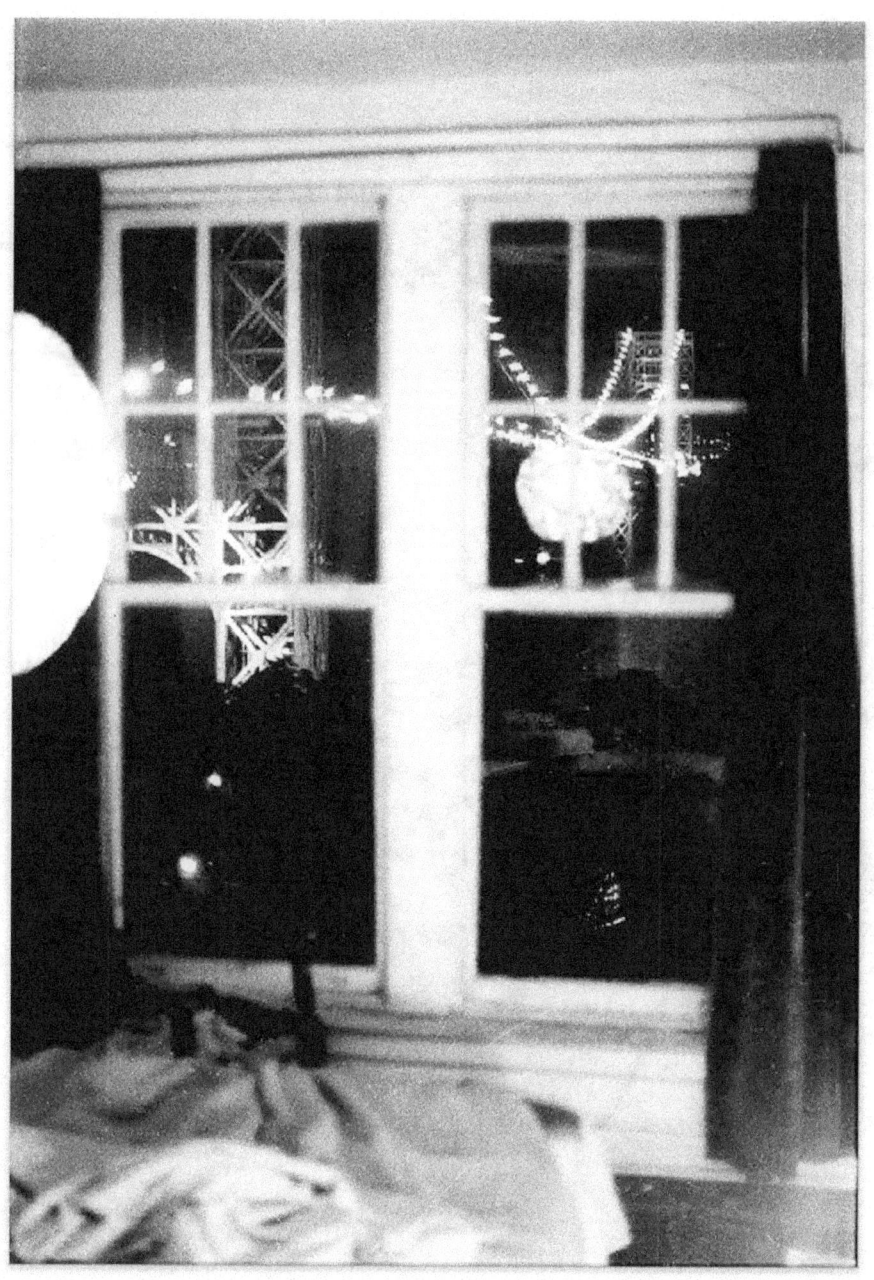

George Washington Bridge, from 5th floor window, 181th Street, Riverside Drive, c. 1973.

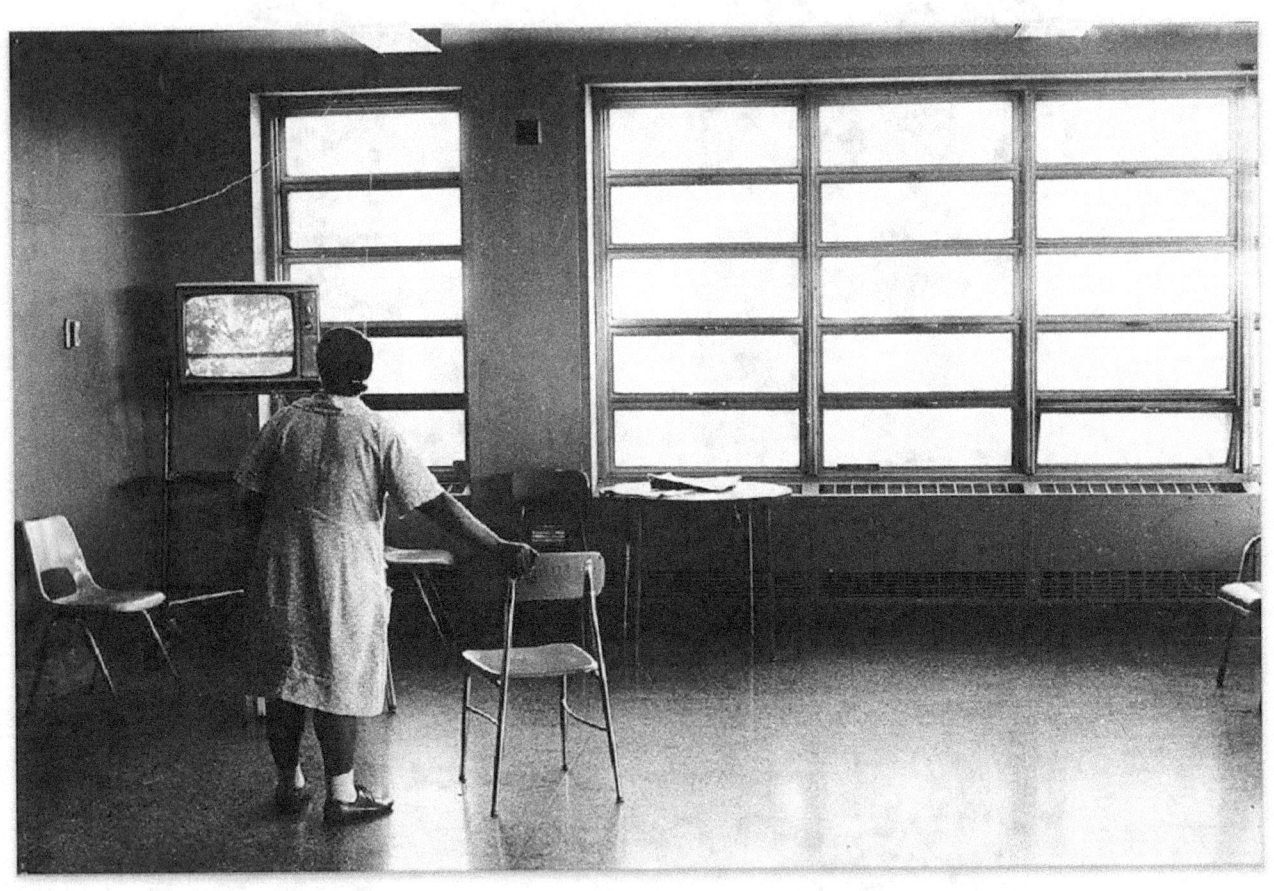

Bronx Psychiatric Center, c. 1973.

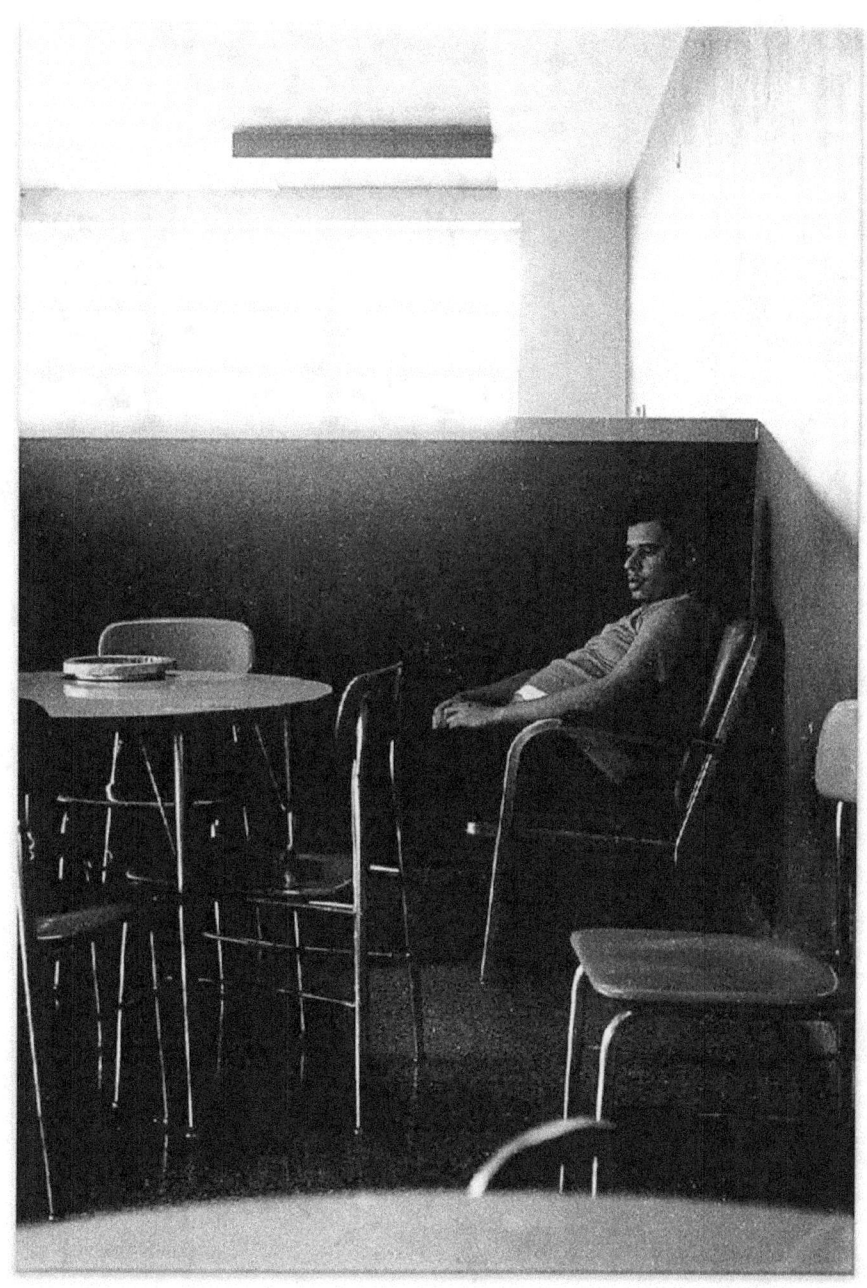

Bronx Psychiatric Center, c. 1973.

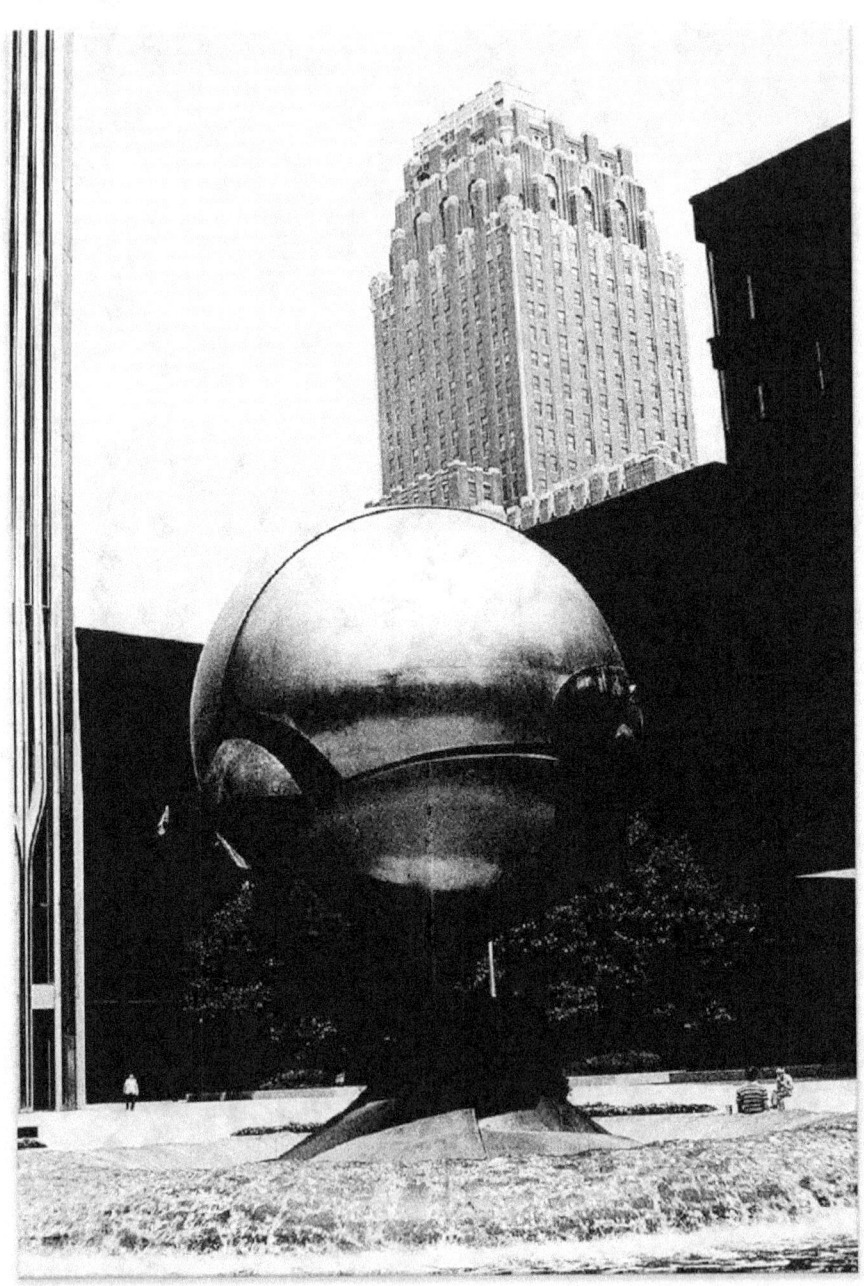

"The Sphere," World Trade Center, Austin J. Tobin Plaza, c. 1974.

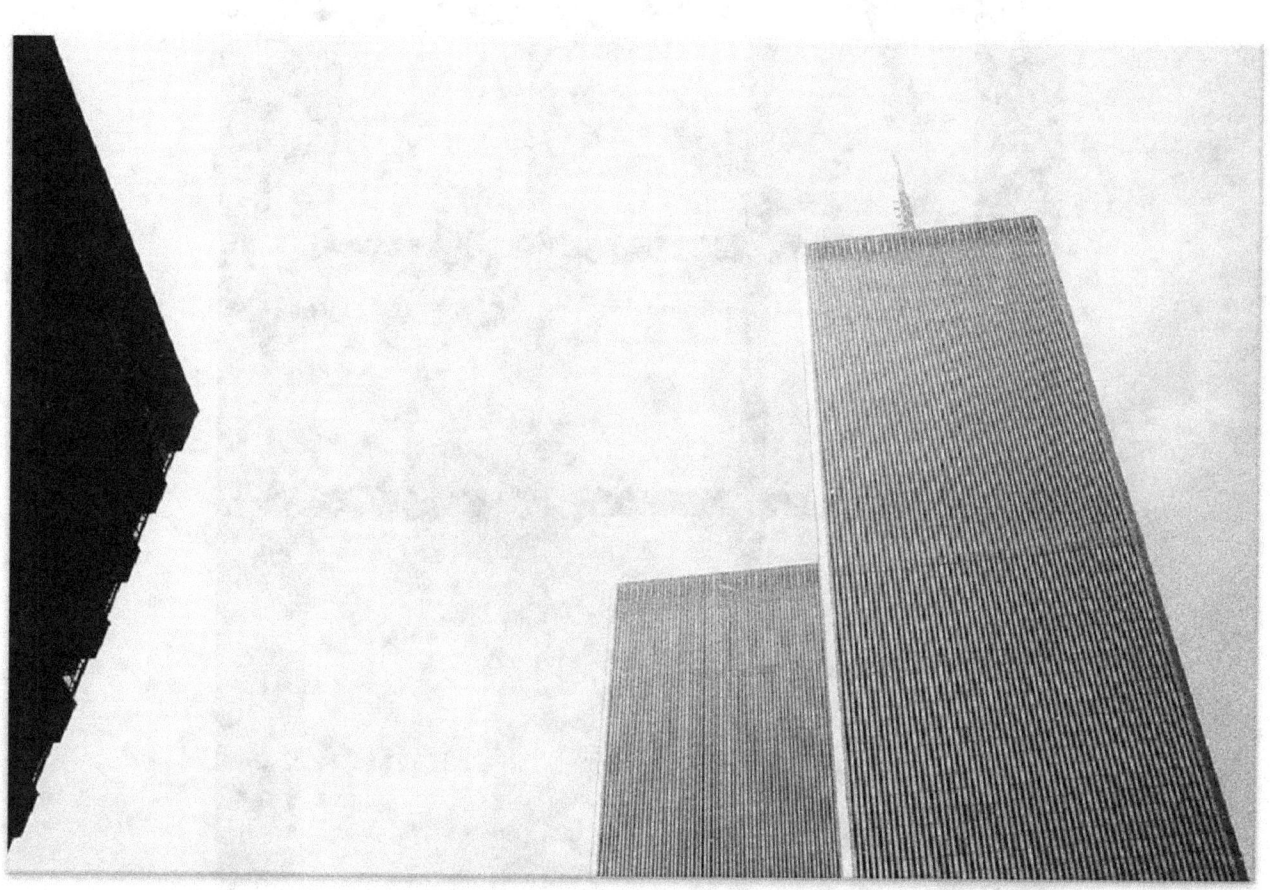

World Trade Center, South Plaza Building, left, c. 1974.

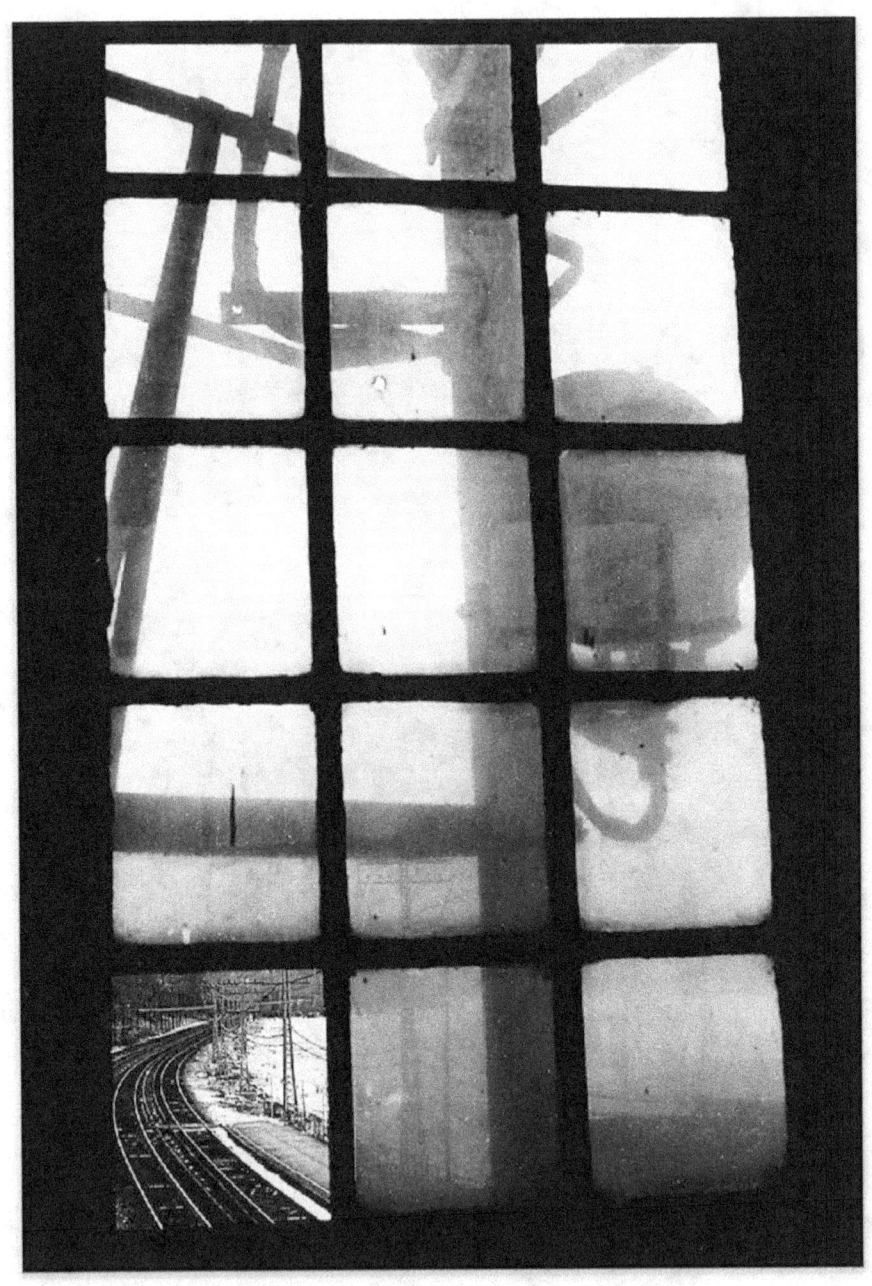

New York Central (Metro North) rail crossing bridge, c. 1965.

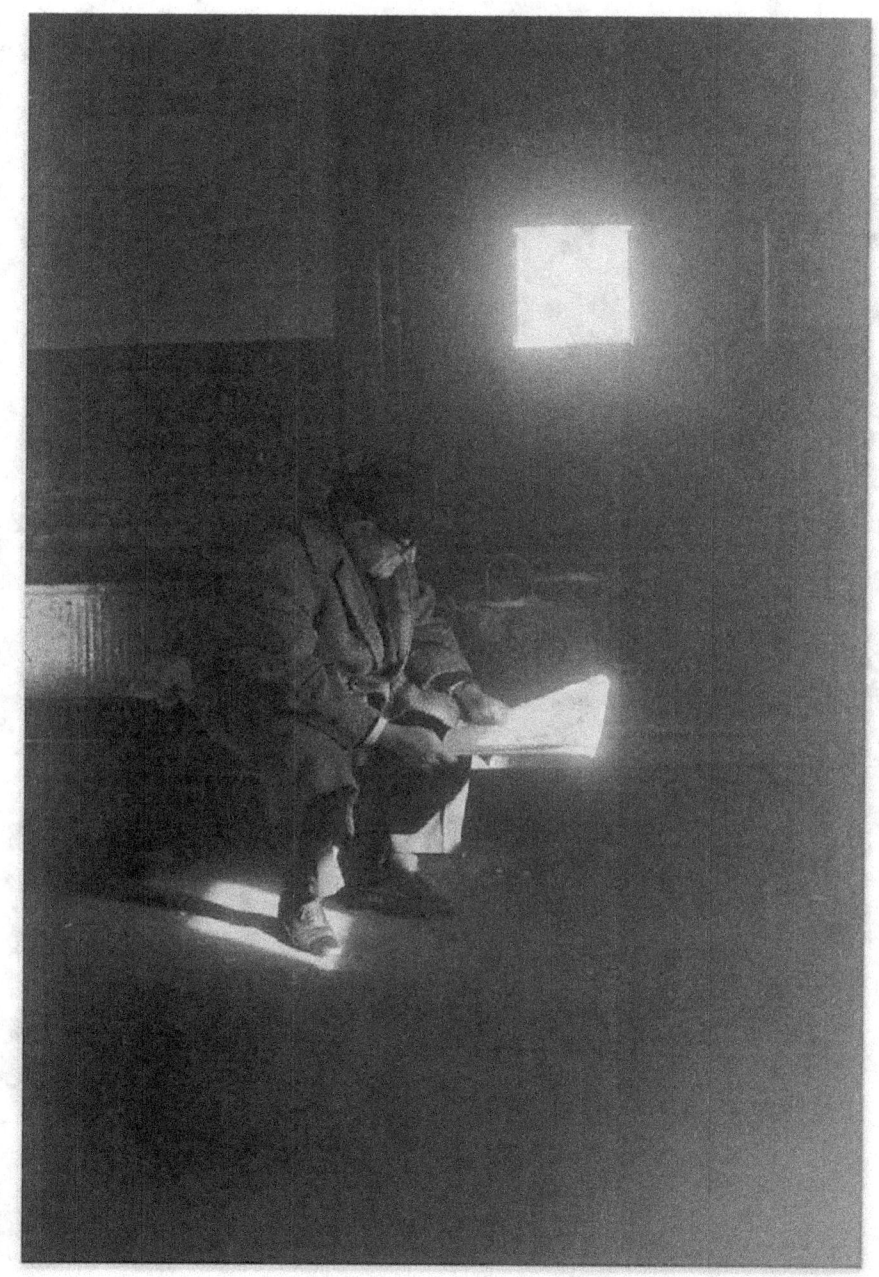

Marble Hill waiting room, New York Central (Metro North), c. 1965.

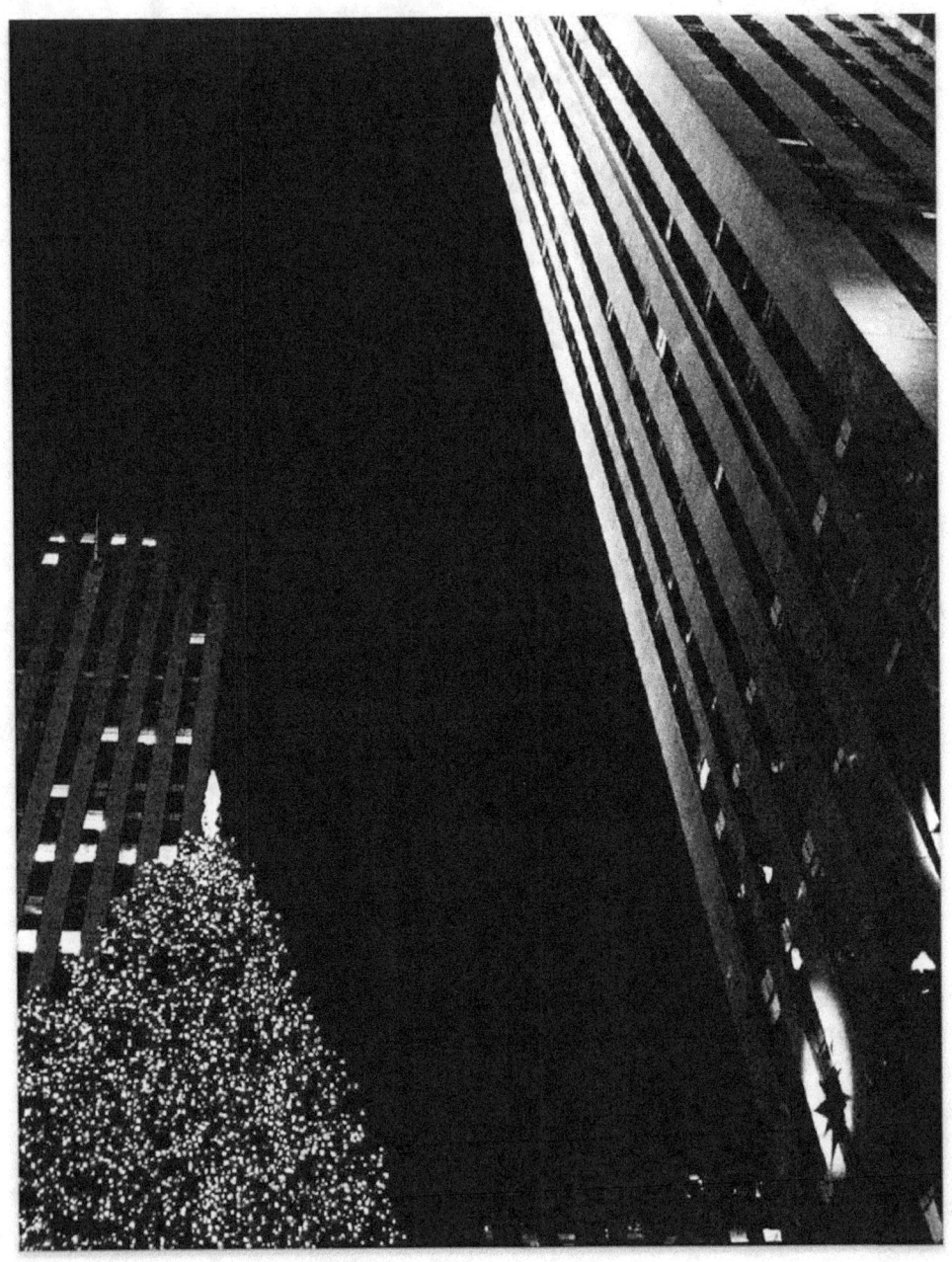

Rockefeller Plaza and 50th Street, facing south,
Comcast Building on right, December, 2009.

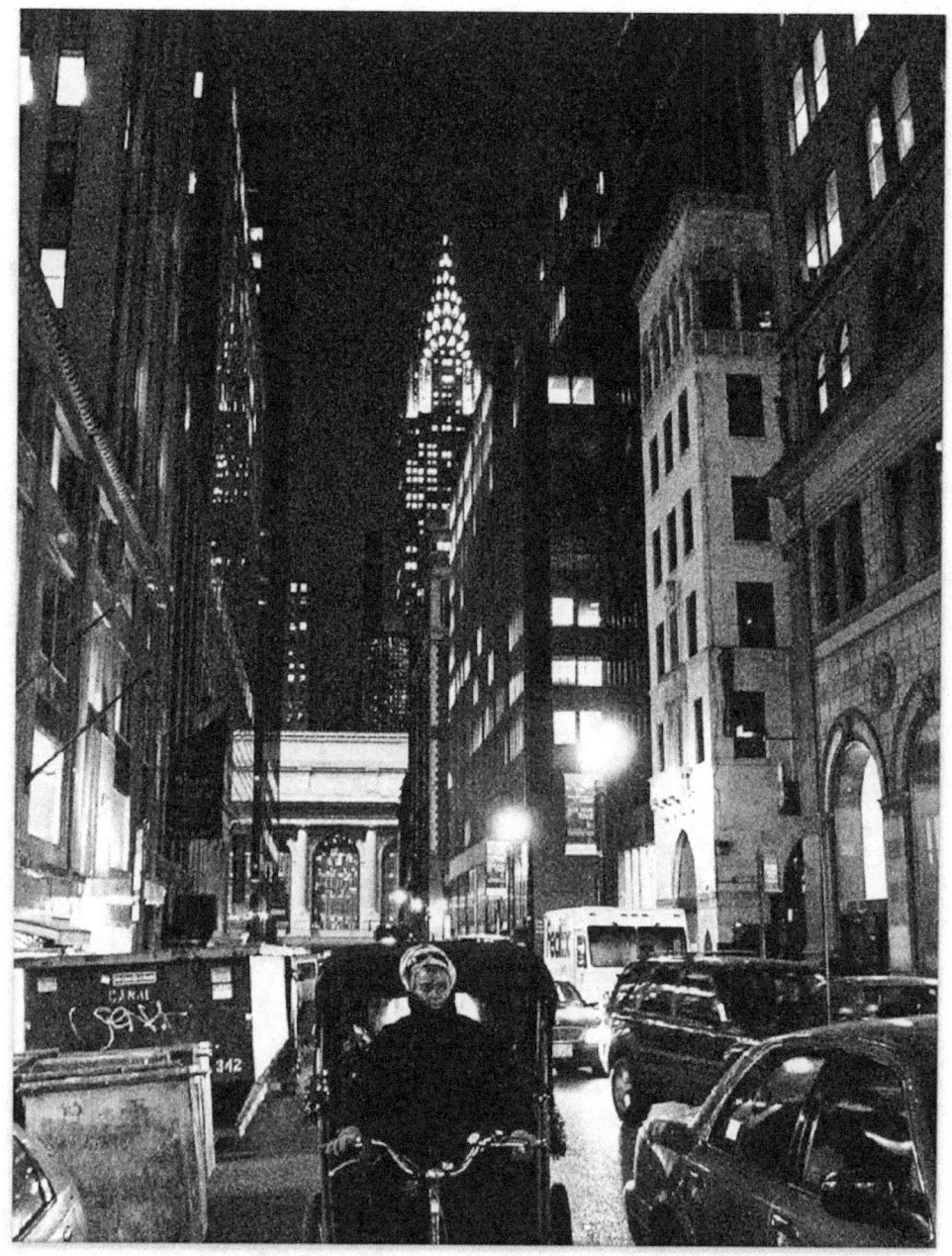

43rd Street, east of 5th Ave., Manhattan, facing east towards Grand Central Station,
Chrysler Building rear right, December, 2009.

West Side, Lower Manhattan, 2018

March 26, 2018, late afternoon: I am sitting in the passenger seat while my friend George drives uptown on West Street, also known as Route 9A. This is lower Manhattan on the western edge of Greenwich Village and traffic is very heavy. We are moving slowly.

It's a great opportunity. I am returning home with nothing to do except look out the window, or if George says something, maybe respond (we're old friends). I have my little point-and-shoot digital camera - not a phone - and I can just click away as we travel at just over walking speed. I mention "not a phone" because I still don't look at phones as cameras. For shooting out a car window like this it probably should not matter what I use – it's psychological I know – but I still like the *idea* of a camera.

This part of Manhattan has been experiencing what I would call intense development: new buildings and other construction almost everywhere I look (2018). This is just north of the World Trade Center site, in a section that once housed the meat-packing point of entry for the city. Now, instead, it has stores, restaurants, and other tourist attractions.

This area also contains the old New York Central rail connections that once moved freight into the district. It really was an amazing transportation idea: freight boxcars on elevated track beds moved to and *through* buildings, making deliveries along the way. Today - and just as amazing - a 1.5 mile section of this elevated track bed, called the High Line, has gardens and a walking path instead of track.

These photographs are shown in the actual order taken. They are full-frame with no manipulation.

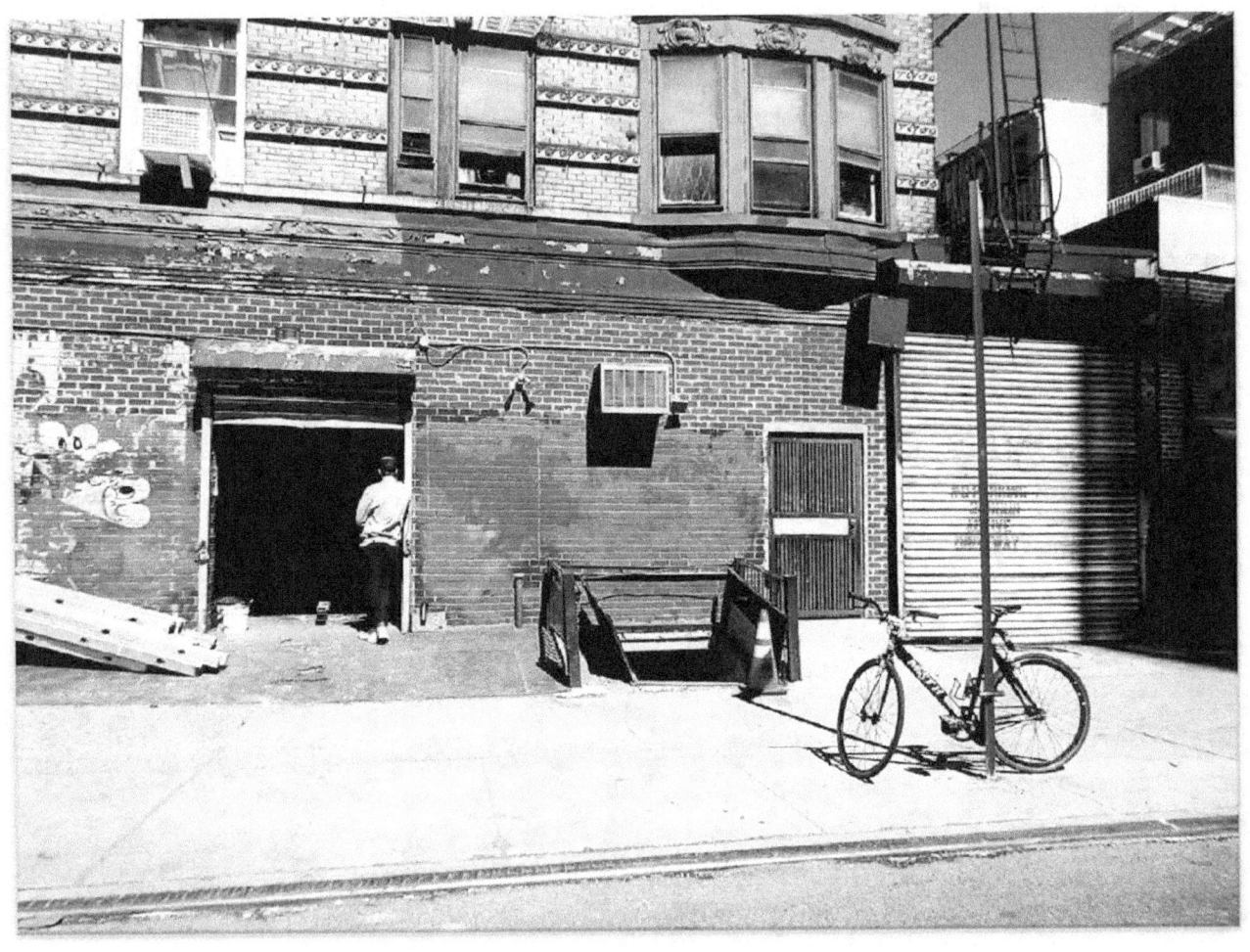

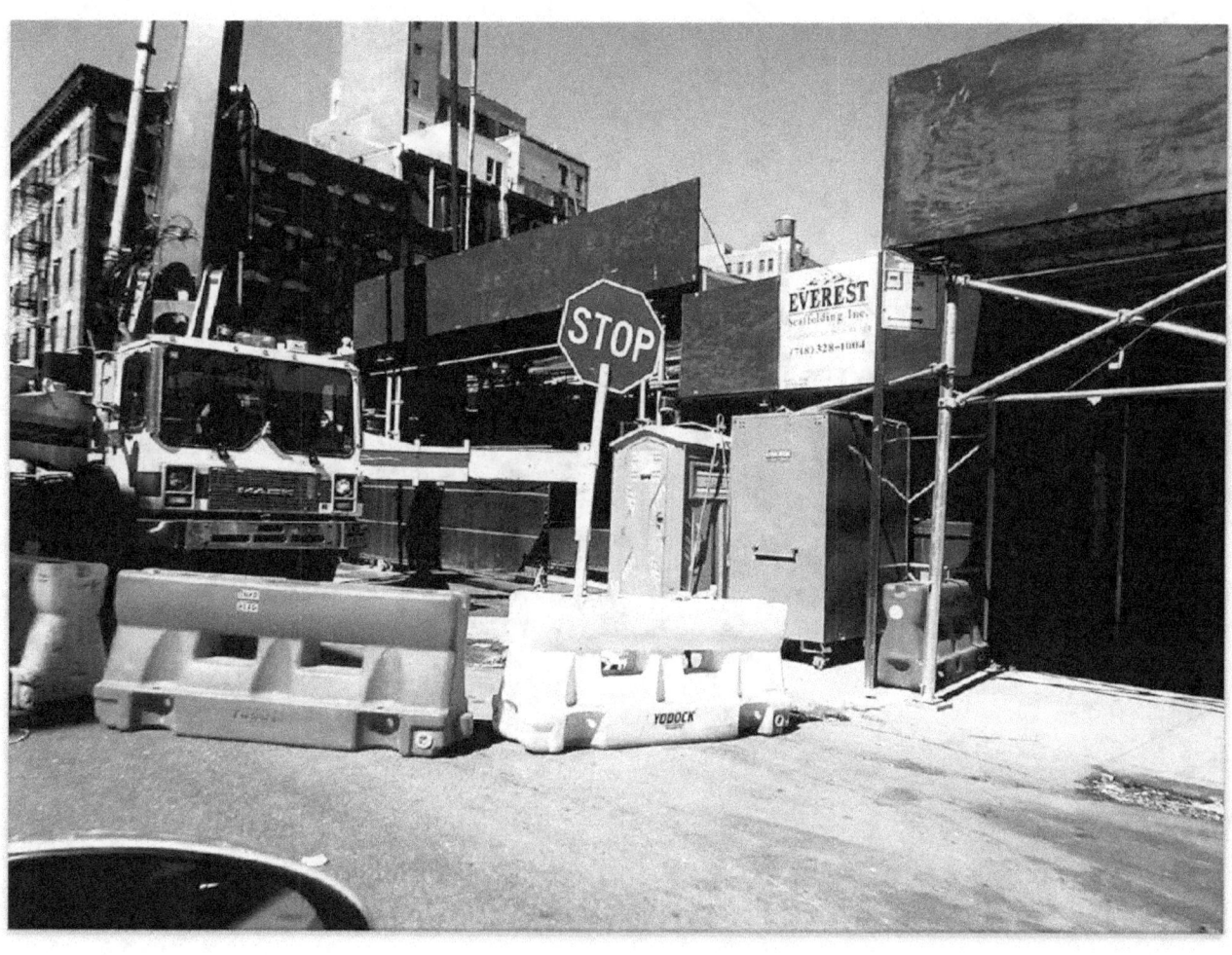

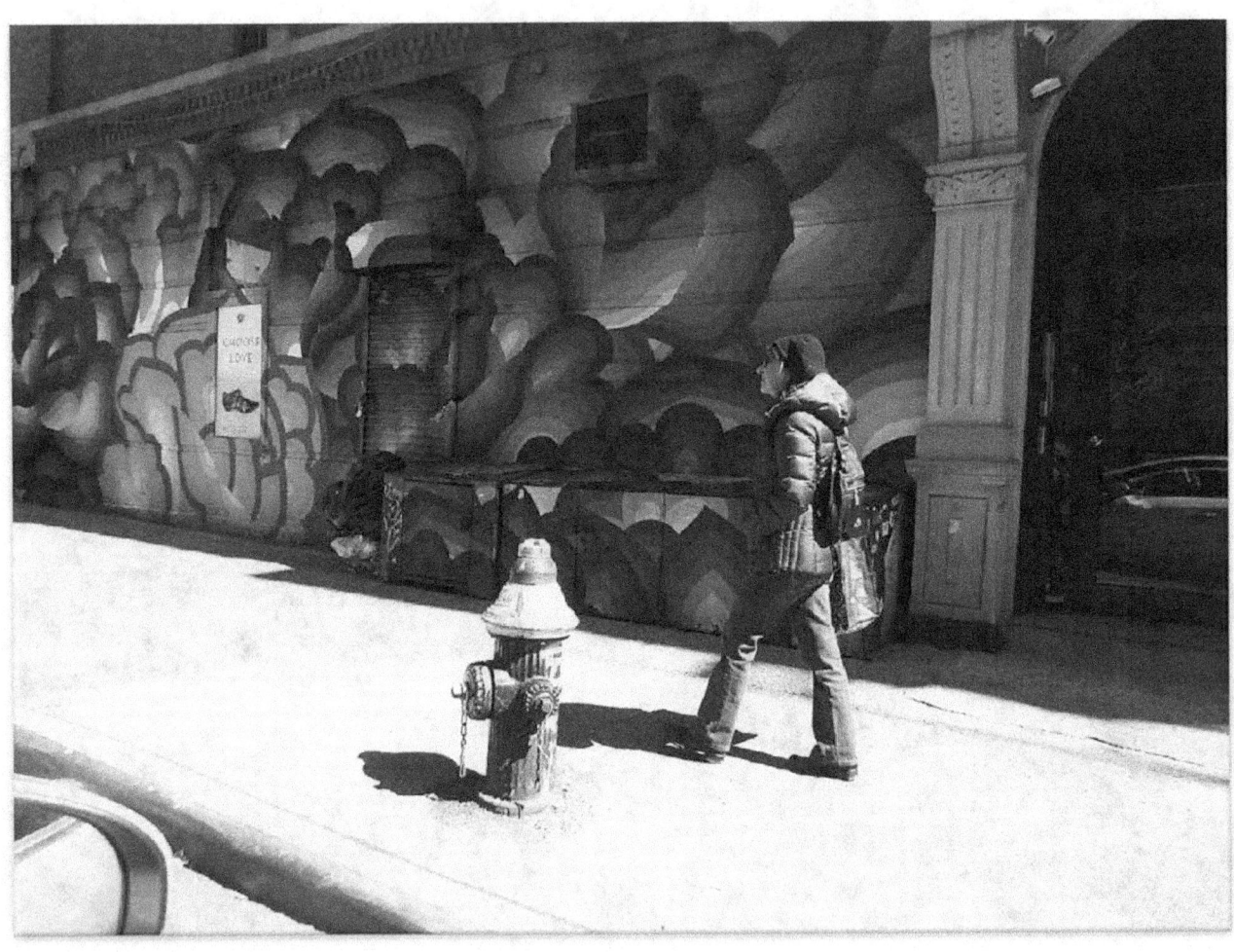

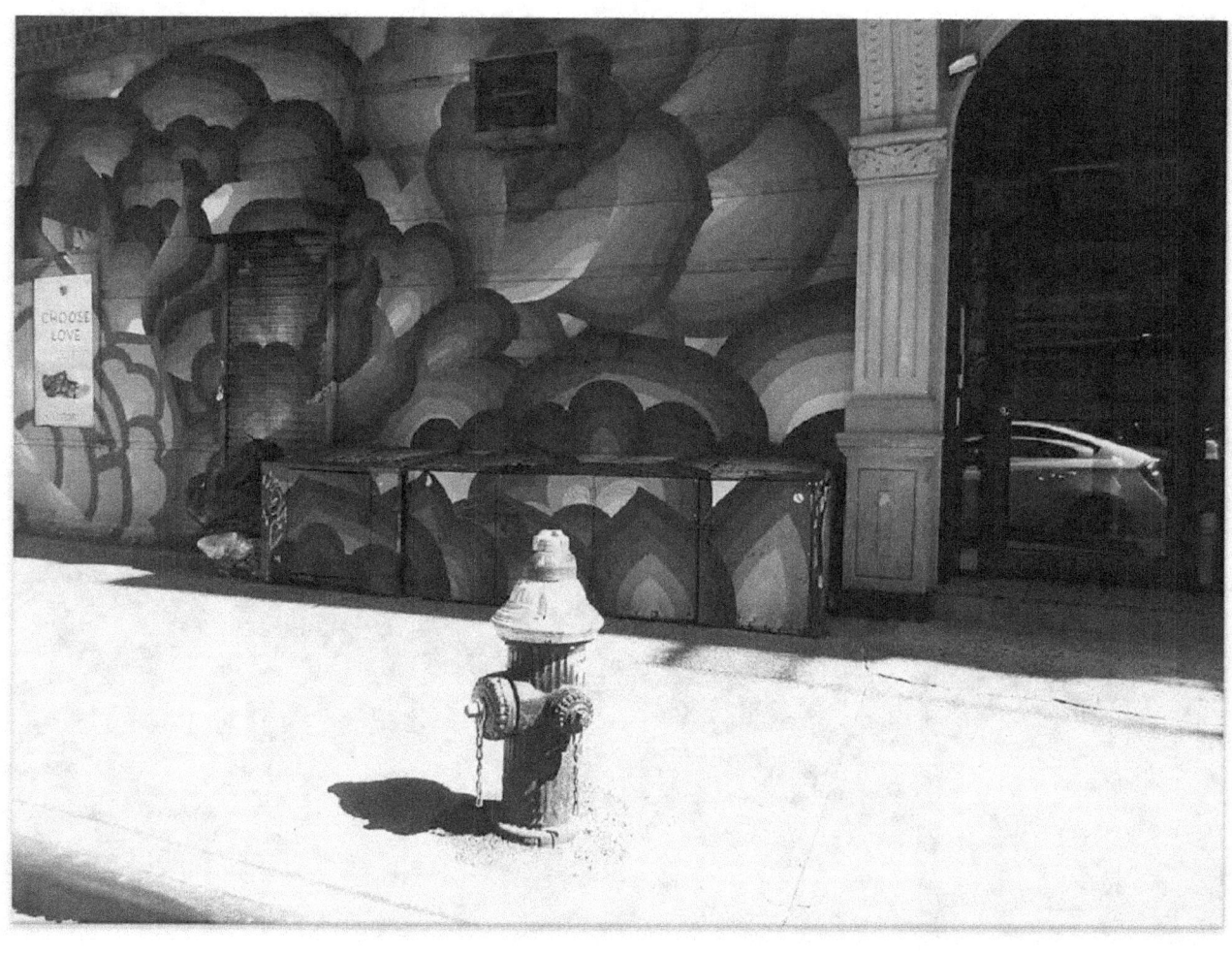

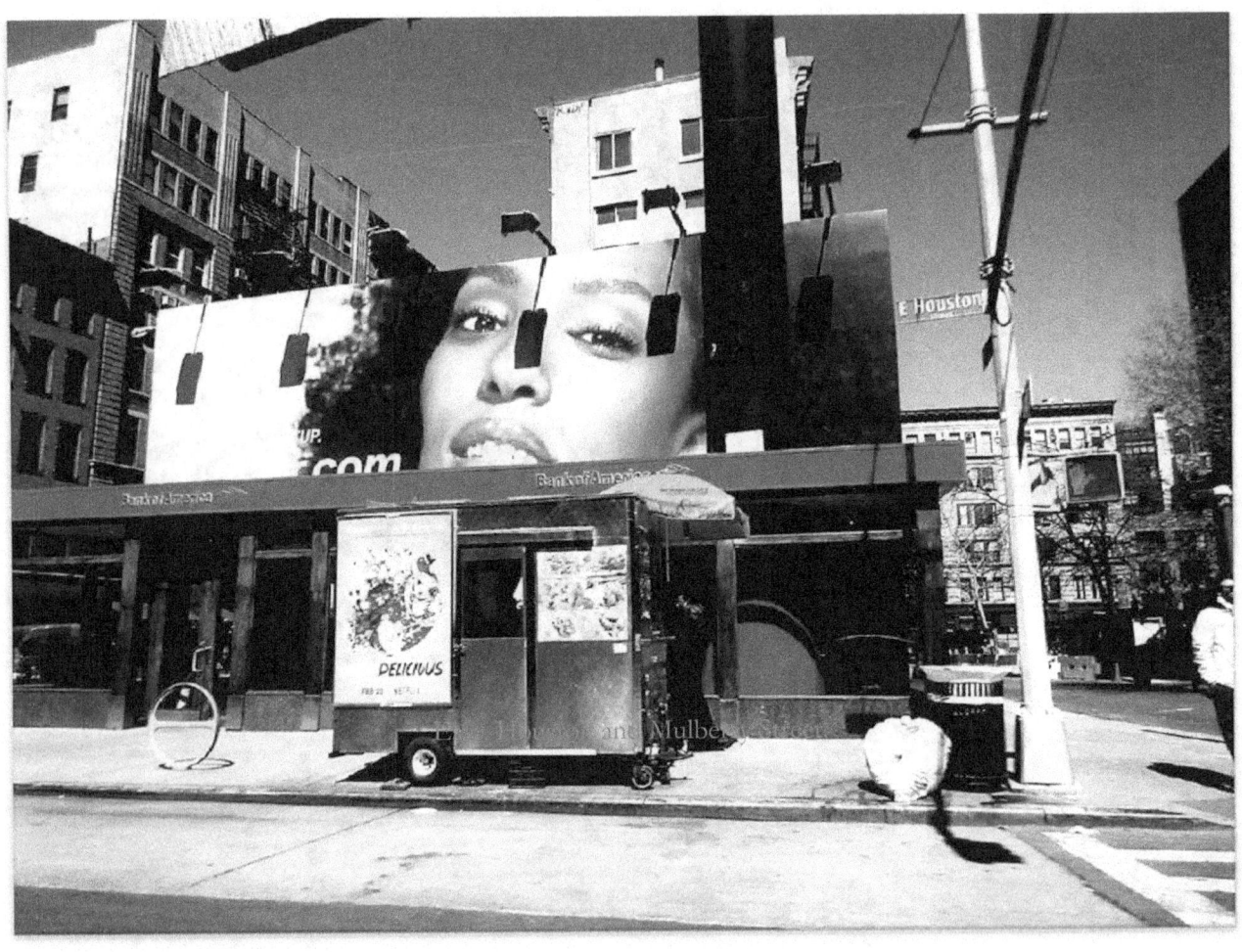

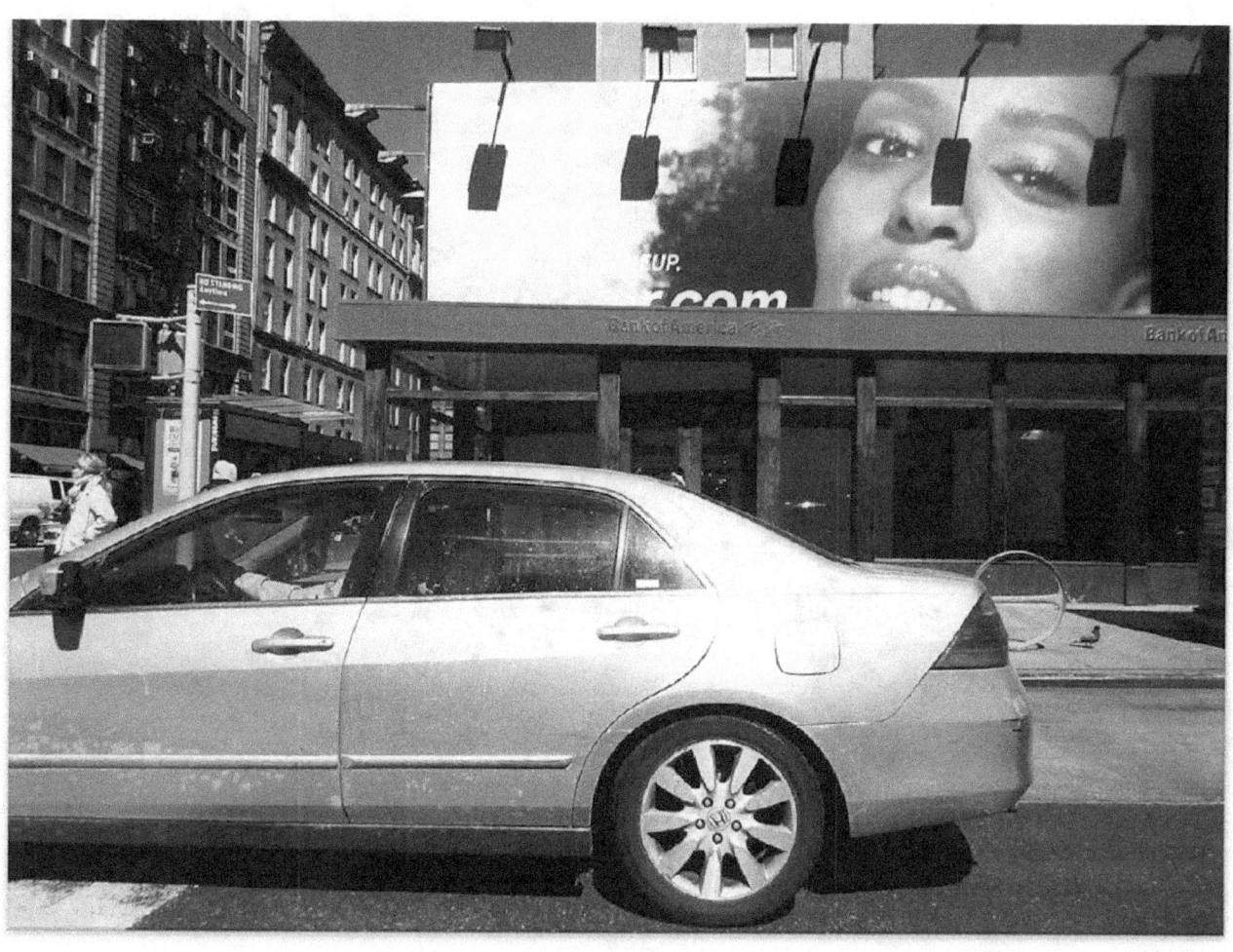

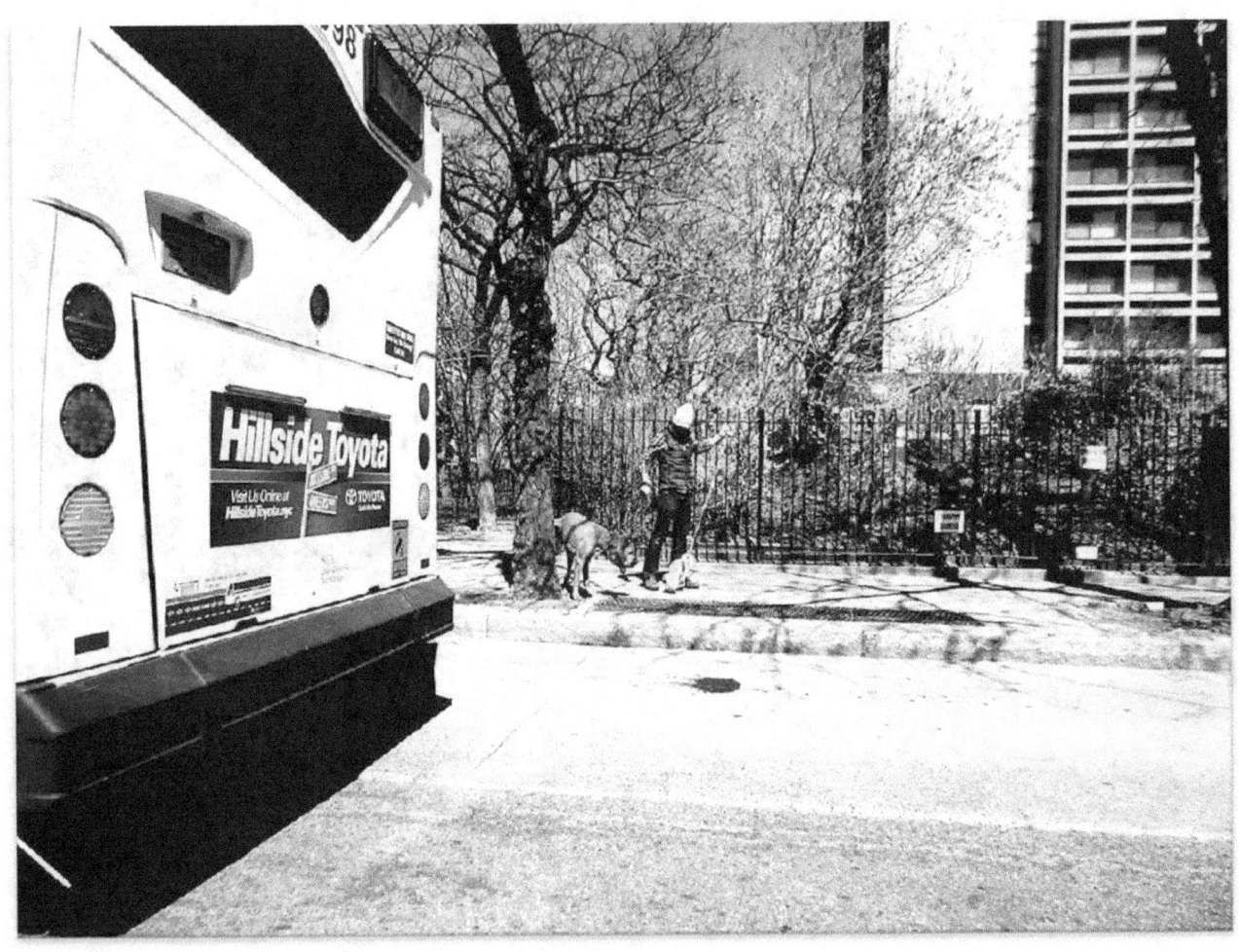

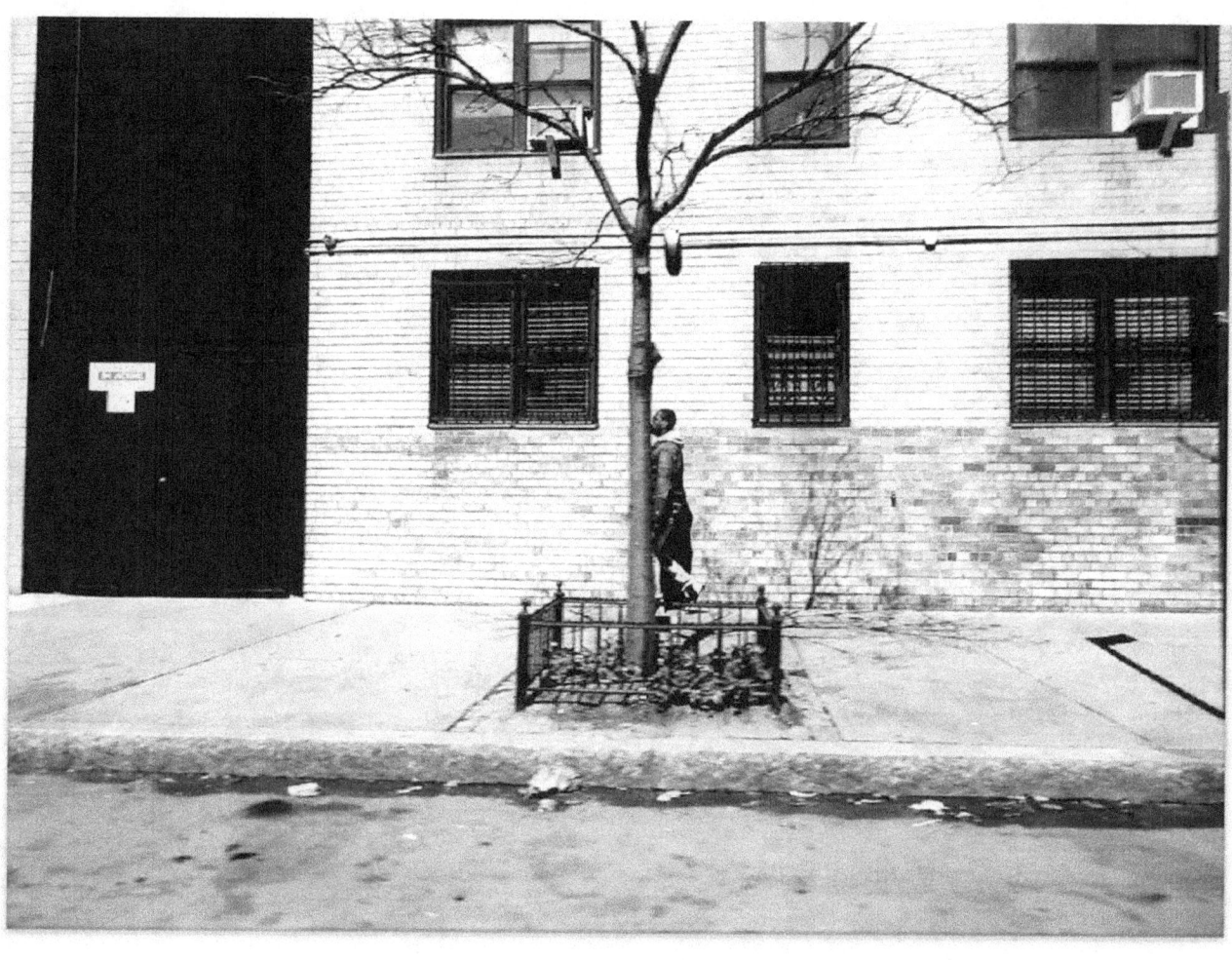

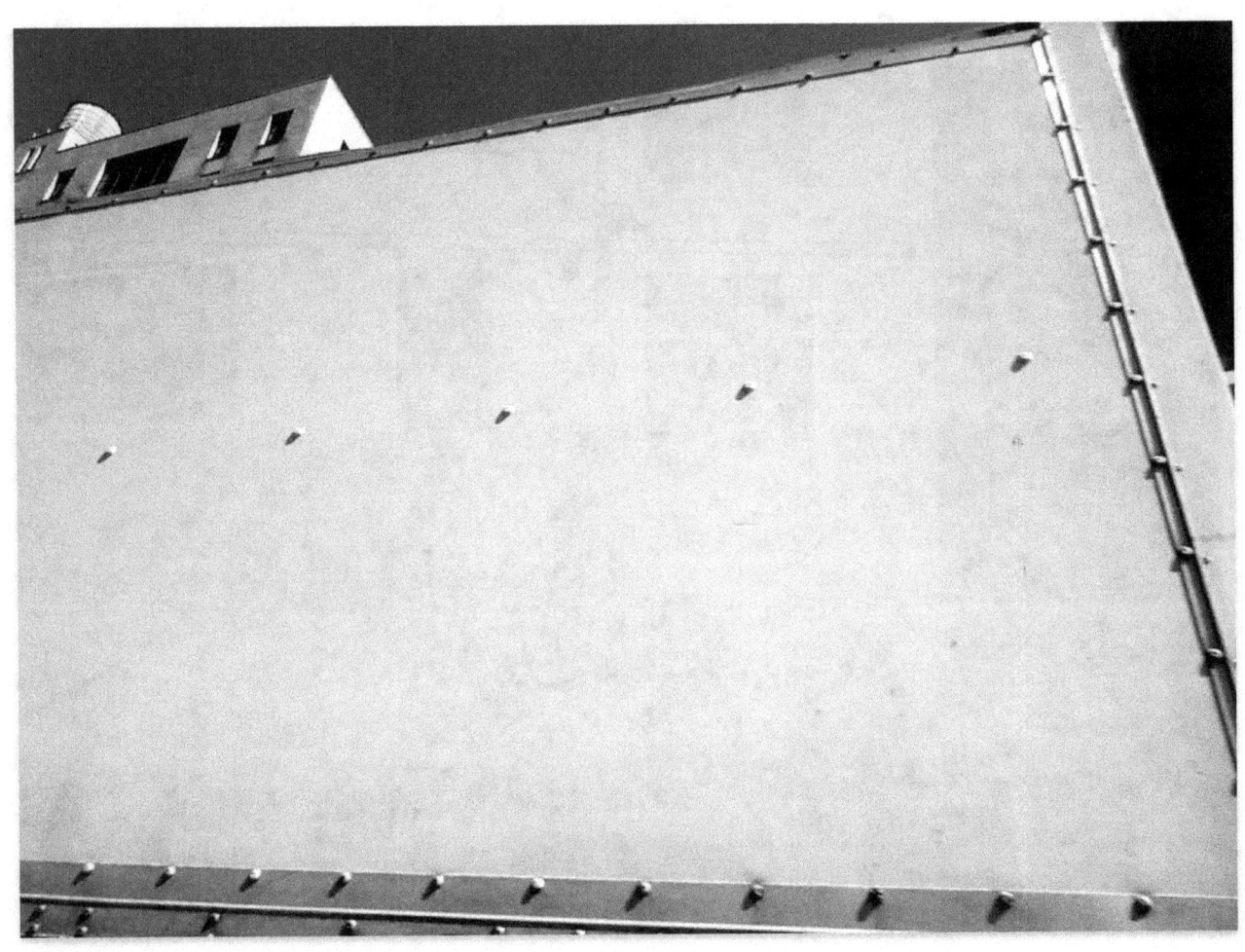

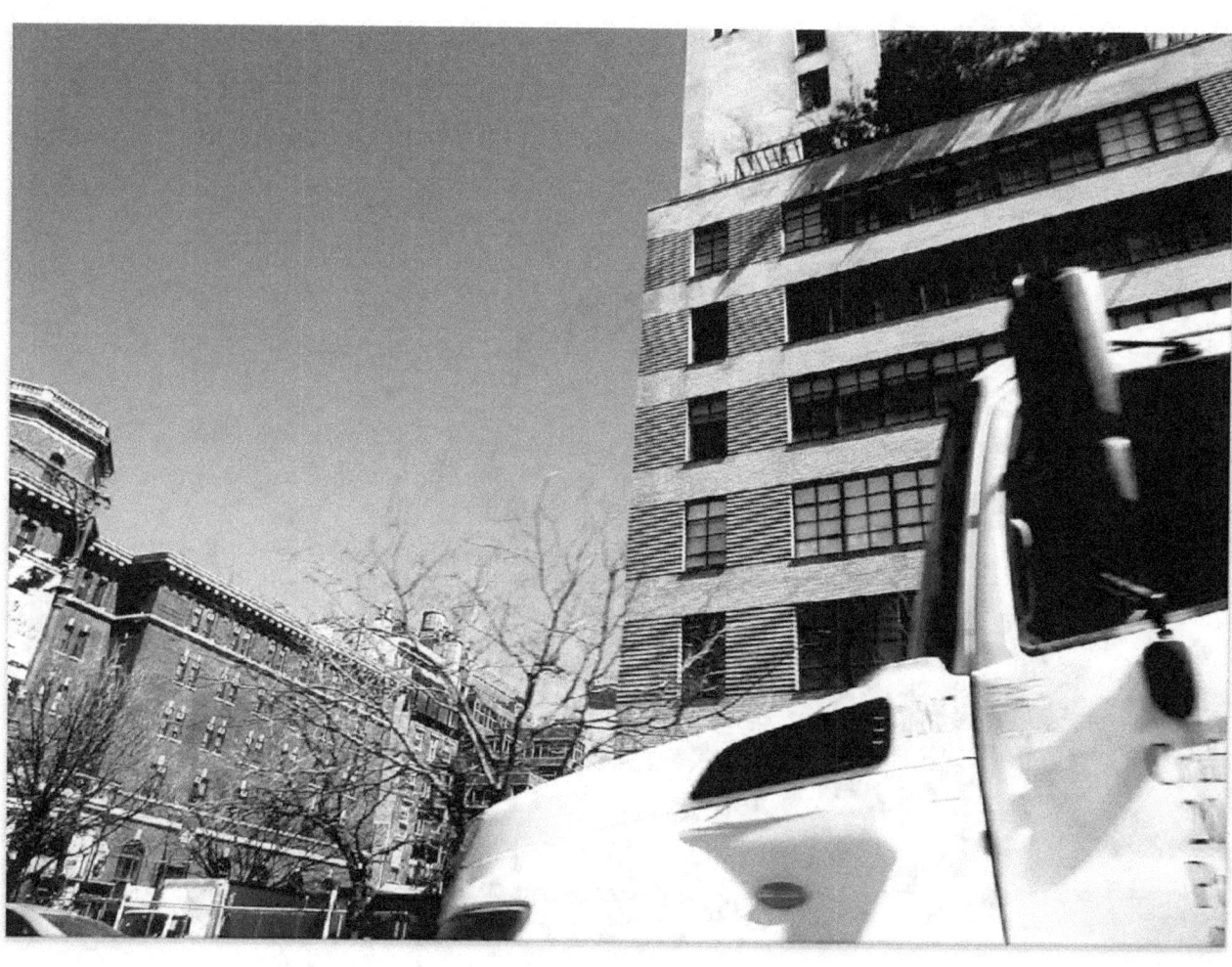

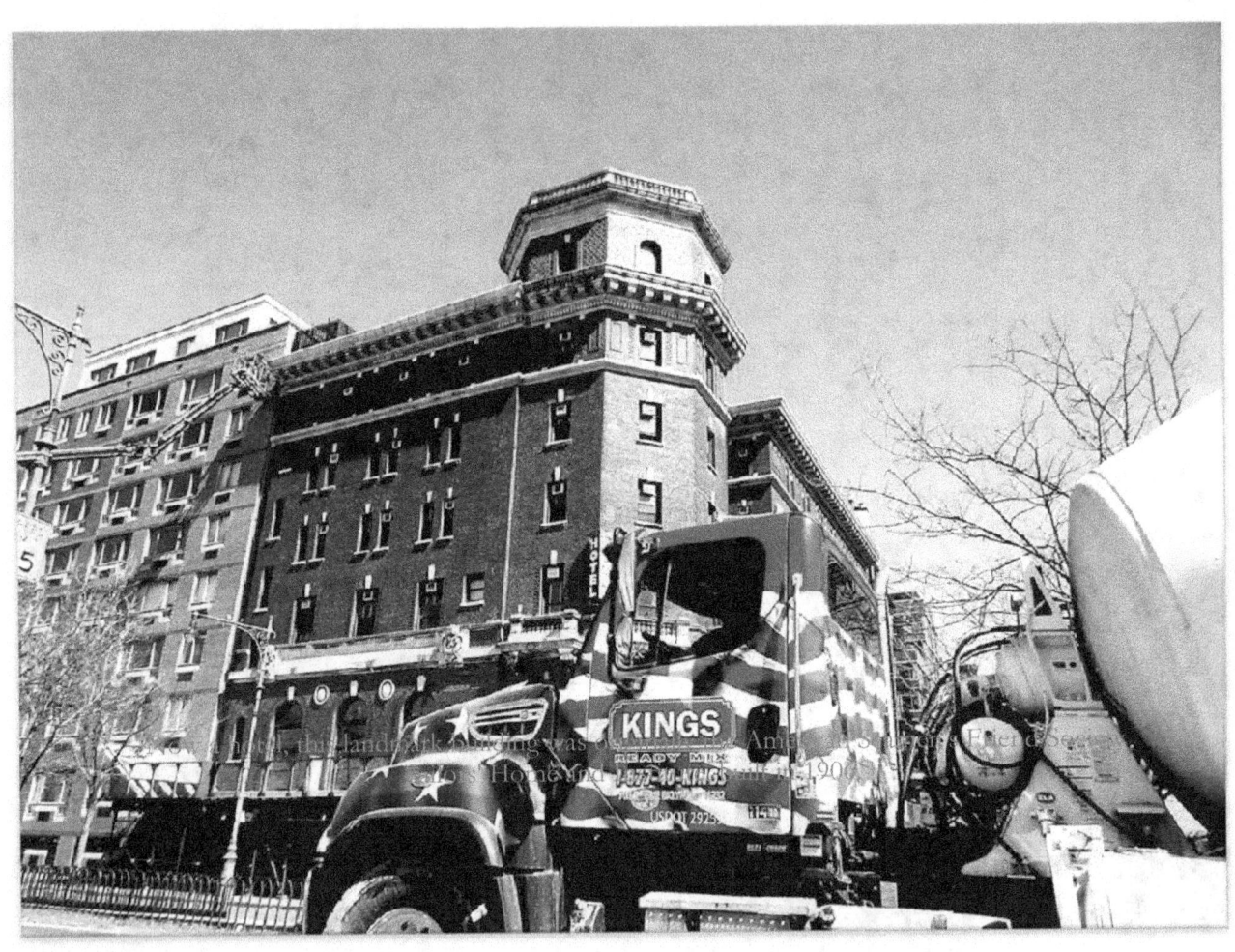

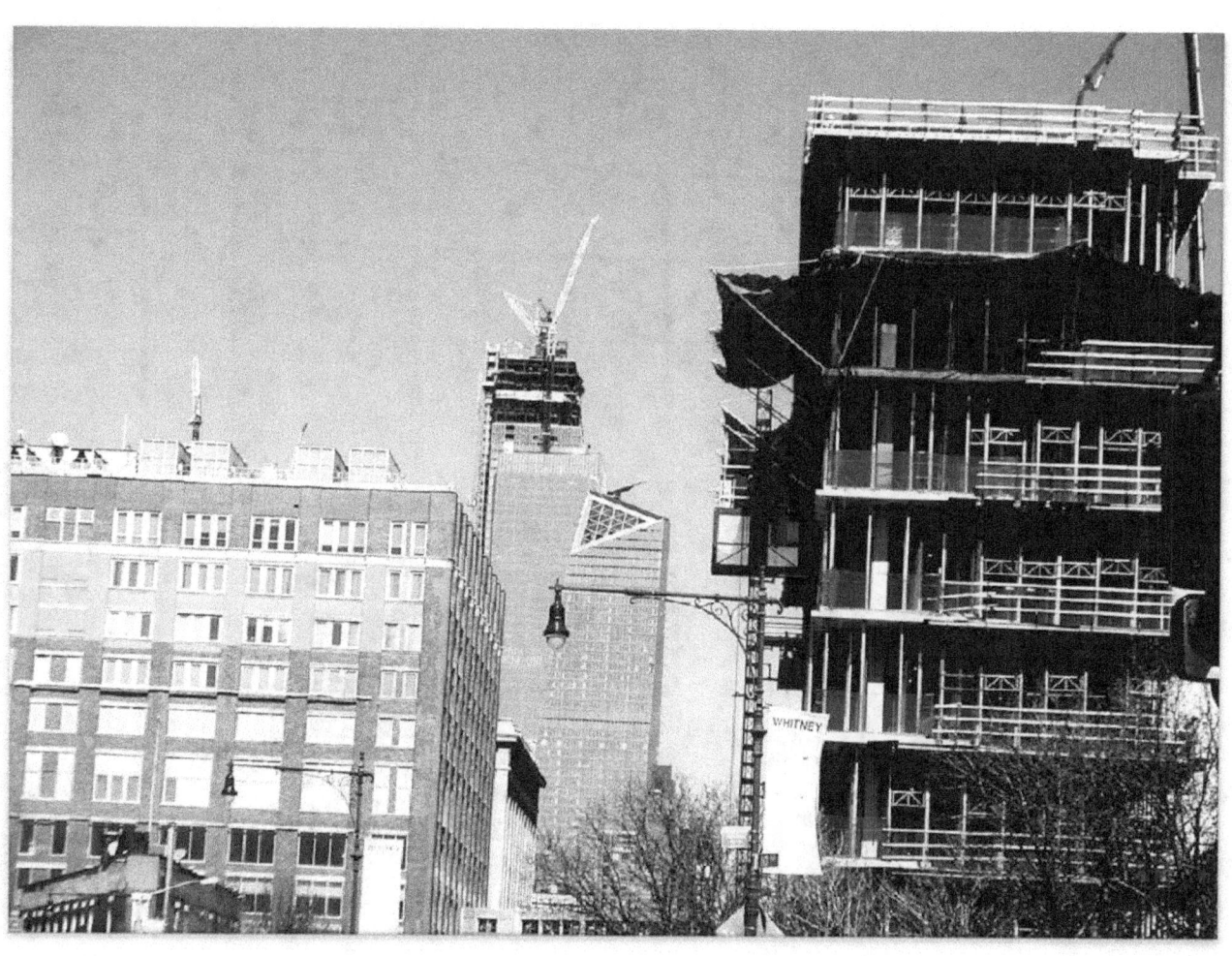

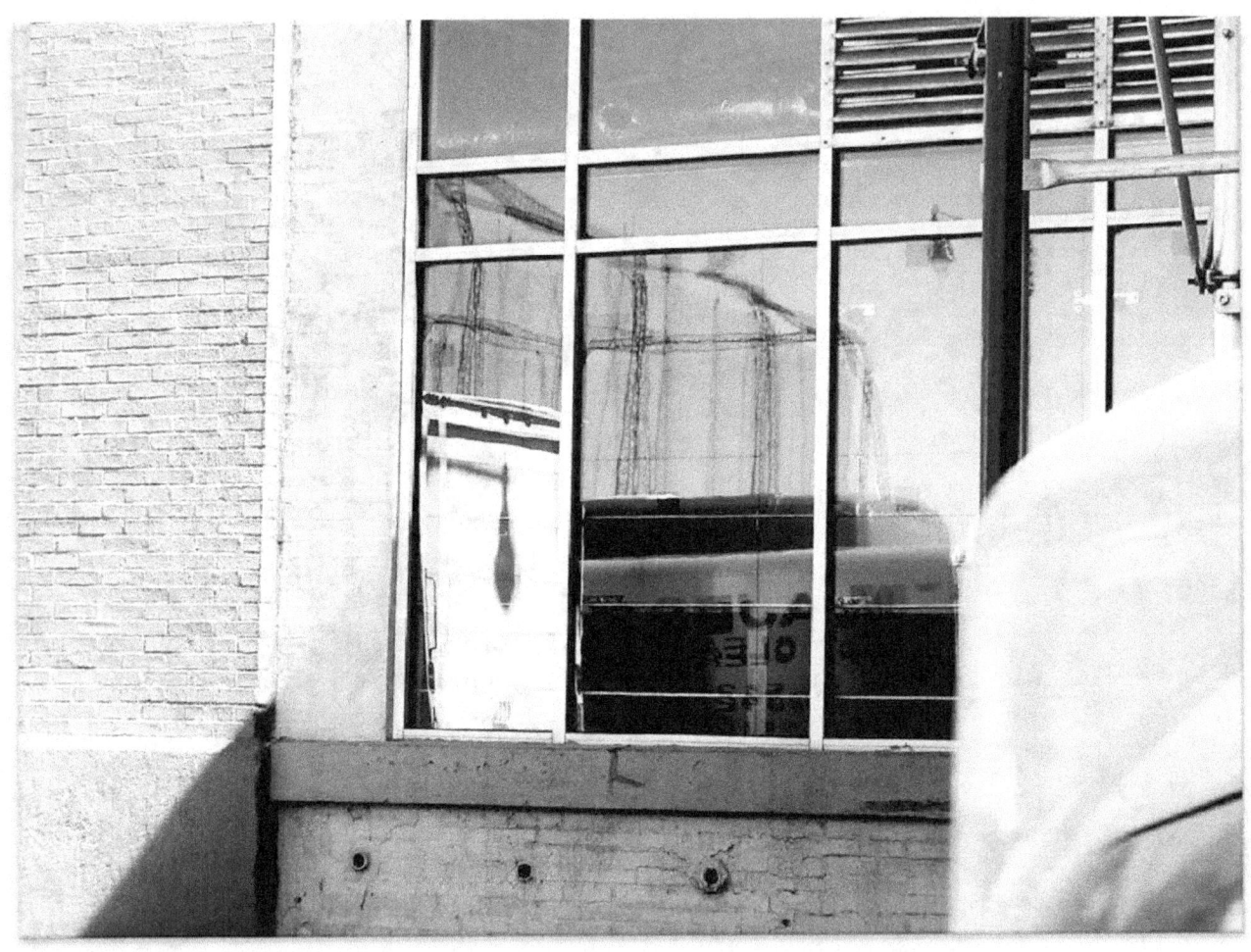

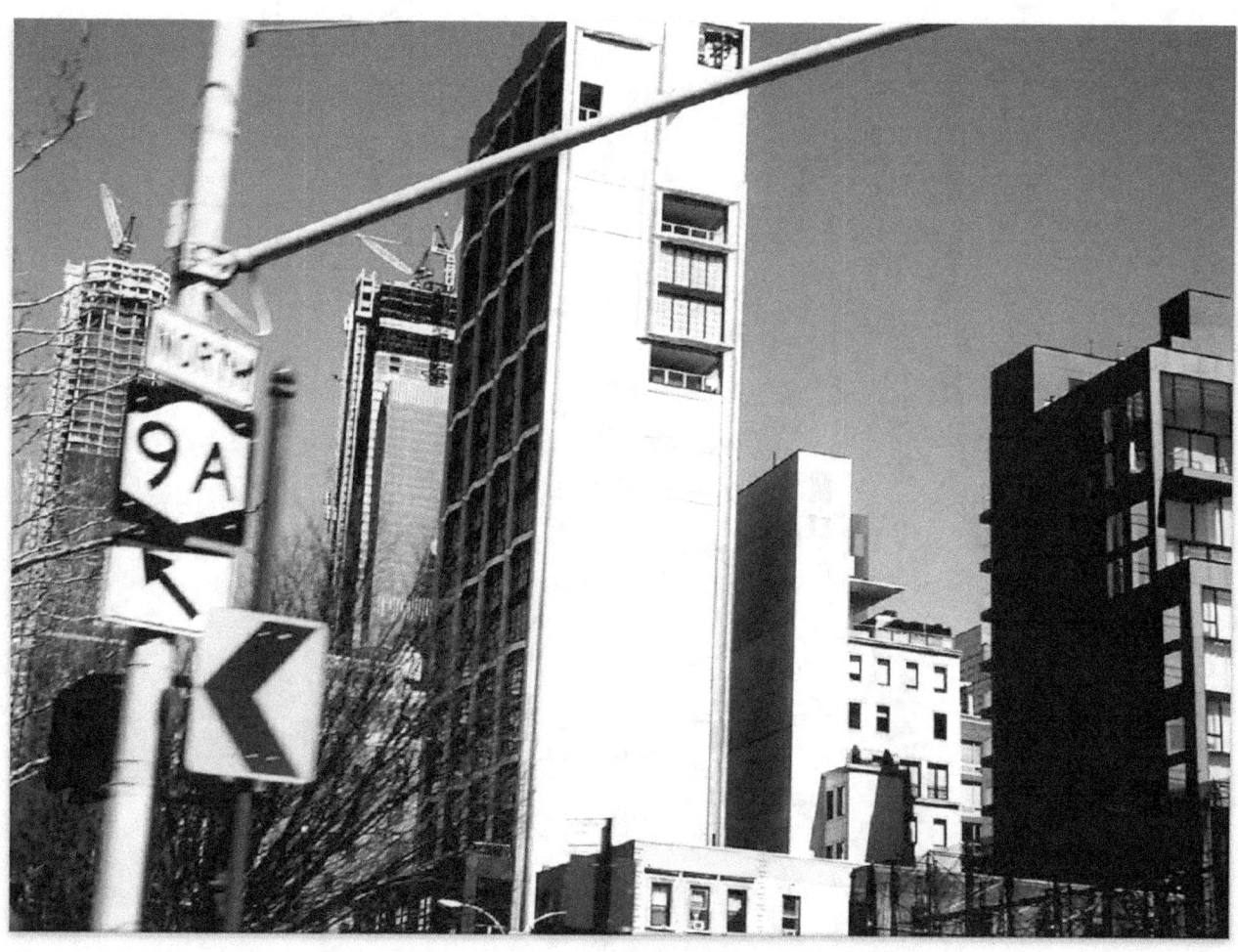

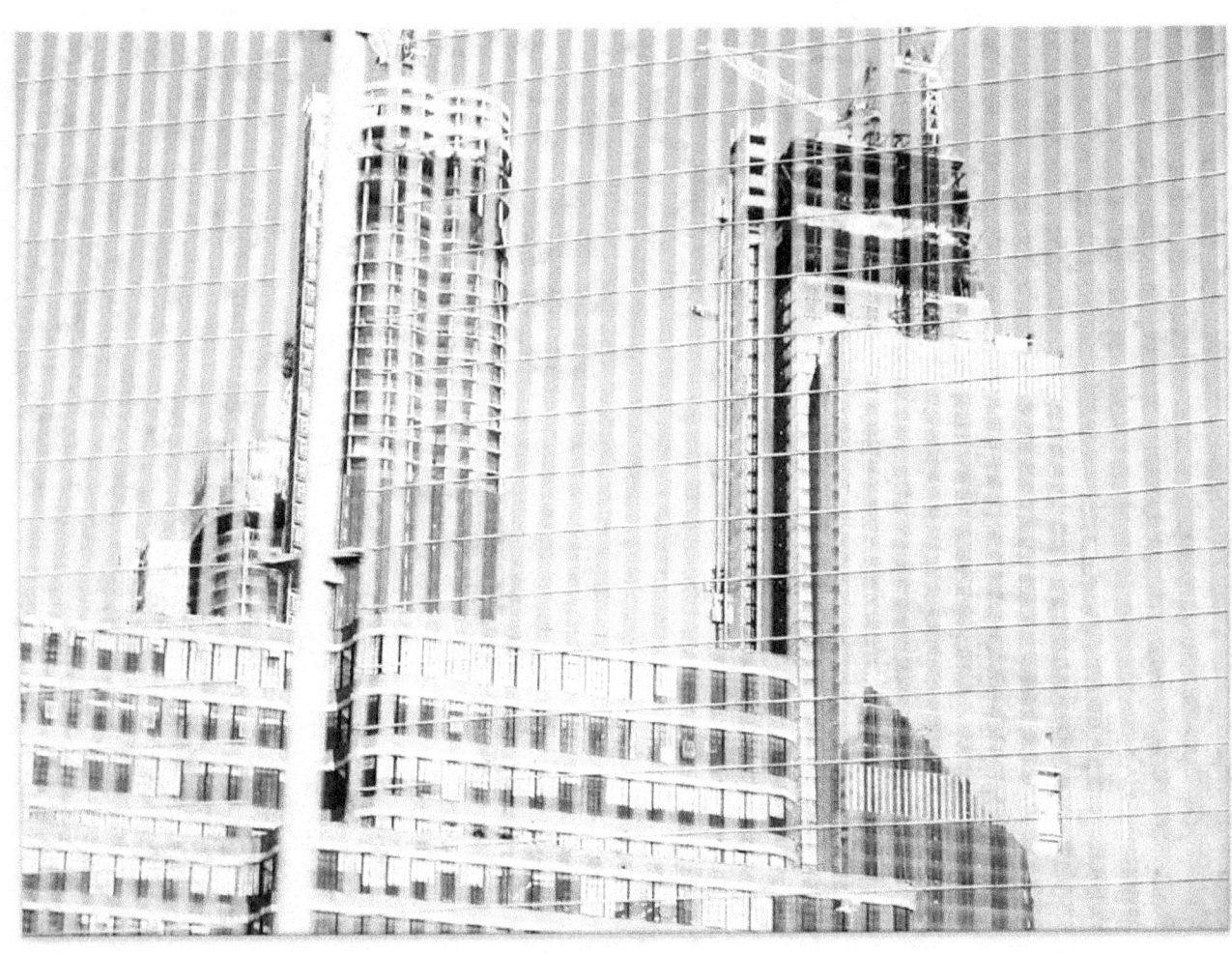

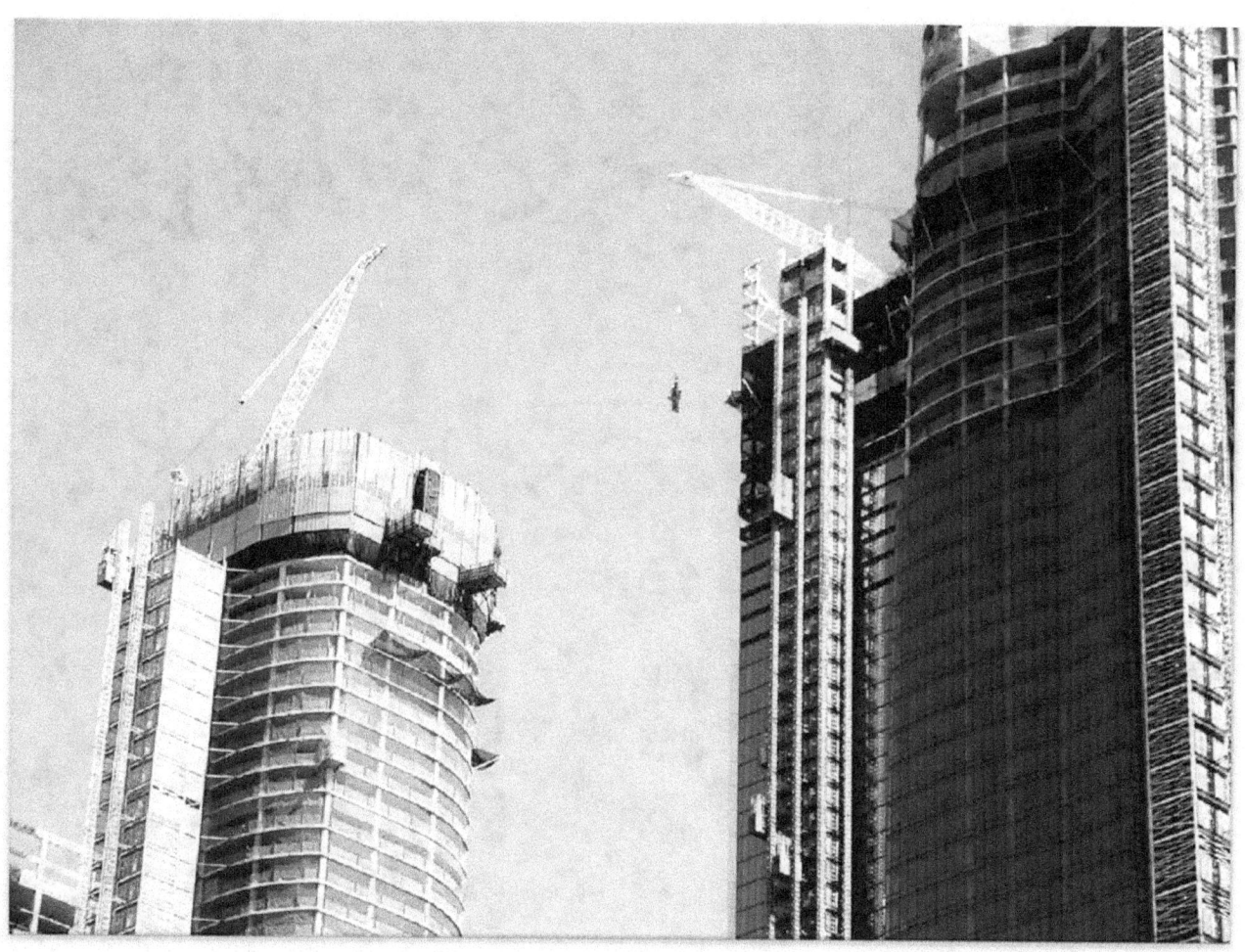

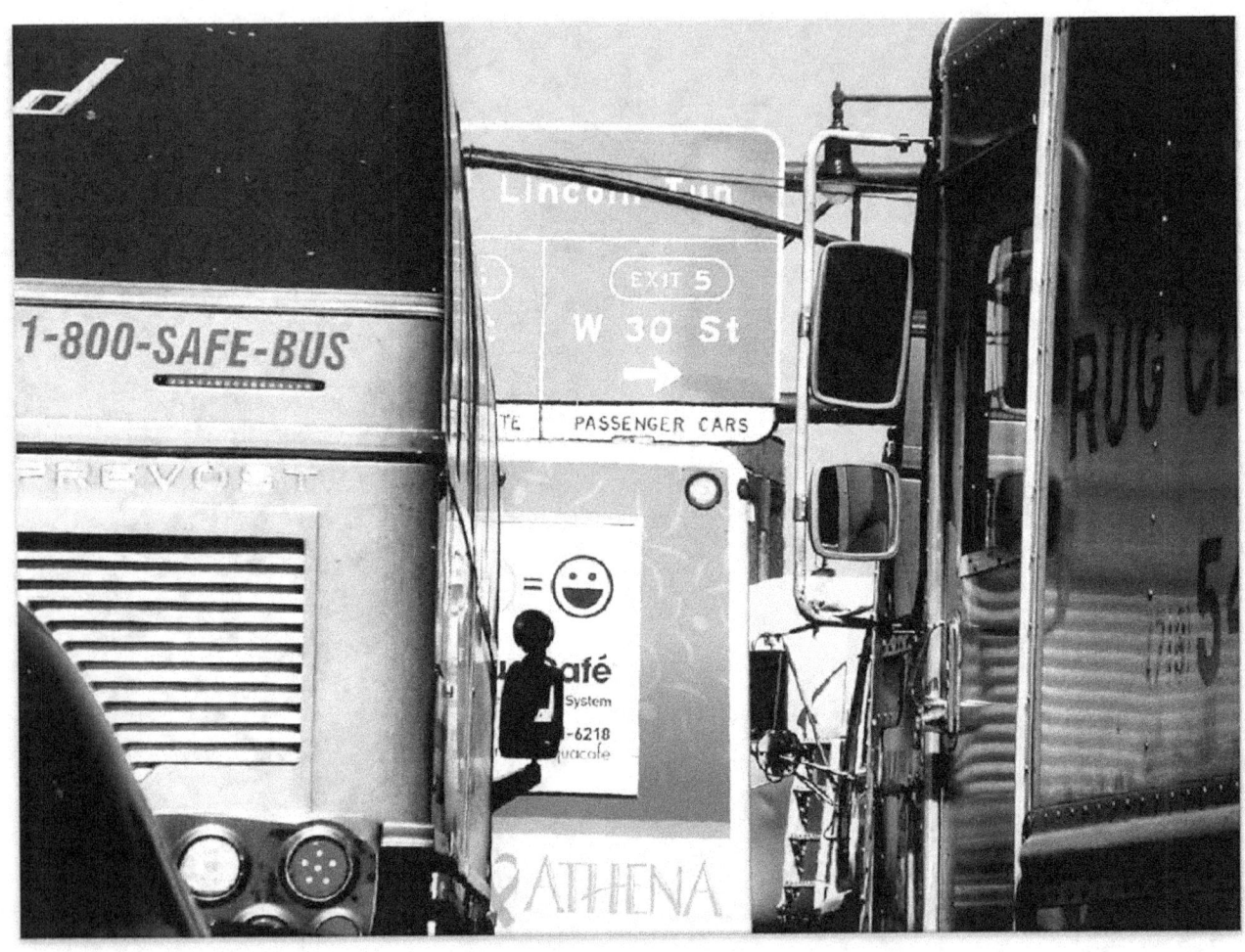

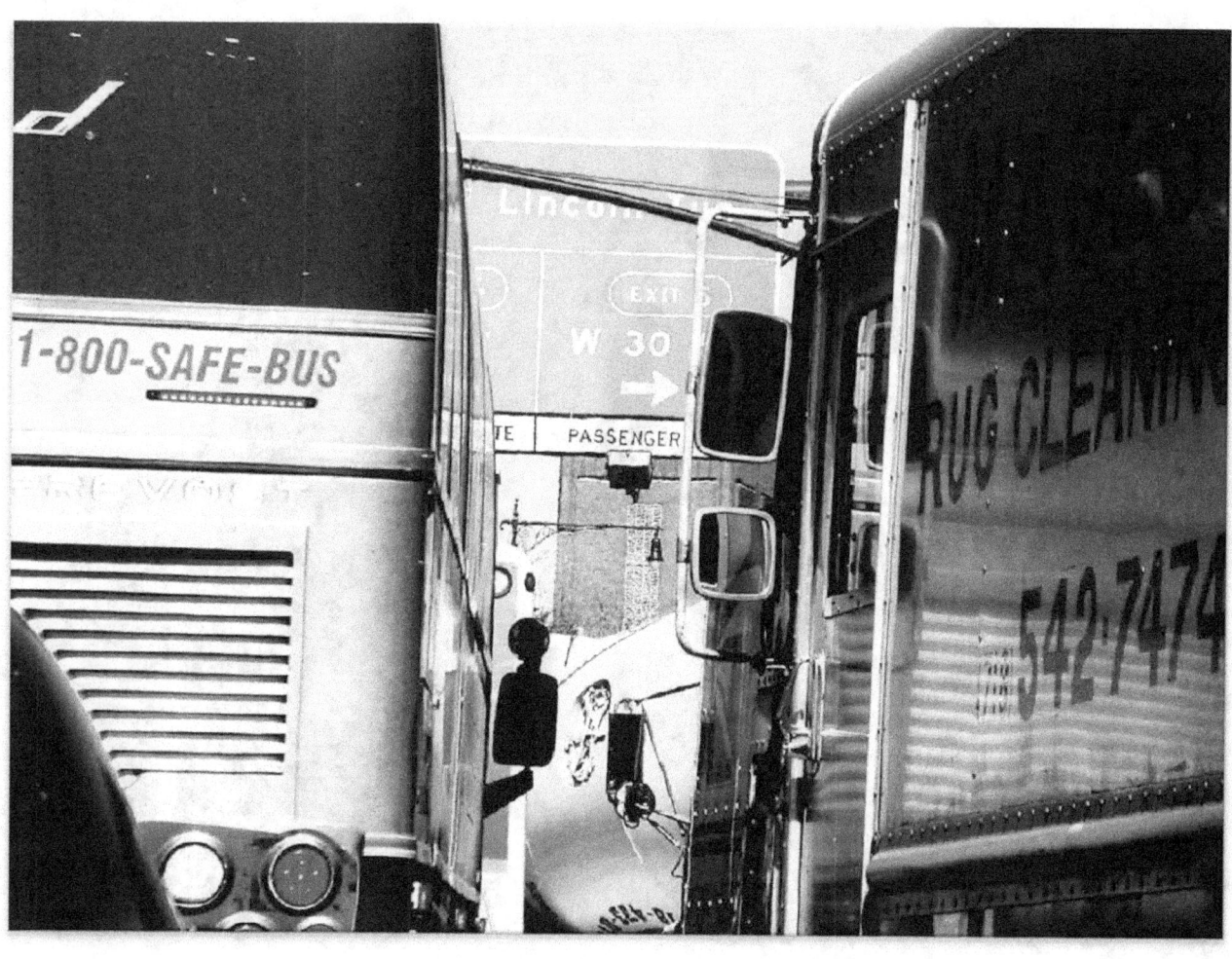

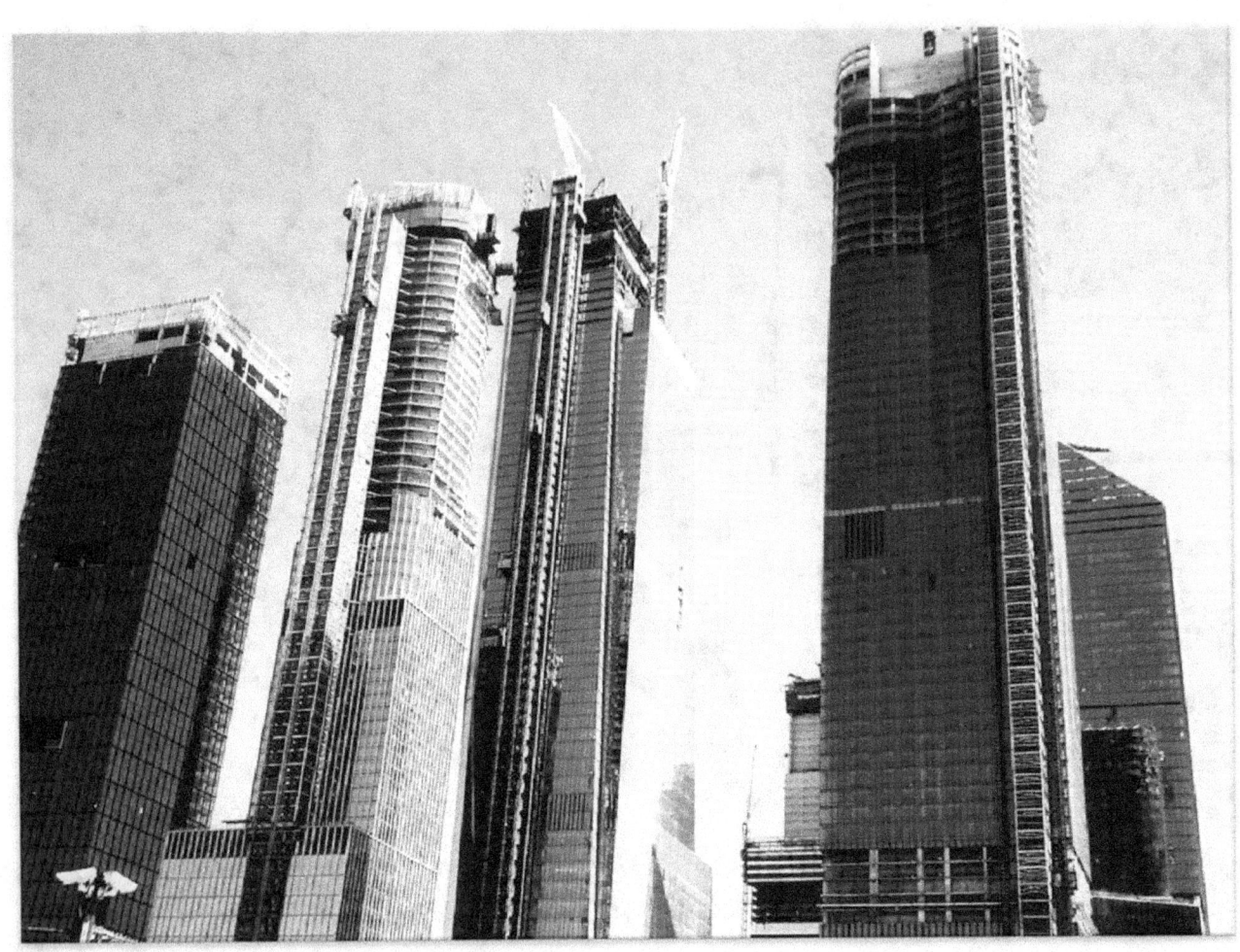

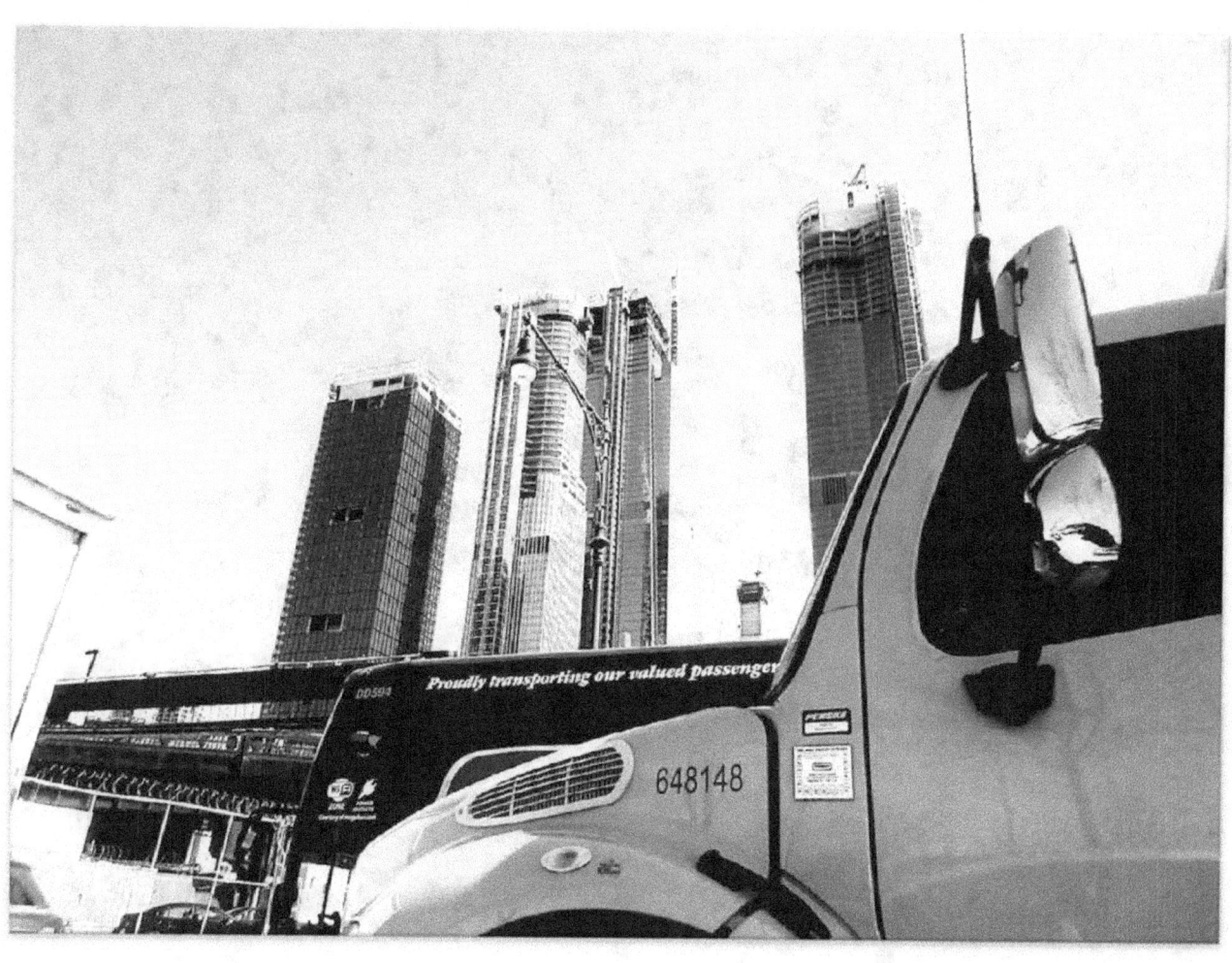

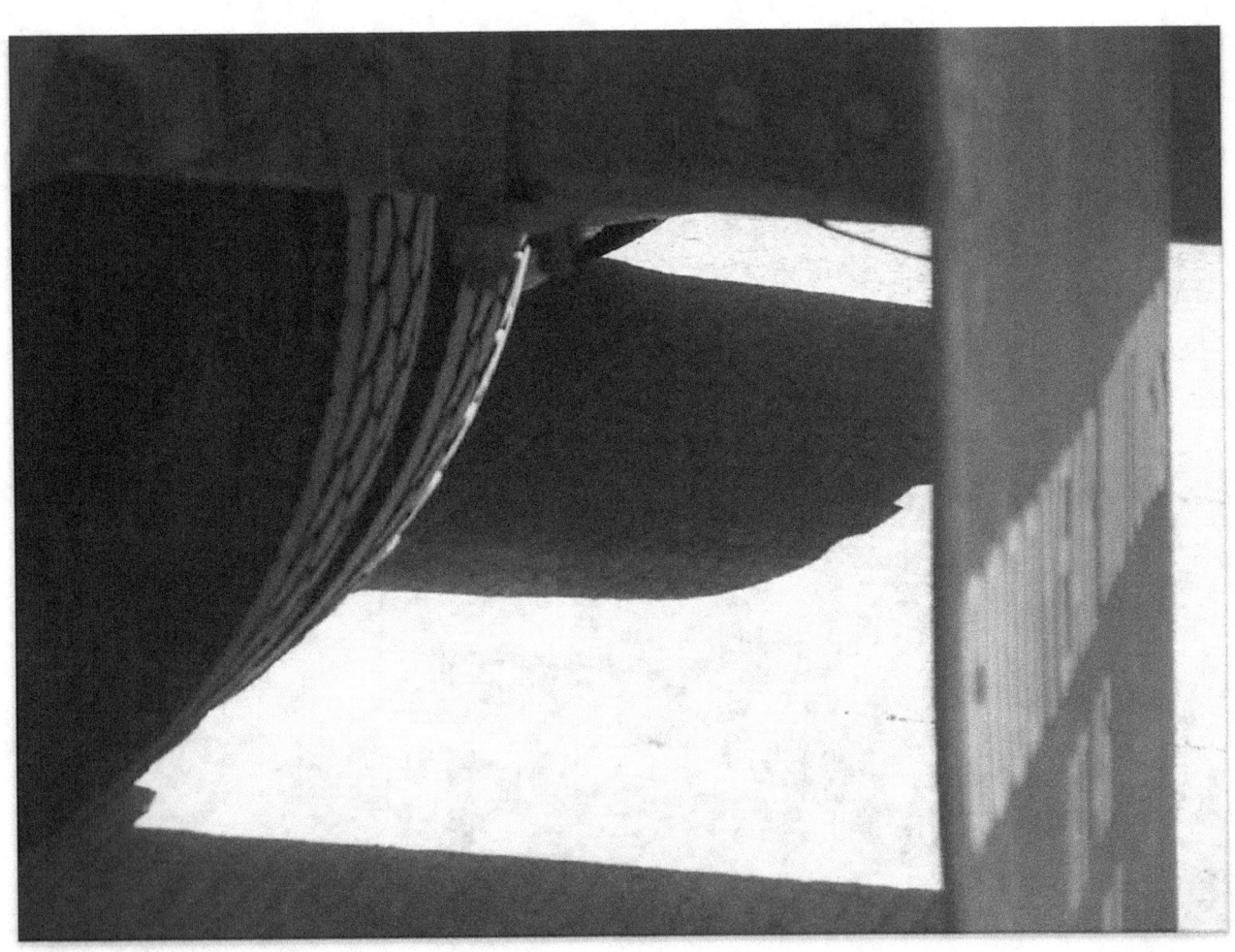

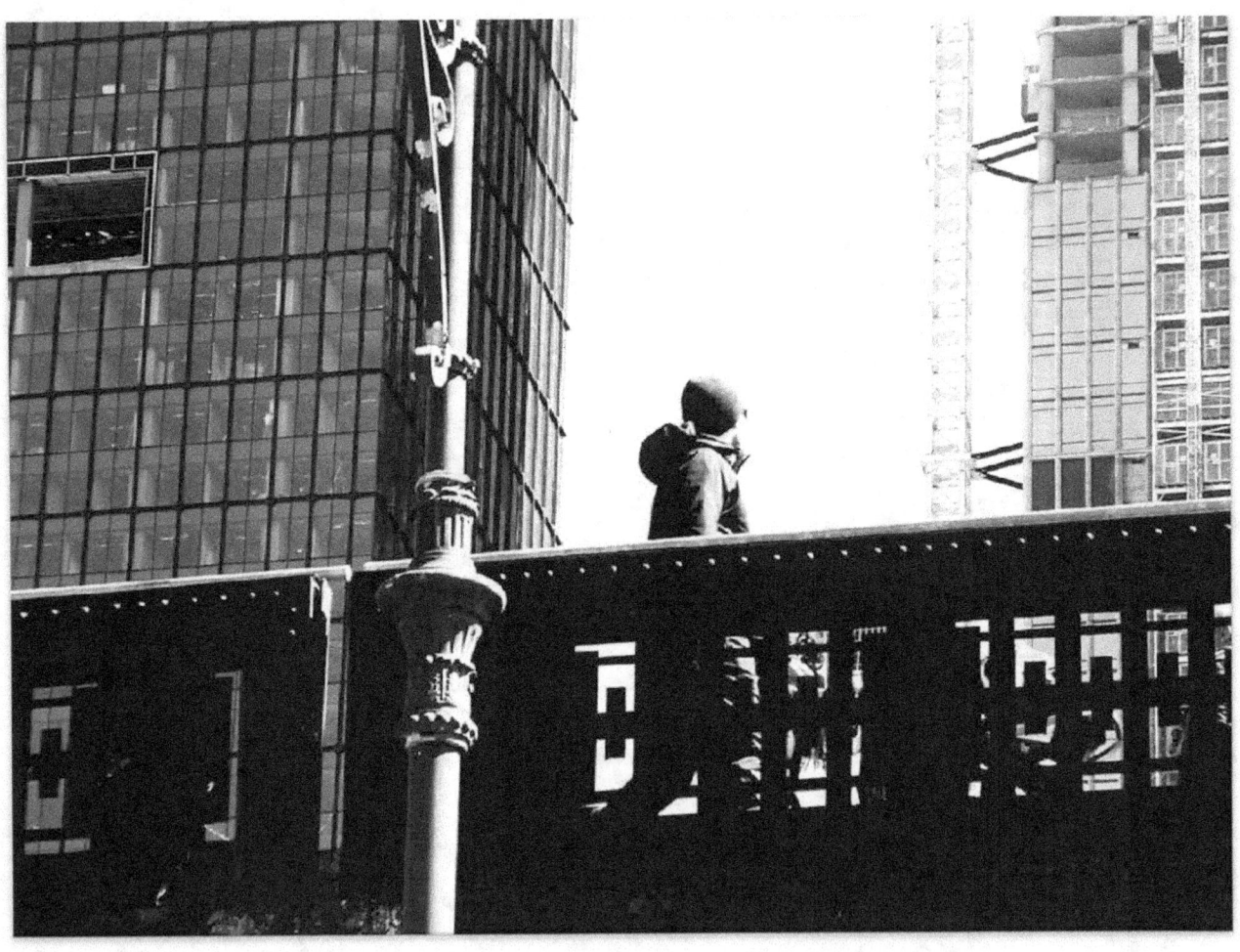

A zoomed in shot of a walker on the High Line.

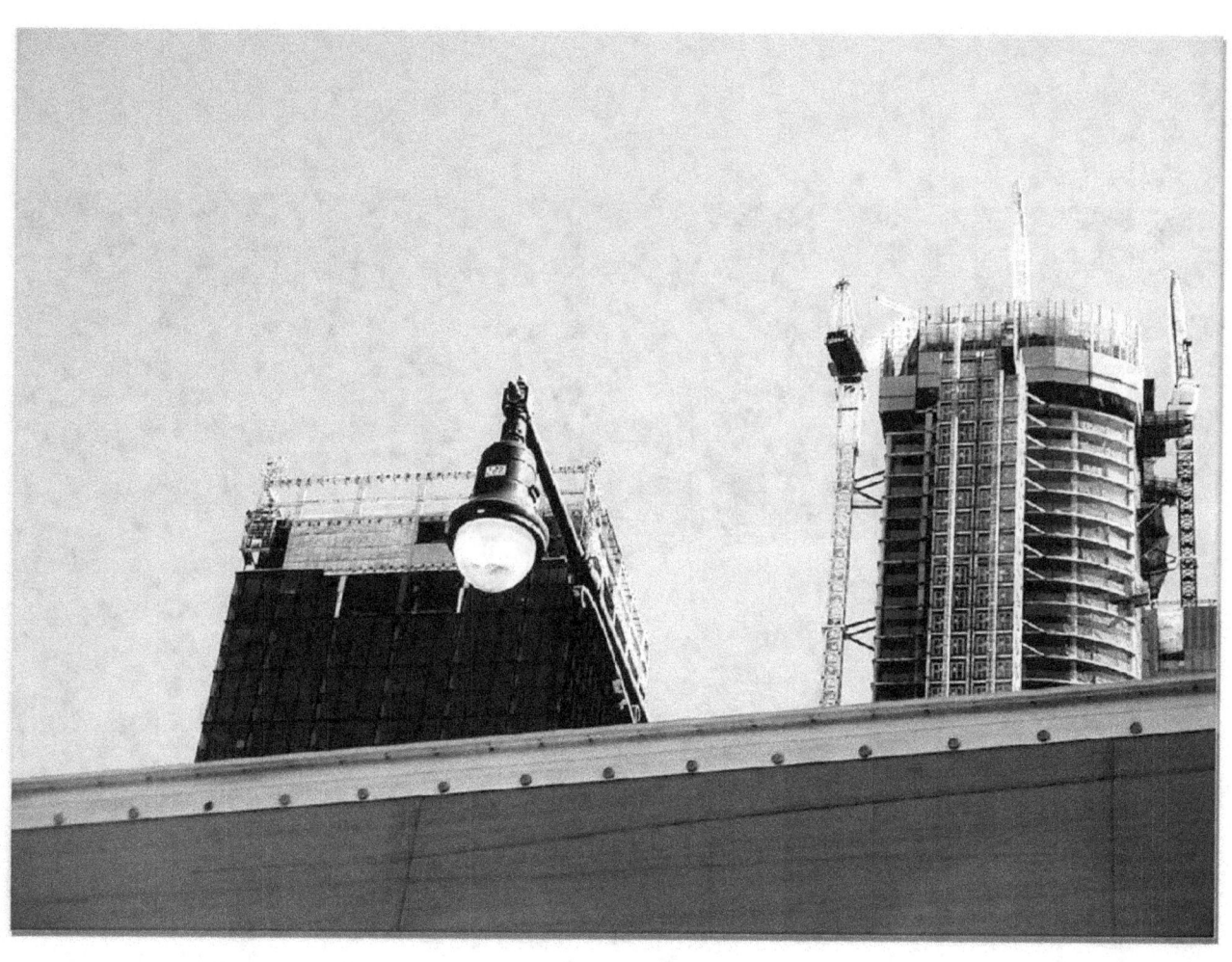

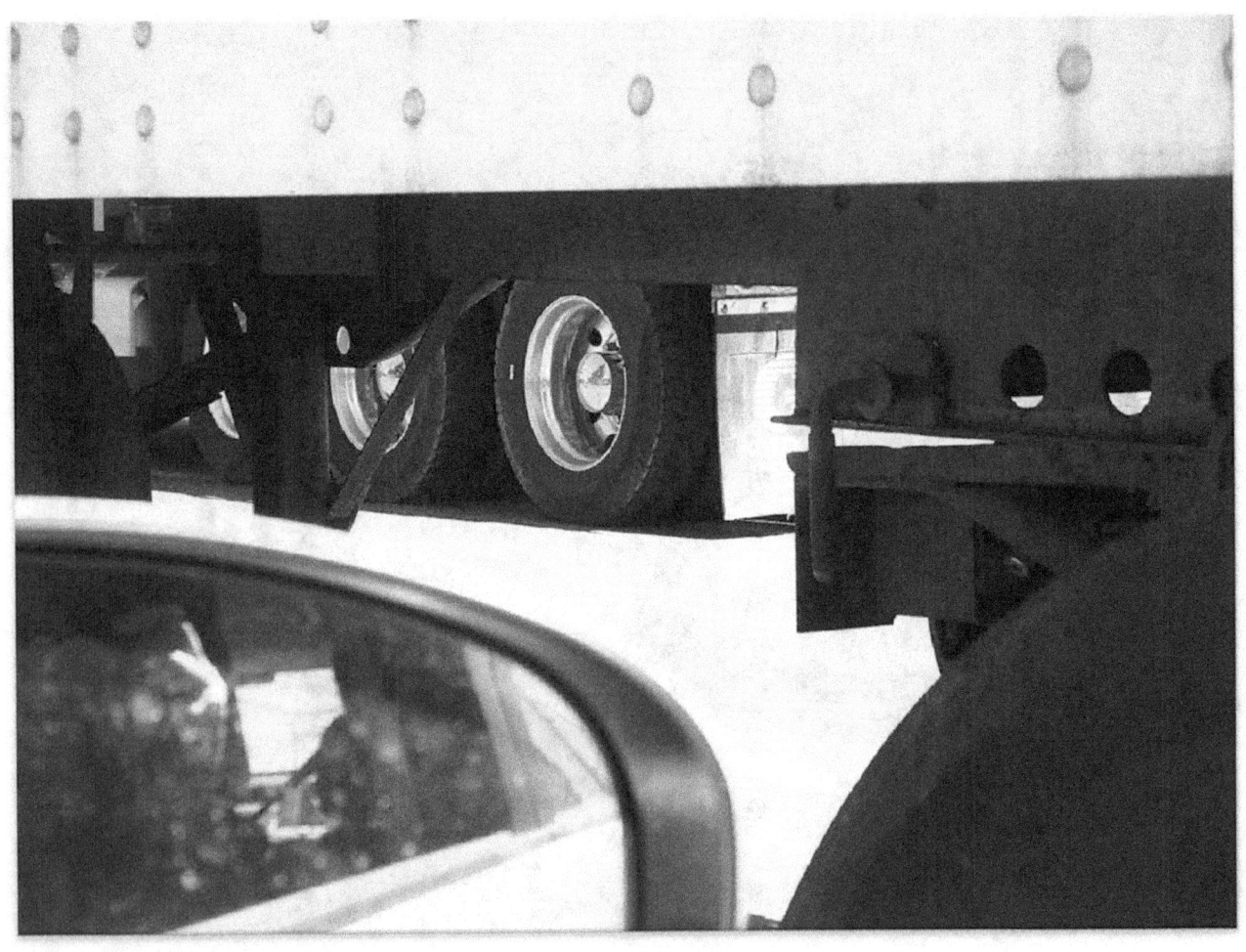

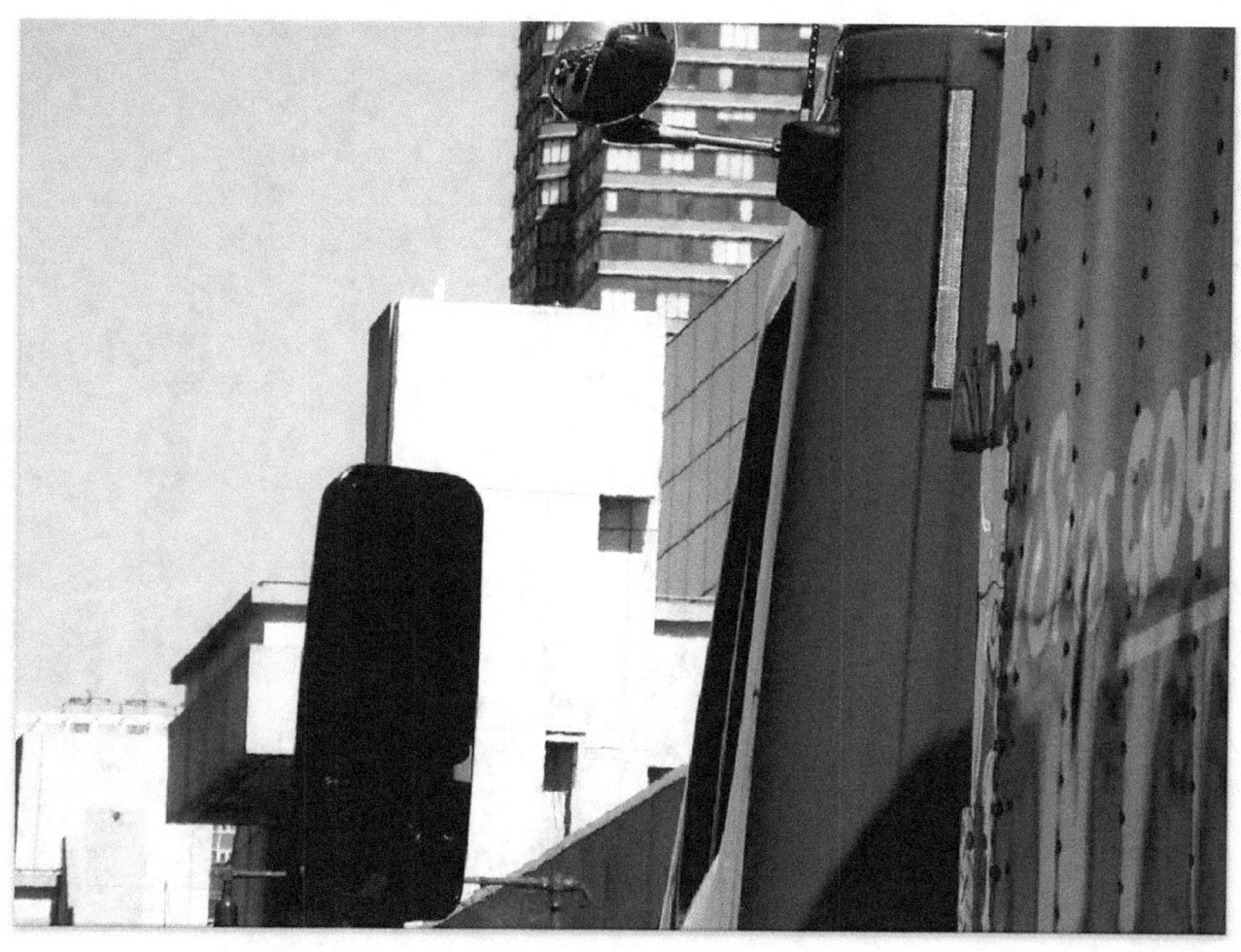

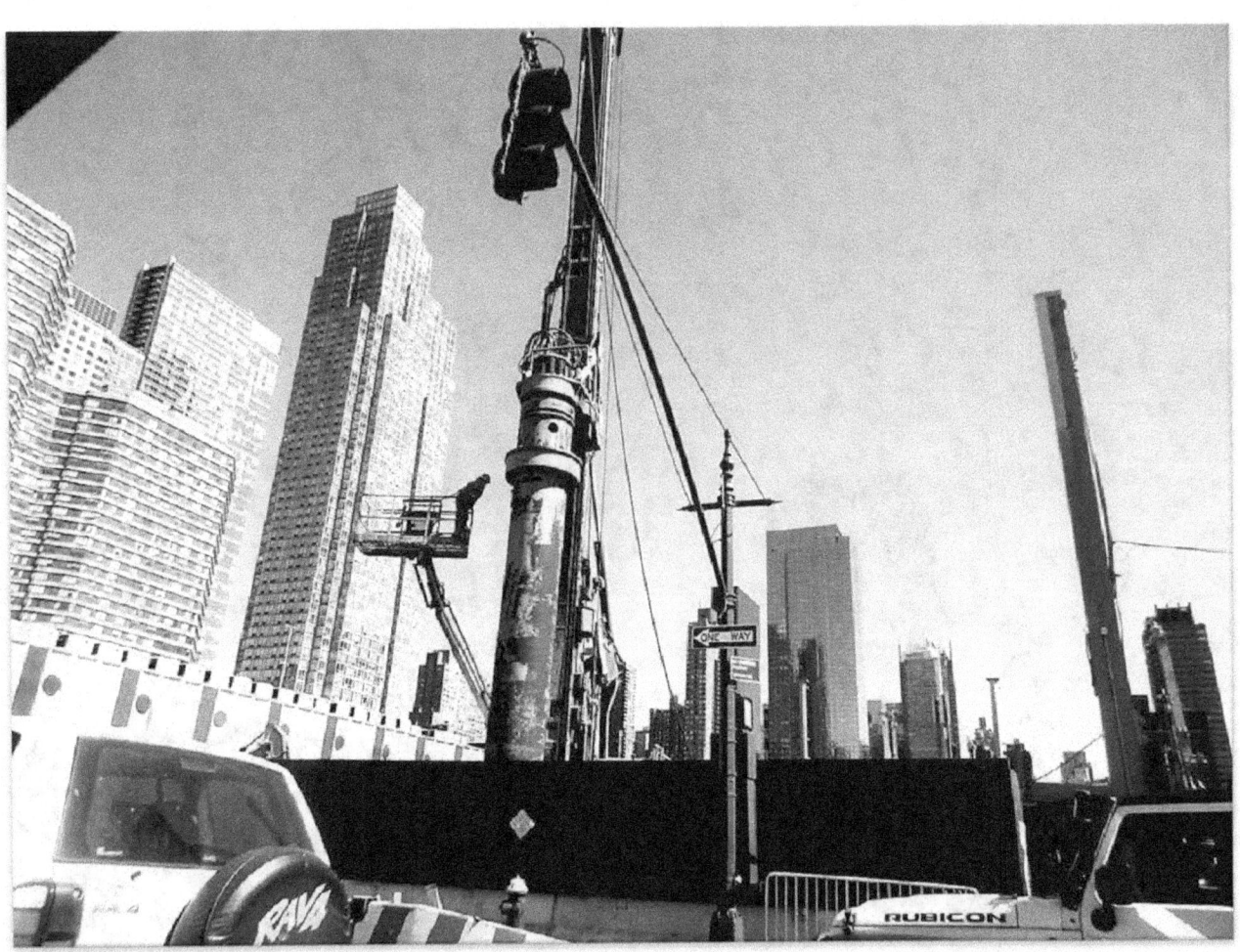

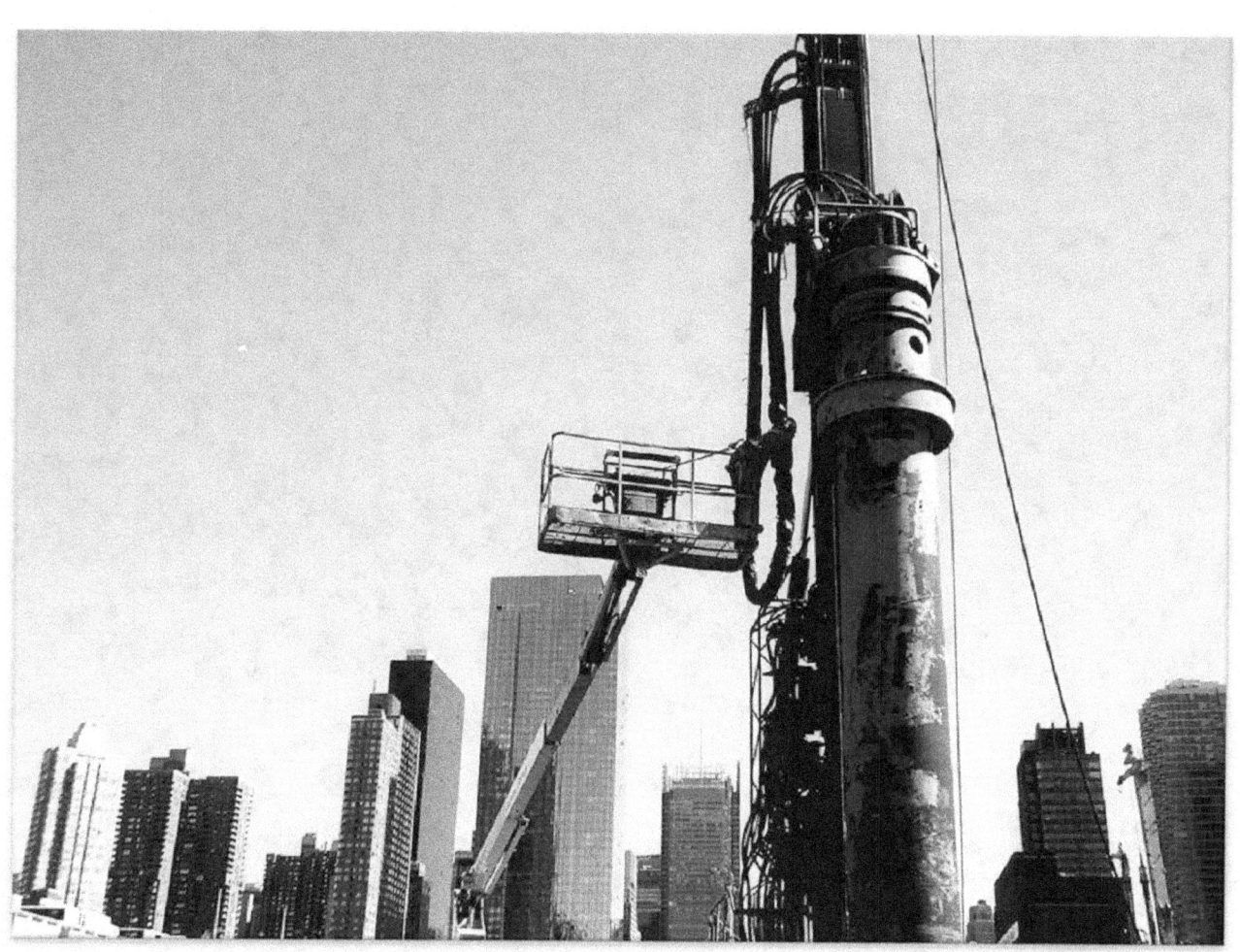

New York City

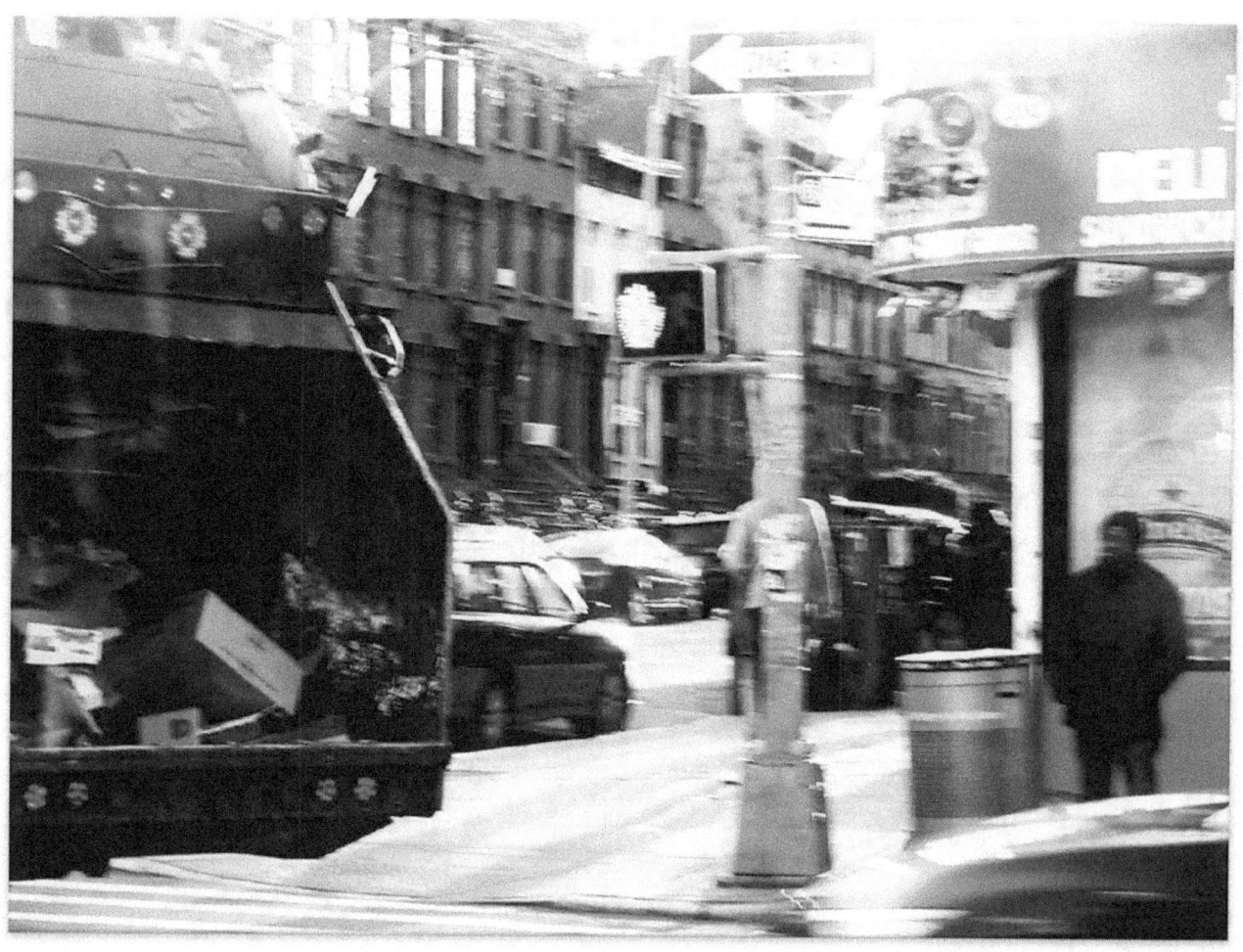

March 16, 2018, 5:30 PM,
Northwest Corner, Nostrand Ave.
Clifton Place, Brooklyn, NY